FEMINIST INTERPRETATIONS OF JOHN DEWEY

RE-READING THE CANON

NANCY TUANA, GENERAL EDITOR

This series consists of edited collections of essays, some original and some previously published, offering feminist re-interpretations of the writings of major figures in the Western philosophical tradition. Devoted to the work of a single philosopher, each volume contains essays covering the full range of the philosopher's thought and representing the diversity of approaches now being used by feminist critics.

Already published:

Nancy Tuana, ed., *Feminist Interpretations of Plato* (1994)

Margaret Simons, ed., *Feminist Interpretations of Simone de Beauvoir* (1995)

Bonnie Honig, ed., *Feminist Interpretations of Hannah Arendt* (1995)

Patricia Jagentowicz Mills, ed., *Feminist Interpretations of G. W. F. Hegel* (1996)

Maria J. Falco, ed., *Feminist Interpretations of Mary Wollstonecraft* (1996)

Susan J. Hekman, ed., *Feminist Interpretations of Michel Foucault* (1996)

Nancy J. Holland, ed., *Feminist Interpretations of Jacques Derrida* (1997)

Robin May Schott, ed., *Feminist Interpretations of Immanuel Kant* (1997)

Celeine Leon and Sylvia Walsh, eds., *Feminist Interpretations of Søren Kierkegaard* (1997)

Cynthia Freeland, ed., *Feminist Interpretations of Aristotle* (1998)

Kelly Oliver and Marilyn Pearsall, eds., *Feminist Interpretations of Friedrich Nietzsche* (1998)

Mimi Reisel Gladstein and Chris Matthew Sciabarra, eds., *Feminist Interpretations of Ayn Rand* (1999)

Susan Bordo, ed., *Feminist Interpretations of René Descartes* (1999)

Julien S. Murphy, ed., *Feminist Interpretations of Jean-Paul Sartre* (1999)

Anne Jaap Jacobson, ed., *Feminist Interpretations of David Hume* (2000)

Sarah Lucia Hoagland and Marilyn Frye, eds., *Feminist Interpretations of Mary Daly* (2000)

Tina Chanter, ed., *Feminist Interpretations of Emmanuel Levinas* (2001)

Nancy J. Holland and Patricia Huntington, eds., *Feminist Interpretations of Martin Heidegger* (2001)

FEMINIST INTERPRETATIONS OF JOHN DEWEY

EDITED BY CHARLENE HADDOCK SEIGFRIED

THE PENNSYLVANIA STATE UNIVERSITY PRESS
UNIVERSITY PARK, PENNSYLVANIA

Library of Congress Cataloging-in-Publication Data

Feminist interpretations of John Dewey / edited by Charlene Haddock Seigfried.
        p.   cm.—(Re-reading the canon)
    Includes bibliographical references and index.
    ISBN 0-271-02160-8 (cloth : alk. paper)
    ISBN 0-271-02161-6 (pbk.: alk. paper)
    1. Dewey, John, 1859–1952.   2. Feminist theory.   3. Pragmatism.
  4. Education.   5. Democracy.   I. Seigfried, Charlene Haddock, 1943–   II. Series.
  HQ1190.F452   2002
  305.42′01—dc21   2001021546

It is the policy of The Pennsylvania State University Press to use acid-free paper for the
first printing of all clothbound books. Publications on uncoated stock satisfy the
minimum requirements of American National Standard for Information
Sciences—Permanence of Paper for Printed Library Materials, ANSI Z39.48–1992.

In loving memory of my parents,
Charles and Allene Haddock

Contents

Preface

Nancy Tuana

Take into your hands any history of philosophy text. You will find compiled therein the "classics" of modern philosophy. Since these texts are often designed for use in undergraduate classes, the editor is likely to offer an introduction in which the reader is informed that these selections represent the perennial questions of philosophy. The student is to assume that she or he is about to explore the timeless wisdom of the greatest minds of Western philosophy. No one calls attention to the fact that the philosophers are all men.

Although women are omitted from the canons of philosophy, these texts inscribe the nature of woman. Sometimes the philosopher speaks directly about woman, delineating her proper role, her abilities and inabilities, her desires. Other times the message is indirect—a passing remark hinting at women's emotionality, irrationality, unreliability.

This process of definition occurs in far more subtle ways when the central concepts of philosophy—reason and justice, those characteristics that are taken to define us as human—are associated with traits historically identified with masculinity. If the "man" of reason must learn to control or overcome traits identified as feminine—the body, the emotions, the passions—then the realm of rationality will be one reserved primarily for men,[1] with grudging entrance to those few women who are capable of transcending their femininity.

Feminist philosophers have begun to look critically at the canonized texts of philosophy and have concluded that the discourses of philosophy are not gender-neutral. Philosophical narratives do not offer a university perspective, but rather privilege some experiences and beliefs over others. These experiences and beliefs permeate all philosophical

theories whether they be aesthetic or epistemological, moral or metaphysical. Yet this fact has often been neglected by those studying the
traditions of philosophy. Given the history of canon formation in Western philosophy, the perspective most likely to be privileged is that of
upper-class white males. Thus, to be fully aware of the impact of gender
biases, it is imperative that we re-read the canon with attention to
the ways in which philosophers' assumptions concerning gender are
embedded within their theories.

This new series, *Re-Reading the Canon*, is designed to foster this process
of reevaluation. Each volume will offer feminist analyses of the theories
of a selected philosopher. Since feminist philosophy is not monolithic in
method or content, the essays are also selected to illustrate the variety of
perspectives within feminist criticism and highlight some of the controversies within feminist scholarship.

In this series, feminist lenses will be focused on the canonical texts of
Western philosophy, both those authors who have been part of the traditional canon, as well as those philosophers whose writings have more
recently gained attention within the philosophical community. A glance
at the list of volumes in the series will reveal an immediate gender bias of
the canon: Arendt, Aristotle, de Beauvoir, Derrida, Descartes, Foucault,
Hegel, Hume, Kant, Locke, Marx, Mill, Nietzsche, Plato, Rousseau, Wittgenstein, Wollstonecraft. There are all too few women included, and
those few who do appear have been added only recently. In creating this
series, it is not my intention to rectify the current canon of philosophical
thought. What is and is not included within the canon during a particular historical period is a result of many factors. Although no canonization
of texts will include all philosophers, no canonization of texts that ex-
cludes all but a few women can offer an accurate representation of the
history of the discipline, as women have been philosophers since the
ancient period.[2]

I share with many feminist philosophers and other philosophers writing from the margins of philosophy the concern that the current canonization of philosophy be transformed. Although I do not accept the
position that the current canon has been formed exclusively by power
relations, I do believe that this canon represents only a selective history
of the tradition. I share the view of Michael Bérubé that "canons are at
once the location, the index, and the record of the struggle for cultural
representation; like any other hegemonic formation, they must be continually reproduced anew and are continually contested."[3]

The process of canon transformation will require the recovery of "lost" texts and a careful examination of the reasons such voices have been silenced. Along with the process of uncovering women's philosophical history, we must also begin to analyze the impact of gender ideologies upon the process of canonization. This process of recovery and examination must occur in conjunction with careful attention to the concept of a canon of authorized texts. Are we to dispense with the notion of a tradition of excellence embodied in a canon of authorized texts? Or, rather than abandon the whole idea of a canon, do we instead encourage a reconstruction of a canon of those texts that inform a common culture?

This series is designed to contribute to this process of canon transformation by offering a re-reading of the current philosophical canon. Such a re-reading shifts our attention to the ways in which woman and the role of the feminine is constructed within the texts of philosophy. A question we must keep in front of us during this process of re-reading is whether a philosopher's socially inherited prejudices concerning woman's nature and role are independent of her or his larger philosophical framework. In asking this question, attention must be paid to the ways in which the definitions of central philosophical concepts implicitly include or exclude gendered traits.

This type of reading strategy is not limited to the canon, but can be applied to all texts. It is my desire that this series reveal the importance of this type of critical reading. Paying attention to the workings of gender within the texts of philosophy will make visible the complexities of the inscription of gender ideologies.

Notes

1. More properly, it is a realm reserved for a group of privileged males, since the texts also inscribe race and class biases that thereby omit certain males from participation.

2. Mary Ellen Waithe's multivolume series, *A History of Women Philosophers* (Boston: M. Nijoff, 1987), attests to this presence of women.

3. Michael Bérubé, *Marginal Forces/Cultural Centers: Tolson, Pynchon, and the Politics of the Canon* (Ithaca: Cornell University Press, 1992), 4–5.

Acknowledgments

"A Toast to John Dewey" (1929), by Jane Addams, originally appeared in *Survey* 63 (15 November 1929): 203–4.

"Experimenting with Education: John Dewey and Ella Flagg Young at the University of Chicago," by Ellen Condliffe Lagemann, is reprinted by permission of The University of Chicago Press and the author from *American Journal of Education* 104 (May 1996): 171–85. Copyright © 1996 by The University of Chicago.

"John Dewey's Pragmatist Feminism," by Charlene Haddock Seigfried, is reprinted by permission of Indiana University Press from *Reading Dewey: Interpretations for a Postmodern Generation*, ed. Larry A. Hickman (Bloomington: Indiana University Press, 1998), 187–216. Copyright © 1998 by Indiana University Press.

"Feminism and Pragmatism: On the Arrival of a 'Ministry of Disturbance, a Regulated Source of Annoyance; a Destroyer of Routine; an Underminer of Complacency,'" by Marjorie C. Miller, is reprinted by permission of The Hegeler Institute from *Monist* 75 (October 1992): 445–57. Copyright © 1992 by *The Monist*.

"Philosophy, Education, and the American Tradition of Aspirational Democracy," by Elizabeth Kamarck Minnich, is a modified version of "The American Tradition of Aspirational Democracy," which first appeared in *Education and Democracy: Re-imagining Liberal Education in America*, ed. Robert Orrill (New York: College Entrance Examination Board, 1997). It is reproduced here by permission of the College Entrance Examination Board.

"The Need for Truth: Toward a Pragmatist-Feminist Standpoint Theory," by Shannon Sullivan, is a modified version of a chapter in *Living Across and Through Skins: Transactional Bodies, Pragmatism, and Feminism* (Bloomington: Indiana University Press, 2001).

Introduction

Charlene Haddock Seigfried

Feminist appropriations of John Dewey's pragmatist philosophy, which began enthusiastically around the turn of the century, were followed by a long period of neglect. They subsequently reemerged only in the last two decades of the twentieth century. In the earlier period, both feminism and pragmatism were being established as movements and as theoretical perspectives that challenged the political, cultural, and economic status quo. In the more recent period, both were already well established as independent perspectives. Feminist theory has in the meantime prolifer-ated into a great diversity of approaches that have eclipsed such earlier divisions as those between liberalism and socialism, humanistic and woman-centered values, incremental and revolutionary approaches to women's suffrage, and race and class as primary issues along with gender. Pragmatism has also become more visible as more satisfying alternatives have been sought to the narrow focus and detached theorizing of mainstream analytic philosophy and the postmodernists' overly symbolic dematerializing of the body as endlessly pliable. Four authors in this volume (Addams, Seigfried, Lagemann, and Fischer) look back to Dewey's original engagement with feminist activists and theorists in an effort to establish that feminism was already deeply rooted in pragmatism from the beginning. It is important to bridge the considerable gap between these first tentative feminist efforts and a contemporary rekindling of interest. In recovering this first fragile but real demonstration of mutual interest and influence, both continuities and discontinuities with more recent feminist positions become available for consideration and open opportunities for criticism, appropriation, and further development.

John Dewey's Philosophy of Emancipatory Experience

John Dewey is one of the founders of American pragmatism. He situates himself in the pragmatist tradition of Charles Sanders Peirce and William James, but credits many of his contemporaries, such as his colleagues in the philosophy department at the University of Chicago, the women administrators and teachers at the Laboratory School, and the women residents of the Hull House Settlement, as contributing to his distinctive version of the Chicago school of pragmatism. In a surprisingly appropriate quirk of fate, John Dewey was born in 1859—the same year Charles Darwin's *The Origin of Species* was published. For Dewey, evolutionary theory heralded a dramatic shift in the way we understand our place in the universe and transformed human understanding. Once we realize that we are in and of nature, not a metaphysical aberration, it is only logical to conclude that

> interest shifts from the wholesale essence [in] back of special changes to the question of how special changes serve and defeat concrete purposes; shifts from an intelligence that shaped things once for all to the particular intelligences which things are even

now shaping; shifts from an ultimate goal of good to the direct increments of justice and happiness that intelligent administration of existent conditions may beget and that present carelessness or stupidity will destroy or forego. (Dewey [1909] 1977, 11)

Philosophy is brought resoundingly back to earth now that we know that understanding what the world is like and what our role in it is cannot be determined by rational introspection or by transcendental leaps, but rather—like other living organisms—we are limited in outlook and learn over time and, unlike them, we can intelligently remember past relationships and foresee future possibilities. The role of philosophy should radically change as a result, and we can at last take responsibility for our own proposals and not attribute them to necessary truths or the nature of the natural world. Instead, we ought to work with others whose everyday lives are already transforming the world so that together we can do so more intelligently, more efficiently, and with more concern for all those affected. This refocusing on how change is actually brought about in concrete experience helps explain the breadth of Dewey's social network, which included women, children, blacks and other ethnic minorities, and the working classes, and the scope of his interests in embracing social changes, from women's changing roles in the industrial revolution to the revolt of the masses in Russia and China.

Now that it is possible to recognize the specific conditions that generate values and the precise consequences of acting on our ideas, Dewey ([1909] 1977, 13) argues that philosophy ought to develop "a method of locating and interpreting the more serious of the conflicts that occur in life, and a method of projecting ways for dealing with them." At the very time that science was identified with value-free inquiry by the Vienna School of Logical Positivism, which was gaining a foothold in the United States, and academic philosophy departments began a trajectory that would lead to the hegemony of epistemology, which assumed the stance of a detached observer, Dewey ([1909] 1977, 13) went against the grain by arguing that philosophy had for the first time the resources required for succeeding as "a method of moral and political diagnosis and prognosis" (see Seigfried 2001). No wonder that women activists of his day found a theoretical basis in pragmatism. Today it can provide intellectual support for feminists who argue that they are not politicizing an otherwise neutral, purely rational philosophical discipline. Susan Hekman (1997, 356) relates feminist standpoint theory to a paradigm shift that was already under way in the second half of the twentieth century; namely, "from an absolutist, subject-centered conception of truth to a conception of truth as situated, perspectival, and discursive." But this shift began much earlier with pragmatism, and Dewey provides much more usable methodological tools than does Hekman in her appeal to Weber's concept of ideal types for resolving the dilemma Nancy Hartsock finds herself in when she asserts both a privileged emancipatory perspective and irreducible diversity and locatedness.

Dewey rejected the epistemological turn because it assumes a subject of consciousness set apart from a world of objects that it somehow has to copy or mirror rather than knowledge as being a certain way of experiencing the world of which one is already a part. Since so much of contemporary philosophical discourse assumes the epistemological perspective, it will be helpful in reading the following essays to keep in mind the radically different meanings Dewey gives to many common and some not so common terms. Although his terminology will continue to be elaborated throughout his later work, a few definitions taken from "The Need for a Recovery of Philosophy" (Dewey [1917] 1980) give sufficient warning not to assume that he means the same thing by the same words in use in other traditions of contemporary philosophy. Experience, for example, is not an inner state of subjective consciousness, nor is it "identical with brain action; it is the entire organic agent-patient in all its interaction with the environment, natural and social" (Dewey [1917] 1980, 26). Knowledge is not a cognitive relation between subject and object; rather, it "*is always a matter of the use that is made of experienced natural events,* a use in which given things are treated as indications of what will be experienced under different conditions" (Dewey [1917] 1980, 33–34). Dewey's method of inquiry into concrete situations replaces the epistemological problem of what knowledge in general is. As a process of knowing, inquiry operates in everyday life and is formalized in scientific experimentation and involves "operations of controlled observation, inference, reasoning and testing" (Dewey [1917] 1980, 37). Intelligence does not refer to the exercise of a universal and homogeneous rationality, but is a complex ability that has evolved over time. It is not neutral for Dewey, which is why he so often uses it as a modifier indicating a proper course of action. Intelligence "is the sum-total of impulses, habits, emotions, records, and discoveries which forecast what is desirable and undesirable in future possibilities, and which contrive ingeniously in behalf of imagined good" (Dewey [1917] 1980, 48).

Misinterpretations of pragmatism can be reduced by keeping in mind Dewey's contention that philosophy ought to concern itself with proximate instead of ultimate questions, with concrete human experience and its potentialities, and that understanding is social through and through. He goes so far as to state that not just social consequences, but "socially *desirable* consequences are bound up with the matter of truth" (Dewey [1911] 1978, 54). The reason is that even if there were such a thing as eternal and absolute truth, unless it is operative in human affairs to help secure a better future, it would be of interest only to "discarnate angelic beings." Unless it is concretely regulative of actual affairs, we would still need to find a substitute that would be.

The task of philosophy must include the criticism of prejudices, because life-experience is saturated with past interpretations that appear to be simply given (Dewey [1925] 1981, 40). Since our understanding of things is imbued with conventional beliefs, knowledge understood as mere representation of things as they are is an inadequate model. What is needed is an experimental method capable of freeing us from bondage to routine and blind repetition of the past by "purposefully introducing changes which will alter the direction of the course of events" (Dewey [1929] 1984, 81). The best tool we have for overcoming the inertia of the distortions and prejudices masquerading as what is simply given is intelligence as a means of action. "Objective truth means interpretations of things that make these things effectively function in liberation of human purpose and efficiency of human effort" (Dewey [1911] 1978, 66). Not just any efficiency will do, because scientific verifications are not fully carried out when they stop short at economic or utilitarian outcomes. "Not till tested in the satisfaction of the most intimate and comprehensive of human needs will they be fully tested, and hence fully be true" (Dewey [1911] 1978, 66). Pragmatic truth can appeal to things *as they are* as long as it is realized that things *are* in shared experience. Until understandings have been shared as a means to human well-being, they have not reached the secure status of truth. Dewey's pragmatism is as far from a value-free instrumentalism as it is possible to be and still provide a critical methodological approach for securing warranted beliefs.

Dewey ([1911] 1978, 52) argues that Aristotle's dictum that "man is a political animal" goes all the way down. Philosophers have for too long been satisfied to quote this saying in the context of discussions of politics, but this would make it a mere tautology. Its force comes from the fact that it applies in regions not usually thought of as political, such as art, religion, and science. It certainly applies to our intellectual life, but outside of more recent marginalized discourses, philosophical analyses of intellect have traditionally and vehemently been segregated from social problems and ends. Dewey ([1920] 1982, 89) seeks to remedy this failure to examine the momentous implications of the social nature of human understanding, beginning with the fact that philosophy itself "did not develop in an unbiased way from an open and unprejudiced origin." He (Dewey [1920] 1982, 90) accuses philosophers from Plato and Aristotle onward of insincerity, on the grounds that they have "professed complete intellectual independence and rationality" while generating systems "in behalf of preconceived beliefs."

One of the more pernicious consequences of the traditional split of theory and practice is that it led to a cognitive quest for absolute assurance such as could be obtained by rational thinking alone and consequently distracted attention and diverted energy from doing something to change actual situations (Dewey [1929] 1984, 29). Pragmatists have been accused of claiming that action is inherently superior to knowledge. Instead, Dewey repeats over and over that what pragmatists propose is nothing less than the "constant and effective interaction of knowledge and practice" (Dewey [1929] 1984, 30). That the practical affairs of everyday life, even intelligently guided practice, is so consistently interpreted as lacking intellectual content or interest confirms Dewey's criticism of the demeaned and depreciated meaning of the practical and the useful in traditional philosophical discourse. Since the purpose of applying the pragmatist method to problems is to obtain "securer, freer and more widely shared embodiment of values in experience" through intelligent action, persistent accusations of pragmatist inquiry as merely instrumental or value free are either misunderstandings based on inadequate textual evidence or indications of a fundamental dispute about what values are (Dewey [1929] 1984, 30).

Context is central to Dewey's philosophy, which therefore is often developed genealogically in order to recall how and why we have come to see and interpret the world as we do. Dewey, in fact, takes the neglect of context as the besetting fallacy of most reflective thinking. Abstract thinking that does not recognize and call into question its own background conditions and embeddedness in social and political power structures inevitably distorts reality and mistakes its own perspective for unbiased access to the truth. In its delusion of carrying on neutral inquiry, developing context-free theory, and reflecting the insights of isolated individuals, it cannot ground or justify the need for including marginalized, ignored, or oppressed persons and groups, nor their interests, as necessary components of theory that claims to reflect on truth, reality, and values. The authors of the first group of chapters in this volume, therefore, develop the earliest expressions of feminist interpretations of pragmatism in order to reveal the persons and issues that shaped it and to make available these historically and concretely grounded models as resources for contemporary theory and practice.

Recovering the Feminist Roots of Pragmatism

A lost tradition of pragmatist feminism is both symbolized by and instantiated in the lasting friendship and cooperative efforts of John Dewey and Jane Addams. When it came to social involvement and pragmatism in action Dewey was tutored first by his wife, Alice Chipman, and then more extensively by Addams. In education, his mentors were Ella Flagg Young and the women, including Katherine Camp Mayhew and Anna Camp Edwards, who taught and developed the curriculum of the University of Chicago Laboratory School. His long and distinguished life of public involvement in the most contentious power struggles between capitalists and workers, whites and blacks, individualistic liberalism and socialism, and other incendiary issues of the day shows how well he learned the lesson.

Dewey's female friends, colleagues, and students also used his pragmatist theories as a basis for their own feminist theories and practices. What Addams celebrated in her essay "A Toast to John Dewey" was his active engagement in the social issues of the day as the expression of what intellectual life at its best should be. She opens her essay by praising his active support of Hull House, which was her own lifelong work, and then continues with detailing his dedication to many issues of social welfare, remarking that such involvement is rare in philosophers. The features of Dewey's philosophy that she also emphasizes in her own thinking and reform efforts include the interaction of individuals and their social and natural environments; deemphasizing the hierarchical relations between student and teacher, client and social worker; intelligence linked with transforming society for the better; and philosophy as continuous education. Philosophy for Dewey involved active engagement in social and political problems, which meant international as well as national collaboration.

Since the occasion for Addams's remarks is a tribute to Dewey on his seventieth birthday, it is not surprising that she gives such a positive assessment. Although Addams more often directs her efforts to women and women's causes and explicitly mentions the efforts of his wife, Alice Dewey, on behalf of women's education in China, she does not see Dewey as differing in his commitment to women's emancipation. She does mention the one time she took a stance that isolated her not only from Dewey but from most people at the time. This was when she remained steadfastly pacifist throughout the World War I, whereas Dewey reluctantly agreed that the crisis demanded a temporary abandonment of pacifism. Since Addams argued that women's interests should enable them to take the lead in rejecting war as a means of settling disputes, Dewey's less unequivocal support of pacifism could be construed as the one breach he made with her feminist goals. But even in this case, she says that she found a reliable guide for her own efforts in his method of judging truth by the practices it leads to. It should be noted that Dewey ([1930] 1984) immediately countered any impression Addams may have made in her tribute that he influenced her while she did not likewise strongly influence him.

Ellen Condliffe Lagemann's essay on Ella Flagg Young (as well as Marilyn Fisher's final essay on Addams) both remind us of and build on this earlier wave of pragmatist feminism. Feminist interpretations of Dewey, therefore, are as much internalist critiques as externalist ones, since we now know that he developed his philosophy through discussions with many women active in the social and political movements of the time. He acknowledges as much, according to his daughter, Jane M. Dewey, who reports that her father said that "personal contacts had, on the whole, more influence in directing his thought than the books he read," and when he publicly protests that Addams and Young attributed to him influential ideas that were actually their own (Seigfried 1996, 47–48, 75, 80–82).

Young was already an experienced educational administrator when she returned to school and enrolled in Dewey's classes. Lagemann argues that Young had a good understanding of the role of politics in education, which influenced Dewey's thinking while he was at the University of Chicago, but which he did not follow up on with the same fervor in his later writings. He did not remain as strong an advocate of teachers in later years, according to Lagemann, and his active involvement in educational experimentation waned as his interests broadened and his colleagues and collaborators were drawn from different disciplines. Perhaps as a consequence of leaving Chicago and losing contact with Young, Dewey never afterward gave primary attention to questions of power in reconstructing education, even though he did deal with issues of conflict in his social and political writings.

The usual way for philosophers to respond to original and challenging thinkers is to critically analyze their major works, expose the strengths and weaknesses of the positions found, and creatively develop the perspective according to their own interests. In the course of this close association with a chosen predecessor, their insights can also be put to use in the service of pressing issues, such as feminist concerns with the constraints and prejudices women encounter both in their role in the family and as they enter more deeply into the public realm. In fact, a pragmatist hermeneutics requires doing so in order to avoid reducing thinking to the mere exegesis of original or recoverable meanings in isolation from the conditions that generated them and the difficult problems we have to think about today. As Dewey's writings are transformed in the course of developing a contemporary pragmatist feminism, questions naturally arise about Dewey's own explicit feminist concerns. His own attitudes do not limit the scope or usefulness of his philosophy, but knowing what they are can shed light on how women saw his work at the time and on how we understand his life and work in hindsight.

Now that Dewey is being reclaimed as a resource for feminist theorizing, it is important to clear up a misconception shared by both pragmatists and nonpragmatists. Despite the fact of his active support of women's rights and of antiracist causes, it has been claimed that he never wrote on women or racism.[1] The problem is that what he did write is scattered here and there throughout his philosophical writings or else appeared in his more polemical speeches and political tracts that were not reprinted in the standard collections. I have therefore thought it important in my chapter, "John Dewey's Pragmatist Feminism," not only to trace what an earlier generation of women found valuable in his philosophy, but also to bring together in one place and analyze most of his reflections on women. In the process, it becomes obvious that he did take a uniquely pragmatist feminist perspective on issues, even though he occasionally fell short of consistently adhering to it. Knowing what Dewey's own feminist positions are provides a needed corrective to speculation on this point and can deepen the theoretical context of the various approaches taken in this volume. The fact that until very recently pragmatist scholars were skeptical of claims that Dewey could be called a feminist philosopher or that he had taken feminist positions in his writings is prima facie evidence that concerns about women's subordinate status and efforts to rebut the misogynist philosophical tradition were not central to his philosophy. However, they were not totally absent, either.

In "John Dewey's Pragmatist Feminism" I begin piecing together Dewey's explicit feminist concerns from scattered and often obscure texts, published and unpublished. The publication of the critical edition of all of Dewey's writings, social and political speeches and manifestos as well as his recognized philosophical books and articles, has made it possible to see more clearly the close link between his theorizing and his political activism.[2] His concern with feminist issues also comes into clearer focus and makes it possible for the first time to examine the nature of his own pragmatist feminism. As would be expected when examining a life as long and as involved with social and political issues of the day as Dewey's was, it is evident that his positions evolve as conditions change and as feminist thought itself changes in response to them. Some themes and attitudes persist as well. It is now possible to say that he explicitly argued for the possibility and desirability of women's special angle of vision, as long as this is not taken to be invariant, unchangeable, or monolithic, but attributable instead to similarities of cultural roles assigned to women and to the same negative social, legal, and political constraints they endured. One could deduce that such a position is consistent with pragmatist theories of perspectivism and pluralism, but it is revealing to find out that he himself explicitly drew this corollary, since so many otherwise commendable philosophical positions were not seen as applicable to women by their authors. In fact, much feminist theory has involved pointing out, exploring, and criticizing such discrepancies.

However, such an opportunity to examine his writings on women also reveals that he was not always so consistent or insightful about feminist issues. The longest, most explicit discussion of women's situation occurs in the last chapter of both editions of *Ethics* under the heading "The Family," in the first edition, and "Marriage and the Family," in the second edition, contexts that skew the analysis. The pitfalls of a view of women seen solely from a male perspective, even that of a sympathetic male, are most apparent in these extended analyses. Insightful comments on the changing status of women are found together with reactionary ones. Both the earlier 1908 edition (Dewey [1908] 1978) and the later

1932, extensively rewritten edition (Dewey [1932] 1985), express considerable perplexity about where all these changes are leading, and the central concern is to defend the institution of the family from attack.[3] That
these chapters in both co-authored editions were written by James H.
Tufts problematizes Dewey's authorship. However, both claim that their
collaboration extended over all parts of the books.

Recognition of the ubiquity of selective bias led pragmatists to devise
the pragmatic method as a way of overcoming it. Dewey specifically uses
the genetic method to trace the history and causes of prejudice. The
theory of inquiry that he develops and then uses in his own analyses of
issues throughout his writings always includes this component of recognizing and subverting distorting and demeaning preconceptions. But because he underestimated the force and virulence of prejudice and the
myriad forms of drives for power and domination, he often underestimates
what is required for overcoming them. Since whether and to what extent
Dewey recognized prejudice, oppression, and the will to dominate, as well
as what resources he has to offer in overcoming them, are central issues
for feminist interpretations, I develop both issues in detail, especially as
they relate to women and blacks.

Dewey's positions on this and other feminist issues can also be used to
assess their further development by feminist philosophers throughout this
book. These include the subjugation of slaves and women as the source
of Aristotle's dualism of theory and practice; the economic basis of racism
and need for coalition building to overcome it; the democratic basis of
women's right to the franchise, which precludes militant methods; opposition to settling disputes by force, since the weaker members of society
are disproportionally vulnerable and better methods are needed to empower them; a pragmatist standpoint theory encouraging women's contributions to knowledge, but which also requires diversity of perspectives
and plural interactions to overcome its own limitations; criticism of patriarchy and the role of industrialization in oppressing women; rejection of
liberal atomism for multirelated selves in a democratic society requiring
coalition building among all disadvantaged groups, not favoring any one
over others; rejection of theories of an innate human nature, which only
serve to rationalize social inequalities and prejudices and further entrench
habits; a defense of heterosexual marriage in the face of the disintegrating
forces of World War I and women's changing roles; and, finally, support of
the legalization of birth control as a means of intelligent family planning.

In the last essay in the first section on recovering a usable past, Marjorie Miller makes an impassioned plea for rejoining the traditions of feminism and pragmatism, which share the dubious distinction of being regarded by more mainstream philosophical approaches as ushering into the sacred groves of academe "a ministry of disturbance, a regulated source of annoyance, a destroyer of routine, an underminer of complacency." She makes the intriguing suggestion that the many points on which United States feminist analyses of women's experiences overlap with those of the American Tradition, of which Dewey is a part, might be due to these feminists' unconsciously drawing on the reconceptions of experience provided by this tradition. She goes even further, in suggesting that the many feminist criticisms of the disguised maleness of the dominant philosophical concepts of reason are more closely aligned with the function of similar criticisms in Dewey's philosophy than they are with many other philosophical versions with which feminists have consciously aligned themselves. An additional area of significant overlap concerns the nature of philosophy itself. Despite the diversity of feminist theories, it is difficult to find any that do not seek to account for the concrete, historical multiplicity of women's situations; to theorize from the perspective of plural locations; and to actively engage in the reconstruction or transformation of various oppressions. Miller argues that in all these areas feminists are rediscovering and developing further major themes in the American Tradition of philosophizing.

The Personal and the Political

Dewey's earliest interests and writings involve education. It was so important to his philosophical outlook that the first book in which he sought to develop his own philosophical perspective was *Democracy and Education* (Dewey [1916] 1980). The title links education with his other lifelong interest; namely, the democratic outlook that he argued was indispensable for individuals to fully develop as persons for whom the welfare of others is indispensable to their own, no matter how differently they are situated by color, gender, class, ethnicity, or nationality. In an essay with a similar title, "Philosophy and Democracy," Dewey ([1919] 1982) defended the explicit connection of philosophy with the social and political goals of democracy without relinquishing the duty of philosophers to provide "an intellectual warrant for our endeavors." Dewey's own feminism and criticisms of many of the same harmful assumptions of our inherited Western philosophical tradition that feminists have condemned can largely be credited to his working so closely with women involved in early childhood education and with the Hull House women who saw their role as social reformers bound up with adult education. It is therefore appropriate that the first group of topical essays concerns education.

The authors of the two chapters on educational theory and practice emphasize that pragmatist education subverts rigid dichotomies between theory and practice, teacher and student, the personal and the political, dominant and marginal cultures, even between ego boundaries and social realities. Both explore issues of self-identity in a social context that simultaneously seeks to suppress and undermine and to recognize and celebrate multiple, diverse relationships and attachments. Elizabeth Kamarck Minnich and Ana M. Martínez Alemán demonstrate the practical and theoretical gains to be achieved in the mutual transformation of the personal, the political, and the theoretical that pragmatist educational theory encourages.

In relating her love affair with pragmatism, Minnich situates herself and her own coming of age as a philosopher and educator within the long tradition of aspirational democracy. She shows how the various movements demanding equal rights for the many groups of people historically denied them, followed by agitations for a fuller recognition of the diversity and value of multiply identified persons, not only affected her own self-understanding, but also challenged the political and moral sensibilities of the educational professions. Looking back, she marvels at the remarkable intertwining and the emancipatory force of the personal and the political that her educational encounter with Dewey's pragmatist philosophy both reflected and encouraged. Like Addams's ([1916] 2001) reflections on how past memories can be valuable tools for transforming the present, Minnich's graduate school attraction to the socially transformative possibilities of pragmatism, despite its neglect by more professionally driven philosophers, testifies to its continuing capacity to challenge received views. By also situating her discourse within a chorus of voices, which includes, besides William James and Dewey, Carter G. Woodson, Anna Julia Cooper, Jane Addams, W. E. B. Du Bois, Fred Newton Scott, and Mary Parker Follett, Minnich not only enacts the fruitful human interrelatedness and interdependency central to her pragmatist feminist theory and practice, but also seeks to recenter philosophy in a democratizing educational vision. Minnich's recital of the long history of contradictions between high-minded political goals and sordid reality and of the voices raised in protest against oppressive practices does not just remind us of how far we have yet to go. She also expands the network of pragmatist thinkers available to us and brings out the cogency of their analyses as resources for contemporary theory as well as for morally informed practical action.

Alemán, imagining herself as a space between syncopated beats, also approaches her topic autobiographically, but as a fractured subject encompassing Cuban feeling and knowing overlaid with Ango-American schooling. She brings her struggles with multiple identities into the classroom, where similar struggles are being worked through. Alemán finds Dewey's way of bringing together the intellectual potency of identity with educational practice helpful for explaining how multiply situated persons such as the Jamaican author Michelle Cliff "journey to speech." For Dewey, identity is dynamic and unfolding and our potentialities are elicited through interactions with the world. For Alemán, this means that her identity is not only who she is but also what she does; it is cultural, linguistic, political, gendered, and more. In the classroom, as in life, identity is something to be achieved, to be worked toward between teacher and pupil. Since, according to Dewey, thinking is contextual and presupposes experience that implies individuality and historic identity, his approach is helpful in developing a multicultural feminist classroom. Alemán also relates self-realization to the full exercise of each person's powers in contributing to the common good of a democratic society.

Since Dewey originally develops his theory of how individuals grow and develop over time and in interaction with their natural and social environment in his educational writings, it is not surprising to find some of the same issues that have already been raised recurring in the section on subjectivity. Erin McKenna argues that both the ethics of care and the ethics of justice are inadequate because they are based on incomplete theories of the self. A more complex and dynamic notion of the self can be found in pragmatist feminism, which gets beyond minimal notions of responsibility to promote social connections and individual growth. McKenna first explains how Sarah Hoagland and John Dewey criticize not only social justice models of contract theory and liberal individualism, but also organicist/care approaches to ethics. McKenna's pragmatist account of individuals radicalizes both the spatial and temporal perspectives of the self developed by Peter French; and she uses Hoagland's lesbian ethics to extend and correct Dewey's concept of the self.

Paula Droege focuses on the subject or subjective experience as a necessary part of a robust feminist epistemology. She therefore addresses postmodernist criticisms of appeals to women's experience as being either incoherent or dangerous and she rejects postmodernist assumptions that such appeals exhibit an indefensible essentialism and the fiction of a unitary subject. Refusing the modern linguistic turn that collapses experience into language, Droege adopts Dewey's explanation of two levels of experience, noncognitive and cognitive, to defend an experience-based epistemology. The advantage of this perspective becomes apparent when she is able to defend women's subversive knowledge claims against community standards, despite the social nature of confirmation.

Situated Perspectives

In the first of two chapters in the section on objectivity and truth, Eugenie Gatens-Robinson utilizes the insights of John Dewey and Donna Haraway to develop a theory of objectivity that can give full weight both to the reality of natural objects and to the mediating influence of the attitudes of persons for whom they are objects. She wants to bring together Dewey's pragmatically optimistic account of the object of knowledge with Haraway's edgier postmodern account of objectivity in order to lead to a more liberating and less alienating theory of knowledge. The plurality of perspectives, so important to feminist accounts of the value of diversity, cannot do without a persuasive explanation of the objectivity of the relations that shape our shared interests or that undermine them. Objectivity in the sense of passively reflecting a set of mind-independent objects has become progressively problematized. Moreover, if women have distinctive contributions to make to human understanding and if the depredations of supposedly neutral scientific results are to be rejected as miscarriages of valid inquiry, then the received model of objectivity has to be rejected for a better account.

For Dewey, scientific objects are ways of handling things to reach desired ends. As features of our interactions with the world, they cannot be arbitrary without negative consequences. Nonetheless, they are thoroughly historical and dynamic. The aim of scientific inquiry is make ourselves at home in the world. For Haraway, to be objective is to be locatable and thus responsible for how one comes to see. Her history of the object in the biological sciences as reflecting capitalist and patriarchal domination of nature reveals deeply pragmatic insights. Rather than seeking to control a world subject to our whims, she urges a fidelity to a world that has the capacity to hoodwink us. Gatens-Robinson concludes by developing in more detail the ecological view of objectivity that both Dewey and Haraway share. In their different emphases, Haraway seeks to fray the boundaries separating organisms and machines, while Dewey is more concerned to weave organisms and the natural environment together in a dynamic process of meaningful experiences.

Given the centrality of experience and perspectivism in pragmatist philosophy, it would be odd, indeed, if Dewey did not formulate an earlier version of feminist standpoint theory (see Seigfried 1996, 45, 144, 154–56). It is alluded to in many of the chapters in this book, but Shannon Sullivan develops a full-blown explanation of a pragmatist version of standpoint theory.[4] She explicitly takes up a central problem some feminists have found with Sandra Harding's version of feminist standpoint theory in order to resolve them from a Deweyan perspective. The issue that keeps being raised is how to both recognize human situatedness and still provide epistemological standards. Sullivan argues that the problem with even Harding's latest revisions of standpoint theory is that she still assumes a foundational ideal of truth as mirroring reality. Dewey ([1919] 1982, 51), in fact, makes an even more radical criticism of this theory of truth when he says that any philosophy that claims to have unconditional insight into the nature of reality or ultimate truth "inevitably works in behalf of a regime of authority," and that it is not accidental that most philosophies have been used to justify the particular religious or political order that happened to exist at the time.

As an alternative to a correspondence theory of truth, Sullivan develops Dewey's explanation of knowing as a method of experimental inquiry engaged in to satisfy our desires and needs. She also shows that perspectives are not just dualistic, as in subjugated and dominant perspectives, but are plural. Pluralizing perspectives does not undermine the values and epistemic importance of women's situated objectivity according to pragmatist feminism, but in explaining knowing as a process of mutual transformation of self and others, of self and world, it instead provides a methodology for warranting such claims. Following this methodology herself, Sullivan concludes by showing how well Dewey's and Harding's positions work together by each supporting the other's strong points and transforming and correcting their weak points. The privilege Harding attributes to subjugated women, for example, is the same privilege found in any situated perspective, to be subjected to the same tests, but women's contributions to knowledge are no less real for this qualification.

Theory and Practice

No feminist interpretation of Dewey would be complete without addressing his relevance for social and political issues. Initial experience sets the problems for Dewey's pragmatism and a reconstructed experience warrants our intellectual judgments. Because concrete experience is so central, experimental inquiry rather than formal logic is the appropriate method for pragmatist philosophers, and because the goal of inquiry is the transformation of a presently troubling or oppressive situation to a better, more emancipatory one, social and political issues are implicated in all the areas of philosophy. Social reconstruction arises from the interactive nature of theory and practice and is guided by the inclusion and empowerment of those neglected or abused by the current structures of power.

Dewey has been called the last of the great public intellectuals because his own practice informed his theory and his theory was carried out in practice. His active support of women's causes, of antiracism, of anticolonialism, and of organizations opposed to predatory capitalism was early, persistent, and quite public. He supported coeducation when it was under attack and was outspoken about enfranchising women, raising the status of women teachers, and the right to birth control. He was a co-founder of the National Association for the Advancement of Colored People (NAACP) and the American Federation of Teachers, traveled to China to lend his support to democratic reforms, marched with striking workers, and supported the United Nations against nationalistic isolationists.

Lisa Heldke opens the section on social and political philosophy by questioning how down to earth Dewey's appeals to the practical actually are. Judith Green reminds us of the importance of democratic transformation in those pragmatist and feminist perspectives with which we have been concerned in this book. And—echoing Lagemann's analysis of the relations between Young and Dewey—Fischer finds that Addams's critique of capitalism as patriarchal is more radical than Dewey's criticisms of industrial capitalism.

Heldke's suggestion to rename theorizing "thinking about practice" or "thoughtful practice" recognizes Dewey's intention to radically recon-struct philosophy toward what Michael Eldridge (1998) calls intelligent practice. For Dewey the experimental method is a model for how activi-ties can be made more intelligent. It operates already in everyday experi-ence, which, however, can be made more efficacious by consciously incorporating some of the insights gained through more methodically carried-out scientific experimentation. Science liberates commonsense knowing from application solely to individual situations and thereby frees up its practical power in a wider range of analogous situations. But Hel-dke argues that Dewey ignores the ways that foodmaking and child care employ the experimental method. She says that he also ignores the fact that they employ a nonexperimental method that offers insight into how to avoid separating knowing and doing. According to Heldke, Dewey does not show how "childbearing, foodmaking and carpentry might be accorded similar value by philosophers." He does think that there is a learning curve and that earlier observations on the outcome of transfor-mations of particular situations will, with further experience and the learning of various methodologies, develop into better approaches.

Judith Green begins by showing how the reduction of democracy to capitalist economics has caused global problems for women and depressed regions of the world. She argues that a Deweyan model of a democracy, which is inclusive of women's voices, values, and experience-based vi-sions for a preferable future, should replace the managerial model of capi-talist liberal democracy. According to Dewey, human potentialities are actualized primarily through social action, which democratic institutions can facilitate, rather than from the actions of isolated individuals each seeking to maximize her or his own well-being. Women of diverse back-grounds must become key players in deeper processes of democratization to develop their own potentialities and contribute their much needed values and insights to local communities and global associations.

The first essay in this book is an appreciation of John Dewey by Jane Addams. We come full circle by concluding this last section on social and political philosophy with Marilyn Fischer's chapter showing not only how much Addams and Dewey have in common, but also what Dewey could have learned from Addams. Her demonstration of the patriarchal nature of capitalism shares many features of Dewey's criticism of indus-trial capitalism, but goes beyond it. Addams develops specific features of the ways in which it subordinates persons to profit that Dewey ignores or leaves underdeveloped. And whereas Dewey tends to idealize families, Addams's work among the immigrant poor leads her to a better understanding of the negative effects on family life of industrial capitalism. Fischer explains that Addams criticized socialism as well as capitalism for being too ideological, and that she arrived at this conclusion through her concrete experiences in the Hull House Settlement. Addams was also engaged in a widespread experiment to reconstruct the nature of the family; on the one hand, by demonstrating that the private nature of families is an illusion in neighborhoods where poor sanitation, crime, and adverse working conditions can claim the lives of even the most sheltered children; and, on the other hand, by the nature of the intimate and wider social relations of the female residents of the Hull House "family."[5] Addams's theorizing from a rich variety of women's experiences is an invaluable contribution to Dewey's appeals to experience as the origin and test of knowledge.

A Foreseeable Future

Where do we go from here? The essays in this book are part of the revival of interest in Dewey's philosophy on the part of feminists. The recency of this renewed interest means that there are many areas of feminist theory developed independently of it, so I will briefly indicate those that would benefit from a rapprochement as well as directions in which some Deweyan feminist scholarship is already moving. Because of its unbroken interest in Dewey's educational theory, the discipline of education has continued to be fertile ground for feminist theorists. I would urge feminists in all disciplines to likewise explore areas of mutual concern. In his time, for example, Dewey was recognized as the preeminent philosopher of democracy, who emphasized the importance of diversity and the harms caused by privilege of all sorts. He therefore sought inclusiveness without subordination, consensus building without coercion, and cooperation in setting and working toward common goals without diluting diversity. As current feminist scholarship continues to open new perspectives in global, anticolonialist theories of democracy as a logical extension of its emphasis on the inseparability of gender, race, ethnicity, class, and sexual orientation, the times seem ripe for a broader reassessment of Dewey's theory of democracy.

Dewey also excoriated radical individualism and showed that social relations enter into every aspect of human organic and cultural development, including ethics. His naturalized ethics is both similar to, and differs from, such versions of feminist ethics as the ethics of care, social ethics, and lesbian ethics. This volume would have greatly benefited from a section on value theory in which feminists engaged Dewey's emphasis on specificity, criticism of received views and institutions, and the social dimension of value change. Pragmatist theorizing of the multiple and dynamic relationships through which persons are constituted in interaction with their natural and social environment finds new relevancy in feminist theorizing of situated subjectivity, the widespread devaluation of women, the public and private split, and ecofeminist theory.

There are other areas in which feminist and Deweyan perspectives seem to be converging. His antiessentialism, antireductionism, and logic of inquiry that requires multiple points of view, to justify both warranted assertions and value judgments, represent a theoretical position continuous with contemporary feminist efforts to deconstruct 'woman' into its concretely racial, class, sexual, and globally multicultural dimensions. He was an outspoken critic of logical positivism and developed a theory of knowledge and inquiry that acknowledged perspectivism and incorporated emotional and value dimensions. Feminist criticisms of the biases hidden in epistemological claims to the transparency of truth or the neutrality of judgments have an ally in pragmatist theories of knowledge. In *The Quest for Certainty*, Dewey ([1929] 1984) anticipated many poststructuralist themes but also argued that unless deconstruction leads to reconstruction, to more valuable ways of organizing experience, its radical potential remains unrealized.

Finally, in *Art as Experience* Dewey ([1934] 1987) criticized museum art and opened up the aesthetic dimension of everyday experience. Although such themes are congenial to issues of feminist aesthetics, I would like to see in which direction Deweyan scholarship would go when it explicitly incorporates feminist analyses of the ways in which women's bodies are constructed by societal expectations, advertising, and the beauty industry and when it addresses such varied cultural practices as beauty pageants, anorexia, and genital mutilation. There are also opportunities for bringing queer theory to bear on Dewey's philosophy and for recognizing the contributions of Native American philosophers to issues and outlooks central to pragmatist theory.

Notes

1. To support his critical view of pragmatism, for example, John Patrick Diggins (1999, 261) claims that Dewey "stayed completely clear of the controversial issues of race and the status of women."

2. The collected works of John Dewey are organized chronologically into *The Early Works, 1882–1898*, vols. 1–5 (1969–72); *The Middle Works, 1899–1924*, vols. 1–15 (1976–83); and *The Later Works, 1925–1953*, vols. 1–17 (1984–90), ed. Jo Ann Boydston (Carbondale: Southern Illinois University Press).

3. It would be worthwhile to compare the 1908 *Ethics* and the post–World War I 1932 *Ethics* for their respective analyses of the marital crisis that women's changing demands and position are causing. Only the first section of the chapters on the family are the same in both editions. In many ways the analyses in the first edition are more radical.

4. Dewey explicitly formulates a feminist standpoint in "Philosophy and Democracy" ([1919] 1982, 45) and qualifies it in "Context and Thought" ([1931] 1985, 20–21).

5. During the Progressive Era, women created in the social settlement movement an alternative institution, outside traditional families, in which they could both find affection and support and make important contributions to society. See Sklar 1998.

References

Addams, Jane. [1916] 2001. *The Long Road of Woman's Memory*. Reprint, with an introduction by C. H. Seigfried, Champaign: University of Illinois Press.

Dewey, John. [1908] 1978. *Ethics*. Vol. 5 of *The Middle Works*. Edited by Jo Ann Boydston. Carbondale: Southern Illinois University Press.

———. [1909] 1977. "The Influence of Darwinism on Philosophy." In *The Middle Works*. Vol. 4. Edited by Jo Ann Boydston, 3–14. Carbondale: Southern Illinois University Press.

———. [1911] 1978. "The Problem of Truth." In *The Middle Works*. Vol. 6. Edited by Jo Ann Boydston, 12–68. Carbondale: Southern Illinois University Press.

———. [1916] 1980. *Democracy and Education*. Vol. 9 of *The Middle Works*. Edited by Jo Ann Boydston. Carbondale: Southern Illinois University Press.

———. [1917] 1980. "The Need for a Recovery of Philosophy." In *The Middle Works*. Vol. 10. Edited by Jo Ann Boydston, 3–48. Carbondale: Southern Illinois University Press.

———. [1919] 1982. "Philosophy and Democracy." In *The Middle Works*. Vol. 11. Edited by Jo Ann Boydston, 41–53. Carbondale: Southern Illinois University Press.

———. [1920] 1982. *Reconstruction in Philosophy*. In *The Middle Works*. Vol. 12. Edited by Jo Ann Boydston, 77–201. Carbondale: Southern Illinois University Press.

———. [1925] 1981. *Experience and Nature*. Vol. 1 of *The Later Works*. Edited by Jo Ann Boydston. Carbondale: Southern Illinois University Press.

———. [1929] 1984. *The Quest for Certainty*. Vol. 4 of *The Later Works*. Edited by Jo Ann Boydston. Carbondale: Southern Illinois University Press.

————. [1930] 1984. "In Response." In *The Later Works*. Vol. 5. Edited by Jo Ann Boydston. 418–23. Carbondale: Southern Illinois University Press.

————. [1931] 1985. "Context and Thought." In *The Later Works*. Vol. 6, *1931–1932*. Edited by Jo Ann Boydston, 3–21. Carbondale: Southern Illinois University Press.

————. [1932] 1985. *Ethics*. Vol. 7 of *The Later Works*. Edited by Jo Ann Boydston. Carbondale: Southern Illinois University Press.

————. [1934] 1987. *Art as Experience*. Vol. 10 of *The Later Works*. Edited by Jo Ann Boydston. Carbondale: Southern Illinois University Press.

Diggins, John Patrick. 1999. "Pragmatism: A Philosophy for Adults Only." *Partisan Review* 66 (2): 255–62.

Eldridge, Michael. 1998. *Transforming Experience: John Dewey's Cultural Instrumentalism*. Nashville: Vanderbilt University Press.

Hekman, Susan. 1997. "Truth and Method: Feminist Standpoint Theory Revisited." *Signs* 22 (21): 341–65.

Mayhew, Katherine Camp, and Anna Camp Edwards. 1936. *The Dewey School: The Laboratory School of the University of Chicago, 1896–1903*. New York: D. Appleton-Century.

Seigfried, Charlene Haddock. 1996. *Pragmatism and Feminism: Reweaving the Social Fabric*. Chicago: University of Chicago Press.

————. 2001. "Beyond Epistemology: From a Pragmatist Feminist Experiential Standpoint." In *Engendering Rationalities*, edited by Nancy Tuana and Sandi Morgen, 99–121. Albany: State University of New York Press.

Seigfried, Charlene Haddock, and Hans Seigfried. 1995. "Individual Feeling and Universal Validity." In *Rhetoric, Pragmatism, Sophistry*, edited by Steven Mailloux, 139–54. Cambridge: Cambridge University Press.

Sklar, Kathryn Kish. 1998. "Hull House *Maps and Papers*: Social Science as Women's Work in the 1890s." In *Gender and American Social Science: The Formative Years*, edited by Helene Silverberg. Princeton: Princeton University Press.

Westbrook, Robert B. 1991. *John Dewey and American Democracy*. Ithaca: Cornell University Press.

Part One

A Usable Past

1

A Toast to John Dewey

Jane Addams

John Dewey was a member of the first board of Hull-House trustees. It consisted of two or three business men, two or three philanthropic women, and the philosopher, to keep us from becoming either hard-boiled or sentimental in this new undertaking, which the English somewhat heavily called "residential study of the problems of the job: he took Julia Lathorp's Plato Club for a series of Sunday afternoons one midwinter, some days so stormy that only the "cranks" came.

The Plato Club was an epitome of all discussions held on social questions in the nineties. You propounded your theory and stuck to it through thick and thin, and no compromise was permitted! You either belived in heredity or you believed in environment, and the very highschools debated the question with the same fervor brought to bear upon the problem of the priority of the chick or the egg. It was therefore most significant when John Dewey, who came to the new University of Chicago in 1894, announced the theory, or rather when the theory slowly leaked out, of an ever changing society in constant need or exploration and rediscovery; but stranger still was his ultimate test of the utility of any social scheme. Even Mr. Dooley said to Mr. Hennessy, in the Chicago Tribune itself, "The question is, Hennessy, does it work? The jawing isn't worth a tinker's dam."

It was still more useful then, when John Dewey began a little practice school which he established near the University of Chicago, and demonstrated among other things the inter-action between the individual and his environment. He studied the response of each child, not to a static environment but to various surroundings largely produced by the child himself. An historic period having made itself at home in the child's imagination, he energetically dug, built, wove and cooked according to his needs in a primitive hut or a moated castle.

John Dewey's little yellow-covered book, School and Society, made so clear the necessity for individualizing each child that it is quite fair, I think, to say that his insistence upon an atmosphere of freedom and confidence between the teacher and pupil, of a common interest in the life they led together, profoundly affected all similar relationships, certainly those between the social worker and his client. We were used to saying that the welfare of the community is a mutual responsibility, but John Dewey told us that the general intelligence is dormant, with its communications broken and faint, until it possesses the public as its medium.

He, who had so highly individualized the children in his school as to drive their parents into alarmed protest, warned us not to make exceptions of ourselves in regard to the experiences of life. But as he had socialized the children by giving them an almost empirical consciousness of the race life, so he individualized us by the corollary that the dear public itself—for which we were so much concerned—comes into existence through the extension of the acts of individuals beyond those personally involved.

Perhaps the entire psychological approach to the problems of social welfare was implicit in the situation when that group of brilliant men formed the Department of Philosophy at the new University of Chicago. Most of them had been attached in some way to the University of Michigan. There were James Tufts, John Dewey, George Mead and James Angell, if I may be permitted to use Quaker nomenclature. This philosophic department was one of those which incorporated pedagogy within itself. Many educators had been philosophers and a few philosophers had been educators, but this department broke down those invisible walls which so stubbornly separate one academic department from another. There is nothing in all creation like it, excepting the unbreakable division walls between the different departments of the United States government.

Perhaps we may trace back to this new group of men the movement now culminating in the brand new psychiatric social workers and in the institutes of juvenile research. It began, in Chicago at least, when a student of John Dewey's was put in charge of the Child Study Department in the public schools. It was largely the prestige of Dr. Dewey himself which enabled the department to come into existence and perhaps it is not a mere coincidence that it was Chicago that founded the first psychopathic clinic attached to its Juvenile Court which in its turn had been the pioneer ten years earlier, because children were entitled to a court adapted to their own needs. We are impatient for the time when such a treatment may be extended to the adult criminal. At the moment the data supplied by the psychologists is often left on the hands of the embarrassed judge as extra-legal material; he cannot permit it to affect the judicial decision, although it may be convincing enough to weigh heavily upon his conscience.

Whatever may be the outcome of these newer experiments, many of John Dewey's contemporaries are certain of one thing: that the problems of social welfare in our own time have never been so squarely faced as by the philosopher who deliberately made the study of men and their intelligences a foundation for the study of the problems with which men have to deal. In those years when we were told by the scientists, or at least by the so-called scientists, that the world was in the grasp of subhuman forces against which it was absurd to oppose the human will, John Dewey calmly stated that the proper home of intelligence was the world itself and that the true function of intelligence was to act as critic and regulator of the forces which move the world.

Perhaps the greatest tribute to this worldly wisdom of his—the most impressive acknowledgement of his contribution to social welfare—has been the confidence with which one distracted nation after another has called him into their councils. We were in China only a few months after the Deweys had been there. The Philosophy Club at Peking was voluble with admiration, insisting that the philosophy of Dewey and his concepts of conduct could be compared to no one but to Confucius himself. It may have been this pious juxtaposition which moved one of these nascent philosophers gravely to remark, that it was a pity that when America needed a new religion the citizens had not called upon John Dewey to found it instead of Mrs. Eddy. Following the Dewey technique, Alice Dewey had inaugurated the office of Dean of Women at the National University at Nanking, to make clear that co-education was feasible in China as elsewhere. I shall always remember the tribute of affectionate appreciation given by her Chinese successor.

I do not know much personally of Dr. Dewey's journey to Turkey, although I have no doubt it was as successful as his others were, but I do wish that I might reproduce to you the enthusiasm on the part of the young Mexicans; of Saenz, the present minister of education; of Vasconsalez, who previously held that office; of the school of gifted artists who, as they decorate the vast walls of the education building with scenes from this history of the Aztecs and other Indians, always bear in mind the educational theory as they conceive John Dewey propounded it to Mexico. They showed us a wall in the boys' school upon which the paintings had been deliberately defaced because they violated the canons of the new education and had imitated the frivolities of a dead art.

It is hard to exaggerate the gratitude of the young Russian intelligentsia in this country for the report that Dr. Dewey gave of the contemporary Russian experiment not only in education but in rebuilding the social structure itself. The representatives of a misunderstood and unpopular cause are devoted above all others to the recognized authority who becomes the champion of their cause through a clear and objective statement of the facts. He has done this many times. Years ago, before trade unions had proved their social utility and when it was scarcely respectable to be identified with them, John Dewey made it clear to them and for all their Chicago friends. Later he entered into a contest with the unions themselves that they might not curtail freedom in their educational enterprises.

That John Dewey should take an active part in the successful movement for the outlawry of war, is prehaps a corollary of his wide acquaintance with this world of ours and his desire for a stable foundation for those super-structures of social welfare of which we venture to dream.

Only once in a public crisis did I find my road taking a sharp right angle to the one he recommended. That fact in and of itself gave me pause to think, and almost threatened my confidence in the inevitability of that road. Our rough journeyings thereon often confirmed John Dewey's contention that unless truth vindicates itself in practice it easily slips into futile dogma.

Advocates of peace in time of war, we were perforce thrust into the position of the doctrinaire, although the Dewey teaching saved us from resorting to the ineffable solace vouchsafed to the self-righteous, and as we struggled in one country after another for a foothold in reality and actually found it, we were grateful to him for having taught us a method.

Of course, even in those days when I first knew John Dewey, he bore certain earmarks of the traditional absent-minded philosopher. I vividly remembered when he lost a newly acquired doctor's hood at the fifty years' celebration of the founding of the University of Wisconsin. At the moment I was walking with the venerated president of the University of Michigan, down that path which seems to connect the somber dome of the university with the gilded dome of the State House. Angell and Addams had "swapped" stories of foreign visitors whom we had entertained and we had almost reached a decision to collaborate on a book entitled, Famous People whose Boots We have Blacked, for at that time distinguished foreigners—innocent of the domestic system prevailing on the broad and democratic prairies—confidingly flung their boots outside their bedroom doors, little suspecting that only their hosts would deign to pick them up. President Angell, whose diplomatic services had taken him well over the world, whose tolerant and kindly spirit had appraised many men of many lands, listened delightedly when asked if he had lost a hood, and replied, "Of course, it is Dewey's. The occasion wouldn't be complete unless he *had* lost it!" Turning to me he remarked, "Dewey, of all men on this campus today, will probably make the greatest contribution, in spite of the fact that they have combed the universities from Oxford down for this occasion."

Although Dr. Dewey is not easy to read, nor in the Chautauqua sense, a popular lecturer, through the conscious use of his luminous mind he has almost made over the connotations of the very word philosopher for thousands of people. This has been the result of his deliberate convictions. May we quote his own words which one of his students has placed on the title page of his last book: "Better it is for philosophy to err in active participation in the living struggles and issues of its own age and times, than to maintain an immune monastic impeccability. To try to escape from the snares and pitfalls of time by recourse to traditional problems and interests—rather than that, let the dead bury their own dead." It is such winged words as these which have endeared John Dewey to those who live in settlements or undertake other lines of social welfare.

I remember during certain strenuous days in Chicago when we were under cross-fire in a bewildering situation of a strike turned into a lockout, that I thought with primitive green envy of university professors on the other side of town secure from the bludgeonings of both trade unionists and capitalists. But at least one of these professors promptly entered the industrial arena. It was part of his life-long effort to embody truth in conduct. He has qualified for a preeminent position among all those committed to the long struggle for social betterment.

It is a toast rather than a topic—John Dewey and Social Welfare!

2

Experimenting with Education

John Dewey and Ella Flagg Young at the University of Chicago

Ellen Condliffe Lagemann

Although John Dewey is often described as a "child-centered" philosopher, a careful reading of his writings indicates that he did not believe
children could learn well without teachers to help link their prior experience to the experience available in school. The crucial role Dewey as-

This essay derives from a larger research project on the social history of educational research in the
United States between the 1860s and the 1960s that has been generously supported by the Spencer
Foundation. It was originally presented as a lecture at the Centennial Celebration of John Dewey's
Decade at the University of Chicago, 1894–1904. I am grateful to Andrew Mullin for help with the
research on which this article is based.

signed teachers has not been fully recognized because Dewey said relatively little about teachers in his major educational writings, including *Democracy and Education* (1916). During his Chicago years, while working closely with teacher advocate Ella Flagg Young, Dewey wrote incisively about teachers and the political constraints that limited their effectiveness. However, after leaving Chicago, this was not a focal point of his major educational works. The significance of this oversight is explored in this article, especially in relation to Dewey and Young's brief but close and important collaboration.

However appealing John Dewey's thought may be, there is no denying that it lacks a sense of realpolitik. Dewey's descriptions of democracy as associated living, of schools as embryonic communities, and of politics as the education of publics have stirred the imagination of many people because they resonate with deeply humane and widely shared values. His most memorable phrases, for example, "what the best and wisest parent wants for his child, that must the community want for all of its children" (Dewey [1899] 1976a, p. 5) portray worthy social ideals and important social relationships with unusual clarity. Despite that, when one reads Dewey's writings wanting to know *how* the kind of democracy, education, or politics he described might be developed, one comes up lacking.

Perhaps a philosopher should not be taken to task for failing also to be a reformer. Surely there is a need for social criticism even when it is not joined to plans for social improvement. That notwithstanding, it seems fair to fault Dewey for not attending more centrally to strategic concerns because he called for a philosophy that would illuminate the real problems of this world. My purpose, however, is not so much to judge Dewey as to understand what his ideas do and do not offer and to call attention to significant problems he failed to address. More specifically, I hope to suggest that by acknowledging the shortcomings of Dewey's thought, educators today can move beyond the common use of Dewey's name as an icon in order to grapple afresh with what he believed.

Such reengagement could yield many benefits including the dispelling of myths that have long clouded understanding of crucial aspects of Dewey's educational thought. Among these, none has been more pervasive or pernicious than the claim that Dewey advocated child-centered education. Although it is true that Dewey thought learning had to build from the experience of the child and did not think teachers should impose discipline on children or rely on directive, authoritarian teaching methods, he was firmly convinced that teachers played a central role in education. He did not believe children could learn well if left totally to their own devices. Teachers, he maintained, should link the experiences children brought to school with the activities, relationships, and materials that could be marshaled in school to help them grow. In Dewey's thought, teachers were indispensable guides and organizers of the educational process and the success of educational reform would depend on their effectiveness (Dewey [1902] 1976*b*, p. 285; [1903] 1977, p. 235).

Although Dewey was clear in his disavowal of child-centered education and therefore cannot be held responsible for misinterpretations that portray him that way, he was responsible, I believe, for widespread misunderstanding of the important role he assigned teachers. Though clearly stated in his writings (and demonstrated throughout his life), the importance of teachers was not featured in *Democracy and Education* or in other major educational works. The silence is unfortunate and difficult to understand, but examining Dewey's relationship with Ella Flagg Young may shed light on why it occurred.

A longtime Chicago schoolteacher and administrator, who studied and worked with Dewey from 1895 until 1904, Young was one of Dewey's most important tutors in education and especially important in shaping his understanding of teachers and teaching. According to Dewey's recollections of his Chicago years (1894–1904), Young exercised more influence on his educational ideals, especially "his ideas of democracy in the school," than anyone else except his wife, Alice Chipman Dewey (Jane Dewey 1951, p. 29; Boydston 1975). Although Young's influence on Dewey was thus acknowledged and profound, it was also partial. Young had a clear understanding of the subtlety and centrality of politics in education, which Dewey echoed briefly while they worked together in Chicago but never fully incorporated into his educational thought. It is therefore to what Dewey did and did not learn from Young that one must turn, I think, to understand his failure to emphasize the significance of teachers, which helped skew interpretations of his thought and limited the practical value of his philosophy.

Ella Flagg Young: A Teacher Advocate

At the time Ella Flagg Young became John Dewey's student, public schooling in the United States was undergoing very significant change.

More children were staying in school beyond the elementary grades, and the administration of schools was more and more likely to be treated as a function distinct from and superior to classroom instruction. Increasingly, too, universities were establishing departments and schools of education, which were seeking to train principals and other educational leaders and to engage in research. As a result, schools came to be linked to universities in a variety of hierarchical relationships. University professors developed tests and texts for school use. They also served as outside consultants to school boards and, as was true of Dewey himself, interpreted educational problems in their speeches and writings.

As Ella Flagg Young knew from her own observations and experience, many of these changes had negative consequences for teachers. Thanks to increasing bureaucracy and professionalization, teachers in metropolitan centers like Chicago lost autonomy and status in palpable ways. Increasingly subject to work rules that specified how they could and could not relate to the youngsters in their charge, teachers became ever more subordinate to administrators, and, because elementary teachers tended to have fewer years of schooling, they were losing rank relative to high school teachers (Murphy 1990).

A strong advocate for teachers, Young was extraordinarily astute in her understanding of the changes going on around her, and she shared her insights with Dewey. Fifty years old when she became Dewey's student, Young was tough, savvy, articulate, and deeply intellectual. One acquaintance claimed she was rather "brusque and plain looking with piercing looking eyes that could read people through and through" (Dora Wells, in Donatelli [1971], p. 89). Another stated that "in fighting for a principle, Mrs. Young could be as 'hard as nails,' and she could match her wits with anyone" (Elmer A. Morrow, in Donatelli [1971], pp. 241–42). Margaret Haley, the longtime leader of the Chicago Teachers' Federation, who was one of Young's great admirers, remembered her as "the nearest approach I have ever seen to thought in instantaneous action" (Reid 1982, p. 141). According to Haley, "her intellect was a machine gun," but "it was her moral courage rather than her mental capacity that made her a leader of women" (Reid 1982, p. 140). Dewey simply said: "I have hardly known anyone who made the effect of genuine intellectual development the test and criterion of the value of everything as much as she" (Dewey, in McManis [1916], p. 121).

As a student in Dewey's seminar at the University of Chicago, Young was the undisputed star. One of her peers remembered the class as a two-way conversation between Dewey and Young that pretty much excluded everyone else (McManis 1916, pp. 102–3). Because she had quite literally grown up as a teacher, Young had a great deal of hands-on experience to contribute to Dewey's emerging educational thought. In turn, Dewey believed he had "a specific intellectual point of view and terminology" to offer Young, which gave her "greater intellectual assurance" (Dewey, in McManis [1916], p. 120).

Having moved to Chicago from Buffalo, New York, with her parents and two older siblings in 1858, when she was 13, Young had attended elementary school and then the Normal Department of the high school before beginning to teach at the age of 17. Thereafter she had moved steadily up the administrative ladder, becoming a principal in 1876 and a district superintendent of schools in 1887. She had remained in that post until 1899, when she resigned in protest. Chicago's new superintendent of schools, E. Benjamin Andrews, former president of Brown University, was attempting to centralize control of the curriculum, which Young vehemently opposed. In fact, she had recently proposed the organization of teachers' councils in all the Chicago schools to facilitate the involvement of teachers and principals in decisions concerning curriculum. According to Margaret Haley, Young had made this suggestion because she insisted that "the experience gained by teachers in the actual work of teaching should not be ignored" (Reid 1982, p. 88). The Chicago Board of Education did not agree. Although some teachers' councils were established on a voluntary, outside-of-school basis, the board would not give them official status. This defeat, combined with her sense of being "in discord professionally with her superiors in office," led to Young's departure (Young to Mary Lynch, June 9, 1899, in Donatelli [1971], p. 133).

Reforming the Laboratory School

Young's resignation was fortunate for Dewey. Free of administrative responsibilities within the Chicago schools, she was now willing to accept an appointment in Dewey's department at the University of Chicago and to become supervisor of instruction at the University Elementary School that Dewey had just organized. "The Laboratory School," as Young dubbed it, was an outgrowth of Deweys growing disenchantment with philosophy conceived as abstract theorizing and his growing interest in determining whether and how education might provide philosophy with a basis for empirical experimentation (Young, in Donatelli [1971], p. 7). Personally important to Dewey because his children were students there, the Laboratory School was also vital to Dewey's intellectual develop-ment. That Young was able to help him understand the workings of the school in terms that were quite literally relevant to his philosophical queries helps explain the great influence Dewey attributed to her.

Although the Laboratory School was growing in size when Young joined its staff, its place within the university was not as secure as Dewey would have liked. To Dewey, the importance of the school was clear. As he had told the university's trustees, he was convinced that trying to teach pedagogy without an experimental school "partakes of the nature of a farce and imposture—it is like professing to give thorough training in a science and then neglecting to provide a laboratory for faculty and students to work in" (Dewey to [university trustees], [spring 1896], in McCaul [1961] p. 153). University of Chicago president William Rainey Harper agreed, but he also worried about the school's management and its expense and insisted that the university could not and should not provide the school with the levels of financial support Dewey thought it required.

Respected by Harper, who was active in Chicago school politics and aware of the high regard in which Chicago teachers held Young, and trusted by Dewey, Young was able at least for a time to advise Dewey and reassure Harper. Soon after beginning at the university, she told Harper that she and Dewey were working on plans "to make the work of the Elementary School really available in the pedagogical depart-ment" and that she was preparing "a study of the working out of theory and method of the school as a preliminary to an expert report, thorough and searching, to Mr. Dewey" (Young to Harper, December 2, 1899, in Smith [1979], pp. 69–70). Presumably it was this that prompted Dewey subsequently to remark that "in the reorganization of the laboratory school after certain weaknesses in its original scheme of administration had become apparent (due largely to my inexperience in administrative matters) her influence with that of Mrs. Dewey were the controlling factors. It is due to these two that the laboratory school ran so much more systematically and definitely—free from a certain looseness of ends and edges—in its last three or four years" (Dewey, in McManis [1916], p. 120).

From the start, Dewey had held weekly meetings with the Laboratory School teachers to discuss the activities of the week in different classes and to consider how those pertained to the school's general principles. The "principles," he explained later, were equivalent to "a kind of working hypothesis," and "their application was in the hands of the teachers," who were totally free to apply them as they saw fit (Dewey, in Mayhew and Edwards [1936], p. 371). Although the meetings were intended to promote cooperation in the experimental aims of the school, Dewey believed they were not initially successful in doing that. They were too centered on "practical" problems, he thought, "too much given to matters of immediate import and not sufficiently intellectual in content" (Dewey, in Mayhew and Edwards [1936], p. 371). Apparently the school was in a rather chaotic state, the teachers' concern with "practical" problems likely having arisen from a lack of clear expectations and clearly designated responsibilities.

After Ella Flagg Young and Alice Dewey became involved, however, things changed. They instituted a departmental structure, which helped alleviate some of the problems that had been so troublesome previously and ensured that one person with special knowledge and experience in a particular area would bring a weekly report to the teachers' meetings, presenting "the results of testing certain educational theories in the actual practices of her classroom" (Dewey, in Mayhew and Edwards [1936], p. 374). This ensured the smooth running of the school. It also produced the kind of cooperation on questions of educational theory and practice that Dewey was searching for and proved to him, he said later, that freedom combined with intellectual cooperation provided a better way to ensure effective teaching than "supervision, critic teaching, and technical training" (Dewey, in Mayhew and Edwards [1936], p. 371). Opposed to the growth of central supervisory personnel in the schools, Dewey became convinced that "primary teachers should have the same power, the same freedom (and the same pecuniary recompense that now goes to university and, in less measure, to high-school teachers)" (Dewey, in Mayhew and Edwards [1936], p. 372). He wrote later that "in recollection of many things in our school practice and results that I could wish had been otherwise, there is compensation in the proof our experience affords that the union of intellectual freedom and cooperation will develop the spirit prized in university teachers, and that is sometimes mistakenly supposed to be a monopoly of theirs" (Dewey, in Mayhew and Edwards [1936], p. 372).

"I Was Constantly Getting Ideas from Her"

Even though Dewey was careful to couple his wife, Alice Chipman Dewey, with Ella Flagg Young in discussing positive changes in the operation of the Laboratory School, it is abundantly clear that it was Young who was his primary tutor. Candidly confessing that he was "constantly getting ideas from her," Dewey explained that "It was from her that I learned that freedom and respect for freedom mean regard for the inquiring or reflective processes of individuals and that what ordinarily passes for freedom—freedom from external restraint, spontaneity in expression, etc.—are of significance only in their connection with thinking operations" (Dewey, in McManis [1916], p. 120). Young's suggestions for the Laboratory School apparently showed Dewey that giving teachers clear expectations and assignments did not constrain them. Quite the opposite was the case. More important, her suggestions demonstrated that what was crucial for good teaching were opportunities to think and experiment within a context of frank exchange and full respect.

Exemplified at the Laboratory School, Young's views about the importance of freedom for teachers were also embodied in the dissertation she wrote under Dewey's supervision and defended in 1900. This offered another medium for intense and profoundly educative exchange.

Entitled *Isolation in the School*, Young's dissertation presented a compelling description of what was needed to improve education at all levels. Most important, Young argued, was social equality between and among all the participants in the educational system—students and teachers, teachers and administrators, and school and university teachers. This was a prerequisite to the cooperation and the continuous, collaborative discussion, modification, and reaffirmation of aims that made effective education possible. Not surprisingly, given the importance she assigned to intellectual and pedagogical autonomy for teachers, Young was critical of "non-teaching supervisors" (Young 1901, p. 29). They were costly and their presence demeaned the actual work of "class teachers," she said. As would always be the case when "the highest ranking officer is a person *in* power rather than a person *of* power," they were also a source of "petty jealousy," she observed (Young 1901, p. 30).

In *Isolation in the School*, Young revealed herself to be a master of practical philosophic application. Although the study could be read as a treatise on Deweyan psychology, its focus was problems of educational policy

and practice. It contained a great deal of theory—ideas about the importance of will, the value of knowledge rooted in experience, and the inseparable relationship between character and conduct. But it did not present
these constructs as ends in themselves. It used them to explain the
thoughts, emotions, ideals, and behaviors of real people, in real situations.

From *Isolation in the School*, it is also clear that Young was willing to
speak forthrightly and critically about the subtle, yet powerful changes in
education that were transforming the actual work of teachers as well as
causing a decline in their status. "The young men who look toward the
schools wish to undertake some new line of work, not of instruction, but
of investigation; to measure and weigh the little ones with machines,"
she noted with not a little sarcasm (Young 1901, p. 42). Disdainful of
university professors bent on research into child hygiene, she was also
suspicious of "the young women of parts [who] wish to be special teachers—to teach the teachers, not the children" (Young 1901, p. 42). She
understood, however, that a wish to escape the elementary classroom was
not a personal failing but was rather a reflection of public thinking. "So
closely associated with drudgery is the ideal of teaching the young, that
trained minds and cultivated personalities shrink from entrance into the
direct work," she explained realistically (Young 1901, p. 42). But "close
supervision," which was "un-American" and undemocratic, in Young's
view, and would not be tolerated within colleges and universities, was
also at fault.

In *Isolation in the Schools* and in others of her writings, Young demonstrated a keen sensitivity to the differences of gender, class, age, status,
and profession that can lead to competition and conflict between and
among groups of people.[1] She wryly observed, for example, that "woman
was far behind man" in understanding her "inherent right" to express
herself through work (Young 1901, pp. 40–41). Men, said Young, would
not tolerate the low salaries or "the mechanism, drudgery, and loss of
individuality which the method of organization and administration has
tended to make characteristic of the graded school" (Young 1901, p. 41).
On another occasion, she applauded the involvement of "club women"
in literacy campaigns among the foreign born, while carefully noting that
"it should always be remembered that it is the teachers and not the club
women who are experts in education, and while the club women may
lead in the movement, when it comes actually to doing the work they
should leave it to the teachers" (Young 1916a, p. 1). Describing the gen-

der politics involved in teacher unionization, she explained on yet another occasion that teachers had learned through long and hard experience that "the men, in their own station and rank in life, the college-bred men, were not ready to do anything for them; therefore they were compelled to go in with those who had felt the oppression and the grind of the power of riches" (Young 1916b, p. 358).

However intellectual Young may have been, she was first and foremost a teacher advocate and a seasoned politician. Whether it was this or other aspects of her experience that account for her powerful insights into politics is difficult to discern from extant sources about her life. Like others among her equally strong, equally feminist, and equally intellectual female contemporaries, notably Jane Addams, Young lived much of her adult life with other women (she had been deserted by her husband after a very brief marriage), one of whom, Laura Brayton, became her intimate, lifelong companion, and this relationship may have contributed to the strength, independence, and feminism that supported her political vision. Whatever its sources, Young's grasp of the politics of education was unusually subtle and deep.

During Dewey's last years in Chicago, Dewey and Young were engaged in conversations that were "so continuous and detailed that the influence resulting from them was largely insensible," Dewey said later (Dewey, in McManis [1916], p. 119). In fact, even assuming mutual influence, it is striking how much *Isolation in the School* presaged views Dewey subsequently expressed. One particularly interesting example of this was an article Dewey published three years after Young's dissertation was presented, which, tellingly, was entitled "Democracy in Education." Commenting on the politics of education in a style that was nearly as forthright and critical as Young's and using language that was characteristic of her, Dewey spoke out against the "close supervision" of teachers and urged "the adoption of intellectual initiative, discussion, and decision throughout the entire school corps" (Dewey [1903] 1977, p. 232). He argued further that a lack of freedom for both teachers and students was the greatest barrier to developing a school system that would prepare people for life in a democracy. He insisted that freedom was necessary to recruit able people into teaching. And he maintained that all other reforms were "conditioned upon the reform of the quality and character of those who engage in the teaching profession" (Dewey [1903] 1977, pp. 196, 198). In "Democracy in Education," John Dewey was an unflinching teachers' advocate.

Democracy and Education

Sadly, the close collegiality that Dewey and Young shared at the time Dewey wrote, "Democracy in Education" was not to last. In the fall of 1903, the Laboratory School was merged with a school that had been founded by Colonel Francis Parker, and Alice Dewey was appointed principal of the new venture. Her appointment alarmed many of the teachers in the former Parker School because she was known to be critical of the school and was believed to be willing to fire teachers of whom she did not approve. The protests of the Parker School teachers caused President Harper to promise that Alice Dewey would only be allowed to serve for one year, though Harper did not make that clear to either of the Deweys. When he refused to reappoint Alice as principal in the spring of 1904 both Deweys therefore resigned. Though evidence is scant, Young apparently sided with the teachers against Alice Dewey. After the Deweys left Chicago in 1904, Young never saw them again.

After Young's untimely death from influenza in 1918, Dewey wrote warmly of her influence on his thought. And yet, despite that, after 1904, he seems to have turned away from consideration of "democracy *in* education" to concern himself instead with the broader issues of "democracy *and* education." Even though *Democracy and Education*, the title for his post-Chicago masterwork, was selected by the book's publisher, it accurately reflected the direction of Dewey's thought. Although he continued to be deeply interested in education throughout his life and remained active in many educational organizations, after leaving Chicago direct participation in educational experimentation was no longer an important part of his life. At Columbia, Dewey was a member of the Department of Philosophy and his closest colleagues were found there and in the various Columbia social science departments. On occasion, Dewey lectured at Teachers College, which was affiliated with Columbia, but his contact with Teachers College was sporadic and quite limited. It is perhaps not surprising therefore that the essential outlines of his educational thought did not change a great deal after he left Chicago, even though other aspects of his thought, including the political dimensions, changed, evolved, and matured quite fundamentally (Lagemann 1989; Westbrook 1991). In *Democracy and Education*, Dewey simply brought the various strands of his thinking together.

Focusing in *Democracy and Education* on the aims of education in a democratic society and what would be required to realize those aims, Dewey provided a lengthy discussion of school curricula but rarely mentioned teachers (in fact, teachers are not even a subject category in the book's index). The few comments he did make were entirely compatible with his earlier calls for intellectual freedom, to wit, the claim that a "distrust of the teacher's experience" was translated into a "lack of confidence in the responses of the pupils" (Dewey [1916] 1980, p. 116). But comments of this kind were too brief and sketchy to provide a clear understanding of why the circumstances under which teachers worked were so important. What is more, there was no indication given in the book that freedom, respect, equal pay, classroom autonomy, and intellectually challenging professional training—democracy in education—were necessary conditions for democratic education.

In other post-Chicago works, Dewey took positions that were also compatible with the views he had expressed in "Democracy in Education" (Dewey [1933] 1986, pp. 127–35; [1937] 1987, pp. 217–25). From *The Sources of a Science of Education*, one could discern, for example, that he was not in sympathy with advocates of a formally defined, university-generated "science of education." He thought a science of education should include "any portions of ascertained knowledge that enter into the heart, head and hands of educators, and which, by entering in, render the performance of the educational function more enlightened, more humane, more truly educational than it was before" (Dewey [1929] 1984, p. 39). In pointing this out, he might well have noted that a formally defined, university-generated "science of education" eclipsed the intellectual freedom of teachers, but he failed to do that. That advocates of this kind of educational science were helping to create and legitimate hierarchical relationships between the mostly male professors who were to generate knowledge about education and the mostly female teachers who were to apply that knowledge went unremarked. Even though Dewey understood and criticized the validity and usefulness of so-called laws of learning, he failed to appreciate and comment upon the social functions such formulas fulfilled as different groups vied for relative rank and power.

What all this suggests, I think, is that Dewey learned only a part of what Ella Flagg Young was willing, able, and eager to teach. Although he deeply respected teachers and acquired from Young a clear sense of the importance of intellectual freedom to the teaching art, he did not enduringly learn that because the status and authority of teachers was contested terrain politics had to be a first priority in promoting educational change. To be sure, Dewey did join the teachers' union in New York City and he did write in support of progressive political causes that would enhance teachers' power. However, it was only while he was conversing with Young on a daily basis that changing the distribution of power in education achieved the kind of central place in his writing that Young would have thought was deserved. Very different from Young, Dewey's understanding of conflict between people of different interest and position was more episodic than enduring. It was at the periphery rather than the center of his concerns. Certainly, Dewey knew that conflict existed and certainly he knew that it had social sources. He made that abundantly clear in *The Public and Its Problems*, *Liberalism and Social Action*, and *Individualism Old and New*, as well as in others of his political writings. However, in his major educational writings, he did not give primary attention to questions of power.

Because he did not feature the central importance of politics *in* education, Dewey could write about education *and* democracy without saying much about the wherewithal necessary to connect the two. He said a good deal about the importance of the child's experience because that point was essential to the psychology on which he based his conception of learning. But he said little about teachers and the circumstances required to enable them to teach effectively. That was not necessary because he seems to have assumed that once education and democracy and their relation were rightly understood, rational people of good will would follow the dictates of science and collaborate in an educational reformation. To be fair, Dewey was not naive and he did argue that "a reorganization of education . . . can only be accomplished piecemeal, a step at a time" (Dewey [1916] 1980, p. 144). Nonetheless, the point remains that understanding and analyzing the political aspects of educational reform was not his strong suit. He was better at describing the aims of education than he was at considering how those aims might be achieved, not merely in an unusual school or classroom, but more generally throughout the nation's schools. In consequence, he said too little about teachers and did not provide anything like a comprehensive analysis of the myriad relationships and circumstances that defined what teachers could and could not do. This did not cause misinterpretations of Dewey's views as child centered, though it may have opened the door to them. But it did unwittingly obscure the complex social and political aspects of educational reform.

Temperament, perspective, and Dewey's characteristic habits of mind may help to account for the fact that he did not enduringly absorb all aspects of Ella Flagg Young's perspective, despite his great admiration for it. Perhaps because he never totally shed his essentially Hegelian mental template, he was not nearly so incisive as Young about the irreconcilable differences of interest that can and do exist between and among different categories and groups of people (Dewey, in Adams and Montague [1930], p. 21; Frankel, in Cahn [1977], p. 13; and Bernstein 1986, p. 271). A moralist, Dewey held an unshakable, essentially religious faith in rationality, science, and the ultimate goodness of all people, and that, too, had a profound effect on his perceptions (Rockefeller 1991, chap. 5). So did his persistent optimism, which enabled him tenaciously to hope that science could help peopole transcend the differences in which politics begins. Whatever the reasons, Dewey did not fundamentally incorporate Young's penetrating sense of the centrality of politics into his own philosophy of education.

Obviously, that does not invalidate or even lessen the brilliance of other aspects of Dewey's thinking about democracy and education. But it does require attention, I think, if erroneous attributions of child centeredness are to be shed in favor of reanalysis of what Dewey's ideas can mean in the world today. Once one recognizes that Dewey's perspective requires not only study of the child and the curriculum, but also of relationships between teachers and educational scholarship—all that Dewey would have included in a science of education—then one can move from thinking of educational reform in terms merely of school redesign and curriculum change to thinking of it also in terms of relationships between schools and all the institutions that help shape what teachers can do. Central among these, of course, are universities where new knowledge is developed and teachers are educated, not only or most importantly about what and how to teach, but more subtly and essentially about the ways in which education is regarded in American society. Sadly, as Ella Flagg Young understood with typical incisiveness, if universities have participated in the improvement of education, they have also constrained the effectiveness of teachers in many, often subtle ways. The place of schools and departments of education within universities and the attitudes of noneducation students and faculties to education have often had a corrosive influence on would-be teachers and have sometimes helped siphon off the most able to other fields and professions. Clearly, then, if teacher effectiveness is important to the effectiveness of education, university reform must be considered.

Not a central theme in Dewey's writings, the importance of university reform to the development of democracy in education is nevertheless evident when one turns to the strategic questions of implementation and concrete reform that Dewey left aside. It is but one example of what can be seen when the implications and peripheral concerns of Dewey's major educational writings are given the emphasis they deserve. Approaching Dewey this way involves making connections between democracy *in* education and democratic education that Dewey slighted after he left Chicago. If doing so rekindles possibilities that the sad ending of Dewey and Young's relationship foreclosed for a time, then perhaps the isolation of schools and of education, which concerned them both, may finally begin to decrease.

Notes

1. Obviously, differences of race can also lead to conflict, but, to my knowledge, Young never wrote about race.

References

Adams, George P., and William Pepperell Montague, eds. *Contemporary American Philosophy: Personal Statements*. New York: Macmillan, 1930.

Bernstein, Richard. *Philosophical Profiles: Essays in a Pragmatic Mode*. Philadelphia: University of Pennsylvania Press, 1986.

Boydston, Jo Ann. "John Dewey and the New Feminism." *Teachers College Record* 76 (February 1975): 441–48.

Cahn, Steven M. *New Studies in the Philosophy of John Dewey*. Hanover, N.H.: University Press of New England, 1977.

Dewey, Jane M. "Biography of John Dewey." In *The Philosophy of John Dewey*, edited by Paul Arthur Schilpp. 2d ed. LaSalle, Ill.: Open Court, 1951.

Dewey, John. *The School and Society* [1899]. In *John Dewey: The Middle Works*, vol. 1 of *The Collected Works of John Dewey, 1882–1953*, edited by Jo Ann Boydston. Carbondale: Southern Illinois University Press, 1976a.

———. *The Child and the Curriculum* [1902]. In *John Dewey: The Middle Works*, vol. 2 of *The Collected Works of John Dewey, 1882–1953*, edited by Jo Ann Boydston. Carbondale: Southern Illinois University Press, 1976b.

———. "Democracy in Education" [1903]. In *John Dewey: The Middle Works*, vol. 3 of *The Collected Works of John Dewey, 1882–1953*, edited by Jo Ann Boydston. Carbondale: Southern Illinois University Press, 1977.

————. *Democracy and Education* [1916]. In *John Dewey: The Middle Works*, vol. 9 of *The Collected Works of John Dewey, 1882–1953*, edited by Jo Ann Boydston. Carbondale: Southern Illinois University Press, 1980.

————. *The Sources of a Science of Education* [1929]. In *John Dewey: The Later Works*, vol. 5 of *The Collected Works of John Dewey, 1882–1953*, edited by Jo Ann Boydston. Carbondale: Southern Illinois University Press, 1984.

————. "Education and Our Present Social Problems" [1933]. In *John Dewey: The Later Works*, vol. 9 of *The Collected Works of John Dewey, 1882–1953*, edited by Jo Ann Boydston. Carbondale: Southern Illinois University Press, 1986.

————. "Democracy and Educational Administration" [1937]. In *John Dewey: The Later Works*, vol. 11 of *The Collected Works of John Dewey, 1882–1953*, edited by Jo Ann Boydston. Carbondale: Southern Illinois University Press, 1987.

Donatelli, Rosemary V. "The Contributions of Ella Flagg Young to the Educational Enterprise." Ph.D. dissertation, University of Chicago, 1971.

Lagemann, Ellen Condliffe. "The Plural Worlds of Educational Research." *History of Education Quarterly* 29 (Summer 1989): 185–214.

Mayhew, Katherine Camp, and Anna Camp Edwards. *The Laboratory School.* New York: D. Appleton-Century, 1936.

McCaul, Robert L. "Dewey and the University of Chicago. Part I: July, 1894–March, 1902." *School and Society* 89 (March 1961): 152–79.

McManis, John T. *Ella Flagg Young and a Half-Century of the Chicago Public Schools.* Chicago: A. C. McClurg, 1916.

Murphy, Marjorie. *Blackboard Unions: The AFT and the NEA, 1900–1980.* Ithaca: Cornell University Press, 1990.

Reid, Robert, ed. *Battleground: The Autobiography of Margaret A. Haley.* Urbana: University of Illinois Press, 1982.

Rockefeller, Steven C. *John Dewey: Religious Faith and Democratic Humanism.* New York: Columbia University Press, 1991.

Smith, Joan K. *Ella Flagg Young: Portrait of a Leader.* Ames: Iowa State University Research Foundation/Educational Studies Press, 1979.

Westbrook, Robert B. *John Dewey and American Democracy.* Ithaca: Cornell University Press, 1991.

Young, Ella Flagg. *Isolation in the School.* University of Chicago Contributions to Education, no. 1. Chicago: University of Chicago Press, 1901.

————. "Los Angeles Schools Ten Years in Advance of Times." *Journal of Education* 83 (February 1916): 1a.

————. "A Reply." *National Education Association, Proceedings* 54 (1916): 356–59b.

3

John Dewey's Pragmatist Feminism

Charlene Haddock Seigfried

Making a Case for Pragmatist Feminist Philosophy

There can be little doubt that pragmatist philosophy in general and John Dewey's philosophy in particular are not part of the impoverished tradition of discourse that feminists criticize. It is not among those philosophies that can "talk about the power of reason but not about the power of empathy," that can talk about rational knowledge but not the understanding brought about by a sense of compassion, one that robs feeling of any rationality. It fulfills Phyllis Rooney's (1991, 97–98) call for a way to speak "about experience as embodied humans," and it answers the feminist need for "an empowering reason, one that doesn't require an opposing force over which it needs to gain transcendence."

Dewey's political activism included support for the many women's issues for which feminists were campaigning at the time, including women's suffrage, women's right to higher education and coeducation, unimpeded access to and legalization of birth control, and just wages and worker control of the conditions of work for women as well as men. Explicit references in his philosophical writings to issues as they differentially affect women or to feminist theory are sporadic but insightful and consistently supportive even when critical of some feminist approaches in favor of others. His feminist perspective is surprisingly consistent with his pragmatism. It is surprising given the widespread lack of congruence of most white, male philosophers' theories of rationality and human nature with their claims about race, ethnicity, class, and women that has been explored and documented in decades of feminist research.

Pragmatist theory itself provides strong resources for feminist thinking, since many of its positions address current feminist interests and debates. Among these are a pluralism and perspectivism that go beyond theory to advocate the actual inclusiveness of appropriately diverse viewpoints, including those of class, color, ethnicity, and gender, as a precondition for resolving problematic situations, whether these involve political, economic, epistemological, or ethical issues. This position unites earlier feminist interests in nonhierarchical leadership styles and a belief in "a woman's voice" with more recent recognitions of the diversity of women and the complexity of multiple identities besides gender, as well as commitments to "letting the subaltern speak." The pragmatist understanding of the developmental processes that characterize persons who dynamically interact with their physical and social environments dissolves a knot of problems evident in controversies over feminist standpoint theories as well as over the oscillation between affirming the individual subject as a unique Promethean entity or as a passive social construct.

The complex and nuanced understanding of experience and its role in questions of understanding and inquiry that informs Dewey's rejection of the epistemological turn opens a whole new approach to questions of knowledge and reality (see Seigfried 2001). His explanation of the interactive character of experience, as both passive and active, subjective and objective, provides a way for feminists to escape from false dualisms generated by the contemporary tendency to reduce philosophy to epistemology and sharply demarcate a privileged realm of theory from its applications in the real world. The unproductive debate between realism and interpretivism can be ignored. We do not have to defend either a version of empiricist epistemology in order to objectively ground claims about women in reality or a version of postmodernist deconstruction of truth and assumption of the self-referentiality of texts in order to recognize the subjective character of understanding, the denial of which has contributed to rejecting the validity of women's experiences and perspectives.

However, the wealth of feminist scholarship about the explicit and implicit role of gender at every level of social, cultural, economic, political, religious, and intellectual organization enriches, critiques, and transforms pragmatist theories. Dewey's conversion of a commitment to social democracy into an emancipatory agenda that affects all aspects of human individual and social development becomes more robust and effective insofar as it takes into account the barriers to inclusiveness exposed in feminist research on racism, classism, sexism, and homophobia. He recognized that democracy can only work where there is faith in individuals as unique resources and not in the superior insights of elites who claim privileged access to reality. Individuals develop and flourish as persons only in interaction with others in society. He showed how these insights, in turn, require a changed conception of intelligence that is really a changed psychology, one that demonstrates that autonomy cannot develop except in situations of interdependence and that learning requires attention to the ways that those around us use things that lead to anticipated outcomes. It also signals a rejection of the model of truth as correspondence and as a function of a priori deduction and the development instead of a model of sympathetic inquiry into actually problematic conditions leading to desired outcomes. The democratic ideal Dewey [1908] 1977, 40) seeks, which is the recognition that the achievement by individuals of their own freedom and prosperity requires the achievement of these goals by all, cannot be obtained without the "conscious articulation of genuinely modern tendencies" that inform the situation in which we find ourselves.

Although he analyzed many of these tendencies in his later writings, in 1908 Dewey ([1908] 1977, 40) said that such insight into the current conditions of life had not yet been satisfactorily achieved and that until it had been, the ethics that characterizes our lives also remained undescribed. Feminist philosophers have made great strides in the exploration of the concrete contexts influencing philosophical reflection. They have shown how unexamined assumptions of sexual, racial, and class superiority have distorted claims about reality and adversely affected the lives and opportunities of exploited members of society. They have consequently not escaped criticism from those who imagine that they themselves express a view from nowhere and who therefore severely criticize feminist theory for developing just such analyses of current cultural, economic, and political situations and for showing how the unanalyzed assumptions informing these various ways of life bias philosophical thinking (see Code 1995).

Because Dewey's ([1931] 1985, 17) philosophy was also concerned with concrete human experience in both its specificity and generality, he also had to defend himself against those who "seem to accept a dogma of immaculate conception of philosophical systems" and think it "derogatory to link a body of philosophic ideas to the social life and culture of their epoch." Pragmatist philosophy as envisioned and practiced by Dewey is therefore continued, deepened, and expanded by those feminist theorists who link knowledge with action, who take the goal of thinking to be emancipation, who recognize the multiple conditions that affect understanding, who demonstrate how a disembodied rationality distorts rather than reveals the world in which we find ourselves, who recognize the interpretive character of experience and who therefore deflate claims about the nature of reality as such and develop instead morally responsible intellectual criteria for adjudicating specific claims about particular realities.

The First Generations of Feminist Pragmatists

In 1949 in *The Second Sex* Simone de Beauvoir ([1949] 1974, xxii) argued that one reason women did not organize themselves to dispute male sovereignty was that they had no past, no history, no solidarity of work and interest comparable with that of the proletariat. But in the same book she began to recover just such a past, as had Jane Addams (1916) in *The Long Road of Woman's Memory*, written more than thirty years earlier. There is now evidence that earlier generations of women studying pragmatist philosophy found resources in it for their own emancipation and that women contributed to pragmatist theory and practice. Even before Dewey moved to Chicago and inaugurated a pragmatist school of thought, Addams had invited him to be on the board of directors of the Hull House Settlement, which she and Ellen Gates Starr had founded, and they worked together to counter the civic and industrial exploitation of immigrants flooding into Chicago at the turn of the century. They collaborated in settlement work and discussion, and they read each other's books.

The first generations of women to study pragmatist philosophy found two aspects of it particularly empowering. One was the pragmatist principle that theory arises from experience and is accountable to it. This changed the subject matter of philosophy from continued rehearsals of the works of generations long dead and the formalism of problem solving based on purely logical considerations to concern with the "the perplexities, the trouble, and the issues of the period in which a philosophy arises" (Dewey [1931] 1985, 17). The changed focus also allowed them to trust their own experiences as a starting point for reflection even when they contradicted the received views of the time. The other principle was that the purpose of inquiry into experience was not to replicate it, but to interrogate problematic situations in order to satisfactorily resolve them. Not all resolutions are satisfactory, because not all fulfill Dewey's ([1934] 1987, 23; see 42–44 and 142–45) criterion of a consummatory experience, that is, one that is the fulfillment of our being in interaction with the conditions of existence, a temporary state of harmony that is at the same time the beginning of further enriching interactions. Because experience is a transaction between organisms and their physical and social environment, such resolutions are a means of growth for the self as well as a means of transforming oppressive situations into liberating ones.

Pragmatism's experimental method undermines the conservatism that seeks to preserve old standards despite changing conditions. According to Dewey ([1929] 1984, 218), "What is needed is intelligent examination of the consequences that are actually effected by inherited institutions and customs, in order that there may be intelligent consideration of the ways in which they are to be intentionally modified in behalf of generation of different consequences." Women of many different ethnic groups and classes, and other groups whose lives were severely circumscribed by convention and who bore the brunt of sexist, ethnic, and racial prejudices, found a powerful resource in a philosophical position that questioned rather than justified convention and whose goal was transformation of given conditions to better meet the just needs of individuals and communities. Through reflections on the consequences for thinking of the Darwinian evolutionary model, pragmatists understood that a metaphysics of being could no longer be defended once the pervasiveness of temporality was acknowledged. To succeed in understanding things as they are, for example, requires a prior examination of how they came to be and is continuous with interest in how they will turn out. Accurate anticipation of outcomes that we have helped to bring about, not accuracy of representation, is the goal of knowledge.

But what did women bring to their reflections that derived from and challenged their particular situation? Lucy Sprague Mitchell is one example of a female undergraduate who has left evidence that her experiences were at odds with what she was hearing in the philosophy classroom. I first came across her name in my efforts to discover whether I, as a woman for whom pragmatism was an invaluable resource for developing feminist theory and practice, had any predecessors. Higher education for women was still the exception rather than the rule for women when Mitchell entered the class of 1900 at the Harvard Annex, the forerunner of Radcliffe College. She studied with William James, Josiah Royce, George Santayana, Hugo Munsterberg, and George Palmer and was the only one in her class to receive Honors in Philosophy. I was not surprised to learn that in an essay written for Royce she had rejected the knower as isolated subject because it was solipsistic and argued instead for a relational self. But I was intrigued by her rejection of free will in another paper. Recognizing that her belief in determinism was in fundamental disagreement with both Royce's and Palmer's beliefs, she also denied that reality was ultimately benevolent and rational, and asserted instead that "the reality of evil and disappointment" was one of her "strongest beliefs" (Antler 1987, 62).

Mitchell, who became a lifelong friend of John Dewey, had already met him; his wife, Alice; and Jane Addams in Chicago, read all of John Dewey's writings on education, avidly followed Addams's work, and later attended Dewey's lectures at Teacher's College, Columbia University. I do not know whether the positions expressed in her undergraduate essays continued into her pioneering work in higher education for women and in progressive education, but her youthful sense of being determined by conditions over which she exercised little control and her recognition of the pervasiveness of evil and disappointment do not reflect the optimistic meliorism associated with pragmatist philosophy. They are more characteristic of the experiences of marginalized members of society whose choices are severely circumscribed and who bear the brunt of adverse social, economic, and physical conditions. Mitchell was privileged by her upper-class status and wealth, but was still subject to the limitations imposed by patriarchal traditions of family life. She suffered from tuberculosis throughout her college years, but after graduation, although chronically ill herself, assumed her role as dutiful daughter and cared for her mother until her mother's death from tuberculosis and then continued to care for her ill and despotic father.

The sense of frustration she experienced growing up under continuous constraint in an authoritarian household and in deferring her own goals to meet the needs of others jars with the meliorism, creative possibility, and openness to the future characteristic of pragmatist philosophy. Her situation, like that of W. E. B. Du Bois, who studied philosophy at Harvard a decade earlier than Mitchell, illustrates the disruptive changes of attitude, tone, and subject matter evident when pragmatism is approached from the perspectives of those differently positioned from the norm by gender, race, or class. In Du Bois's (1980, 146–47) 1890 commencement speech, for example, he says that "to say that a nation is in the way of civilization is a contradiction in terms and a system of human culture whose principle is the rise of one race on the ruins of another is a farce and a lie." White commentators were predisposed to label such viewpoints "bitter" and to resent their militancy (Aptheker in Du Bois 1975, 14). But such sentiments expose the limitations of their awareness of the unjust relations endemic in American society. Their lack of understanding of the suffering caused by racism unwittingly reveals their privileged positions as whites. Such marginalized perspectives as those Mitchell and Du Bois express, though, are not necessarily opposed to the hopeful tone of the pragmatist faith in reconstruction. If anything, such an emancipatory agenda can resonate with particular force for those traditionally excluded or oppressed, as Mitchell (1953, 74) acknowledged when she said that Dewey freed her from her father's patriarchal attitudes and as is evident in Du Bois's (1975, 134–59) calls for a social democracy.

Prejudice, Alienation, and Oppression

Of central importance for a feminist interpretation of Dewey is the determination of whether he recognized and censured sexual, class, and racial discrimination and of whether his pragmatist philosophy can accommodate marginalized persons and alienated perspectives. What resources has it to offer in overcoming such alienation and discrimination and changing the social, economic, and political conditions that have brought them about? Over the years Dewey's political writings became increasingly radicalized in response to continued warfare, the Great Depression, the intransigence of entrenched economic and political forces, and the growing virulence of public discourse. But all his writings show an awareness of the negative effects of past unjust beliefs and practices and a desire to develop the resources needed for everyone, but especially those presently excluded, to overcome these obstacles and to be enabled to contribute to a better future for themselves and others.

Dewey argues that reflective thinking begins with the existential situation of everyday experience. He deliberately seeks to undermine the prevailing practice of philosophizing in a vacuum, as though rationality was a characteristic of disembodied minds unaffiliated with others and unaffected by society. He coins the term "body-minds" to emphasize that feeling plays an essential role in human understanding. Because we have the capacity of feeling, our responses to natural and social environments are selective. Our susceptibility to the useful and harmful in our surroundings eventuates in anticipation of consequences and intelligent foresight. Feelings, therefore, reveal and direct us toward objective features of experience. They are also affected by past experiences and beliefs: "Comfort or discomfort, fatigue or exhilaration, implicitly sum up a history whereby . . . the past can be unraveled and made explicit" (Dewey [1925] 1981, 196–97). Such feelings reveal more than a particular individual's personal history because "experience is already overlaid and saturated with the products of the reflection of past generations and by-gone ages" (Dewey [1925] 1981, 40). Even experiences that seem uniquely one's own are filled with inherited interpretations.

Selective bias in interactions with social and physical environments is inevitable, which is why "philosophy is a critique of prejudices." None of us escapes bias, because "interest, as the subjective, is after all equivalent to individuality or uniqueness" (Dewey [1931] 1985, 15). To be a person, an individual center of action, is to uniquely undergo and actively apprehend the world of which one is a part. These undergoings and doings are expressions of a history, habits, and perspectives.[1] Critical reflection is needed in order to determine whether these inherited interpretations, welded onto the genuine materials of firsthand experience, will eventuate in a fuller and richer grasp of our situation or will impoverish it through distortion. One great task of philosophy, therefore, is to emancipate us from prejudice (Dewey [1925] 1981, 40). Dewey's pragmatist philosophy is thus allied with other emancipatory theories such as feminism that aim at exposing prejudices and that work to empower the oppressed.

But although his analyses reveal the ubiquity of unconscious biases, some of which are helpful and some of which are harmful, Dewey never-theless thinks that "deliberate insincerity and hypocrisy are rare." What seems to be hypocrisy is more often a reflection of the difficulty we have in consistently integrating theory and practice, attitudes and responses (Dewey [1929] 1984, 224). His lack of suspicion of the motives of others leads him to underestimate the extent and depth of misogyny, racism, homophobia, and classism in personal habits and societal institutions and to neglect the development of an account of the more irrational sides of human understanding and use of power. This has paradoxical results for his analysis of feminist issues.

On the one hand, Dewey's realization that selective interest plays a necessary role in our ability to organize our experiences satisfactorily, even when the organization is intellectual, motivates him to develop a methodology of inquiry that takes such bias into account. Recognizing that we cannot achieve impartiality merely by wanting to do so, he makes inclusiveness of others in decision-making processes a condition of objec-tivity. It is not just morally wrong to refuse to include in deliberations that affect their lives those members of society that are believed to be inferior. It is also an intellectual fallacy to suppose that limiting points of view to those of an intellectual elite would more adequately achieve the objectivity expressed in the resolution of problematic situations than a more inclusive approach would. Dewey also makes emancipation from prejudice a central concern of pragmatist philosophy and a necessary part of the steps needed to accomplish its goal of reconstructing society.

On the other hand, once having recognized the sources of oppression in the intention of ruling elites to preserve their power and after demon-strating the negative effects this has had both in theory and practice, he fails to follow through with an account of the role that power plays in human affairs. He seems curiously uninterested in accounting for the vir-ulence of prejudice and its persistence or in exploring in detail how it alters the lives of those affected by it. By locating conflicts in different approaches to life and not in struggles for power, he frequently underesti-mates what is required to overcome them. He seems to think that once someone has participated in a rational process of inquiry, she or he would not persist in holding onto prejudices or unilateral power. I am not claiming that he ignores the forces opposing personal and societal liberation—quite the contrary—but only that his analyses often do not go far enough.

Dewey sometimes attributes stubborn intransigence to the force of habit that tends to conserve and reinforce traditional models of behavior long after they have ceased to be intellectually justified. He consistently links the traditional dualisms that still distort contemporary philosophical reflections to the origins of philosophy in an ancient Greek ruling class whose leisure was secured through slave labor. He therefore seeks to dismantle the assumptions through which such oppressive beliefs continue their hold on us, but does not address the means by which the ruling power was secured in the first place. At other times he locates the source of oppression in capitalist economics. He holds that the deliberate rejection of moral standards as the basis of economic decision making in industrialized countries is responsible for the unjust state of affairs in which we find ourselves. He ([1929] 1984, 225) also blames moral philosophers for placing economic considerations "on a lower level than either morals or politics." They make a great mistake because "the life which men, women and children actually lead, the opportunities open to them, the values they are capable of enjoying, their education, their share in all the things of art and science, are mainly determined by economic conditions."

He does not, however, pursue the sources of oppression far enough to reflect on why the need to develop and consolidate one's own power is so often understood as requiring denying it to others. The initial optimism I felt when first coming across references to women's subordination in hitherto unsuspected places in Dewey's writings was often followed by a feeling of disappointment that the examples were used to illustrate some other point and were not introduced in order to deepen a feminist analysis. In *Democracy and Education*, for example, Dewey ([1916] 1980, 260–70) criticizes Aristotle's theoretical separation of the practical and the intellectual because such a metaphysical position legitimates and extends an unequal and unjust social order. He attributes Aristotle's hierarchical dualism to the fact that he wrote when most men and all women were stuck in menial labor and were used as mere means for the intellectual ends of others. Dewey's explicit goal is to promote social democracy and the educational practices and theory necessary to achieve it. He therefore encourages the development of a curriculum that uses intelligence and theory as "a guide of free practice *for all*." Both his genetic account of the origin of the separation of theory and practice in the inequalities of class and gender and his liberatory intent to transform education to be inclusive are feminist positions worth developing. They are insufficient, however, insofar as they fail to name the patriarchal appropriation of slave and women's labor as one of exploitation or oppression or to follow up by exploring how the working classes and women are affected by such oppression. Such explicit analyses are necessary in order for his recommendations for overcoming the illicit separation of theory and practice to be effective.

These strengths and weaknesses are illustrated in two talks Dewey gave in which he directly addressed issues of discrimination, one concerning the plight of blacks and the other supporting women's suffrage. In his "Address to the National Association for the Advancement of Colored People" in 1932, Dewey recognizes the greater discrimination and suffering that blacks endure in the midst of the Great Depression, but he thinks this is a quantitative rather than a qualitative difference. He ([1932a] 1985, 225) says to them that blacks as a group have doubtless "suffered more than any other, more keenly, more intensely. Doubtless you are the first, on the whole, to lose employment and the last to be taken on. You are quite likely the last to get an equal opportunity to share in whatever measures of relief or constructive public work, to tide over the depression, undertaken. But none the less, the causes from which all are suffering are the same." Like Marx, he thinks that economics is the basic cause of both racism and classism, that those in control politically and economically consolidate their power through encouraging suspicion and divisiveness among the working-class poor. The solution is coalition building among all minority groups, who should break with both national parties and start a third party "which will help bring about a social and economic reconstruction in the interest of a society which is cooperative and human" (Dewey [1932a] 1985, 230). With the end of economic slavery, all other forms of slavery will also be overcome.

This blindness to the virulence of racial prejudice—exacerbated no doubt by the severe economic crisis—makes Dewey's analysis of the problem and suggestions for resolving it less effective than they could be. Dewey ([1932a] 1985, 229–30) says to the NAACP audience: "I submit to you the thing I would submit to any white group that is also at a disadvantage, since your fundamental difficulties do not come through color or any other one thing." But he then says that they *are* due to one thing: "Why were you kept in slavery except for economic reasons? What was slavery except a manifestation of the motive for private gain? Why is it that the denial of civil liberty, of cultural equality still continues except as an aftermath of that economic oppression from which you once suffered?" This economic aftermath is so devastating because of its emphasis on competition: "What is the economic order in which we live today excepting one of competition? Fundamentally, the disadvantages, or the inequalities—civil, political, and cultural,—of the colored group, of every under-privileged group in this country, exist because we are living in a competitive order which, because it is competitive, has to set man against man, brother against brother, group against group" (Dewey [1932a] 1985, 229).

He denies that racism is the fundamental problem for blacks, attributing the cause of slavery, persecution, and the denial of civil liberties to capitalistic economic oppression. He contends that "those who want the greatest profits and those who want the monopoly, power, influence, that money gives, can get it only by creating suspicion, dislike and division among the mass of people." They secure their own power by setting disadvantaged groups against one another. He recognizes that blacks have been discriminated against more than others, but thinks that they only suffer to a more intense degree what all laboring groups suffer. The depression has thus disclosed a community of interest among all the minority and oppressed groups of the country, but they have not yet realized that they suffer from a common victimization. Only a coalition of minority and disadvantaged groups can effectively challenge the entrenched political and economic powers. "A cooperative economic and social order is the only kind of order in which there will be a genuine possibility for equality among human beings irrespective of race, color and creed, and of the other things which are now played upon to divide people in order that a few may have a monopoly of privilege, power and influence" (Dewey [1932a] 1985, 230).

I concur that a cooperative economic social order that breaks the monopoly of privilege and power would be a powerful means for blacks to advance on many levels. I also agree with Dewey's condemnation of capitalistic exploitation and with his stress on the importance of subjugated groups joining together to fight oppression. But the economic position of blacks by itself does not begin to address the question of why they are feared and despised as well as discriminated against in jobs and housing, why they are the last hired and the first fired, why they are most often at the bottom of the heap in any competitive situation, or why they are scapegoated for crimes and general social unrest. Coalition building among disadvantaged groups is a valuable means for successfully opposing entrenched political and economic power, but it is unlikely to go forward in an atmosphere of hate and discrimination.

In another political forum, Dewey shares Addams's belief that the strongest argument for women's suffrage is that it is necessary to complete the democratic movement. Dewey ([1911] 1978) says in "A Symposium on Woman's Suffrage" in 1911 that unless it is completed, the evils due to the imperfect state of democracy will be attributed to democracy itself. In answer to four questions addressed to each of the symposiasts, he says that it is reactionary to put limits, such as moral or property restrictions, on women's access to the vote. He clearly rejects any double standard in morality by arguing that since men's moral standard does not affect their right to vote, then neither should women's. And property restrictions only strengthen the strong influence on government already wielded by those with economic power. "It is the masses—the poor—who most need the protection of the ballot." As Du Bois (1940) also forcefully argues in regard to blacks in *Dusk of Dawn*, literacy tests are likewise irrelevant in determining social and political intelligence.

Dewey does not think that militant methods are necessary to secure women's suffrage in America, and therefore it would not be wise to use them. English political life, by contrast, does not make changes except under great pressure and under those conditions "women certainly needed some way of demonstrating that they were in earnest." This analysis does not take into account why granting votes to women, an extension of the franchise that is so obviously in keeping with the democratic principles Americans profess, was so fiercely resisted for so long in America, or why women should patiently continue to use tactics year after year that were obviously not succeeding. A glimpse of what women were up against can be gathered from a few incidents out of many in the years following Dewey's remarks, such as the brewers' complicity in the brazen vote-counting fraud in the 1912 suffrage referendum in Michigan, a vote against suffrage that was not overturned "despite tremendous public uproar and attempts by the Governor to insure a fair count"; the near riot caused by a suffrage parade organized by Alice Paul, Crystal Eastman, Mary Beard, and others the day before Woodrow Wilson's inauguration in which troops of cavalry and a protecting wall formed by male student volunteers from Maryland Agricultural College were needed to enable the marchers to make their way through a hostile, jeering crowd; and

Carrie Chapman Catt's 1916 report to the board of the National American Woman Suffrage Association that "the first anti-suffrage organization of importance to be effected in the South has been formed in Alabama with the slogan: 'Home Rule, States Rights, and White Supremacy'" (Flexner 1975, 268, 272–73, 284).

In these and in other writings Dewey does consistently argue against the subjugation of women, racial or ethnic and other minorities, and the working class, and for their emancipation and full participation in society. He thinks that these goals can be accomplished through rational persuasion, coalition building, a willingness to use the experimental method, and when all these fail, overt resistance, such as strikes and public pressure. What is needed to complete his analyses and proposals is a more penetrating account of the sources of inherited prejudice and motivations for beliefs ranging from indifference, to distrust, derision, and violent antipathy toward select groups of people. Since he also believes that agitation and confrontations, especially violent ones, expose a breakdown of communicative inquiry, he also ignores the issue of how to resolve conflicts when those in more powerful positions stubbornly persist in suppressing others. He does recognize that violence can take more subtle forms and that the use of even overt violence can be effectively hidden by those in power to make it look as if confrontation is always the fault of those protesting a misuse of authority. But this recognition does not lead him to revise his theory concerning problematic situations or his methods of resolution.

Perhaps there is no way to persuade those who willingly use force to impose their will on others to stop doing so, except by a more powerful counterforce. Dewey appeared to concede as much when he gave up his pacifism in the face of the enormity of the attack on peoples and nations and the failure of the institutional safeguards of freedom in the two world wars. He was keenly aware of the horrible price to be paid in settling disputes by force, however, and returns again and again to the question of what needs to be done in the present in order to stave off such confrontations in the future. In doing so, he joins Addams in developing a pacifist feminist model of resistance to the brute use of force to settle disputes as well as a positive program of what should be done to avoid the need or expectation of violence as a legitimate recourse.

Women who are victims of domestic violence, blacks, homosexuals, lesbians, and others in society who undergo unprovoked assaults have, if anything, a greater stake in peaceful resolutions of conflicts as long as their just demands are met. But they also need to be heard and their causes recognized, and this often involves violent opposition by the forces of the status quo that are oppressing them. Dewey ([1939] 1988, 228) thinks that conflicts of all sorts arise through the alienation of others and that the democratic spirit requires breaking down the barriers that divide us into opposing groups: "To take as far as possible every conflict which arises—and they are bound to arise—out of the atmosphere and medium of force, of violence as a means of settlement into that of discussion and of intelligence is to treat those who disagree—even profoundly—with us as those from whom we may learn, and in so far, as friends." This is indeed a worthy ideal, but what recourse do subjugated groups have when those who disagree with them are implacable foes?

Dewey's philosophy took a more radical turn because of the threat to the survival of democratic forms of government posed by the totalitarian regimes of fascist Germany and Japan in World War II. Unlike many other intellectuals of his time, he did not embrace jingoistic nationalism and instead took the unpopular position that such "America First" movements expressed the very same attitudes that produced the totalitarianism they were supposedly repudiating. Rather than use the popular revulsion stirred up against enemies in Europe and the Far East to engage in chauvinistic self-congratulation and the stifling of dissent, Dewey warned that the same factors that led to the loss of freedoms abroad were already at work in the United States. He repudiated the identification of democracy with economic individualism, which actually undermines the will to work together, the essence of cooperation. Uncoerced cooperation as the intent to link one's own well-being with the well-being of all others is central to Dewey's ([1939] 1988, 226) theory of social democracy, which is based on two premises: (1) belief in the potentialities of every human being "irrespective of race, color, sex, birth and family, of material or cultural wealth"; and (2) the need for providing conditions that will enable these potentialities to be realized.

In the face of totalitarian threats to democracy, Dewey therefore calls for strengthening and deepening these two fundamental positions. In doing so, he ([1939] 1988, 226) begins developing a more acute account of prejudice as an obstacle to his ideal of participatory democracy. He points out that "to denounce Naziism for intolerance, cruelty and stimulation of hatred amounts to fostering insincerity if, in our personal relations to other persons, if, in our daily walk and conversation, we are moved by racial, color or other class prejudice; indeed, by anything save a generous belief in their possibilities as human beings, a belief which brings with it the need for providing conditions which will enable these capacities to reach fulfillment." Merely verbal expressions of one's allegiance to democracy remain sentimental unless put into practice every day and are no protection against intolerance and using others for one's own gain.

Dewey ([1941] 1988, 277) specifically singles out the evils of racism and anti-Semitism, in addition to classism: "Our anti-democratic heritage of Negro slavery has left us with habits of intolerance toward the colored race—habits which belie profession of democratic loyalty." And he points out that religion has too often been used to foster anti-Semitism before concluding that "[t]here are still many, too many, persons who feel free to cultivate and express racial prejudices as if they were within their personal rights, not recognizing how the attitude of intolerance infects, perhaps fatally as the example of Germany so surely proves, the basic humanities without which democracy is but a name." In a 1940 essay, "Contrary to Human Nature," Dewey ([1940] 1988) demonstrates that his appeal to habit as the vehicle of prejudice does not necessarily preclude unmasking and condemning the role of power in societal relations. In this more radical side of Dewey's examination of the place of habit in human development, he shows how those whose power is entrenched not only subjugate others but also entice them to collude in their own subjection.

Feminist analyses of misogyny, homophobia, and racism would complement these accounts by calling attention to specific issues that need to be addressed if the effort to develop persons who are sufficiently tolerant and concerned for the welfare of others that they will not resort to violence to settle disputes is to succeed. Charlotte Perkins Gilman, W. E. B. Du Bois, Jane Addams, and Alain Locke certainly recognized the importance of dealing with these issues, and began the process of deepening and expanding Dewey's pragmatist account.

Dewey's Pragmatist Feminist Theory

For pragmatists, it is not isolated individuals who make up the basic unit of existence or theory, but concretely interrelated persons within a natural and social environment. Because Dewey takes the active transaction of organisms and environment as the basis of human action, which is specifically characterized as striving for goals, its feminism is perspectival and pluralistic. Rationality has evolved over time as the power to reflect on the results of our actions on the environment and its effects on us. It is the ability to imagine a future different from the present, to anticipate and feel strongly about future as well as present states of affairs, and to retain from present experiences something that will be of value to future experiences. It is, therefore, exhibited in the everyday lives of women as well as men, of the underprivileged as well as the elite, educated classes, and is not reducible to consistency within formal systems. Women's and men's different experiences lead to different perspectives on the world and different values, not because of their biological differences as such, but only as such biological and psychological differences lead to different experiences and only as they are mediated through specific beliefs, customs, value systems, and institutions.

In "Philosophy and Democracy," one of Dewey's more radical addresses, he explicitly uses his pragmatist principle of perspectivism to argue that women's experiences differ significantly enough from men's to affect the philosophies they develop. He ([1919] 1982, 45) says that "[w]omen have as yet made little contribution to philosophy. But when women who are not mere students of other persons' philosophy set out to write it, we cannot conceive that it will be the same in viewpoint or tenor as that composed from the standpoint of the different masculine experience of things." Dewey ([1931] 1985, 20–21) also argues in "Context and Thought" that such differing standpoints will exhibit the limitations as well as the strengths of their point of view and need to be corrected by listening to and interacting with others differently situated. In a couple of letters written to Scudder Klyce in 1915 and 1920, Dewey developed further his views of male domination and women's perspectives.

He (1915) criticizes Klyce for claiming that women, as a class, have been restricted by men and that these restrictions have negatively affected their development without his also recognizing that men must also be analyzed as a class shaped by their privileged position. Klyce's failure to do so shows that he takes men as a standard without realizing how his emotional attachment to a masculine viewpoint distorts his judgment. Women who have theorized from their own experiences have recognized that "men are essentially hogs" because they assume that their own work is the most important thing in the world. Moreover, men do not even recognize their own androcentric viewpoint. Dewey also criticizes Klyce for generalizing from too narrow a base of women. In his own experience of "essentially sane women . . . of superior concrete intelligence" Dewey has been struck by how often they surprise him intellectually in ways that men's reasoning never does. He also says that it is his experience that women's observations are more honest than men's and that they are more willing to face the unpleasant facts of life than men are.

Dewey (1920) also criticizes Klyce's stereotypical view that men are more courageous than women. Klyce mistakenly compares "men" with "ladies," a manifestly artificial product of societal distinction. The conventional definition of courage is too one-sidedly taken from men's experiences and their self-aggrandizement, and it should be obvious from women's childbearing alone that they exhibit superior courage. Men tend to judge women in aggregate because they do not recognize the same individuality in them that they see in other men. This is partly due to the division of labor between women and men and the restriction of women to subordinate and poorly paid positions. The "enormous handicaps" from which women suffer in the labor market can only be overcome by experiments through which new facts about their abilities and the nature of work will become perceptible.

Dewey expects that women's entrance into the professions will humanize them, bringing in an element of service to counteract the present overemphasis on profit. Much more experimentation is needed to show what women's potentialities are. As for the criticism that feminists are too shrill and argumentative, Dewey (1920, 6) says the wonder is that there is not more protest. The present unequal division of labor fails to give women an "outlet for their individualized capacities *as* they are influenced by sex." Women have never had a chance to decide for themselves what, if any, division of labor they want because men have settled the question for them purely on the basis of anatomy. Dewey (1920, 6) says that this statement "is the woman question in a nutshell."

Dewey also points out that society has not considered what women should do with their lives beyond their childbearing years. He (1920, 6) admonishes Klyce that he could "learn more from 'even' the extreme feminists than you have been wiling [*sic*] to do." Just as Jesse Taft (1915) had argued in her 1913 dissertation on the Woman Movement, written for the pragmatist philosophy department at the University of Chicago, Dewey attributes the widespread controversies over women's issues to the displacement of their home-based occupations by the industrial revolution. Women who seek fulfillment outside the home are labeled selfish, but he (1920, 7) points out that this judgment is made is from the perspective of the "unperceived 'very' *longtime* Selfishness [*sic*] of men."

Dewey's feminism is rooted in a central value of his pragmatism, which is that democracy as a way of life ought to guide all other aspects of philosophical analysis and activities. Dewey's (Jane Dewey 1939, 30; Kellogg 1969, 171) interpretation of this value was deeply influenced by Jane Addams. Central to his understanding of social democracy is the rejection of the atomistic individualism of liberal democracy as well as of fixed essences and hierarchies. He ([1919] 1982, 52–53) affirms instead that every existent is unique and irreplaceable and "does not exist to illustrate a principle, to realize a universal or to embody a kind or class." Individuality is neither external nor mechanical.

> In social and moral matters, equality does not mean mathematical equivalence. It means rather the inapplicability of considerations of greater or less, superior and inferior. It means that no matter how great the quantitative differences of ability, strength, position, wealth, such differences are negligible in comparison with something else—the fact of individuality . . . [understood as] the incommensurable in which each speaks for itself and demands consideration on its own behalf.

This uniqueness thrives in interaction with other individuals, so that the tendency to isolation and independence inherent in individuality is dynamically balanced in democracy with fellowship or collegiality, that is, continuity, or "association and interaction without limit." Philosophizing from democratic principles can be judged as all other philosophical perspectives are, by whether it leads to better institutions of life. Pragmatist feminists theorize and act against the prejudices and oppressions that hinder the full participation of all in the life of multiple communities of which they are members. Such participation requires the unhindered development of the capacities of each to freely choose and skillfully carry out their choices in interaction with others who are equally valued.

Specific Feminist Issues

In turning from the general contours of Dewey's pragmatist feminist philosophy to his actual explanations of the problems women face in a society organized around men's perspectives and values and in which men wield disproportionate power, the strengths and weaknesses of his own use of pragmatist feminist theory to interpret experience become more apparent. He positively values women's accomplishments and acknowledges their influence on his theories. As we have seen in his support of enfranchising women, he is not afraid to speak out and work for women's radical causes and against misogyny, just as he consistently attacks racial, ethnic, and class prejudice. But sexism is clearly of lesser concern than is classism and racism and he misses many opportunities to follow through in developing specifically feminist analyses. The assumptions underlying his feminist analyses are sometimes quite radical and at other times moderately liberal or even conventional. The way that his pragmatism informs his feminism can be deduced from two specific issues: how privilege and power is hidden behind appeals to human nature and how women are affected by marriage and motherhood.

Dewey continues a long line of feminist analysis at least as old as Mary Wollstonecraft's 1790 work, A Vindication of the Rights of Women, and as new as postmodernist deconstructions of mistakenly essentialized identities when he argues that a frequent ploy for opposing social change is to assert that the proposal goes contrary to human nature. At best, such a defense of the status quo diverts attention from a "critical examination of the actual merits of the proposal in question." At worst, it is merely "an expression of a strong prejudice clothed in the garb of an ideal in order to appear respectable. The use of the idea of the unchangeability of human nature as a means of opposition to special projects for political and economic change belongs to the latter class" ([1940] 1988, 258). Appeal is made to traits that happen at the time to be associated with human nature, the very beliefs and habits that are being challenged.

Since history shows that reforms have always had to overcome the "opposition of habits entrenched in positions of advantage," it is surprising that appeals to human nature have not lost their force.[2] The inertia of established customs is no argument for the constancy of human nature. But people's minds as well as actions are in the grip of habit, "and while the tendency is most marked in the case of those who obtain one-sided advantage from customs as they exist, it is strong enough to hold in subjection many of those who are put at a disadvantage by those customs." Both those who opposed the abolition of slavery and those who opposed the enfranchisement of women "used the argument that it was contrary to the very laws of Nature and of Nature's God. Such facts prove how strong is the tendency to use well-established habits as the proper standard and measure of what is natural and unnatural" ([1940] 1988, 259).

Dewey does not expect that merely exposing the will to power hidden in appeals to a fixed human nature will eliminate its negative consequences, because the conception of human nature also reifies and essentializes the conserving force of habit in human behavior. He says that "although the argument from fixity of human nature is but a 'rationalization' of existing habits, including prejudices and one-sided interest which have become institutionalized, proponents of social changes have something to learn from it." The first lesson is that the stubborn conservatism of habits means that " 'revolutions' never go as far or as deep as they are supposed to go; it takes time, usually a long time and a succession of partial changes, to carry one through, since carrying through signifies the establishment of habits which will be as deep-seated and as 'natural' as those which have been displaced" ([1940] 1988, 260). The second lesson is that features of human nature that are even more constant than habits can be appealed to in order to challenge rather than perpetuate the inequities of the present social order. A healthy, vigorous life is such a feature, which the capitalist economic system can be faulted for not meeting. Means must be found for satisfying other basic human needs besides the need for food and health, such as "the need for companionship, for freedom of choice, for rivalry or emulation, for security, etc." ([1940] 1988, 261).

Both liberal and radical reformers would be less disillusioned if they recognized that no single prescription for transformation of the social order can succeed as its followers expect. This should lead not to discouragement, but to more effective efforts in which the complexity of the conditions of oppression are recognized. Doubtless this makes policy change more difficult to implement, but both history and experience provide evidence that simple solutions, though valuable for energizing reformers and revolutionaries, are bound to fail, because they inevitably leave out some of the conditions contributing to the oppressive situation.

Another set of feminist issues has to do with sex, marriage, and the family. In the first decades of the twentieth century in the United States prohibitions on the open discussion of women's sexuality contributed to psychological problems and unwanted pregnancies. Dewey supported Margaret Sanger, Charlotte Perkins Gilman, and other feminists who challenged the suppression of sexual information and the prohibition of birth control. In 1928, for example, he ([1930] 1990, 127) protested Mary

Ware Dennett's conviction on the charge of sending obscene material through the mails.[3] The supposedly offensive material was an educational pamphlet called *The Sex Side of Life*. In defense of her right to publish on issues of sexuality, Dennett responded to criticism of her activities with *Who's Obscene?* and included Dewey's letter of support in it. He wrote that as both an educator and father of seven children, he welcomed the distribution of *The Sex Side of Life* to parents and youth and condemned its suppression, since there was nothing obscene or indecent in accurate information on sex, but there was in the suppression of such information.

Although Dewey often recognized how patriarchal forms of marriage and family life oppressed women and therefore sought to eliminate their negative effects, he did not always adopt such a feminist perspective. It is mostly absent, for example, in "The War's Social Results," written in 1917, in which Dewey made some uncharacteristically utopian predictions about the new social democracy that would emerge after the Allied victory in World War II. He predicts that supply-and-demand capitalism will be replaced by industrial democracy. The domination of the upper classes will cease and the great amounts of money taken from them for the war effort will continue to be exacted by the state after the war but will instead be spent on the needs of the common people. Although he ([1917] 1990, 23) says that "it is not at all clear what the reign of the hitherto submerged classes will be like," he thinks that the family will undergo a most radical change and may even cease to exist. Love, marriage, and romance may come to mean very different things from what they do in the present.

He is not so optimistic about whether these changes will be for the better. He is careful to say, for example, that he is not advocating changing the ideals of marriage or a revolution in sexual morality, but only observing that tremendous changes are on the way. Most of the changes have to do with the diminished role of the father, who was at one time supreme. The change is due primarily to the transition from feudalism to capitalism. Under capitalism, the individual, not the family, became the economic unit, and it was natural "that children threw off the yoke of patriarchal rule" (Dewey [1917] 1990, 24). Dewey does not explicitly name women's oppression by patriarchal rule, but he does say that its overthrow is most clearly illustrated in the free selection of marriage partners and the increasing importance of romance. Marriage, however, was not thereby strengthened, but divorce has become more common.

According to Dewey, the war has accelerated a new economic epoch, and with it has come "three most startling changes in the social status of women." With millions of eligible young men killed or rendered unfit for marriage, women will vastly outnumber men and many cannot expect to find husbands. Even more important, "women never had so little use for husbands as they have in France and Germany today" (Dewey [1917] 1990, 24). During the war women took men's jobs and many proved that they were more efficient than men. Having acquired economic power, women were starting to gain political power. They could decide to abdicate in favor of men after the war in order to get husbands, but with little prospect of that for most women, he wonders what they would receive that would cause them to relinquish these gains. Finally, with the great loss of lives, all the nations have advocated childbearing and the states have granted children a right to be born and to be educated. In the state's assuming responsibility for children, fathers and husbands are left with less responsibility than ever. Dewey predicts that changes will occur in morality to fit the new conditions. Exactly what they will be he cannot say except to note that there will be some shifting from the ideals of "marital monopoly."

In analyzing this essay it is clear that Dewey both predicts and supports radical changes in the postwar period. He hopes that a socially responsible industrial democracy will replace the predatory practices of unbridled capitalism and that the lower classes will be emancipated from the control of the upper classes. But his assessment of the results of the emancipation of the submerged class of women is ambiguous. He seems more worried that the status quo will be overturned than confident that a new era in gender relations will emerge that will be beneficial to women and to society in general. His masculinist biases are revealed by the fact that he recognized the great social and economic changes in women's lives brought about by the war, but only seems concerned with the impact of such changes on men's lives. He does not emphasize women's newfound economic independence and freedom from patriarchal control in marriage as a necessary step in their emancipation or even call them positive gains. In fact, he distances himself from radical challenges to the institution of marriage and to sexual morality. He is more concerned with the rising divorce rate as a result of the diminishment of the supreme role of the father than he is with its impact on women's subordination.

Since Dewey recognizes that economic changes accelerated by the war have led to three startling changes in the social status of women, he raises our expectation that the significance of these changes for women and for society will be examined. Instead, he treats them as causes for alarm. What he is really worried about is how women's changed status will affect men's. He notes that women have made real economic and political gains and as a result have little use for husbands to support them. What this might mean for women is not considered. He wonders what will happen if women do not voluntarily abdicate their newly acquired economic power when men return home from the war. He does not raise the issue of why women should want to abdicate power or why men should expect them to do so. Oddly enough, the third change only indirectly concerns women, but it does have a direct impact on men's traditional role of supporting a family. It has to do with the state's newfound zeal for children's rights, because of the importance of replacing people lost in the war. Dewey's only comment on this changed state of affairs is that giving more responsibility for children to the state will diminish men's responsibilities.

Dewey concludes the essay by predicting that whatever changes men have undergone as a result of their war experiences will largely determine postwar society. Despite his recognition of women's very different war experiences and newfound emancipation from economic dependency and patriarchal control, no such claim is made about their experiences or influence. So, despite his call for a reconstruction of morality due to changed conditions, he failed to follow through with developing or even advocating a feminist ethics adequate to postwar realties.

By 1930 Dewey seems to have made a complete about-face. He ([1930] 1984, 276) clearly asserts that "present ideas of love, marriage, and the family are almost exclusively masculine constructions." Rather than lamenting men's reduced role in the family, he recognizes that upholders of conventional marriages and traditional beliefs about love and sexuality promote "idealizations of human interests that express a dominantly one-sided experience," namely, that of men. "They are romantic in theory and prosaic in operation." Dewey's findings have long been recognized by an earlier wave of feminist theory that has emphasized the suffocating restrictions such prosaic practices imposed on women and by later waves of feminists, who have explored the even more deadly consequences of domestic abuse. Dewey also connects men's sentimental idealization of relationships developed to further their interests with a legal system that supports men's dominance. He counters such sentimentalization and legalization by appealing to the realities of the relationships of men, women, and children, which have been covered over in both the idealizing accounts and the legal system. He ([1930] 1984, 276) now asserts, furthermore, that "the growing free-dom of women can hardly have any other outcome than the production of more realistic and more human morals. It will be marked by a new freedom, but also by a new severity. For it will be enforced by the reali-ties of associated life as they are disclosed to careful and systematic inquiry, and not by a combination of convention and an exhausted legal system with sentimentality." Since Dewey's own pragmatist ethics begins with the realities of associated life, he is deliberately including feminist concerns with the domestic sphere within pragmatist ethics (see Seigfried 1996, 224–58).

But in the fuller explication found in "Marriage and the Family," which is the last chapter of his 1932 *Ethics*, Dewey ([1932d] 1985), along with his co-author, James Hayden Tufts, takes the realities of associated life as a strong argument for supporting the permanence of commitment to heterosexual marriage, which should combine sex with friendship.[4] He responds to the assaults on the institution of marriage that emanate from the new Freudian emphasis on sexual satisfaction and the modern em-phasis on individual fulfillment. Several things are troubling about the exposition from a feminist perspective. The first section, which is a brief sketch of the history of the family, clearly states that—except for a short matriarchal period—the present form of marriage derives from a patriar-chal model of "father right" that was not even displaced by the Protestant Reformation, which retained the "subjection of women" in marriage. The problem is that this insight does not inform the rest of the analysis. In fact, this first section is the only part of the chapter not rewritten from the 1908 version of the *Ethics*, where a more radical critique of women's oppression by the patriarchal family was introduced. Where the first edi-tion emphasizes and is plainly concerned about women's alienation, the second edition is mainly concerned that women's economic, educational, and political emancipation threatens the institution of marriage. The earlier sources of conflict between women and men are now merely "irri-tations" not needing further reflection.

As was intimated in "The War's Social Results," divorce is seen as a mostly selfish act by those not willing to make the sacrifices necessary to continue the institution of marriage. The forces encouraging "casual attachments instead of permanent unions" are examined first from "the point of view of man and woman" and then as they affect children ([1932d] 1985, 447). Despite the acknowledgment that women's social

roles have been more profoundly changed than men's as a result of industrialization, and that the working classes' experiences differ from the middle class's, women's interests are not considered separately from men's
nor from the perspective of the middle-class family. By contrast, in the
first edition, the conflicts generated by the fact that women and men's
perspectives diverge due to their different situations and social pressures,
combined with the fact of men's blindness to women's plight, were such
important issues that Tufts and Dewey ([1908] 1978, 525) spoke of a
"masculine fallacy" and a "feminine fallacy" by analogy with William
James's term "psychologist's fallacy." The psychologist's fallacy, according to James, was confusing one's own point of view with that of other
persons in the situations under examination. By assuming that women's
and men's interests in preserving marriage are the same and in discount-
ing the effect on newly emancipated women of Dewey's admonition to
subordinate their selfish interests to the good of the family, Tufts and
Dewey commit the very masculine fallacy that they had earlier warned
against. Jane Addams ([1902] 1964, 71–101) had already argued in 1902
that the priority of higher social values over individual good could not
be used to condemn women for being selfish for refusing to subordinate
themselves to family claims when it was their very recognition of wider
social demands that led them to choose a career outside the home in the
first place.

An indication that the more reactionary aspects of the chapter on
marriage in the 1932 *Ethics* may be attributable to Tufts rather than to
Dewey ([1932d] 1985, 460) is the fact that in it, birth control clinics—
which were as controversial then as abortion clinics are today—are defended as legitimate, but specifically in that they function to reeducate
"the poor and the ignorant" and substitute medically approved procedures for their violent and criminal methods.[5] Dewey's defense of birth
control in the same time period was not class based, and he supported
it unequivocally as part of his effort to wrest science and technology
away from military and capitalistic control and use it instead for social
good and individual empowerment. In "Education and Birth Control,"
for example, he says that opposition to the birth control movement is
part of the larger resistance to newly discovered knowledge that affects
the conduct of life (Dewey [1932c] 1985). "Ignorance, prejudice,
dogma, routine, tradition" come into play in the ongoing conflict between the old and entrenched and new ideas and discoveries. Such con-

flict is inevitable in human beings affected by a past and anticipating a future.

Knowledge always means increased control and the birth control movement provides a means for intelligently controlling the processes of procreation and conception. It puts a blind natural process under human direction. Laws and public sentiment formed in ignorance of such means of control newly developed by science block public access to knowledge that will give persons more complete control of their conduct. Since "suppression and secrecy breed unfairness, mental and moral disorder," arbitrary restrictions to the intelligent control of nature must be removed. Dewey points out that mass education was being criticized for failing to develop the individual capacities of children, but policies whose effect is to increase the numbers of people born without any regard to their quality of life work against this very respect for the individual. If parents had the power to make the quality of life supreme in their homes, then the problem of mass education would disappear.

The issues at stake in a bill seeking to legalize birth control, which was introduced in the United States Senate in the early 1930s, have chilling parallels with contemporary debates over abortion rights. In "The Senate Birth Control Bill," Dewey ([1932b] 1985) asks, for example: "Can anything more absurd be imagined, than that clinics should be established for the care of women, and that a reputable physician should be guilty of a crime if he gives information as to the location of these clinics, to a woman needing care?" In lobbying for the bill he seeks to broaden its appeal by diffusing accusations that it is too radical. He points out that it is conservative in restricting those authorized to give out information to those deemed competent, such as the government, medical societies, schools, and journals. He predicts that later generations would compare criminalizing those distributing scientific information about birth control to the dark ages when witches were hunted down. The bill is also conservative in that it seeks to "conserve human life and well-being, that of mothers, of children, of families." Unimpeded access to safe forms of birth control would lessen the need for abortions and it would lessen the injury caused by unscrupulous quacks. The bill neither compels those opposed to it to distribute information about birth control nor does it prohibit groups from dissuading their members from employing contraceptive measures. But it would be "un-American, undemocratic, and despotic" for such groups "to attempt to use legislation to create crimes, in order to impose their special moral views on others."

Conclusion

Dewey's pragmatist feminism has many facets, only a few of which have been explored in this chapter. Most important, he argues for the continuity of theory and practice and that philosophy has an explicitly emancipatory goal. Because of his recognition that experience is had before it is interpreted, he astutely criticized the intellectualist fallacy represented today in the exaggerated claims of formalist epistemology, and he developed a powerful model of concrete experience. These positions have many resources for contemporary feminist analyses, just as contemporary feminist theory reveals absences and failings in the earlier pragmatist theory. The background conditions of the context of understanding and the operation of selective interest opens a space for recognition of the multiple prejudices that feminists examine. Reflection on these background conditions also reveals the embeddedness of human understanding in the histories, values, and multiple relationships through which persons are constituted in interaction with others. The limitations of perspectivism that follows from its particularity also suggests a remedy to pragmatist feminists in that it requires inclusiveness of points of view as a means to achieve objectivity and therefore a justification for including those traditionally excluded.

Intelligence is explicitly linked to "free communication; the method of conference, consultation, discussion, in which there takes place purification and pooling of the net results of the experiences of multitudes of people." That this is no trivial requirement is emphasized by Dewey's ([1941] 1988, 276) pointing out that during World War II when this assertion was made, "hundreds of thousands of persons who have been tortured, who have died, who are rotting in concentration camps, prove that talk may also be tragically costly, and that democracy to endure must hold it immensely precious." The multiplicity of points of view as well as the multiple relations constitutive of persons support feminist claims to having insights to contribute to philosophizing that have so far been missing and whose absence has distorted what is there. It also gives good reasons for deemphasizing essentialist analyses of gender and provides a model for theorizing about the multiple relationships through which we are constituted and that have been distorted through homophobia, racism, classism, and colonialism, as well as sexism. As in quotations where Dewey links the conditions for objectivity in knowledge with democratic values, his emphasis on the continuum of means and ends deliberately collapses the distinction of pure and applied theory. It thus supports the specificity of feminist analyses of housework, sexual relations, abortion, job discrimination, and the myriad problematic situations that women in all our variety encounter, as necessary steps to theorizing about reality as well as to attaining justice.

Notes

1. For Dewey's explanation of experience as the interaction of persons and some aspect of the world in terms of undergoing and doing, see *Art as Experience* (Dewey [1934] 1987, 50–52, 137); in terms of action-undergoing, see *Experience and Nature* (Dewey [1925] 1981, 28–30).

2. Dewey uses a strange circumlocution; isn't it the case that it is persons, and not habits, that are entrenched in positions of advantage?

3. Dennett's conviction was later reversed (Dewey [1930] 1990, 560 n. 127.5). See also Chen 1996.

4. Although Tufts wrote the chapter on marriage, the preface to the first edition was reprinted along with the new preface, and it states that because of suggestions and criticisms by each of the other's work, Dewey and Tufts consider the book to be jointly authored throughout.

5. Among these reactionary positions are blaming women's newfound opportunities in the public realm for the instability of marriage and the declining birthrate and further analyses encouraging stereotypical gender roles.

References

Addams, Jane. 1916. *The Long Road of Woman's Memory*. New York: Macmillan.
———. [1902] 1964. *Democracy and Social Ethics*. Reprint, with an introduction by A. F. Scott, Cambridge: Harvard University Press.
———. [1910] 1981. *Twenty Years at Hull-House*. New York: Signet Classic.
Antler, Joyce. 1987. *Lucy Sprague Mitchell*. New Haven: Yale University Press.
Beauvoir, Simone de. [1949] 1974. *The Second Sex*. Translated by H. M. Parshley. New York: Vintage.
Chen, Constance M. 1996. *"The Sex Side of Life": Mary Ware Dennett's Pioneering Battle for Birth Control and Sex Education*. New York: New Press.
Code, Lorraine. 1995. *Rhetorical Spaces: Essays on Gendered Locations*. New York: Routledge.

Dewey, Jane M. 1939. "Biography of John Dewey." In *The Philosophy of John Dewey*, edited by Paul Arthur Schilpp. Evanston: Northwestern University Press.

Dewey, John. [1908] 1977. "Intelligence and Morals." In *The Middle Works*. Vol. 4. Edited by Jo Ann Boydston, 31–49. Carbondale: Southern Illinois University Press.

———. [1908] 1978. *Ethics*. Vol. 5 of *The Middle Works*. Edited by Jo Ann Boydston. Carbondale: Southern Illinois University Press.

———. [1909] 1977. "The Influence of Darwinism on Philosophy." In *The Middle Works*. Vol. 4. Edited by Jo Ann Boydston, 3–14. Carbondale: Southern Illinois University Press.

———. [1911] 1978. "A Symposium on Woman's Suffrage [Statement]." In *The Middle Works*. Vol. 6. Edited by Jo Ann Boydston, 153–54. Carbondale: Southern Illinois University Press.

———. 1915. Letter to Scudder Klyce, July 5, from Huntington, New York, number 03542, in the Dewey archives of Southern Illinois University, Carbondale, Illinois. Also John Dewey to Scudder Klyce, 1915.07.05 (03542). In *The Correspondence of John Dewey*. Vol. 1, *1871–1918*. Charlottesville, Va.: InteLex, 1999.

———. [1916] 1980. *Democracy and Education*. Vol. 9 of *The Middle Works*. Edited by Jo Ann Boydston. Carbondale: Southern Illinois University Press.

———. [1917] 1990. "War's Social Results." In *The Later Works*. Vol. 17, *1885–1953*. Edited by Jo Ann Boydston, 21–25. Carbondale: Southern Illinois University Press.

———. [1919] 1982. "Philosophy and Democracy." In *The Middle Works*. Vol. 11. Edited by Jo Ann Boydston, 41–53. Carbondale: Southern Illinois University Press.

———. 1920. Letter to Scudder Klyce, May 8, from Nanking, China, number 04621, in the Dewey archives of Southern Illinois University, Carbondale, Illinois. Also John Dewey to Scudder Klyce, 1920.05.08 (04621), *The Correspondence of John Dewey*. Vol. 2, *1919–1939*. Charlottesville, Va.: InteLex, forthcoming).

———. [1925] 1981. *Experience and Nature*. Vol. 1 of *The Later Works*. Edited by Jo Ann Boydston. Carbondale: Southern Illinois University Press.

———. [1929] 1984. *The Quest for Certainty*. Vol. 4 of *The Later Works*. Edited by Jo Ann Boydston. Carbondale: Southern Illinois University Press.

———. [1930] 1984. "What I Believe." In *John Dewey: The Later Works*. Vol. 5. Edited by Jo Ann Boydston, 267–78. Carbondale: Southern Illinois University Press.

———. [1930] 1990. "In Defense of Mary Ware Dennett's *The Sex Side of Life*." In *The Later Works*. Vol. 17. Edited by Jo Ann Boydston, 127 and 560n. Carbondale: Southern Illinois University Press.

———. [1931] 1985. "Context and Thought." In *The Later Works*. Vol. 6, *1931–1932*. Edited by Jo Ann Boydston, 3–21. Carbondale: Southern Illinois University Press.

———. [1932a] 1985. "Address to the National Association for the Advancement of Colored People." In *The Later Works*. Vol. 6. Edited by Jo Ann Boydston, 224–30. Carbondale: Southern Illinois University Press.

———. [1932b] 1985. "The Senate Birth Control Bill." In *The Later Works*. Vol. 6. Edited by Jo Ann Boydston, 388–89. Carbondale: Southern Illinois University Press.

———. [1932c] 1985. "Education and Birth Control." In *The Later Works*. Vol. 6. Edited by Jo Ann Boydston, 146–48. Carbondale: Southern Illinois University Press.

———. [1932d] 1985. *Ethics*. Vol. 7 of *The Later Works*. Edited by Jo Ann Boydston. Carbondale: Southern Illinois University Press.

———. [1934] 1987. *Art as Experience*. Vol. 10 of *The Later Works*. Edited by Jo Ann Boydston. Carbondale: Southern Illinois University Press.

———. [1939] 1988. "Creative Democracy: The Task Before Us." In *The Later Works*. Vol. 14. Edited by Jo Ann Boydston, 224–30. Carbondale: Southern Illinois University Press.

———. [1940] 1988. "Contrary to Human Nature." In *The Later Works*. Vol. 14, *1939–1941*. Edited by Jo Ann Boydston, 258–61. Carbondale: Southern Illinois University Press.

———. [1941] 1988. "The Basic Values and Loyalties of Democracy." In *The Later Works*. Vol. 14. Edited by Jo Ann Boydston, 275–77. Carbondale: Southern Illinois University Press.

Du Bois, W. E. B. 1940. *Dusk of Dawn: An Essay Toward an Autobiography of a Race Concept*. New York: Harcourt, Brace.

———. 1975. *Darkwater: Voices from Within the Veil*. With an introduction by Herbet Aptheker. Millwood, N.Y.: Kraus-Thomson.

———. 1980. *The Autobiography of W. E. B. Du Bois*. New York: International.

Flexner, Eleanor. 1975. *Century of Struggle*. Cambridge: Harvard University Press.

Kellogg, Paul. 1969. "Twice Twenty Years at Hull-House." In *Eighty Years at Hull-House*, edited by Allen F. Davis and Mary Lynn McCree. Chicago: Quadrangle Books.

Mitchell, Lucy Sprague. 1953. *Two Lives*. New York: Simon and Schuster.

Rooney, Phyllis. 1991. "Gendered Reason: Sex Metaphor and Conceptions of Reason." *Hypatia* 6 (2): 97–98.

Seigfried, Charlene Haddock. 1996. *Pragmatism and Feminism: Reweaving the Social Fabric*. Chicago: University of Chicago Press.

———. 2001. "Beyond Epistemology: From a Pragmatist Feminist Experiential Standpoint." In *Engendering Rationalities*, edited by Nancy Tuana and Sandi Morgen. Albany: State University of New York Press.

Sklar, Kathryn Kish. 1998. "Hull House *Maps and Papers*: Social Science as Women's Work in the 1890s." In *Gender and American Social Science: The Formative Years*, edited by Helene Silverberg. Princeton: Princeton University Press.

Taft, Jessie. 1915. *The Woman Movement from the Point of View of Social Consciousness*. Menasha, Wis.: Collegiate Press, George Banta.

Westbrook, Robert B. 1991. *John Dewey and American Democracy*. Ithaca: Cornell University Press.

4

Feminism and Pragmatism

On the Arrival of a "Ministry of Disturbance, a Regulated Source of Annoyance; a Destroyer of Routine, an Underminer of Complacency"[1]

Marjorie C. Miller

A philosophic tradition makes its mark through the growth and extension of the vocabulary it develops, the categories it articulates, the distinctions it illuminates, and the connections it draws. The power of a
philosophical tradition is revealed in the recurrence of its problems and
themes, the fecundity of its methods, the durability of its structures and
insights. It may be that such power is shown not by generating academic
approval and attention, but (on the model of Dewey's discussion of the
reflex arc as circuit)[2] by a tradition's ability to *reconstruct*: through persistent inquiry to create the conditions for its own relevance; by its discover-

ies to open the way to its own rediscovery. Rediscovery in this sense may be recognized by the emergence, after a period of eclipse, of: a vocabulary, a set of categories, a concern with particular distinctions and connections, a focus on problems and a development of themes which had been previously articularted in a powerful philosophic tradition. I shall argue that this emergence may be viewed as "rediscovery" even if those articuating the new positions are unaware of their direct or indirect debt to the earlier tradition; and I shall argue that just such a rediscovery of the American Tradition is apparent in the work of contemporary feminist philosophers.

I am all too aware of the problems inherent in the approach I have . suggested: neither the "Classic Tradition in American Philosophy" nor "Feminist Philosophy" can reasonably be treated as undifferentiated wholes. Further, it is now a commonplace to group feminist philosophers according to the affinity of particular theories to the commitments, assumption, and principles of the philosophic traditions out of which they more-or-less self-consciously emerge: i.e., feminists are identified as liberal, Marxist, Socialist, radical, existentialist, psychoanalytic, or post-structuralist, among others.[3] The standard feminist texts do not yet label a group as "Pragmatists" or "Classic American Traditionalists," although important work along these lines is beginning to appear in print.[4] The rediscovery I wish to examine here goes beyond the obvious sort.

Some fruitful claims may be made involving three thematic concerns: the problematizing of experience, the privileging of "reason," and the conception of philosophy. For each theme, I shall look at the way particular feminists have raised, addressed, and developed that theme—and at the way their approach may be viewed as a "rediscovery" of the "classic tradition." Each of these themes are important to both feminists and "classic" American philosophers, and the particular examinations pursued here may suggest the value of extending the comparison and discussion.

I

First, "experience" has been a central theme in feminism for a number of reasons: feminist theorizing in several fields has stressed the uniqueness of women's experiences; women have encountered discrepancies between *theoretical accounts* of what they do and undergo, and their own living-through of such experiences (of sexuality and motherhood, for example); and identity politics has focused attention on the potential power of women's articulation of our own experiencings.

I have not yet read a feminist metaphysics of experience. The focus is not on "experience" as metaphysical category, but rather on substantive concerns about the nature of women's experience(s): their coherence, validity, and relation to theory. By "coherence," I mean the extent to which women may be said to have experience in common—as women; the extent to which these experiences may be said to constitute a coherent domain or universe—women's "world"; finally, the extent to which such experiences may be siad to be uniquely coherent—to constitute a domain which is other than men's world. By "validity" I mean, on one hand, the degree to which the experiences women have must be separately and appropriately consulted in the development and validation of face- and value-claims about *the* world; and, on the other hand, the degree to which women's experience(s) are adequate to women's world(s). With respect to the relation between women's experience and theory, the question is raised about the nature of theory construction as practiced: is there something intrinsically distorting in the rational account of experience? Does such rationalized accounting necessarily "defeminize" or delegitimize women's experience(s)?

Claims for the uniqueness of women's experience are actively debated within the feminist literature. Apart from the suspect claim for a unique women's reality, or a unique experience of that reality, there remains an encountered dissonance between theoretical accounts of reality (historically and traditionally provided by men) and the experiences of many women. Response to such dissonance is often initially personal (doubting the legitimacy or reliability of one's own experience). After discovering not only that other women share the dissonnance, but that the inadequacies of theoretical accounts often serve a function—to legitimate existing structures of dominance and control—some feminists turned away from "theory," addressing the legitimacy of women's experiences through developing forms of "woman-culture."[5] More philosophically sophisticated feminists, however, have adopted or developed versions of anti-positivism ranging from critical theory through various forms of post-structuralism and post-modernism. Feminists draw on Derrida, Foucault, and Habermas as sources for the attack. With the exception of Charlene Haddock Seigfried and Mary Mahowald, as well as, less directly, Nancy Fraser,[6] Lisa

Heldke,[7] and Susan Bordo,[8] few make explicit reference to American Pragmatists. Nevertheless, I shall argue that not only do important elements of feminists' attempts to reconstruct the concept of experience parallel views expressed by the philosophers of the American Tradition, but also that the press of feminist concern has added force to processes set in motion by that earlier tradition—creating that theoretical and experiential climate wherein it can be *rediscovered* that experience is theory-laden (and that theory is experience-laden):[9] "Theories are not value-free. They arise in social contexts and out of particular human interests and concerns, and cannot be understood in isolation from these. They also imply conceptions of social and political relationships. . . ."[10] Thus "experience is not the raw material knowledge seeks to understand, but rather knowledge is the active process which produces its own objects of investigation, including empirical facts."[11] These quotations are taken neither from Dewey nor from James—but clearly, there are resonances here. Before we look more closely at the resonances, I should like to extend the references to feminist positions.

Many feminist discussions responding to these questions draw on conceptions of experience which, first, deny the spectator account of experience (Adrienne Rich and Sandra Harding, from very different directions, emphasize this point).[12] Second, they recognize experience as broader than perception (for example, de Beauvoir in one way and Irigaray in quite another both address this concern).[13] Third, they contest the notion of experience as that which is passively undergone. (Again, Irigaray's insistence on the active voice, part of her attack on the usefulness of the conception of experience, is relevant here.)[14] Fourth, they insist on the significance of the affective and the emotive for an adequate account of experience. (This occurs in at least two different ways: in the radical feminist insistence on the embeddedness of embodied individuals in a natural world—dreamers, lovers, tasters, touchers as well as cognizers[15] and, more narrowly, in the insistence that cognitive experience itself includes the affective and the emotive.)[16] Fifth, they challenge the conception of "general" or "universal" experience.[17] And finally, they "understand experience not only as material for knowledge but as the medium through which the individual person lives and develops."[18] (Many feminist philosophers would stress this point, but Jane Flax makes the point with special clarity).[19]

These are also points emphasized by John Smith as elements of the reconception of experience in Peirce, James, and Dewey.[20] While not self-consciously drawing on the works of the American Tradition, feminist philosophers are indeed relying on conceptions of experience available by virtue of the reconstruction of philosophy to which that tradition has contributed. Further, the rootedness of feminist philosophy in the project of overcoming oppression, while nourished by socialist and Marxist traditions, also finds resources in the conception of experience as transformative so central to Dewey's thought. Dewey's recognition that "experience in its vital form is experimental, an effort to change the given; [that] that is characterized by projection, by reaching forward into the unknown; [that] connection with a future is its salient trait,"[21] is a recognition which provides a context for the centrality of the questions concerning experience as they emerge in feminist philosophy. Dewey insists on the connectedness of adequate philosophical theorizing to experience. In *Experience and Nature* he suggests:

> a first-rate test of the value of any philosophy which is offered us: Does it end in conclusions which when they are referred back to ordinary life-experiences and their predicaments, render them more significant, more luminous to us, and make our dealings with them more fruitful? Or does it terminate in rendering the things of ordinary experience more opaque than they were before, and in depriving them of having in 'reality' even the significance they had previously seemed to have?[22]

The failure of traditional theories to account for women's experiences represents a failure of this test. The articulation of the insistence that a theory must illuminate and not erase represents the possibility of understanding philosophic theory in a way which would force it to do so. Finally, Dewey's insistence on the reality of all that is done and undergone—all that is experienced[23]—is a ground for the radical critique of views of experience which relegate to the "merely subjective" or to the "purely psychological," aspects of experience which have been ignored by the tradition but have been all too real to women.

II

The issue about the privileging of reason has at least three dimensions in feminist philosophy:

1. As Genevieve Lloyd points out in *The Man of Reason*, the ideal of reason, the very notion of reason, is one which historically emerged in a dichotomization which came to characterize "universal" "objective" "unsexed, unclassed" rationality as that which excluded the characteristics identified and symbolized as female: materiality, unlimitedness, indefiniteness, passivity, potentiality.[24] The conception of reason which is founded on such exclusion is challenged by feminists as being incoherent: it demands universal validity while identifying itself in terms which, in Seyla Benhabib's phrase, involve substitutionalist universalism rather than genuine universalism.[25]

Further, Lloyd notes that the development of Reason after Bacon is a development which can be characterized by the metaphor of rational (read as: limited, formal, objective, male) control over nature (read as: unlimited, material, chaotic, female).[26]

Hence, this dimension of the critiques lies along the axis of "the maleness" of Reason: feminists here argue that the privileging of Reason is the dominance of that conception whose origin lies in the exclusion of the characteristics inscribed as female, and which has been developed in the context of control of the symbolically female.

2. As Alison Jaggar points out, the emphasis on the equation of cognition and rational cognition obscures the rich cognitive resources of emotional, affective, desiring experience.[27] The feminist critique which is generated in this dimension focuses on the privileging of Reason as an arbitrary limitation of the conception of knowledge—one rooted, indeed, in the "maleness of Reason" as just described, but one criticized not only for its oppressively sexist consequences, but also for its production of a defectively limited epistemology.

3. Finally, feminists, along with other philosophers from the diverse theoretical traditions emerging in the postmodern era, have come to stress the contingent, historical nature of rationality itself. Again, this dimension overlaps "the maleness" and "arbitrary limits" above, but "the privileging of Reason" is here criticized for its hypostatization of an ahistorical, universalized, objectivating "faculty" or "method." Such privileging leads to an inadequate account of judgment and provides an inadequate connection to plural, historical, social realities: it provides no theoretical basis for clarifying normative choices and political practices.[28]

While it is crucial to recognize that the privileging of Reason has been challenged by Marx, by Nietzsche, by Foucault and by Derrida, as well as by the many branches of the traditions influenced by their work, this critique has also been central to the pragmatic/naturalist tradition. Further, while the *grounds* of the latter critique differ from those most often alluded to by feminist theorists, the *function* of that critique, especially in Dewey's work, is, I would argue, more closely aligned to practical imperatives implicit in the feminist stance than are those versions of the critique to be found in the traditions with which feminists more consciously align themselves.

The critique proceeds along several lines. For C. S. Peirce, in regard to the first dimension above, although the ideal of Reason and of the development of "concrete reasonableness" remains crucial, his is a conception of reason which is not essentialist, not defined by excluding or dominating or controlling a Nature conceived as Other. Remembering the Peircean maxim: Do not block the road to inquiry! we note that, as Richard Bernstein put it:

> All basic distinctions are relative to the stage of the development of inquiry and there is no conceptual distinction that cannot be revised, modified, or even abandoned in light of further inquiry. . . . Peirce's theory of inquiry stands as one of the great attempts to show how the classic dichotomies between thought and action, or theory and praxis can be united in a theory of a community of inquirers committed to continuous, rational, self-critical activity.[29]

In Dewey, Reason—as a philosophic category—is finally replaced by the conception of intelligence.[30] And intelligence is "the sum-total of impulses, habits, emotions, records, and discoveries which forecast what is desirable and undesirable in future possibilities, and which contrive ingenuously in behalf of imagined good."[31] Unlike Reason, intelligence is neither product nor component of a "mind" which is articulated in contradistinction to a "body." Further, while intelligence is understood as an active function, the activity of intelligence clearly does not exclude passivity. Doing and undergoing involve one another:

> Just as there is no assertive action, no aggressive attack upon things as they are, which is all action, so there is no undergoing which is not on our part also a going on and a going through. (p. 63)

Finally, intelligence is a function of a live creature, developed through transactions between that creature and the world in which it is enmeshed—a world understood as physical, biological, social and cultural. Neither the organism, nor the world, nor functioning intelligence, is given and fixed antecedent to the interaction. They emerge in conjunction with one another. Intelligence could not be conceived of as an ahistorical or universal category. Since "impulses, habits, emotions, etc." evolve, so must intelligence. It is historically and culturally specific.

Turning to a latter-day representative of the American Tradition, Justus Buchler argues against the privileging of Reason because the category has been inconsistently developed and inappropriately applied. He argues that the essential process of reason is articulation in furtherance of query. Articulation is defined as the extension of meaning,[32] and as "the manipulation . . . of products as ends in themselves; that is, as subjects of communication for the sake only of further communication."[33] And such articulation is relevant to all forms of query and of human production. Hence,

> The attribute of reason must be applicable to the whole of human production and not merely to the forms of talk and thought; to inventive communication in all its forms and not merely to that exemplified by assertive query.[34]

Buchler's (like Dewey's) approach to these questions, in *reconceptualizing* reason, manages to preserve a notion of purposive and validatable utterance without requiring that purposiveness emerge in dichotomous opposition of mind to body, objective to subjective, active to passive, or—in other ways—out of a dichotomy which defines reason in terms of categories symbolically associated with the male and derived in exclusionary or dominating relation to traits symbolically associated with the female.

Further, this conception, in insisting on the variety of forms of judgment and query—none of which is to be understood as either primary or paradigmatic, insists also "that even assertion cannot be understood adequately if understood merely as the product of mind."[35]

With respect to the privileging of reason, then, not only has much of the discussion taking place in feminist philosophy developed concerns which have been central to the American Tradition, but also that Tradition can be shown to include formulations responding usefully to the concerns articulated. While other traditions have more directly addressed the notion of Reason as "male," the Pragmatic/Naturalist tradition has taken, as focal concern, the development of conceptions of experience, cognition, and judgment undermining the traditional dichotomies on which "reason" has been inscribed as the not-female. That is, without the mind/body, objective/subjective, active/passive dualisms as categorical frames within which experience is conceptualized; without the primacy of the epistemic dimension of experience or of assertive judgment, there is the possibility of a conceptualization of knowing and judging which preserves openness to the diversity of experiences and experiencers without losing the possibility of validation. Further, the significance of emotion and habit, of culture and relations, of embodiment and situatedness, are central to at least the Jamesian and Deweyan versions of the tradition's accounts, as is the emphasis on the historicity of the category of reason and its bearing on the emergence of meaning in the reconstruction of political life. There are conceptual tools in this tradition—tools which might be developed to address the crucial liberatory concerns raised by feminist critiques, but not yet fully and satisfactorily clarified in current theories.[36]

III

Perhaps the most significant theme to be examined is the conception of the nature of philosophy and of philosophic activity. No question has been more consistently interesting to philosophers than the question of what it is that philosophers do—and, in the contemporary world, of whether there is indeed any role for us at all. Whether seeing itself as queen or as "underlabourer," philosophy has been required to define its voice in relation to both science and poetry. Empirical and/or imaginative renderings are not meant to be the "stuff" of philosophic production; neither the particular nor the concrete have been thought to be the central concerns of philosophers. Further, philosophy has tended to see its milieu in the largest of arenas—the meta-theoretical analyses of the laws and structures governing the physical, social, and cultural universes—rather than in twists of the nautilus' shell, in the repetitive movements of the assembly worker, or in the whispers of the bedroom. The voice meant to carry in such large arenas is one modulated by objectivity, honed in rational analysis, made resonant by long practice in the agonistic art of argumentative discourse.

From Hegel, through Marx, Nietzsche, critical theory and poststructuralism, the conception of philosophy as a "purely" theoretic/descriptive discourse has been powerfully attacked—and has been mortally wounded. Nevertheless, the echoes of the vast arena remain enshrined in the voice of academic philosophy. Even, surprisingly, in those discourses most directly derived from various versions of critical theories. Still, the "philosophical voice" is one which rings with measured tones, speaks only of important things, and utilizes the vocabulary and the cadences of the past—modified to conform to the style of the discourse of the particular movements with which it identifies.

Feminist philosophy, united in almost no other respect, consistently views philosophy as a discipline which must account for women's concrete, historical, plural situations; which must be inflected with the diverse accents of plurally located theorizers; and which must serve, in some manner, as an instrument in the reconstruction/transformation of an oppressive social order. In 1920, Dewey argued that what was wrong with prior philosophies was:

> They are all committed to the logic of general notions under which specific situations are to be brought. What we want light upon is this or that group of individuals, this or that concrete human being, this or that special institution or social arrangement. . . . We need guidance in dealing with particular perplexities in domestic life, and are met by dissertations on the Family or by assertions of the sacredness of individual Personality.[37]

Later, he characterized philosophy as "criticism of criticisms,"[38] whose

> function is to regulate the further appreciation of goods and bads; to give greater freedom and security in those acts of direct selection, appropriation, identification and of rejection, elimination, destruction which ensnare and which exclude objects of belief, conduct and contemplation.[39]

In short, it is indeed the pluralistic and specific clarification of social experience in the service of its reconstruction.

*   *   *

Women, struggling to become feminists, often have passionate, wavering, tentative, even querulous voices—the philosophic voice does not articulate their confusion, frustration, anger, or terror. Feminist philosophers, on the other hand, have generally mastered the voice, but have used it (with some discomfort) precisely to address the residue of unarticulated feelings and experiences of their sisters. Put gently, Jean Grimshaw notes:

> feminism makes a difference to philosophy. The difference it makes is that women, in doing philosophy, have often raised new problems, problematised issues in new ways and moved to the centre questions which have been marginalised or seen as unimportant or at the periphery.[40]

In a slightly more strident tone, Carol Gould argues:

> Insofar as traditional philosophy has distorted the theoretical account of social reality by leaving women out, the critical inclusion of women as a philosophical subject matter must begin with a critique of philosophy.[41]

Nancy Foster, in the recent work *Unruly Practices*, pushes for a fully engaged voice:

> social transformation requires struggle in the sense of engagement with one's opponents. In academic arenas this means challenging ideological distortions built into mainstream perspectives and, insofar as possible, compelling their adherents to respond.[42]

Dewey, in the introduction to *Reconstruction in Philosophy*, approvingly cites C. D. Darlington's comment (originally offered in another context):

> We need a Ministry of Disturbance; a regulated source of annoyance; a destroyer of routine; an underminer of complacency.[43]

Feminist philosophy has arrived to fill the need. In reconstructing the urgent sense of the demand for precisely the engaged, critical voice provided, feminist philosophy has rediscovered what is central to the American Tradition in philosophy.

Notes

1. C. D. Darlington, Conway memorial Lecture on *The Conflict of Society and Science*, quoted in John Dewey "Introduction," *Reconstruction in Philosophy*, 2nd ed. (Boston: Beacon Press, 1948 [1920], p. xvii.

2. See John Dewey, "The Reflex Arc Concept in Psychology" (EW 5:96–109); see also Ralph Sleeper's discussion of the reflex arc as circuit in *The Necessity of Pragmatism: John Dewey's Conception of Philosophy* (New Haven and London: Yale University Press, 1986).

3. These labels are widely used to identify groupings of feminists; see, for example, Josephine Donovan, *Feminist Theory: The Intellectual Traditions of American Feminism* (New York: Frederick Ungar, 1985); Jean Grimshaw, *Feminist Philosophers: Women's Perspectives on Philosophical Traditions* (London and New York: Harvester Wheatsheaf, 1986); Alison M. Jaggar, *Feminist Politics and Human Nature* (Totowa, N.J.: Roman and Allanheld, 1983); and Rosemarie Tong, *Feminist Thought: A Comprehensive Introduction* (Boulder and San Francisco: Westview Press, 1989).

4. See especially: "Symposium on Pragmatism and Feminism," *Transactions of the C. S. Peirce Society: A Quarterly Journal in American Philosophy* (Fall 1991). Charlene Haddock Seigfried, ed.: Special Issue on Pragmatism and Feminism, *Hypatia* 8/2 (Spring 1993). Charlene Haddock Seigfried, *Pragmatism and Feminism: Reweaving the Social Fabric* (Chicago: University of Chicago Press, 1996). See also Margaret Jane Radin, "The Pragmatist and the Feminist," *Southern California Law Review* 63/6 (1990); Richard Rorty, "Feminism and Pragmatism," *Michigan Quarterly Review* 30/2 (Spring 1991).

5. See, e.g., Judy Chicago, *Embroidering Our Heritage: The Dinner Party Needlework* (Garden City, N.Y.: Anchor Books, 1980); Carol Christ and Judith Plaskow (eds.), *Womenspirit Rising* (San Francisco: Harper and Row, 1979); Tee Corrne, Jacquiline Lapidus, and Margaret Sloan-Hunter, *Tantras of Womanlove* (Tallahassee: The Naiad Press, 1982). M. Lugones and E. Spelman, "Have We Got a Theory for You! Feminist Theory, Cultural Imperialism, and the Demand for 'The Woman's Voice,' " *Women's Studies International Forum*, (6), 1983.

6. Nancy Fraser, *Unruly Practices: Power, Discourse, and Gender in Contemporary Social Theory* (Minneapolis: University of Minnesota Press, 1989).

7. Lisa Heldke, "John Dewey and Evelyn Fox Keller: A Shared Epistemological Tradition," *Hypatia*, vol. 2, no. 3 (Fall 1987), 129–40.

8. Susan R. Bordo, *The Flight to Objectivity: Essays on Cartesianism and Culture* (Albany: State University of New York Press, 1987).

9. I owe this formulation to Morris Grossman.

10. Grimshaw, *Feminist Philosophers*, p. 91–92. She is referring to Liz Stanley and Sue Wise, *Breaking Out: Feminist Consciousness and Feminist Research* (London: Routledge and Kegan Paul, 1983).

11. Diana Fuss, *Esssentially Speaking: Feminism, Nature and Difference* (New York and London: Routledge, 1989), p. 118.

12. Adrienne Rich, *Of Woman Born: Motherhood as Experience and Institution* (New York: W. W. Norton, 1976), and Sandra Harding, *The Science Question in Feminism* (Ithaca, N.Y.: Cornell University Press, 1986). For a critique of the visual metaphor which underlies the spectator view, see also Evelyn Fox Keller and Christine R. Grontkowski, "The Mind's Eye," in Sandra Harding and Merrill B. Hintikka (eds.), *Discovering Reality: Feminist Perspectives on Epistemology, Metaphysics, Methodology, and Philosophy of Science* (Holland/Boston: D. Reidel, 1983), pp. 207–25.

13. Cf. Luce Irigaray, 1974, *Speculum de l'autre femme*, Gillian C. Gill (trans.); *Speculum of the Other Woman* (Ithaca, N.Y.: Cornell University Press, 1985). Irigaray, "This Sex Which Is Not One," in Elaine Marks and Isabelle de Courtivron (eds.), *New French Feminisms* (New York: Schocken Books, 1980), and Simone de Beauvoir, *The Second Sex*, trans. H. M. Parshley (New York: Vintage, 1974). See also the discussions of feminists in the Marxist, radical, socialist, and post-modern tradi-

tions as explored in Donovan, *Feminist Theory*, 1985; Tong, *Feminist Thought* 1989; and, especially, Jaggar, *Feminist Politics and Human Nature*, 1983.

14. See Luce Irigaray, "Is the Subject of Science Sexed?" in Carol Mastrangelo Bove (trans.), *Hypatia* 2, no. 3 (Fall 1987).

15. See, for example, Mary Daly, *Beyond God the Father: Toward a Philosophy of Women's Liberation* (Boston: Beacon Press, 1973), and *Gyn/Ecology: The Metaethics of Radical Feminism* (Boston: Beacon Press, 1978).

16. See, e.g., Alison M. Jaggar, "Love and Knowledge: Emotion in Feminist Epistemology," in Jaggar and Susan R. Bordo (eds.), *Gender/Body/Knowledge/Feminist Reconstructions of Being and Knowing* (New Brunswick, N.J.: Rutgers University Press, 1989).

17. This challenge is obviously the one addressed in the concerns about women's experience—but it is also addressed in the general concern about false universalisms as expressed, for example, in the work of Seyla Benhabib and Carol Gilligan.

18. John Smith, "The Reconception of Experience in Peirce, James, and Dewey," *The Monist*, vol. 58, no. 4 (1985), 554.

19. Jane Flax, "Political Philosophy and the Patriarchal Unconscious: A Psychoanalytic Perspective on Epistemology and Metaphysics," in Harding and Hintikka, *Discovering Reality*, 1983.

20. Smith, in *The Monist* (1985), 540, 543.

21. John Dewey, *Creative Intelligence: Essays in the Pragmatic Attitude* (Holt, Rinehart and Winston, 1917), in J. J. McDermott (ed.), *The Philosophy of John Dewey* (Chicago: University of Chicago Press, 1981 [1973]), p. 61.

22. John Dewey, *Experience and Nature* (New York: Dover Publications, 1958), p. 7.

23. See in the work cited above:

> "I take it that an uncorrupted realism would accept such things [evil, error, dreams, hallucinations, etc.] as real events, and find in them no other problems that those attending the consideration of any real occurrence—namely, problems of structure, origin, and operation. . . . 'reality' is a *denotative* term, a word used to designate indifferently everything that happens. Lies, dreams, insanities, deceptions, myths, theories are all of them just the events which they specifically are. Pragmatism is content to take its stand with science; for science finds all such events to be subject matter of description and inquiry—just like stars and fossils, mosquitoes and malaria, circulation and vision. It also takes its stand with daily life, which finds that such things really have to be reckoned with as they occur interwoven in the texture of events." (p. 89)

24. Genevieve Lloyd, *The Man of Reason: "Male" and "Female" in Western Philosophy* (Minneapolis: University of Minnesota Press, 1984), esp. pp. 1–50.

25. Seyla Benhabib, "The Generalized and The Concrete Other: The Kohlberg-Gilligan Controversy and Moral Theory," in Eva Feder Kittay and Diana T. Meyers, *Women and Moral Theory* (Rowman and Littlefield, 1989). See also Carol C. Gould, "Philosophy of Liberation and the Liberation of Philosophy," in Carol C. Gould and Marx W. Wartofsky (eds.), *Women and Philosophy: Toward a Theory of Liberation* (New York: Perigee Books [G. P. Putnam's Sons], 1976).

26. Lloyd, *The Man of Reason*, pp. 10–19.

27. Jaggar, "Love and Knowledge. . . ," in Jaggar and Bordo (eds), *Gender/Body/Knowledge* (1989), pp. 145–170.

28. With respect to this dimension, see Susan R. Bordo, *The Flight to Objectivity*, and "The Cartesian Masculinization of Thought," Carol Gilligan, *In a Different Voice: Women and Moral Development*, Nancy Fraser, *Unruly Practices: Power, Discourse and Gender in Contemporary Social Theory*. And, of course, see especially the feminist theorists who root themselves in the post-structuralist tradition (e.g.: Kristeva, Irigary, Spivak, and others).

29. Richard J. Bernstein, *Praxis and Action* (Philadelphia: University of Pennsylvania Press, 1971), p. 199.

30. Cf. Ralph W. Sleeper, *The Necessity of Pragmatism: John Dewey's Conception of Philosophy* (New Haven: Yale University Press, 1966), p. 179.

31. John Dewey, "The Need for a Recovery of Philosophy" (originally published 1917), in John J. McDermott (ed.), *The Philosophy of John Dewey* (Chicago: University of Chicago Press, 1973/1981), p. 96.

32. Justus Buchler, *Toward a General Theory of Human Judgment*, 2nd ed. (New York: Dover, 1951/1979), p. 33.

33. Ibid., p. 46.

34. Justus Buchler, *Nature and Judgment* (New York: Columbia University Press, 1955), p. 98.

35. Ibid., p. 29.

36. I.e., in Jaggar's discussion of the role of emotion in cognition (cf. Jaggar, "Love and Knowledge. . . ," in Jaggar and Bordo), she is necessarily tentative as she gropes toward an adequate account of cognition; Lloyd (cf. *The Man of Reason*) provides an illuminating critique, but does not offer a developed constructive response; the post-structuralist feminists (e.g., Kristeva, Irigaray, Butler, et al.) likewise provide extraordinarily valuable critiques of Reason—but little in the way of sustained account of how judgment is to be validated or political reconstruction purposively assessed.

37. John Dewey, *Reconstruction in Philosophy*, enlarged ed. (Boston: Beacon Press, 1957 [original 1920, enlarged 1948]), pp. 188–89.

38. John Dewey, *Experience and Nature* (New York: Dover, 1958 [reprint of 2nd ed., 1929]), p. 398.

39. Ibid., p. 404.

40. Grimshaw, *Feminist Philosophers*, 1986, p. 260.

41. Gould, "The Woman Question: Philosophy of Liberation and the Liberation of Philosophy," in Gould and Wartofsky, p. 32.

42. Nancy Fraser, *Unruly Practices: Power, Discourse, and Gender in Contemporary Social Theory* (Minneapolis: University of Minnesota Press, 1989), p. 13.

43. p. xvii (cf. n1, above).

Part Two

Democracy and Education

5

Philosophy, Education, and the American Tradition of Aspirational Democracy

Elizabeth Kamarck Minnich

Democracy is a way of life controlled by a working faith in the possibilities of human nature. . . . That belief is without basis and significance save as it means faith in the potentialities of human nature as that nature is exhibited in every human being irrespective of race, color, sex, birth and family, of material or cultural wealth.
—John Dewey, "Creative Democracy: The Task Before Us"

The future woman must have a life work and economic independence. She must have knowledge. She must have the right of motherhood at her own discretion. The uplift of women is, next to the problem of the color line and the peace movement, our greatest modern cause. When, now, two of these movements—woman and color—combine in one, the combination has deep meaning.
—W. E. B. Du Bois, "The Damnation of Women"

[N]o woman can possibly put herself or her sex outside any of the interests that affect humanity. . . . She stands now at the gateway of this new era of American civilization. . . . To be alive at such an epoch is a privilege, to be a woman then is sublime.
—Anna Julia Cooper, A Voice from the South

I speak about pragmatism as someone who, if you'll forgive my putting it this way, falls in love again every time I return to it. Despite years in which "Oh, do be more pragmatic!" meant, in popular speech, something like calm down, get sensible! and when, in academic circles, "the pragmatists" referred to a small group of what were generally agreed to be rather sloppy American thinkers who might be taught (if taught at all) in U.S. cultural or intellectual history courses, I have retained that pas-

Extensively revised; first published as Minnich 1997.

sionate response. I read the works of pragmatists with intellectual excite-ment, political and moral relief, and the particular emotional pleasure that tells me I am in the company of friends. I confess that I also read them as an equal, not because I have inflated notions of myself (reading them always fills me with awe, in fact), but because I come to them now as one among the many who have been called into philosophizing as into action by a deep commitment fed by the same spring as theirs—a commitment to making democracy, and the education upon which it so essentially depends, surpass its own failures in a renewed attempt to real-ize its aspirations.

Thinking today about pragmatism, progressive education, and femi-nism, then, I am particularly aware that I draw on a historically shared mixture of knowledge and moral and political values as well as my own contemporary experiences. Most particularly, I draw on my experiences as a philosopher and educator working during the past thirty-five-some years of what seems to me to be to a striking degree an *age of movements* that have affected us as a nation in two large waves. (There is in an important sense nothing new about the United States being swept by movements, of course; as I will observe shortly, there are striking similari-ties between those of our times and those of the last turn of the century when the pragmatists flourished.)

The first wave I find it useful to think of now as having been focused on struggles for civil rights, *equal rights,* for those long categorically denied them—for black people; women of all groups; American Indians; poor people; people with disabilities; farmers; migrant workers; lesbian, gays, bisexuals, transgendered people; racially ethnicized groups; old people; rank-and-file union members; students; welfare recipients; tenants; peo-ple who are by current prescriptions "fat"; and others. Obviously, I am thinking of groups and movements for which we could cite names—the civil rights movement, the women's liberation movement, the American Indian Movement, the disability rights movement, fat liberation, the Grey Panthers, and others, and major movement events, such as Martin Luther King Jr.'s "I Have a Dream" speech, the Poor Peoples' March on Washington, student strikes at the University of California–Berkeley and across the nation, welfare rights activists marching on the White House, the Stonewall rebellion, and much more from the turbulent, effective political theater of the times. I do not mean, however, to reduce longer-term, far less media-covered, crucial community-based organizing in all these and more areas to such dramatic moments; that would continue the falsifying heroic United States myth that movements are made by individuals, by street-theater events, by "spontaneous" uprisings rather than by the day-by-day stubbornly inspired but often repetitive, slogging work and usually hand-to-mouth existence of hundreds and hundreds of long-term activists and community leaders. I do, however, mean by using the most visible markers that a movement has been built by such work to underscore just how many, how large, and how broad their reach was: the world knows that "the sixties" (which were actually also the forties, fifties, and far more visibly the seventies) were momentous times in which a great deal changed.

Discrimination on the basis of ascribed membership in a devalued group was challenged, in this equality-seeking wave of the age of movements, particularly insofar as it publicly disadvantaged people. To seek equality then was, in a sense, to seek to be deprivatized, to be fully free and empowered to speak and act effectively among equalized others in public life: quite literally, to demand the right safely to come out.

More recently, a second wave emerged more fully from the first, within which of course it was already present. This wave has been characterized by agitation for the full *recognition* that goes beyond even as it depends upon the granting of rights. Standing (figuratively: some, for example, sat in wheelchairs) out there in public, long privatized—closeted, domesticated, hidden away, devalued (even if sometimes also romanticized), insulted—groups have claimed cultural, social, and personal acknowledgment, respect, and value for themselves not as the dominant culture has defined *them*, but in their own terms. Identity politics, academic research and teaching in new fields (women's studies, queer studies, ethnic studies, among others), curriculum transformation projects, diversity initiatives, multiculturalism, floods of memoirs and autobiographies, these and more have emerged to say, "Here I am; here we are: see us, hear us, take us fully into account, *recognize* us." These are calls that depend on recognition of public rights, but they also ask us to recognize the implication of public rights and life for personal and community contexts. They have thereby perforce reminded us that the rights-bearing individual is a powerful abstraction that, as lived, has never actually been empty of particular gendered, racialized, and otherwise highly culturally shaped content. This wave has taught us that to stand a chance of meaning what we say when we speak of wishing to be able to see, and treat, each person as a unique individual, we need to be able to recognize and value who that person actually is, which, for the creatures of shared meanings that humans are, includes, without ever being reducible to, "where s/he is coming from."

In a sense, then, the wave of movements for recognition comprises claims on a dominant culture to reconfigure many boundaries, including the old public/private division that in practice denied both public and private freedom, rights, and obligations to the majority of those in the United States. In so doing, these movements have raised anew most if not indeed all of the most basic philosophic questions: what does, can, should it mean to be human? What is justice? What can we know? What ought we to do?

In such times, education cannot simply conserve past knowledge and support the creation of new learning that fits smoothly into traditional or professionalized fields. To do so is to take a political and moral as well as intellectual, educational position. It is hardly neutral, objective, disinterested to say to the majority of a nation's people as they are emerging into public and laying claim to the rights, duties, and obligations that make full human, cultural, and individual recognition possible, "I will not recognize you except insofar as the terms of a knowledge tradition within which I was trained already allow, or do not allow, me to see, hear, and take you and your 'kind' into account." In times between movements when conventions of many kinds prevail, it is possible not to confront the moral, political significance of knowledge systems, to see them as "pure," and removed from the messy world around them. In times such as ours (and the earlier pragmatists'), it is not.

Swimming through these waves, sometimes lifted up by them, sometimes swamped and gasping, I earned my B.A. at the highly individualistic and embarrassedly privileged but still progressive Sarah Lawrence College, which was, during my time there (1961–65), also one of the homes of the northern students' movement in support of the southern civil rights movement. I was, then, studying at a place in a time in which individual creativity was nurtured in the context of politics that called people into action for moral reasons, in the name of an aspirational democracy. Later, during my work for the Ph.D., first at the University of California–Berkeley in political science and then in philosophy at the Graduate Faculty for Political and Social Science of the New School (when the anti–Vietnam War movement was also sweeping campuses), I studied pragmatism, among other things. I was advised to write my dissertation on John Dewey by my mentor, Hannah Arendt (whose advice it was always in many senses wise to take). She suggested Dewey to me because "Americans should know their own philosophical tradition," but also, and more important to her, because, "Dewey is one of the few philosophers who ever understood and valued action." As a student of and teaching assistant for Arendt, this had particular appeal to me, given that Arendt's lifework involved finding a grounding for ethical action in thinking and judgment rather than in universalized principles or creeds or ideologies. I was increasingly troubled by a radical disconnection between prevailing ways of knowing and constructions of knowledge and the messy, confusing, changeable, yet always morally fraught and compelling realm of action.

One might think that what was troubling me was an obvious impetus to study John Dewey, and that, in times such as the sixties and seventies in this country, Dewey and the pragmatists would have been taken very seriously. But when I went on to defend my dissertation, the first question I was asked was "Tell me: Why would anyone want to study Dewey anyway?" Being a philosopher of and for United States democracy who focused on experience and education, he was in the view of many philosophers of that highly analytical, language-centered, logical positivist time not a candidate for Serious Philosophical Study. Had I not had on my (anxious-graduate-student) side the very weighty Hannah Arendt as well as Richard Bernstein, to whom she sent me for his deep knowledge of Dewey and his own focus on the concepts of *praxis* and *action*, I rather doubt that my dissertation would have been accepted, regardless of how good it was, or how well or poorly I defended it.

Since then I have done many things, taught and been an administrator at very different schools, but throughout my own work has particularly focused on feminism's philosophical, moral, and politically significant challenges to education to critique its intellectual scope, the significance of its subject matters, the reach and adequacy of its methods and pedagogies, its systems and structures, and its grounds for selecting and ways of treating its participants in all roles. Rather to my amazement, I now find that I have been consistent in my choices of schools to study and work with, philosophers and theorists to converse with, critiques to accept as positive challenges, and political/ethical ideals to which to aspire even as they remain open to critique and change. What has continued to impel me to philosophize, to work in education, and to be involved with feminism and diversity work is the belief that democracy is a crucial moral ideal still compromised at its roots in ways that raise the most important of philosophical and therefore of political and educational questions. I am a child of my times, then, one fortunate enough to have found surrogate parents, especially Hannah Arendt and the pragmatists, from whom to have learned something of earlier efforts to connect philosophy, politics, and education.

I refer to my work now, in conceptual shorthand, as an effort to discern how the *given* of human differences was turned into the *problem* of diversity, informing—deforming—virtually all the systems within and through which we struggle to find meaning and to live together. It is clear to me, as it has by no means always been to my colleagues, that this is philosophical work. But then, I have continued to feel that Hannah Arendt and John Dewey, Jane Addams, Anna Julia Cooper, and W. E. B. Du Bois knew very well what philosophy should be, and that it should be intimately related to, rather than severed from, issues of moral action, of politics and public life; and that has helped. My passion for pragmatism has always contained a large dose of gratitude for such company, such teachers and predecessors.

Imagine, for example, how grateful one can be at finding the following in John Dewey when one's colleagues are once again angry about the "politicizing" of academia, the "disuniting" of America, the "obsession" of "those people" with "victimization," and are calling on us to return to a supposedly disinterested academic quest that denies any implication with what *human being* has actually been construed and constructed to mean through the millennia, centuries, years, and daily moments of all-pervasive invidious prejudices:

> [P]hilosophy has been committed to a metaphysics of feudalism.
> . . . [I]t has thought of things in the world as occupying certain grades of value, or as having fixed degrees of truth, ranks of reality.
> . . . Now any such philosophy inevitably works in behalf of a regime of authority, for it is only right that the superior should lord it over the inferior. The result is that much of philosophy has gone to justifying the particular scheme of authority in religion or social order which happened to exist at a given time. . . . Thus for the most part the democratic practice of life has been at an immense intellectual disadvantage. . . . Now whatever the idea of equality means for democracy, it means, I take it, that the world is not to be construed as a fixed order of species, grades or degrees. It means that every existence deserving the name of existence has

something unique and irreplaceable about it, that it does not exist to illustrate a principle, to realize a universal or to embody a kind or a class. (Dewey [1919] 1993, 45–46)

Thus Dewey and in differing but compatible ways other progressives and pragmatists never made the mistake of holding that how we philosophize, the beliefs we hold, and the systems within and through which we act are radically separable. What human being *means* in every sense was for them at the questioning center of politics as it is of morals and philosophy.

In this, the pragmatists joined in their own way a long radical tradition of aspirational democracy that stretches back to the painfully contradictory founding of this nation. The searing if also generative tension between ideals and practices, as we encountered again in our own age of movements, has yet to be fully resolved. The nation began, after all, with a revolution justified by the invocation of basic human rights deriving from a principle of equality even as American Indians were being "removed," betrayed, slaughtered; Africans were being enslaved; and all women, however otherwise privileged, also remained privatized by being denied the rights and protections of public life and citizenship. And yet those and other groups have called on the very ideals their treatment violated to seek redress in the form of rights and recognition.

On this general level of theory in contradiction with practice, but also in more particular ways, we remain today deeply worried by situations very like those the pragmatists faced at the turn of the last century. Then, too, there was an influx of people, and peoples, that some were not sure could or even should become fully a part of the nation. They were also seen as "dark," and culturally alien, as we tend to forget now that their descendants have become "Americanized"—and so "white". Then, too, rapid economic change (in their case, industrialization) was creating dangerously vast gulfs between the rich and poor, gulfs always deeply implicated with the stubborn "race question." Then, too, there was great concern about what they called "tenements" and we call "inner cities." And the pragmatists, too, were leery of Utopia-promising ideologies that nevertheless understandably appeal to those desperately seeking answers, and justice. Facing all this, we, as did the pragmatists, are turning back to the ideals of democracy not as worn patriotic slogans but as challenges to engage close-in with meliorative change (today, broadly engaged through calls to "reinvigorate civic life" as well as through continuing grassroots, national, and international activism).

Also like the pragmatists, we are again today aware of just how central education is to the crucial task of opening and more inclusively informing minds, hearts, and imaginations as well as providing access to opportunity to keep social, cultural, economic and political hierarchies from locking only a few in and the majority out. I have often quoted to audiences of educators today the "credo" from the Bank Street School for Children, written by Lucy Sprague Mitchell (the Bank Street School, begun earlier, was granted a provisional charter in 1931 by the Regents of the State of New York). It is striking how contemporary it sounds:

> What We Believe: A Credo for Bank Street School for Children
> What Potentialities in human beings—children, teachers, ourselves—do we want to see develop?
> A zest for living that comes from taking in the world with all five senses alert.
> Lively intellectual curiosities that turn the world into an exciting laboratory and keep one ever a learner.
> Flexibility when confronted with change and ability to relinquish patterns that no longer fit the present.
> The courage to work, unafraid and efficiently, in a world of new needs, new problems, and new ideas.
> Gentleness combined with justice in passing judgments on other human beings.
> Sensitivity, not only to the external formal rights of the 'other fellow,' but to him as another human being seeking a good life through his own standards.
> A striving to live democratically, in and out of schools, as the best way to advance our concept of democracy.
> Our credo demands ethical standards as well as scientific attitudes.
> Our work is based on the faith that human beings can improve the society they have created. (Mitchell 1931)

Having cited Mitchell, who is not often named as a pragmatist but whose educational work took place at a time and in an intellectual milieu in which Dewey and others were very influential (her husband, Wesley Clair Mitchell, studied with Dewey), I should make explicit what I have had in mind but have not yet stated. It is my conviction that if we are today to consult the wisdom of the pragmatists as it mutually engages democratic aspirations, public philosophizing, and education, we should do so with the passionate, contentious lot of them. "The Pragmatists" included white women, and men and women of color whose philosophizing centered in reflective action as well as, and in many cases more than, writing, and more white men than most of us have heard of. John Dewey, William James, Charles Sanders Peirce, Josiah Royce, and (on some lists) George Herbert Mead do not constitute a quorum. The shrinking of the key figures in pragmatism (which in its time approached the scope of a movement and produced as movements do intense opposition, even persecution, as well as national and international support) to this or some slightly varied short list, as well as subsequent scholars' focus on the least overtly political writings even of that group, have philosophically decentered what is most basic to pragmatism. To depoliticize the pragmatists collectively is to misconstrue them philosophically; the philosophical problems that animate and characterize pragmatism were and remain moral political problems, problems of justice intimately intertwined with questions about how we think.

Far from holding thinking and acting, philosophy and politics, separate, and so also far from believing that only other academic philosophers were his proper colleagues, John Dewey called on his compatriots to undo invidious hierarchies and divisions of all kinds among human beings in order to release our full intelligence. Perhaps his most well known definition of democracy is that it is *organized intelligence*, and by that he meant nothing like a Platonic state devised by philosophers who have seen Justice-Itself but, rather, an ongoing process involving as many as possible that is constantly readjusting itself. Dewey ([1934] 1980, 348–49) characteristically emphasizes that political, economic, and social hierarchies limit and distort everything by resisting free intelligence: "Wherever social divisions and barriers exist, practices and ideas that correspond to them fix metes and bounds, so that liberal action is placed under restraint. Creative intelligence is looked upon with distrust; the innovations that are the essence of individuality are feared and generous impulse is put under bonds not to disturb the peace. . . . Morals are assigned a special compartment in theory and practice because they reflect the divisions embodied in economic and political institutions.

Following Dewey, it seems to me hard to avoid observing that the shrinking of lists of the pragmatists to a few white men who wrote books that were kept in print, and of their works to the least overtly political, itself demonstrates the effects of the "social divisions and barriers" built into a great deal of academicized philosophizing. I believe that we are returning to the pragmatists now, a larger group of them and their works, precisely because the work of this age of movements has once again brought political/moral issues into close conversation with epistemology, thence to education. In 1995, the Association of American Colleges and Universities issued a series of reports from its National Panel and project "American Commitments: Diversity, Democracy and Liberal Learning." As "scribe" for one of those reports, I wrote in far more pragmatist terms than I then realized:

> Liberal learning today as always involves positions on what counts as knowledge, what it means to be human, what social orders are and should be. Thus, today's active, multivocal discussions about the meanings of the liberal arts and their realization through curricula, pedagogies, and institutional structures *matter*. They are about books and subjects, yes, and they are also about ideals in tension with entrenched realities of power. That is why as educators we must care about racism and racialization, sexism, homophobia, class barriers, anti-Semitism, and all other expressions of the failures of aspirational democracy. These are failures of mind as much as they are failures of heart. They have infected epistemologies as well as practices of justice, because what we think and what we know has everything to do with the ways we make judgments and choices, the ways we act, and the systems we establish. (Minnich 1995, 37)

Those opposed to the work of the National Panel, and the work of many others involved with today's efforts to revitalize an education true to aspirational democracy, charge them with "politicizing" academia. Dewey would have recognized, as we do, that this is true, although not in the sense intended, which includes not only the antipragmatist notion that the academy *should* be utterly removed from the realm of action, but also that in fact it *is*. Dewey, in contrast, held that knowledge is already political, and it is our task, as believers in aspirational democracy, to make that explicit, in order to take responsibility for *how* it is political. Dewey ([1915] 1997, 333–34) wrote, "The origin of . . . divisions [in theories of knowing] we have found in the hard and fast walls which mark off social groups and classes within a group: like those between rich and poor, men and women, noble and baseborn, ruler and ruled. . . . So far as these divisions persist and others are added to them, each leaves its mark upon the educational system."

Similarly, but in the terms of his own direct engagement in the specifically racialized dimensions of education, Carter G. Woodson ([1933] 1990, xi) wrote, in *The Mis-Education of The Negro*, "The only question . . . is whether these 'educated' persons are actually equipped to face the ordeal before them or unconsciously contribute to their own undoing by perpetuating the regime of the oppressor." And Mary Parker Follett (1930, 302), who is also being rediscovered today, offered a vision of inclusive, nonhierarchical wholeness that not only does not blur all into sameness (defined by a dominant/dominating culture and its education), but provides equalizing recognition for differences: "We seek a richly diversified experience where every difference strengthens and reinforces the other through the interpenetrating of spirit and spirit, differences are conserved, accentuated, and reconciled in the greater life which is the issue. Each remains forever himself that thereby the larger activity may be enriched and in its refluence, reinforce him."

In the context of such critiques of and alternative ways of thinking about then prevailing constructions of knowledge and education, Dewey's ([1916] 1997, 332) (in)famous definition of philosophy as "the theory of education as a deliberately conducted practice" takes on much richer meaning. It has been read as an expression only or primarily of his "instrumentalism," which relates it to his faith in modern science as a model for democratic thinking. Such characterizations of his philosophy have contributed to its being seen as limited, or even quaintly naive, by the "left" as well as the "right." But his far deeper commitment was to the belief that philosophy must be radically changed so that it can finally stop subverting democratic aspirations and start doing its proper work of providing just, moral democratic practices with an epistemological grounding appropriate to them. This is hardly "merely" instrumentalism, and there is nothing naive about the ways he analyzed barriers to his purposes.

Dewey's critiques of those barriers, like and with those of all the other pragmatists of his times and those of this age of movements, move us into all spheres, from the philosophical through the educational to the political and into the moral. In all these areas—and perhaps especially in epistemology, which in some senses provides a pivot point for them—such critique aims to reveal the mutual implications of legitimated knowledge and ways of knowing, and of injustices systemically as well as interpersonally inflicted on categorically defined and devalued groups. It does so because, as many progressives have said, unjust divisions of human beings subvert not "only" democracy's aspirational ideals, but also the possibility of the unbiased, open inquiry required for human betterment and the education upon which it depends.

We cannot think, or rethink, meanings of human being that are at the core of philosophy as long as hierarchical views of humankind produce and reproduce hierarchical philosophies that divide mind (meaning some few privileged males) from body (meaning females and large groups of men defined by their physical type, labor, or both). As Allison Jaggar and Susan Bordo (1989, 4) write, "The body, notoriously and ubiquitously associated with the female, regularly has been cast, from Plato to Descartes to modern positivism, as the chief enemy of objectivity. . . . But what *is* the body? Within our dominant traditions, the very concept of body has been formed in opposition to that of the mind. It is defined as the arena of the biologically given, the material, the immanent." That is, body has been defined as that which mind must transcend, and rule, philosophically and politically. It is by no means coincidental that white men have been "*head* of state" as well as "*head* of the household" for so long. It is such views, both philosophical and popular (both of which inform cultures) that deform education such that it serves the "vicious intellectualism" against which William James so passionately railed, making education compatible with vicious social/economic systems. "Vicious intellectualism," as James scholar Stephen Rowe (1996, 31) puts it, "is a retreat from the complexities of real life into intellectual formulations that have become sealed off from any new insight or energy from lived experience." This is to the pragmatists—and others trying to undo philosophy's relation to the old hierarchies—philosophically wrong; it is also very dangerous in ways pragmatists and today's educational movement thinker-activists care about. As James ([1909] 1996, 60) further suggested, using an innocuous example to make a point whose sharpness is evident when it is read in the context of what we know about the definitional acts that support prejudices: "[A] person whom you have once called an 'equestrian' is thereby forever made unable to walk on his own feet."

On the positive side, through such critique, progressive, pragmatic, feminist diversity commitments work for an affirming, empowering release of the full capacities of all our minds, hearts, spirits, and bodies individually and relationally, as we saw in the quote earlier from Mary Parker Follett. Pragmatist vision emerges from critique, not from dreamers or schemers who turn away from what they do not like to imagine a new and different world—as if this, too, were not likely to result in a kind of vicious intellectualism. The pragmatists discern through their critiques possibilities not for a brave new world, but for presently possible real actions in support of more fruitful human interrelatedness and interdependency—within ourselves; to one another; across cultural, historical, and regional groupings; to the earth and the worlds humans create on it; and to a less alienating and divisive understanding of the divine than is often found in the actual histories of established religions. Their vision has at its heart something that is no more utopian than egalitarian, face-to-face, creative, engaged discussion among respectfully differing people that is throughout open-minded, exploratory, fallibilistic. Like Socrates, Diotima, Gandhi, they think of truth as an experiment, a quest, not a possession. The thinking and action carried on in this spirit is to be grounded within contexts of mutually communicative, educative action in a world compatibly understood to be inherently transactional rather than composed of discrete entities (such as atomistic individuals) that can only be more or less forcefully related by external means. We should thus, by this model of what they take to be both desirable and most basically given, hold ourselves in conversation with ongoing experience that unfreezes the meanings of abstractions turned into unchanging absolutes, or into the settled technical terms of professionalized academic expertise. In this spirit, Mary Parker Follett (1926, 7) said, pithily, "I think it better when practicable to keep to verbs; the value of nouns is chiefly for postmortems."

Translating such a recentering of philosophy into a democratizing educational vision for today, Maxine Greene (1995) writes:

> Democracy, Dewey wrote, is a community always in the making. If educators hold this in mind, they will remember that democracy is forever incomplete; it is founded in possibilities. Even in the small, the local spaces in which teaching is done, educators may begin creating the kinds of situations where, at the very least, students will begin telling the stories of what they are seeking, what they know and might not yet know, exchanging stories with others grounded in other landscapes, at once bringing into being something that is in between. . . . It is at moments like these that

persons begin to recognize each other and, in the experience of recognition, feel the need to take responsibility for each other.

The great movements for equality of our age, progressing into move-ments for the kind of recognition that presupposes and makes equality more than a political provision, are indeed once again finding strong friends and telling intellectual support among the earlier pragmatists. In an essay widely read among educators as well as historians of ideas and philosophers, "Pragmatism: An Old Name for Some New Ways of Think-ing?" James T. Kloppenberg recognizes that feminist, antiracist, and labor concerns (among other concerns of social justice movements) were com-patible with what he takes pragmatism to have been, although he does not take them to have been central to it as I believe they were. Kloppenb-erg (1996, 127) writes, for example, that:

> Such early pragmatists as James, Dewey, and George Herbert Mead considered pragmatism a weapon in the campaign against restrictive gender roles for the same reason they considered it a weapon against imperialism and racism and for democracy. They allied with feminist activists and championed feminist scholars such as Jessie Taft *because their conception of pragmatism extended beyond language* to an awareness of the experience of people who were denied choices, or unnecessarily restricted in their choices, by prevailing assumptions and patterns of social relations. (Em-phasis added)

I suggest that "feminist activists and . . . scholars" were part of the movement of pragmatism, not separate groups with which the short list of white male academic pragmatists might ally themselves (any more than Dewey "allied" himself with his longtime friend Jane Addams, with whom he learned a great deal, just as Du Bois learned more than has been, or was by him publicly, recognized with his friend Anna Julia Coo-per). I also do not believe that pragmatism had to be "extended beyond language" to reach "the experience of people who were denied choices." Language has been the focus of a great deal of contemporary philosophy; for the pragmatists, however, experience (no more or less a complex and elusive concept than language) is central, and basic.

In a still more influential work retrieving and reconsidering the pragmatists for today, Cornel West (1989, 25), in *The American Evasion of Philosophy*, writes:

> American pragmatism emerges with profound insights and myopic blindnesses . . . resulting from distinctive features of American civilization: its revolutionary beginning combined with a slave-based economy; its elastic liberal rule of law combined with an entrenched business-dominated status quo; its hybrid culture in combination with a collective self-definition as homogeneously Anglo-American; its obsession with mobility, contingency, and pecuniary liquidity combined with a deep moralistic impulse; and its impatience with theories and philosophies alongside ingenious technological innovation, political strategies of compromise, and personal devices for comfort and convenience.

Of course there are "myopic blindnesses" as well as "profound insights" in the earlier pragmatists, whose philosophizing entailed recognition not only of the need but also of the unavoidable reality of ongoing change guided by ideals never realized. But we should be careful here: some of the "blindnesses" turn out to be our own, a result of reading only the short list of pragmatists. Anna Julia Cooper ([1892] 1988, 162–63), who was by no means consistently radical, nevertheless wrote, for example, about America:

> Hither came Cavalier and Roundhead, Baptist and Papist, Quaker, Ritualist, Freethinker and Mormon, the conservative Tory, the liberal Whig, and the radical Independent,—the Spaniard, the Frenchman, the Englishman, the Italian, the Chinaman, the African, Swedes, Russians, Huns, Bohemians, Gypsies, Irish, Jews. Here surely was a seething cauldron of conflicting elements. Religious intolerance and political hatred, race prejudice and caste pride—"Double, double, toil and trouble;/Fire burn and cauldron bubble."
> Conflict, Conflict, Conflict.
> America for Americans! This is the white man's country! The Chinese must go, shrieks the exclusionist. Exclude the Italians! Colonize the blacks in Mexico or deport them to Africa. Lynch, suppress, drive out, kill out! America for Americans!
> *Who are Americans?* comes rolling back from ten million throats.

Who are to do the packing and delivering of the goods? Who are the homefolks and who are the strangers?

The red men used to be owners of the soil,—but they are about to be pushed over into the Pacific Ocean. They, perhaps, have the best right to call themselves "Americans" by right of primogeniture.

The writings of Cooper, herself most centrally an educator, clearly prefigure works of prominent multicultural historians such as Ronald Takaki and share, too, in a tradition of eloquent African American cultural critique of which West is a prime contemporary exemplar, although there are also times when she speaks in ways that can make contemporary analysts uncomfortable. But there is no denying the sweep and purchase of her genuine, central, defining commitment to a vision of an egalitarian, just, inclusive democracy *not* as an extension of a removed philosophy but at its animating, activist core. Such a commitment had everything to do with pragmatists' refusal to divide thinking from action, and so also their refusal to divide activists from philosophers. As Charlene Haddock Seigfried (1996, 21–22), writes:

The pragmatist belief that theory unrelated to practice is moribund inspired some of their radical students to abandon purely conceptual analysis. West points out that C. Wright Mills, a student of Dewey's, gave up philosophy after earning his M.A. and turned to social theory, declaring war on Talcott Parson's sociology because it supported the corporate liberal establishment. W. E. B. Du Bois "also gave up philosophy after studying under William James at Harvard, turning to the study of history and society." . . . If the pragmatists had succeeded in stopping philosophers from turning their backs on active engagement in solving society's most pressing problems, then feminists of our generation would not have had to endure the continuing struggle both to break into academia and to deinstitutionalize and open up academic deliberations to the wider community.

Yes, and more: if the work of the whole movement of pragmatists then had been successful rather than suppressed within and outside academia, Addams's and Du Bois's and Dewey's internationalism might have kept U.S. feminism and other movements from "first world" fallacies; Addams's pacifism might have supported antiwar efforts and antimilitarism in feminism and the labor movement; Anna Julia Cooper's and Carter G. Woodson's and Dewey's and Addams's anti-ethnic-discrimination and antiracist educational work would have kept us from having to struggle again so hard to open and transform all of education for all of us—and this is just scratching the surface. If there were blindnesses among them then, as of course there were, we should in their own spirit catch and correct them—just as they still help us catch and try to correct our own.

Our own errors, like theirs, can be political or philosophical, of course, but perhaps, given the history of severing action from thought, we should be most careful about emphasizing one over the other as we reenter conversation with the pragmatists now. If it was an error to reduce pragmatism to the short list of academic males, and to focus primarily on a depoliticized version of their philosophizing, it would now also be an error to return primarily to their overtly political writings and histories. The pragmatists' characteristic moral and political positions, and actions, can, and should, be translated into philosophical terms. For them, acting and philosophizing, which are both distinguishable from and mutually constitutive of each other, are alternately each other's figure and ground.

Dewey ([1939] 1993, 248), toward the end of his long life, took advantage of an occasion recognizing his work as an eminent philosopher to say, "I *know* . . . that such a manifestation of friendliness as I have experienced is a demonstration of sympathy for the things that make for the freedom and justice and for the kind of cooperative friendship that can flourish only where there is a freedom which untold multitudes possess in common," in which "communication is progressively liberated from bondage to prejudice and ignorance . . . [and we are all] emancipated from oppressions and suppressions."

In his time, it was not necessary to ask, "Why would anyone want to read the pragmatists anyway?" Today, with the efflorescence of scholarship and activism released by our own age of movements, it is again becoming unnecessary. This gives me hope, even as I see signs of reaction not dissimilar to that which nearly erased pragmatism before.

References

Cooper, Anna Julia. [1892] 1988. *A Voice from the South*. New York: Oxford University Press.

Dewey, John. [1915] 1997. *Democracy and Education*. New York: Simon and Schuster, Free Press.

———. [1916] 1997. *Democracy and Education: An Introduction to the Philosophy of Education*. New York: Free Press.

———. [1919] 1993. "Philosophy and Democracy." In *John Dewey: The Political Writings*. Edited by Debra Morris and Ian Shapiro. Indianapolis: Hackett.

———. [1934] 1980. *Art as Experience*. New York: G. P. Putnam's Sons.

———. [1939]. 1993. "Creative Democracy: The Task Before Us." In *John Dewey: The Political Writings*. Edited by Debra Morris and Ian Shapiro. Indianapolis: Hackett.

———. 1993. *John Dewey: The Political Writings*. Edited by Debra Morris and Ian Shapiro. Indianapolis: Hackett.

Du Bois, W. E. B. [1920] 1972. "The Damnation of Women." In *Darkwater: Voices from Within the Veil*, 164–65. New York: Schocken Books.

Follett, Mary Parker. 1926. *The New State*. New York: Longmans, Green.

———. 1930. *Creative Experience*. New York: Longmans, Green.

Greene, Maxine. 1995. "Diversity and Inclusion: Toward a Curriculum for Human Beings." *Teachers College Record* 2:211–21.

Jaggar, Alison M., and Susan R. Bordo. 1989. Introduction to *Gender/Body/Knowledge: Feminist Reconstructions of Being and Knowing*, edited by Allison M. Jaggar and Susan R. Bordo. New Brunswick: Rutgers University Press.

James, William. [1909] 1996. "Monistic Idealism." In *A Pluralistic Universe*. Lincoln: University of Nebraska Press.

Kloppenberg, James T. 1996. "Pragmatism: An Old Name for Some New Ways of Thinking?" *Journal of American History* 83 (1): 100–101.

Minnich, Elizabeth. 1995. *Liberal Learning and the Arts of Connection for the New Academy*. Washington, D.C.: Association of American Colleges and Universities.

———. 1997. "The American Tradition of Aspirational Democracy." In *Education and Democracy: Re-imagining Liberal Learning in America*. Robert Orrill, exec. ed. New York: College Entrance Examination Board.

Mitchell, Lucy Sprague. 1931. *The Bank Street School Credo* [The Bank Street School was chartered in 1931 by the Regents of the State of New York. See Bank Street Web site, copyright 1999].

Rowe, Stephen C. 1996. "Revitalizing Practice: A Conversational Encounter with William James." In *The Vision of James*. Rockport, Mass.: Element Books.

Seigfried, Charlene Haddock. 1996. *Pragmatism and Feminism: Reweaving the Social Fabric*. Chicago: University of Chicago Press.

West, Cornel. 1989. *The American Evasion of Philosophy: A Genealogy of Pragmatism*. Madison: University of Wisconsin Press.

Woodson, G. Carter. [1933] 1990. *The Mis-education of the Negro*. Washington, D.C.: Associated Publishers.

6

Identity, Feminist Teaching, and John Dewey

Ana M. Martínez Alemán

In the following pages I explore John Dewey's assertions on the construction of individuality or in modern terms, identity, and its relationship to learning. Like Dewey, I shall argue that as individuals involved in a dialectical relationship with the world, we are necessarily dependent upon our interactions with those environments, for self-realization, a project critical for learning. More important, I shall remind us, as John Dewey did, that recognition of identity in a culturally, ethnically, and racially diverse democracy is the means and end of intellectual freedom and progress, the means and end of feminist education. This, in an age of feminist cultural curiosity and in an age of intellectual conservativism, seems imperative.

Syncopated Identity

Watching the Cuban cabaret act at the Tropicana Lounge in Miami Beach this past Christmas, with its decor, seating arrangements, and menu spiced with a prerevolutionary Havana flavor, I realized that we Cubans seem to feel everything in that pause between syncopated beats. As couples dancing salsa and merengue, we cradle this interlude with arms, and legs, and hips poised with confident and knowing readiness. We suspend our marimba hammers in the sticky air above their wooden keyboards; maracas are held perfectly still. In the audience, we savor the moment, leaning forward in our seats, edging our bodies and spirits ever closer to the coolly anticipated downbeat.

Driving home after the show in the silent company of sleepy cousins, I think about my own particular place in that pause, in that space between syncopated beats, the space I suspect defines me. I think about why and how my pause between syncopated beats, about how my moment of Cuban feeling and knowing, is followed by a distinctively *anglo* downbeat. How is it that my identity can be framed by epistemic borders of Anglo-American schooling, of Anglo-American teaching and learning, and yet be colored the bright Caribbean hues of *crianza latina*—of Latin upbringing?

In the logic and language of dual personality and consciousness, I reason that I must be a split self, some sort of fractured subjectivity caught between measures. Perhaps I am another version of James Baldwin's Negro "schizophrenic" educated to know that indeed he could become president, but also assured that "he has never contributed anything to civilization" (Baldwin 1988, 4). Or as Plato's thinking about love, union, and separateness may suggest in the *Symposium*, am I two "halves" split and yearning to be "whole"? Or, as Argentina philosopher María Lugones (1994) submits, perhaps my identity is more about *mestizaje*, a consciousness impure and resisting compartmentalization.

In the car that late night, I suspect that much of who I am and am not has been carved out by curricular paths laid out before me—or more accurately, in spite of me. My identity seems bound to my tutelage, tethered to alien landmarks and guideposts of meaningless familiarity. I recall how the well-intentioned Sisters of Mercy at my Catholic grade school, who for a time fashioned an "Ann Marie" from an Ana María, set my curricular compass rigid and precise, assured that knowing, that thinking, that learning, demanded no recognition of a contextualized self, no subscription to the value and the verity of an historic personality. My public high school and state university teachers most often did not see in *all* our faces the richness of racially, ethnically, and sexually marked consciousness, of identities poised at the educative ready. We were not regarded as peculiar and thus intellectually provocative identities eager to make meaning out of texts and formulas.

But I am a teacher now, I remind myself in midthought. How do I treat the varied and developing identities of those faces now settled before me in the multicultural college classrooms of my American present? How do I understand their certain singularities? How do I—or do I at all—recognize the authority of their identities when considering the texts, the theories, the intellectual queries I offer for consideration? And perhaps of greater concern, upon what does the pedagogy that opens the intellectual door for such subjectivity rest?

At the college where I teach, students have begun to demand curricular and pedagogical opportunities that can engage them in an intellectual investigation of this space between syncopated beats; they yearn for the chance at critical inquiry of that intellectual position that marks them individually and perhaps collectively. In the past two years students have become aware of the relationship between their singular and collective cultural identities and knowledge. They have begun to articulate the desire and demand for access to the tools that will enable them to open their canopic jars of knowing. It is as if buried in ancient Egypt, their bodies mummified, they have begun to understand that their intellectual souls, that some aspect of their cognitive viscera, has been sealed by an educational fate. Many students at my college are speaking of cultural, ethnic, and racial identity as a cognition necessary for discerning inquiry. Students black and white, Latina and Asian, have begun to name their educational dissatisfaction as a crisis of identity, as a crisis of knowledge. Like Baldwin's Negro schizophrenic, my students yearn for curricular projects designed to realize knowledge and self; they yearn for what Jamaican author Michelle Cliff (1988) defines as a "journey to speech."

Michelle Cliff believes that as a young author, she wrote through what she describes as an "internalized message of anglocentricism." Educationally and intellectually assimilated, she "struggled to get wholeness from fragmentation" by reclaiming, retracing, and most important, reexamining African, Caribbean, and Jamaican intellectual heritage. In order to "write as a complete Caribbean woman," to write Milton, Wordsworth, and Keats as a reclaimed, reorganized, and whole cultural identity, Cliff embarked on a solitary journey that required her to explore literary forms, to unearth intellectual contributions, and to "co-opt style" (Cliff 1988).

Michelle Cliff's journey to speech is one that I take to mean a journey about cognition and identity, about knowing and individuality. It is a journey fueled by a desire to understand her subjectivity, to understand herself as knower, and finally, to realize her position as an identified and thus individual knower. She writes of a journey designed to reveal the component parts of her identity, to uncover what her education has concealed or defined as inconsequential for knowing. She suspects that the search is fundamentally about a process of self-realization, about the reconstruction of her peculiarity in time, place, and social dimension. To realize that which marks her as knower—her identity, her individuality—is both the impetus for and objective of her journey. To "write as a complete Caribbean woman" is to realize her identity.

Cliff's identity is what John Dewey would consider her "special disposition"—Cliff's "temperament, gifts, bent, or inclination" and her "special station"—Cliff's "situation, limitations, surroundings, opportunities, etc." (Dewey [1891] 1969, 301). Thus, identity, or in Dewey's terms, individuality or self or personality, is a phenomenon of organic peculiarity and the circumstances of associated life. Dewey would view Cliff's "journey to speech" as a journey toward self-realization, or in his words, "function," the union of disposition and station, of capacity and environment. Michelle Cliff, John Dewey would insist, as an individuality organic with her environment, and motivated by interests internal and external, performs her function in relation to her particular surroundings. For Dewey, Cliff's journey toward intellectual wholeness will be a satisfying activity if such an activity's end brings her back to self, back to identity. Motivated by interest born of a distinct identity, Michelle Cliff's journey will reconstruct and reorganize her experience, deepening and appending meaning, broadening the complexity of what and how she knows.

But it is a journey, let's remember, that requires Cliff to go back, to reorganize and reconsider. It is a journey that requires her to undo in order to become. She must move backward in order to move forward; she must reconsider before she can reflect. Cliff must reeducate herself as a self, as a particular identity, in order to realize her distinctive potential, a complete Caribbean woman writer. The irony here is that this becomes a necessary journey because of the very thing that should have assured her the means and opportunity for self-realization in the first place: Michelle Cliff's journey to speech is about counteracting the effects of an education that did not consider identity as its means and end. As a feminist teacher, I believe that this is the journey upon which our college and university students should embark, and indeed, upon which I sense they long to embark. Our students must be given the opportunities in our classrooms to undo their educational crisis of identity in order to become intellectually whole. As feminist teachers we must see identity as the means and end of education.

This journey is especially imperative in the feminist classroom, that classroom in which the learner and the teacher are positioned identities confronted with the task of integrating subjectivity with critical study. It is a pedagogical journey I take to require an understanding of the past as a resource for understanding our historical present; it is a pedagogy driven by positional epistemologies. Such a journey requires, as John Dewey would assert, educational praxis designed to liberate individuality, to liberate identity, an act of self-realization necessary for our democracy. It is the development of individuality or identity, and the attainment of self-realization—an event Dewey succinctly defined as "freedom"—that for Dewey enables each of us to "make [our] own special contribution to a group interest" and to partake in democracy as independent critical thinkers (Dewey 1916, 302).

For the feminist educator, I believe, the philosophy of John Dewey promises some insight into the intellectual potency of identity, and more important, can provide a framework and grounding for educational practice. As Dewey (1916, 305) writes early in this century, "A society based on custom will utilize individual variations only up to a limit of conformity with usage; uniformity is the chief ideal within each class. A progressive society counts individual variations as precious since it finds in them the means of its own growth. Hence a democratic society must, in consistency with its ideal, allow for intellectual freedom and the play of diverse gifts and interests in its educational measures."

In what follows I explore Dewey's belief in the potency of identity (or individuality as he names it), its relationship to learning, and the implications of a pedagogy centered on self-realization or the actualization of identity in a multicultural democracy.

Dewey on Identity and Individuality

The human individual is himself a history, a career.
—John Dewey, "Time and Individuality"

In April 1938 John Dewey ([1940] 1988, 102) asserts in a lecture titled "Time and Individuality" that the nature of time and of change are philosophical problems worthy of exploration, but more deserving of his attention is the connection of time with individuality. He explores with his audience his contention that the human individual is a biographical entity whose life can be viewed as "a temporal event." Such a historical character, reasons Dewey, suggests that individuals are marked by time and by context, impressions that position us in conditions or opportunities for responses or interactions. The peculiarity of our histories is our individuality, an individuality that is not fixed at birth nor, as Dewey (103) writes, "proceeds to unroll as a ball of yarn may be unwound." My individuality, or my "career," as Dewey names it, develops over time as a result of my particular interactions with the world. As he (111) writes about Abraham Lincoln: "[T]he career which is his unique individuality is the series of interactions in which he was created to be what he was by the ways in which he responded to the occasions with which he was presented." Thus, individuality is a contextualized phenomenon, a result of the particularity of the individual, her responses to the conditions of her life.

What makes us peculiar in our humanity according to Dewey ([1940] 1988, 14:109) are the potentialities that are elicited through interactions with the world. Potentiality, "as a category of existence," warns Dewey, is not a disposition in the classic Aristotelian sense; it is not intrinsic nor related to a fixed end that the individual's essence must actualize. Instead, Dewey writes, "potentialities must be thought of in terms of consequences of interactions with other things," interactions he defines as dialectic in nature. Implicit in this idea is the belief that we are not identifiable until we act, until we are in relation to someone or something else. Clearly then, it is in the *how* of interaction and in the meaning that we give to the interaction that our identity is shaped. Thus, what our relations are and are not to us—who constitutes our associations and what meaning we give to these individuals; what characterizes the conditions of these associations—matters most critically for identity. We can understand this to suggest that as associated, culture-bound and politicized beings, our identities will be informed by how we are who we are in the world, and how we are and who we are to the world.

For Dewey, then, I come to have an individuality or an identity—that which distinguishes me as an individual—because of an exactness and concreteness in the world that is evolutionary. As a process unfolding in which time, place, action, and personal meaning are consequential variables, identity situates me as a historical and idiosyncratic being neither compartmentalized nor fractured, nor in discrete psychic stages. My identity is dynamic and unfolding, and in this way, is seen as indivisible and clearly dependent on the character of my interactions with the world. It is an identity that is dependent not only on my uniqueness, but also on how that uniqueness responds to the conditions of the world. Thus understood, my identity is who I am and what I do in the world; it is cultural, linguistic, political, gendered, and so on. Past and existing cultural, material, and historical forces and phenomena—who I am in, and how I engage with relations of power, for example—are consequential for constructed identity, the significance of which weighs heavily on thinking, learning, and teaching.

This is not to say, however, that Dewey completely dismissed the biological distinctiveness of the individual and thus biology's relationship to the development of individuality. In his critique of instinct theory of social psychology (which included his sharp objections to the profound importance placed on sexual impulses to account for human behavior by Freud and other psychoanalytical theorists), he (Dewey 1922, 93) writes in *Human Nature and Conduct: An Introduction to Social Psychology* that "impulses"—natural and unorganized activities—are "native tendencies" that play an important role in human conduct. As original and unlearned, impulses or instincts are responsible for new directions and distinctions in behavior. However, as unlearned phenomena, impulses are meaningless and are consequently of less importance than the acquired habits of individuals. Yet, because learned conduct is the result of an interplay between native tendencies and associated life, an individual's particular idiosyncratic nativity must be seen as a consideration in the development of personality. Dewey (93) goes so far as to say that the particular impulses of individuals, that the native attributes of individuality, are: "the pivots upon which the re-organization of activities turn, they are agencies for deviation, for giving new directions for old habits and changing their quality."

Thus, Dewey views the organic, biological aspects of personality, of identity, as significant. Their significance, according to Dewey (94), is that they are "starting points for assimilation of knowledge and skill of the more matured beings," and as "starting points," they are "agencies for transfer of existing social power into personal ability; they are the means of reconstructive growth." As sources of novelty, then, impulses—an individual's native potentialities—are responsible for the variance in human behavior and more important for Dewey, for the diversification of thought. Thinking, thus dependent on the influence of experience and on the construction of meaning by distinctively particular beings, is dynamic, mutable, and transformable, and more to Dewey's liking, transformative. Thus dependent on identity, thinking, "an individual matter," has the potential of originality, of creativity and freshness, a quality Dewey (1916, 305) regards as the means for a democratic society's growth.

The Relationship Between Identity and Learning

In an essay written in 1926 for the *Journal of the Barnes Foundation* titled "Individuality and Experience," John Dewey ([1926] 1984, 55) writes about the relationship between individuality and its development with "the work and responsibilities of the teacher. " In the essay he (61 and 59) suggests that individuality, "something to be achieved, to be wrought out," is the pedagogical imperative of the teacher, an objective reached by understanding the interests of pupils, by knowing "enough about [the] pupils, their needs, experiences, degrees of skill and knowledge." The teacher is responsible for the development of individuality, for providing students with the opportunities for self-realization, opportunities that must have some connection to the "interests" of the student. In this way, then, Dewey insists on the student's identity as a decisive pedagogical criterion for teachers.

Identity and interest are, in Dewey's mind, one and the same. For

Dewey ([1931] 1985, 15), there is no separation between a person's interests and individuality. Interest, as the "active or moving identity of the self" (1916, 352), is but a trait of individuality, our "capacity *in action*" ([1891] 1969, 304). Further, Dewey (1916, 352) writes in *Democracy and Education*, "the kind and amount of interest actively taken in a thing reveals and measures the quality of selfhood which exists." Thus, those learning situations that most allow us to "be led to further expression" of our individualities ([1891] 1969, 305) shall be those that most elicit our interests, those that most directly target our identity. And if our individualities—our identities—are historic, then it seems plausible to submit that effective pedagogy is that pedagogy that will consider a student's preferences and capacities, a pedagogy in which identity is given primacy. It is a pedagogy in which that individuality—that identity—is the total sum of the individual's bodied and intellectual history. My particularity as an individual is not taken for granted in this type of pedagogy; it is a context or a condition that Dewey finds indispensable for thinking.

If who I am is a necessary consideration for my teachers, how, then, according to Dewey, will my identity be material for thinking and learning? Knowledge, thinking, and learning were for Dewey distinct but integrated. Knowledge, that which is assumed without question, that which is assumed a temporal given, is an unstable contingency always susceptible to the individual, to the identity of the knower, and to the process by which it is comprehended. The identity of the knower, the context of the act of thinking, affects all elements of thinking, consequently implicating both the knower and the known. Knowledge is handed down through learning, a process that is a "personally conducted affair" (1916, 335). The role of identity in knowledge, then, is to inform the process of learning so as to reconsider and transform knowledge. Because thinking starts from "doubt or uncertainty," according to Dewey (1916, 296), it is the role of identity—the context of the knower—to direct the thinking process, and it is responsible for "the redirection and reconstruction of accepted beliefs." In this way, identity is a critical facet of thinking.

How does identity affect learning, how does it inform my thinking? Dewey considers these questions in his essay "Context and Thought" ([1931] 1985, 17) when he directs his attention to philosophic thinking he considers a "dogma of immaculate conception of philosophic systems." Concerned with the absence of context from philosophic discourse of the era, Dewey writes that the critical variables in the construction of philosophic thought are identity and culture. Here he writes of identity as "the range and vitality of the experience of the thinker," which he notes are historic and associational (20). Identity is subjectivity, or that which characterizes such thinking. Together with what Dewey (21) terms "culture," "the significant features and outcomes of human experience as found in human institutions, traditions, impelling interests, and occupations," identity determines the selection of the subject matter and direction of thinking.

Self-Realization and Dewey's Democracy

As a "truly human way of living," democracy is that ethical ideal that for Dewey (1937, 457) allowed individuals to fully develop their individuality. The relationship between self-realization and democracy was in Dewey's ([1888] 1969, 237) view one that was dialectical, one that required a view of society and the individual as "organic to each other" and thus mutually dependent. This dependence, reasoned Dewey, suggests that the realization of individuality or identity is a quality necessary for democracy and that democracy must have individuality as its means and end. Further, democratic arrangements are responsible for stimulating the development of identity, a responsibility simultaneously placed on the individual herself. As Dewey ([1888] 1969, 224) writes in *The Ethics of Democracy*:

> In one word, democracy means that *personality* is the first and final reality. It admits that the full significance of personality can be learned by the individual only as it is already presented to him in objective form in society; it admits that the chief stimuli and encouragement to the realization of personality come from society; but it holds, none the less, to the fact that personality can not be procured for any one [sic], however degraded and feeble, by anyone else, however wise and strong. It holds that the spirit of personality indwells in every individual and that the choice to develop it must proceed from that individual.

So what we have in Deweyan democracy, then, is the implicit assumption that as a social arrangement, democracy both must be about the identity of its members and must engender these identities.

Dewey's vision of democracy as a means for self-realization was founded on the conviction that all individuals deserved the opportunity to effect their potential. He writes in *Ethics* (Dewey and Tufts 1908) that individuals must have equitable access to the opportunities for self-realization. It stands to reason, then, that Dewey must demand of democratic arrangements fertile ground for the development of identity. As a social arrangement, democracy must provide its members the opportunities to self-realize, the opportunities to develop identity. Education in a democracy, according to Dewey, must be that fertile ground. As a process whose end is to liberate and guide individual capacities, democratic education must take the identity of the learner into account if it is to remain an ethical scheme.

Central to Dewey's ethical vision of education in a democracy is the importance of the individual's participation in the structure of that education and its consequences for sociality. Dewey viewed an individual's partnership in the educational process as one that is requisite for the realization of identity, as a partnership that assures the individual the opportunities to contribute to society. For Dewey (1937, 457), inclusion in the educative must be a condition of democracy if democracy is about the belief that "all those who are affected by social institutions must have a share in producing and managing them." Having a "share in producing and managing" education in democracy meant that individuals become invested by virtue of interests and consequently develop feelings of social responsibility. As Dewey (458) writes: "Absence of participation tends to produce lack of interest and concern on the part of those shut out. The result is a corresponding lack of effective responsibility."

Dewey expresses these sentiments in a talk to school administrators about democratic ideals in the management of the school, but his sentiment is based on his belief that the individual realized, that the individual fully identified, is a dynamic resource for society. If an individual is prevented or precluded from education in a true democracy, he argued, the whole of society would be denied the capabilities of the individual (Dewey 1937, 458). Let's remember that society and the individual in Dewey's mind are involved in a dialectical relationship in which each requires the other for positive growth. Depriving one of the resources of the other necessarily weakens and implicates the other.

Of equal concern to Dewey is the antidemocratic sentiment of educators who believe that intelligence and intellectual potential is resident in only but a particular few, thus disabling democracy by impairing the potential of certain individuals. To believe that intelligence resides only among a certain group or groups of individuals in a democracy is to suppress individuality. Whether it be administrators making curricular decisions for their schools or students demanding inclusion in the development of curricula, Dewey (1937, 457–58) would consider the absence of individuals affected by the curriculum from the consideration of its construction and application as "a subtle form of suppression" that "gives individuals no opportunity to reflect and decide upon what is good for them." This reflection, a result of participation, is for Dewey the hallmark of democratic education, a process that has fully utilized individuality, that has freed and directed individual potential, that has affirmed identity. "If education were conducted as [such] a process," writes Dewey" (1922, 270), "it goes without saying that the lives of the young would be much richer in meaning." This richness of meaning, I believe Dewey to intend, is constituted by identity considered, reconsidered, and realized.

Identity, Feminist Teaching, and John Dewey

Frances Maher and Mary Kay Thompson Tetrault's (1994, 1) examination of feminist pedagogy in higher education, *The Feminist Classroom*, begins with the following quotation from Adrienne Rich: "When those who have the power to name and to socially construct reality choose not to see you or hear you, whether you are dark-skinned, old, disabled, female, or speak with a different accent or dialect than theirs, when someone with the authority of a teacher, say, describes the world and you are not in it, there is a moment of psychic disequilibrium, as if you looked in the mirror and saw nothing." In using the metaphor of the mirror Rich brings to our attention the role of identity in the classroom and, more specifically, its importance in feminist pedagogy.

As Maher and Thompson Tetreault argue, identity in the feminist classroom is seen as a point of departure for the examination of ideas, theories, texts, and sociopolitical experience. Recognition of identity as neither fixed nor rigid creates the kind of pedagogical experiences in which students and instructors are positioned epistemologically, an approach the authors' research suggests allows "different forms of identity to be in relation to each other" (1994, 225). Identity, thus implied, is neither fixed nor categorized; it is historic and developmental. Varied influences on the individual and the meaning given to those effects become matters of individual cognition, the markers of racial, class, gendered, and other constructed distinctions. Viewed in this way, and of critical importance for the feminist classroom, identity as individual and historic is especially associational, its character infused with the meanings of our interactions and associations in the world. Thus Rich's "psychic disequilibrium" can be eased in the feminist classroom by the recognition of her very identity.

But as a teacher, how do I know who Rich is and isn't? How do I make possible psychic equilibrium for my students? Is a requisite demographic survey at the beginning of each term enough to know who they are and aren't? Or is my role really about providing the opportunities for that identity to be realized, for intellectual talents to emerge?

As Cornel West (1989, 70) notes, it is Dewey who presented us with a view of higher education that predicated its content, policies, and practices on the "awareness" of the radical contingency and variability of human societies, cultures, and communities. Accordingly, reasons West on Dewey, academia's understanding of "knowledge, power, wealth, and culture" would engage students in the development of what West calls Dewey's "modern historical consciousness." Put another way, writes West (82), what is needed in academia is "not academic complacency but active engagement with the events and affairs of the world," an engagement that according to Dewey required epistemic pluralism, scientific intelligence, and self-creation (98–99). Feminist teaching, then, if it is to take Dewey's lead and make psychic equilibrium possible, must assess course content, its delivery, and its intellectual standards. In our multicultural classrooms, this assessment requires that we decentralize the Western canon and bring to the varied and developing identities before us those texts, speakers, films, and performances which debunk the myth of universal identities and ways of knowing, those pedagogical tools which acquaint students with the varied and complex possibilities for the construction of knowledge. To examine the intellectual foundations of traditions foreign and familiar is for these diverse and particular identities a means toward the realization of self, toward the attainment of critical consciousness necessary in democracy. Content that broadens and deepens consciousness is the responsibility of the feminist teacher; it is, in Deweyan terms, content that liberates the individual and allows for the full expression of identity. Not unlike the "critical consciousness" of Paolo Freire (1970), it is content that frees identity from the confines of educational rigidity.

Thinking in the multicultural feminist classroom requires, I believe, what Dewey (1916) labeled "scientific thinking." It requires that we teach students how to evaluate knowledge by forming and testing ideas, and to discover "the connection of things" familiar and unfamiliar (140). When faced with the unfamiliar, contrary or incompatible, a consequence of resident historic identities, students in our multicultural feminist classrooms can begin intellectual queries from the resulting perplexity, confusion, and doubt, and move to make conjecture, and then to analyze and explore, and finally posit a hypothesis—an understanding—of the phenomenon. Tentative understanding then allows them to take a position, to test their understanding and reflect. Deweyan in character, this conception of thinking and understanding is grounded in the belief that thinking is contextual, that thinking presupposes experience that implies individuality and historic identity.

Further, the multicultural classroom demands for its members the expression of their individualities if only because it is in these expressions that we prevent intellectual and social fixity. Like Dewey's (1933, 175) criticism of empirical inference, a classroom in which "points of unlikeness are [not] as important as points of likeness" is an educational praxis that "follows the grooves and ruts that custom wears and has no track to follow when the track disappears" (192). Identity is in this way a pedagogical asset. It is that initial groove that directs the inquiry but that is particular and individual and ultimately intellectually original.

Deweyan democracy and individuality as central concerns in feminist teaching can foster a universality of consciousness and conduct, which in my view demands a pedagogy distinguished by a "dialogism" in which ideas are historic, in which interests can be revised, and in which all participants as individuals and as members of communities are recognized (Cornell 1985). This idea of dialogism as articulated by Drucilla Cornell (1985) is a means, I believe, of avoiding relative positions in the classroom, those positions that don't allow for the "full and free" exchange of ideas (Dewey 1916) and consequently reinforce intellectual complacency and rigidity. Relativism determined erroneously by the validation of identity in the feminist classroom does not allow for the critical thinking that enables students to create new intellectual possibilities and, more important, cognitive alliances. As Cornell (1985, 301) states, relativism denies "the possibility of critical reflection—the ability to examine one's context and to imagine alternatives." Thus, self-realization is impossible in a relativistic classroom; thus creativity in a relativistic classroom is stifled. To stay interested in understanding and knowing is to maintain the capacity for self-realization, for intellectual growth. It is, as John Dewey would assert, to sentence ourselves to intellectual immaturity. The possibility of growth and that this potentiality is a never ending learning process is what intellectual immaturity is about (1916). Thus, if interest in learning about particular realities either familiar or unfamiliar to me is thwarted by relativistic identity pedagogy, I won't, I am sure, make much of an intellectual commitment to live in the world, to live in a global community. I will simply stay within the confines of intellectual group identity; I will be mired in intellectual sameness. The most costly danger of relativistic positions spawned from the validation of identity in the feminist classroom is the intellectual sameness that can develop among students, among similarly identified individuals. I am convinced that the greatest liability of such relativism is that in the end, I won't know much more about myself, much more about my identity, about my place past, present, and future as knower in the world.

To say, then, that the feminist classroom must take hold of the pedagogical powers of identity is to say that identity—my particular interactions and associations linguistic, cultural, or psychic—will particularize me in such a way as to move me from the realm of "featureless abstraction" and the experience of psychic disequilibrium, to epistemologically significant agents in the classroom (Code 1991, 1). Thus, such things as my Cubanness, my anglo-ness, and my New Yorker sensibilities, will fuel my inquiry, will enable me to think critically about orthodoxy and innovation, and my place within either or both.

As a feminist teacher I must provide these identities poised ready for expression and realization with the opportunities for affirmation, creativity, reorganization, and validation by cutting those curricular paths characterized by the spirit of Michelle Cliff's "journey to speech." I recall my own particular intellectual path for the understanding of gender and its constructions, deconstructions, and revisions that led me to Rousseau, MacKinnon, and Woolf and to Moraga, Alvarez, and Engels; through the work of Derrick Bell and Cuban poet José Martí, I understand more completely the complexity of my whiteness as a marked racial category. Cervantes, Bécquer, and Carlos Fuentes shape my understanding of the rhythms of my cultural habituations; Hannah Arendt explained to me the difference between work and labor. T. S. Eliot, through Prufrock, allows me to ponder the future walking the psychic bilingual, bicultural beach in trousers, bottoms rolled.

Armed with pedagogy grounded in Deweyan ideas of individuality and democracy, with his conceptions of identity and learning, I believe that as feminist teachers we can cut curricular paths for our students, who as learners are identities marked by such broad categories as race, sex, gender, and class, who are identities historical, relational, and individual. I believe that as feminist teachers we are bound to a Deweyan ethics of the promise and power of contextualized and dynamic individual identity and that our classrooms should be the passageways to self-realization in a "democracy multicultural."

References

Baldwin, James. 1988. "A Talk to Teachers." In *The Graywolf Annual Five: Multicultural Literacy*, edited by R. Simonson and S. Walker. St. Paul, Minn.: Graywolf Press.

Cliff, Michelle. 1988. "A Journey to Speech." In *The Graywolf Annual Five: Multicultural Literacy*, edited by R. Simonson and S. Walker. St. Paul, Minn.: Graywolf Press

Code, Lorraine. 1991. *What Can She Know? Feminist Theory and the Construction of Knowledge*. Ithaca: Cornell University Press.

Cornell, Drucilla. 1985. "Toward a Modern/Postmodern Reconstruction of Ethics." *University of Pennsylvania Law Review* 133:291–380.

Freire, Paolo. 1970. *The Pedagogy of the Oppressed*. New York: Continuum.

Dewey, John. 1888. *The Ethics of Democracy*. University of Michigan Philosophical Papers. Ann Arbor: Andrews and Witherby.

———. [1888] 1969. "The Ethics of Democracy." In *The Early Works*. Vol. 1, *1882–1888*. Edited by J. Boydston. Carbondale: Southern Illinois University Press.

———. [1891] 1969. *Outlines of a Critical Theory of Ethics*. In *The Early Works*. Vol. 3, *1889–1892*. Edited by J. Boydston. Carbondale: Southern Illinois University Press.

———. 1916. *Democracy and Education*. New York: Macmillan.

———. 1922. *Human Nature and Conduct: An Introduction to Social Psychology*. New York: Henry Holt.

———. [1926] 1984. "Individuality and Experience." In *The Later Works*. Vol. 2, *1925–1927*. Edited by J. Boydston. Carbondale: Southern Illinois University Press.

———. [1931] 1985. "Context and Thought." In *The Later Works*. Vol. 6, *1931–1932*. Edited by J. Boydston. Carbondale: Southern Illinois University Press.

———. 1933. *How We Think*. New York: D. C. Heath.

———. 1937. "Democracy and Educational Administration." *School and Society* 45 (1162): 457–62.

————. [1940] 1988. "Time and Individuality." In *The Later Works*. Vol. 14, *1939–1941*. Edited by J. Boydston. Carbondale: Southern Illinois University Press.

Dewey, John, and James H. Tufts. 1908. *Ethics*. New York: Henry Holt.

Lugones, María. 1994. "Purity, Impurity, and Separation." *Signs* 19 (Winter): 458–79.

Maher, Frances, and Mary Kay Thompson Tetreault. 1994. *The Feminist Classroom*. New York: Basic Books.

West, Cornell. 1989. *The American Evasion of Philosophy: A Genealogy of Pragmatism*. Madison: University of Wisconsin Press.

Part Three

Subjectivity

7

The Need for a
Pragmatist Feminist Self

Erin McKenna

Much of contemporary ethical debate centers on the differences and similarities between an ethic of care and an ethic of justice. I believe that both models, in all their diversity, rely on incomplete pictures of the self and so both remain inadequate ethical theories. Both theories can enforce only a minimum standard of behavior—neither promotes growth. If we embrace a more complex and dynamic notion of the self—a pragmatist feminist notion of the self—I believe, we will have the necessary foundation for an ethical theory that can accept change and promote growth. I will use the work of John Dewey and Sarah Lucia Hoagland to suggest such a notion of the self.

The Problem

The United States is built on the myth of the rugged individual. Individuals succeed or fail on their own merit and are to be seen as responsible for their individual lives. Ironically we are also a nation that seeks to blame others for every misfortune in our lives; we sue other persons rather than acknowledge our own negligence, stupidity, or just plain misfortune. We seem to be caught in a society that values self-made individuals who need not accept responsibility for themselves or how they influence the lives of others.

From conscious intent or not, most theories of responsibility generated in the United States usually rely on the notion of the individual presupposed in Lockean social contract theory. That is, theories of responsibility focus on what rational contracting agents would agree to refrain from doing to each other. Responsibility becomes mainly an issue of figuring out who transgressed against whom and how the social unit should respond to the transgression in order to prevent more social disruption. In this picture, society is merely the aggregate of individuals bound together by rules that limit their actions toward one another. It is a mechanistic and legalistic picture of human life. While I agree that it is important to be able to blame individuals for violating rules that help maintain social stability, I believe that following such rules is a relatively minor part of what it is to be a responsible person.

Social contract theory gives us a very limited notion of the individual, society, and the relationship between the two. Its skewed picture of the individual traps us into a pattern of seeking an individual or group to blame for social problems and so remaining disassociated from the problem ourselves, doing nothing to make it better. For example, a person might blame the Christian Right for the erosion of certain civil liberties, or s/he might blame "liberals" for such changes. Regardless, the problem is the result of someone else's action rather than that individual's action—or, more likely, inaction—and so the individual doing the blaming feels no responsibility to do anything. Blame often leads to social inaction.

It can also lead to an accumulation of resentment against a person or group who is seen as responsible for a social problem. For example, some see urban black males as the cause of most violent crimes; some see feminists as the cause of what they perceive as dangerous social changes. If action is taken in regard to either of these "problems," it is hostile action against the individual or group instead of constructive action applied to the problem at hand—vigilantism against black youths and harassment of feminists. Furthermore, we rarely see or acknowledge our own possible role in whatever is going wrong—our role in the poverty of inner-city black children or in the oppression of women.

Such attitudes stem from an idea that we are separate from, and inherently separable from, everyone else. We believe we can isolate individuals who are to blame for any given event and so do not share in responsibility. Because we believe in the rugged individual we need to trace every action back to the individual and fix the problem by fixing the individual. We rarely see that there may be social causes that cannot be "fixed" by fixing (punishing) the individual. Our mechanistic and legalist approach to assigning responsibility is the result of our belief in the basic separateness of individuals, and our view of individuals serves to reinforce feelings of separateness.

When theories of responsibility do not rely on the social contract notion of the individual, they tend to rely on an organicist notion instead. This also has problems. Organicist theories entail the idea of the individual and society as an inseparable organism. On such a model no individual is to blame for anything in particular because all actions are interconnected. Any idea of individual responsibility is an arrogant and misguided presumption about one's ability to affect the whole. The web of relationships has priority over any particular individual. In this picture the individual tends to blend into the whole and is often seen as necessary but not significant in itself. This organicist view has had less impact on thinking in the United States than the social contract model.

Another way to think about this division is provided by Carol Gilligan in her book In a Different Voice, and in the large pool of literature that responds to her work. Here, I think, we see the social contract model aligned with the voice of justice (a masculine, not male, voice) and the organicist model aligned with the voice of care (a feminine, not female, voice). On the justice model one is concerned with satisfying a principle and tends to see relationships as secondary to the individual. On the care model one is primarily concerned with maintaining relationships and tends to see the individual as but one among many to be considered.

> The moral imperative that emerges repeatedly in interviews with women is an injunction to care, a responsibility to discern and alleviate the "real and recognizable trouble" of this world. For men, the moral imperative appears rather as an injunction to respect the rights of others and thus to protect from interference the rights to life and self-fulfillment. Women's insistence on care is at first self-critical rather than self-protective, while men initially conceive obligation to others negatively in terms of noninterference. (Gilligan 1982, 100)

The justice model's reliance on a notion of responsibility as noninterference can, I think, be equated with the social contract model's reliance on a "no harm" principle. The care model's reliance on a notion of responsibility as maintaining one's part in a web of relations can, I think, be equated with the organicist model's reliance on a notion of responsibility as blending into the whole and thereby maintaining its integrity. While all four of these models are more rich and complex than these brief sketches indicate, I think these fundamental resemblances hold, and I will, in the rest of this essay, maintain that the notion of self and responsibility that underlies social contract and justice models is basically the same and that the notion of self and responsibility that underlies organicist and care models is basically the same.

Given the focus on the individual in the United States, it is not surprising that we tend to resist organicist/care models of society and self. But what of communal models that retain a strong notion of the individual, but still see society as something more than a mere aggregate of individuals? Is such a model possible in the United States and would it help us get beyond mere blaming? Can we combine the social contract and organicist accounts of the individual? Can we interweave justice and care?

The difficulty with both the social contract/justice and the organicist/ care models is that they rely on a disembodied notion of the individual. Neither, alone, takes the lived experience of persons seriously (though the care perspective does this more), and neither can account for both the dynamic and relational qualities of human life. Both theories entail notions of the self that are dangerous abstractions and so they seek a universal response that denies or overlooks the particularity of human beings. The social contract/justice model reduces humans to rational calculators deciding among rules and principles.[1] The organicist/care model reduces humans to roles and positions within a larger whole.[2] Neither easily embraces a multifaceted and multipositional human being with changing relations and responsibilities. They both rely on an impoverished sense of self.

The result is a society that can only try to enforce a minimum universal standard of behavior. Little can be said, for instance, about what particular positive actions of care one might be responsible for doing. On either model I will probably be punished if I violate my responsibility to care, for example, by harming children or nonhuman animals. I may be punished if I am neglectful of my responsibilities, if I neglect children and nonhuman animals. But little is done to encourage or reward proper caring. Society only addresses itself toward enforcing the minimum standard. When someone does more, we are often uncomfortable. We see such social crusaders as overstepping the boundary of the individual—as their moving outside their boundary and into ours.

If one takes seriously, however, the idea of individuals as socially embedded from the start of their lives to the end, we need to get beyond the sense of a minimal responsibility to avoid harming others to explore a richer notion of responsibility that entails promoting social connections and individual growth in mutually reinforcing ways. I believe much of pragmatist and feminist (as distinct from feminine) social theory gives us such a model. In all their diversity, both pragmatist and feminist models start with a notion of a dynamic and social individual with multiple ties and projects in the world—a combination of the perspectives of justice and care.[3]

Social Contract and Justice Models

There are many contemporary critiques of social contract theory and ethics based on a justice perspective. Communitarians, feminists, and pragmatists have all voiced their concerns over theories that assume that humans "spring up like mushrooms" and build most of their relationships on antagonism and conflict of interest. As later in this essay I will be developing an alternative model of the self out of the works of John Dewey and Sarah Lucia Hoagland, I will also briefly trace here some of their particular concerns with the social contract/justice model of ethics.

Social contract theory came into full force in the seventeenth and eighteenth centuries. It has many proponents. The three most central figures are Thomas Hobbes, John Locke, and Jean-Jacques Rousseau. Each gives us a different picture of the condition of humanity before the contract and the society that results from the contract. In this essay I will be dealing with the Hobbesian and Lockean perspectives of human psychology and mostly with Locke's picture of civil society. This is a *very* brief and general view of social contract theory.

According to Hobbes and Locke each individual is in competition with every other individual. Hobbes's picture of this state of nature is more severe than Locke's to be sure, but in the end both rely on a notion of individuals who are at odds with one another and so need a sovereign to settle disputes and protect their individual rights and property. Therefore, rational, autonomous individuals are supposed to freely give over to a state their individual power to govern themselves—they form the social contract. Ironically, the state then has the power to limit individual freedom. For Hobbes the sovereign has unlimited power—power over and above that of any particular individual. For Locke, such an expansion of power and rights must be guarded against. The state cannot be granted any power not held by the individual in the state of nature. The power of the state is based on a theory of natural rights. Under the influence of Locke, much of classical liberal theory focuses on limiting state power and protecting the rights of individuals. It is more about freedom from constraint (negative freedom) than freedom to do anything in particular (positive freedom).

In critiquing liberal individualism, both Dewey and Hoagland focus on the need for a more positive notion of individual freedom. For both, this entails a different concept of the individual. Both thinkers want to find a central place for the individual in the social order, but both find the individualistic nature of classical liberalism problematic. Rather than seek the source of social conflict, liberalism assumes that conflict is the natural state of human interaction, and then it seeks to explain sociality and cooperation. As Hoagland (1988, 71) says,

> Machiavelli (1469–1527) captured men's minds by portraying them as motivated by greed and fear. . . . Galileo (1564–1642) developed a method of scientific explanation whereby to explain something is to isolate its parts and show how they must be combined to form the whole. Applying this to the social sphere, we find the idea that individuals per se lack qualities which would

permit them to function in a society. As a result, *how* individuals can be made to cooperate becomes a central problem of social organization.

In the theories of Hobbes and Locke, the role of the state is the limitation of the individual for the protection of all. So, rather than promote freedom, this atomistic, antagonistic view of the self entails the need to restrain individuals in order to allow for a minimum level of social cooperation and stability. It does not, however, have the theoretical capacity to push beyond stability to growth. As Dewey ([1935b] 1987, 30) points out in *Liberalism and Social Action,*

> The underlying philosophy and psychology of earlier liberalism led to a conception of individuality as something ready-made, already possessed, and needing only the removal of certain legal restrictions to come into full play. It was not conceived as a moving thing, something that is attained only by continuous growth. Because of this failure, the dependence in fact of individuals upon social conditions was made little of . . . Social arrangements were treated not as positive forces but as external limitations.

Liberalism's protection of the individual ironically makes individuality very difficult. It tends to result in a social system in which those with power, consciously or not, seek to remain in a dominant position by frustrating the emergence of individuality in those who are subordinate.

> Because a wholly unjustified idea of opposition between individuals and society has become current, and because its currency has been furthered by the underlying philosophy of individualistic liberalism, there are many who in fact are working for social changes such that rugged individuals may exist in reality, that have become contemptuous of the very idea of individuality, while others support in the name of individualism institutions that militate powerfully against the emergence and growth of beings possessed of genuine individuality. ([1935b] 1987, 31)

One problem with the liberal model is that it presupposes ready-made and static individuals who exist basically in isolation. By relying on such a view of the individual, liberal theory actually works to remove the ground for real individuality and individual agency. We rely on force, coercion, and censorship to maintain stability and so frustrate growth.[4]

Organicist and Care Models

Both Hoagland and Dewey also have concerns about the organicist/care approaches to ethics. Critiques of such models are usually concerned with the loss of the individual and the risk of totalitarian systems or oppressive relationships dominating one's life. On the organicist/care model you are who you are in great part because of how you are in relation to others. The idea of a separate self is inherently problematic. One's obligations to others set the parameters of who you are. The basic idea of the organicist model is that we are all interrelated in a complex social order. Everybody has a particular role in that order and the whole functions best if each individual stays within his/her role. The care model picks up on the organicist's idea of a web of relationships and focuses on how who we are is a function of how we are in relationship to others. Who we are and how we should act is governed by our responsibilities in our relationships to others. Such theories focus on building relationships rather than on promoting or restraining individual freedom.

As Dewey ([1935b] 1987, 33) says,

> The dissolving atomistic individualism of the liberal school evoked by way of reaction the theory of organic objective mind. But the effect of the latter theory embodied in idealistic metaphysics was also hostile to intentional social planning. The historical march of mind, embodied in institutions, was believed to account for social changes—all in its own good time. . . . [T]he idealistic theory of objective spirit provided an intellectual justification for the nationalisms that were rising. Concrete manifestation of absolute mind was said to be provided through national states. Today, this philosophy is readily turned to the support of the totalitarian state.

Hoagland's critique is more narrowly focused. On her account such models elevate "feminine" virtues of altruism, self-sacrifice, and vulnerability (values that hardly appear in social contract/justice models,) over individualistic self-reliance. Hoagland argues that these can be dangerous and personally debilitating virtues, however. Even stopping short of a totalitarian state, damage is done in that oppressed groups are "nonreciprocally open, loyal, and dependent. . . . Altruism, self-sacrifice, and vulnerability—as virtues of subordination—function to channel women's energy and attention away from their selves and their own projects" (1988, 83).

Where the social contract/justice theories accept selfishness, organicist/care theories pose the danger of encouraging self-sacrifice. For example, in her book *Caring: A Feminine Approach to Ethics and Moral Education*, Nel Noddings suggests an ethic of care that encourages the engrossment of one's self in the projects and goals of another—the one cared-for. To be sure, on her view, this caring is ideally received well and reciprocated, but nonetheless it is a dangerous position for the one-caring. I think she is right to see our relatedness as more basic than our separateness (a position compatible with pragmatism), and this can be a useful correction to the social contract/justice models. However, her call to "ethical heroism" can lead to the submergence of the individual and the loss of the self. "A caring relation requires the engrossment and motivational displacement of the one-caring, and it requires the recognition and spontaneous response of the cared-for. When caring is not felt in the cared-for, but its absence is felt, the cared-for may still, by an act of ethical heroism, respond and thus contribute to the caring relation" (1984, 78). When I am asked to care in the continued absence of receptivity, reciprocation, or both, I am no longer engaged in a process that sustains my self, but rather my self is being used up. While I am not required to move to ethical heroism on this model, its very mention is a dangerous ideal.[5]

As Sarah Hoagland (1988, 91) says, such "[s]elf-sacrifice is not a means of engaging." Self-sacrifice requires that we submerge our self and our individuality for some other. Not only does this fail to challenge the other to think critically and be flexible, but it also leads to burnout and disengagement from others when one's energy is gone. "Yet lesbian burnout results from self-sacrifice in political projects. . . . She may work frantically, as if responsible for the whole situation . . . until something snaps and she ceases to care, ceases to be able to respond" (90–91). It would seem that organicist/care theories that call for self-sacrifice, at best, like social contract/justice theories, maintain a status quo, but do little to promote growth and the development of individual agency.[6] We need a theory that starts with a socially related self, but retains the concept of individual agency. Curiously, this need may be demonstrated by Charles Dickens's *Bleak House*.

Spatial and Temporal Ethics

In "Time, Space, and Shame," Peter French suggests that ethical theories based on liberal individualism generally rely on a temporal account of the individual and ignore the spatial perspective. He uses the narration of Charles Dickens's *Bleak House* to demonstrate this point. In *Bleak House* the story is told through two different narrations. One is told in the past tense by a main character in the story—the temporalist account. The other is told in the present tense from a third-person point of view—the spatialist account.

In discussing the temporalist account French (1992, 57–58) says, "Because the past tense has duration, events are describable. Actions occur, have prior causes, a history, and they move on to effects. Actors endure through time and reveal plans, goals, and hopes: the elements of action that are the foci of the Kantian and the utilitarian. The moral perspective is act or agent centered. Human relations are shaped by events and, therefore, in and over time." French suggests that the temporalist perspective follows the liberal tradition of focusing on isolated persons. The temporalist "derives his identity not from social organization and institutions, but from his own actions" (59–60). "Temporalists tend to be defenders of some or all of the following: individual liberty, rights, self-determination, and (even) romance" (60).

This picture of the individual does seem to fit with the individual presupposed by the social contract/justice perspectives. However, French then adds some elements that seem to challenge this simple identification of perspectives. He says,

> Where Dickens's present-tense spatial narrator is notably clinical about the sufferings of the downtrodden (describing slum dwellers as filthy, illiterate, diseased, and dying). Esther [the past-tense temporalist narrator] dwells on feelings, motive, and the consequences of choices. The contrast between the two narrators is never clearer than when the corner sweep is discussed by both.

For Esther he is someone to nurse, shelter, to try to save. For the spatial narrator he is another of the innumerable denizens of the depths of the social system who must be kept in their places to control the spread of infection in the body politic. (58)

The social contract/justice perspective is usually seen as governed by rules and principles, caring little for persons in themselves, much less entailing feelings. Yet it is the temporalist French describes as getting personally involved, establishing relationships, and caring.

In other places French's description of the spatialist perspective seems to embody the notion of the individual presupposed by the organicist/care models. The spatialist narrator "provides marvelous insights into the social interdependency of all levels" (57). The spatialist is lost when s/he "has lost his lord, his kin, and his friends in war. All social ties severed, he has no place or identity, and seems to have no moral responsibilities either" (59). "Spatialists focus on roles, station, and communal unity. For spatialists, the temporalist's individual actors, when stripped of their social relations, are revealed to be not isolatable egos, but mere abstractions of no particular moral or metaphysical significance" (60).

This sounds very much like the critique of the social contract/justice perspectives given from the organicist/care perspectives. This critique suggests that the isolated liberal individual is a dangerous fiction that encourages us to be impartial and that allows us to treat people as objects.[7] The organicist/care perspective, like the spatialist account, suggests the importance of realizing that people are who they are in great part by virtue of the relationships they are in.

> Individuality for spatialists like Bradley is a far cry from the (romantic) individualism of the Humean, the Kantian, and the act-utilitarian. Individuals, as Bradley defines them are "organs of the whole," only real because they are social entities, pulse-beats in the system. Bradley explains that one individual human being, insofar as he or she is "the object of his [or her] self-consciousness," is characterized and penetrated "by the existence of others." In short, the content of a self is a pattern of relations within a community. "I am myself by sharing with others, by including in my essence relations to them, the relation of the social state." (61)

Given this relational aspect of the spatialist perspective, how is it that it is the spatialist narrator who takes the distanced, rationalist approach to the suffering boy? I think the answer lies in the impossibility of separating the justice and care perspectives; we are beings who exist in both time and space.

Gilligan herself suggests that we need a combination of the care and justice perspectives. Either on its own is an abstraction of the human individual and both entail dangerous presuppositions about who we are and how we relate to others.

> Development for both sexes would therefore seem to entail an integration of rights and responsibilities through the discovery of the complementarity of these disparate views. For women, the integration of rights and responsibilities takes place through an understanding of the psychological logic of relationships. This understanding tempers the self-destructive potential of a self-critical morality by asserting the need of all persons for care. For men, recognition through experience of the need for more active responsibility in taking care corrects the potential indifference of a morality of noninterference and turns attention from the logic to the consequences of choice. (Gilligan and Murphy, 1970; Gilligan, 1981)

> In the development of a postconventional ethical understanding, women come to see the violence inherent in inequality, while men come to see the limitation of a conception of justice blinded to the differences in human life. (Gilligan 1982, 100)

I think liberal theorists still tend to use the abstracted justice approach and feminine ethicists still tend to use the abstracted care approach (John Rawls and Nel Noddings, respectively, for example). Nothing productive comes from squaring these two off against each other except the uncovering of the inadequate concepts of the individual which underlie each. To have a constructive ethic we need to move beyond these two to draw a picture of an individual who understands her embeddedness and sociality and who is able to act as an individual agent and make choices for herself and her life. As Hoagland (1988, 12) says, "I mean to invoke a self who is both separate and related, a self which is neither autonomous nor dissolved: a self in community who is one among many, what I call autokoenony." Later (145) she says, "What I mean by 'autokoenony' is 'the self in community.' The self in community involves each of us making choices; it involves each of us having a self-conscious sense of ourselves as moral agents in a community of other self-conscious moral agents. And this is not a matter of us controlling our environment but rather of our acting within it and being a part of it." One cannot act as an individual within a social environment in a changing and multifaceted way on either the temporalist or spatialist accounts or from the social contract/ justice and organicist/care perspectives. Each limits what the individual can be and so limits moral agency.

These views do not account for the dynamic aspect of the self. They want a fixed self to serve as a foundation for the theoretical perspective.[8] On a pragmatist account, however, the self is always emerging, always changing. One's spatial location is always changing and so is one's temporal space. Beyond that, one's perspective on his/her spatial/temporal location changes and so new meanings are continually emerging. The past determines the present, but new future goals can result in a reinterpretation and changing of the past. "[W]e look forward with vivid interest to the reconstruction, in the world that will be, of the world that has been, for we realize that the world that will be cannot differ from the world that is without rewriting the past to which we now look back" (Mead 1959, 3). The past itself does not change, but what it is for us in the present is something to which we are asked to apply our critical and creative intelligence in order to move us toward a desired future. "The long and short of it is that the past (or the meaningful structure of the past) is as hypothetical as the future" (Mead 1959, 12).

A pragmatist account radicalizes both the spatialist and temporalist perspective. Space and time become very fluid and gain their meaning and purpose through human agency instead of the reverse. Mead says the self can only emerge in a social setting—in relationships with others (spatialist). He further says that the self then is an agent who constructs meaning out of the temporality of our lives—we change the past in the present to move toward a specific future (temporalist). Such radicalization and integration of the spatial and temporal perspectives is, I think, what is occurring in the ethical theories of John Dewey and Sarah Lucia Hoagland.

The Pragmatist Individual

It seems that most theories of ethics rely on a unidimensional account of the self. The social contract/justice model relies on the abstract, atomistic, antagonistic, rational self; the organicist/care model relies on the abstract, caring, partial, relational self. The temporal and spatial models discussed above show the inadequacy of such disembodied/displaced selves. Dickens needs both narrators in order to give us a complete picture. What does the individual look like when located in both time and space? I think it looks very much like the individual who emerges from the work of the American pragmatists—specifically Charles S. Peirce, William James, John Dewey, George Herbert Mead, Jane Addams, and Charlotte Perkins Gilman. Here I will focus mainly on the work of Dewey, using the others to support and expand his thought.

In Peirce we find the beginnings of the concept of an individual embedded in a context, making judgments in relation to how s/he is situated. In all judgments there is the self, the other, and the relationship between the self and other to be considered. Very much a spatialist account. Peirce calls the relational aspect thirdness. James took this concept very seriously as he developed his psychology. For James the self is irreducibly social; it is inasmuch as it is in relationship to others and its environment. However, it is also temporal—becoming through time. Taking Charles Darwin seriously, James had "a respect for the temporal and becoming aspect of things" (McDermott 1991, xxi).

Selves are constituted by a consciousness that is continually changing and choosing; it is malleable and active; it is a process and an agent. Every experience changes our brain and so no experience is had twice. You are always in a different relationship to the object. Who we are is as much to be found in the changing relationships as in any particular brain state. Our selves are also to be found in the interests that direct our attention. We cannot attend to the whole of any experience. Instead we select parts of the experience relevant to our current interests—this is agency. The self is not a passive object of experience, but actively participates in the world. As John Smith says, James gives us "a radically new account of how the self penetrates and is penetrated by the world" (McDermott 1991, xxx).

Gilman and Addams also develop this notion of an active relational self. They push us to see the social obligations that accompany our connectedness with others. They warn against perceiving too much distance from others. However, they also warn against failing to see the other because all you see is your problems reflected in the other or see the other only as presenting a chance to do good. Gilman says we need to see ourselves as individuals in a collective. She (1912, 330–31) says,

Ethics is a social science. Virtue is a social development. Social advantage is all our goodness is for. Yet against this beautiful and natural development stands the ego-minded past, telling each of us to "mind his or her own business," to cultivate his own soul. We generally believe that goodness is a private affair, and self-development our duty. Yet any of us can see how natural it is to study the conduct of others instead of our own, to try to reform others instead of ourselves. . . .

If the brain-power, nerve-power, will-power—the vital force of humanity—were poured forth as it should be along well-planned lines of social improvement, we should all of us develop the needed human virtues at far less expense.

Addams ([1910] 1981, 76), in a similar vein, says, "I am not so sure that we succeeded in our endeavors 'to make social intercourse express the growing sense of the economic unity of society and to add the social function to democracy.' But Hull-House was soberly opened on the theory that the dependence of classes on each other is reciprocal; and that as the social relation is essentially a reciprocal relation, it gives a form of expression that has peculiar value." We find ourselves in socially complex and reciprocal relationships that demand a social, rather than an individualistic, ethic.

Dewey picks up on this emerging picture of an embedded, relational, changing, active, agent self. Not only is such a self more appealing as a basis for Dewey's theory of social ethics, but it also has empirical support from physiology, psychology, and anthropology. Dewey's critique of liberalism (see above), and the atomistic individual entailed therein, stems from his process view of the self.[9]

According to Dewey, individuals are not given, ready-made, into the world. Rather they are formed, though not determined, by their society. He says ([1935a] 1987, 291),

[A]n individual is nothing fixed, given ready-made. It is something achieved, and achieved not in isolation but with the aid and support of conditions, cultural and physical:—including in "cultural," economic, legal and political institutions as well as science and art.

The real fallacy [of liberalism] lies in the notion that individuals have such a native and original endowment of rights, powers and

> wants that all that is required on the side of institutions and laws is to eliminate the obstructions they offer to the "free" play of the natural equipment of individuals. . . . Since actual, that is, effective, rights and demands are products of interactions, and are not found in the original and isolated constitution of human nature, whether moral or psychological, mere elimination of obstructions is not enough. ([1928] 1984, 100–101)

Since individuals are social beings, society must be arranged to help them develop and be free. Dewey means by freedom the ability to apply a critical and flexible intelligence to any problem. He ([1928] 1984, 108) says, "[F]reedom consists in a trend of conduct that causes choices to be more diversified and flexible, more plastic and more cognizant of their own meaning, while it enlarges their range of unimpeded operation. . . . Our idea compels us . . . to seek for freedom in something which comes to be, in a certain kind of growth. . . . We are free not because we statically are, but insofar as we are becoming different from what we have been." We develop intelligence and freedom through social interaction. He says ([1929] 1984, 67) that "[a]ssured and integrated individuality is the product of definite social relationships and publicly acknowledged functions."[10]

The problem we face now (and when Dewey was writing in the 1920s and 1930s) is that there are few stable "social relationships and publicly acknowledged functions." We live in a constantly changing world, and new technology has vastly increased the rapidity of such change. Changing economic structures have moved us into a corporate world. Unfortunately we still cling to the old ideal of static, ready-made, rugged individuals. As a result, individuals feel lost and alone and so are vulnerable to external forces molding their commitments. He ([1929] 1984, 73) says there are "[c]onspicuous signs of the disintegration of individuality due to failure to reconstruct the self so as to meet the realities of present social life."

The reality of our social world is that it is corporate and collective. If we retain our old notion of the individual based on individualism, the individual will be swallowed up and individuality lost. In order to maintain space for creativity and difference, individuality must be maintained. To do this, we need a new concept of the individual, an integrated individual, a social self. Dewey calls this the "unified individual." Such an individual is attentive to his/her context; s/he acts more than s/he is acted upon; s/he is involved in and responsible for his/her own creation. S/he is not thrown around by natural or social forces, but uses such forces with intelligence, purpose, and foresight. Without this new concept of the self we will find ourselves being moved by external forces; we will experience a loss of agency. The individual must be remade so that people, not economic forces and new technologies, set the social agendas.

> Originality and uniqueness are not opposed to social nurture. . . . The positive and constructive energy of individuals, as manifested in the remaking and redirection of social forces and conditions, is itself a social necessity. A new culture expressing the possibilities immanent in a machine and material civilization will release whatever is distinctive and potentially creative in individuals, and individuals thus freed will be the constant makers of a continuously new society. ([1929] 1984, 109)

If we lose the individual, society will become static.

We must realize our interconnectedness with others and our capacity for intelligent direction of the future. "To gain an integrated individuality, each of us needs to cultivate his own garden. But there is no fence about this garden; it is no sharply marked-off enclosure. . . . By accepting the corporate and industrial world in which we live, and by thus fulfilling the precondition for interaction with it, we, who are also parts of the moving present, create ourselves as we create our unknown future" ([1929] 1984, 122–23). Dewey conceives of the individual as essentially part of a community. The self both effects changes in its community and is changed by it. It is the unified, integrated individual that can get us beyond the abstracted notions of the self found in the social contract/justice models and the organicist/care models.[11]

The Feminist Individual

There is no one feminist view of the individual nor one feminist ethics, but there are some assumptions common to most ethical theories that identify themselves as feminist. As Alison Jaggar (1991, 95) says,

These include the view that the subordination of women is morally wrong and that the moral experience of women is worthy of
respect. . . .

The feminist commitment is incompatible with any form of
moral relativism that condones the subordination of women or
the devaluation of their moral experience. It is neutral, however,
between the plural and local understandings of ethics on the one
hand and the ideal of a universal morality on the other. Feminists
are committed to ethical theories that do not rationalize women's
subordination or devalue their moral experiences—but there may
be many such theories.

Further, Claudia Card (1991, 26) identifies four things she believes feminist ethics needs to do. "One, we need to identify our possibilities for
agency in oppressive contexts. Two, we need to distinguish modes of resistance that would make our survival and our deeds worthwhile from those
that would not. Three, we need to articulate ideals of the person and
community that can acknowledge our histories and yet provide bases for
pride in ourselves and each other. And four, we need to be alert to the
dangers of becoming what we despise."

I cannot hope to do justice to the great variety and richness of contemporary feminist ethics. Therefore, for the purposes of this essay I will be
focusing on Sarah Lucia Hoagland's *Lesbian Ethics*. Her view of the self as
"one among many" provides a nice link between feminist and pragmatist
thought. I think that Hoagland's views provide a positive extension and
corrective of Dewey's concept of the self.

There is of course the question of whether it is appropriate to use
Hoagland's lesbian ethics in this way. She (1988, 22) says, "I want to add
that what I have in mind concerning the shifts in perception which I am
calling Lesbian Ethics are meant to be used in lesbian community, among
ourselves, as we weave new value, as we try to work out of the habit of
dominance and subordination, thereby becoming beings who are not
used to it. Whether these values can be developed from a different angle
as part of a political strategy to confront patriarchy is an open question."
I think her challenge to the values of heteropatriarchy can be used outside of lesbian community to resist old views of who we are as individuals
and to re-form our selves. She provides us with a very fundamental and
necessarily dynamic and social sense of the self—a pragmatist self.

Hoagland argues that heterosexism establishes the relationship of domination and subordination as the normal way of relating. Traditional ethics, as part of the heteropatriarchal structure supports this way of relating. She (12) says,

> My thesis about traditional ethics is this: (1) The focus and direction of traditional ethics, indeed its function, has not been individual integrity and agency (ability to make choices and act) but rather social organization and social control. (2) The values around which traditional ethics revolve are antagonistic, the values of dominance and subordination. As a result, (3) traditional ethics undermines rather than promotes individual moral ability and agency. And (4) these aspects of traditional ethics combine to legitimize oppression by redefining it as social organization. Appeal to rules and principles is at the heart of this endeavor.

She argues that while traditional ethics has ostensibly been about liberating and supporting individual agency, it has, in fact, undermined the individual. Because the traditional social contract/justice models assume that individual selves are naturally selfish and antagonistic, they rely on rules to limit individual choice. The argument is that such rules, and the consequent subordination of certain individuals, are necessary for social order. Further, social order is the most we can hope to achieve given our "natural" conflict of interests, so we should gladly embrace such order even if it requires the subordination of certain individuals or groups.

In a heteropatriarchy, homosexuals and women are at least two groups whose voices would disturb the social order. Their interests must be seen as subordinate to, and dependent on, the interests of the heterosexual male norm. They can have no interests of their own—no selves of their own. Traditional ethics, therefore, consciously or not, defeats its own purported purpose. In the end such theories subordinate the individual to the social order. This is true of theories based on the social contract/justice models and of theories based on the organicist/care models (see her critique of the ethic of care above). A new model is needed.

At least one thing this new model needs to do is provide and rely on a different sense of self. We need a picture of the self that is less abstracted from social context, not internally partitioned (mind not separated from body, nor reason from emotion), and that is perceived as an integrated, but constantly changing, whole. We need to integrate mind/body, reason/emotion, and self/other. "Rather than perceive our selves as essentially related to all others antagonistically, we can perceive our selves in a form of cooperative relationship with each other. Rather than perceiving our selves as essentially isolated, as unlimited and hence thwarted, even threatened, when we come across another, we can perceive our selves as one self among many and so enhanced by others" (237–38). Hoagland says ethics should be "about our ability to interact, to connect, to be intimate, to respond" (12). To do this we need self-understanding and the power to create ourselves—not the submergence of the self in others. This is both an empowering and creative act that both requires us to choose for ourselves and provides a firmer ground for future choices about who we want to be.

Another difficulty with the traditional ethical perspectives is that because they rely on an individualistic/antagonistic model, choices are perceived as junctures in our lives where we are vulnerable to the desires of others and where, whatever we choose, we have lost something. Choices are always perceived as either/or situations on such models and are rarely revisited. Moral maturity and moral agency come to be measured by one's ability to make the choice, make the best of the situation, and go on. Hoagland feels this is (1) an impoverished sense of agency, and (2) not a sense of agency available to everyone.

First, agency need not involve such a sense of loss. Agency can be about creating opportunities, not just making the best of choices as they are presented.[12] Second, not everyone can "make the best of the situation," because not everyone is in control of the situation. As Hoagland points out, agency in traditional ethics requires that one have some control over the choices one faces, the actual outcome of such choices, or both.[13] In a heteropatriarchy, however, this sense of agency is available only to those in the dominant position—the rest are seen as victims. To get beyond perceiving ourselves as victims, Hoagland suggests a different notion of agency. "She is a moral agent who makes judgments within a context of oppression in consideration of her own needs and judgments" (50). Rather than see women simply as victims of heteropatriarchy, we need to recover a sense of agency.

> By perceiving women's behavior, not through the value of 'femininity', but rather as actions of moral agents making judgments about their own needs and abilities in coerced and oppressive circumstances, we can begin to conceive of ourselves and each other as agents of our actions (though not creators of the circumstances

we face under oppression). And this is a step toward realizing an ethical existence under oppression, one not caught up with the values of domination and subordination. (50)

As Hoagland suggests, withdrawal from situations of domination and subordination may be necessary in order to develop and nourish this new sense of agency. Withdrawal may be necessary to form the basis of a moral revolution. By removing oneself from the context of domination and subordination one may gain room to create new values—to create new selves.[14]

I do not intend to debate the efficacy of separation here. What is important for the purposes of this essay is Hoagland's realization that withdrawal alone does not create new values—withdrawal alone does not equal a moral revolution. Such a revolution requires constant and intense self-reflection and self-creation. Her new sense of agency and choice is a first step. "Now, if we decide to regard choice as a creation, not a sacrifice, situations requiring difficult decisions will still arise between us. However, we can regard our ability to make choices as a source of power, an enabling power, rather than a source of sacrifice or compromise" (93). Moral agency is the ability to choose and act in the face of ambiguity.[15] We need not see such choice and action as final because one is involved in a continual process of understanding one's self as it is in relation to others. We may see past actions differently when future purposes change or our understanding of our self and others is transformed. Hoagland (139) says, "I have been arguing that paternalism does not serve us; it leads us to pursue power as control and as a result we undermine our own and each other's moral agency. . . . Paternalistic thinking, the belief that it is appropriate to act for (not with) someone, keeps us believing that we can do things without knowing others or understanding their perceptions and world-views in relation to our own (often called "objectivity" in science), it encourages atomistic individualism." Hoagland's sense of agency requires interactive understanding. "I am suggesting that we can develop moral agency by developing our attending and intelligibility, by our perceiving ourselves as one among many, autokoenonously" (246). We need to replace the relation of antagonism, along with its accompanying view of ethics as our holding one another accountable for failures to live up to rules and principles. In its place Hoagland suggests relationships based on attending and intelligibility. Such relations require being with someone in an active and attentive way in order to understand who they are and in order to be understood oneself. It requires getting clear on who one is and into whom one is evolving. Ethics, then, becomes about understanding one's self and others, not just about making them behave.[16] "In my opinion, the heart of ethical focus, the function of ethics, and what will promote lesbian connection, is enabling and developing individual integrity and agency within community. I have always regarded morality, ideally, as a system whose aim is, not to control individuals, but to *make possible,* to encourage and enable development" (285). I think there is clearly an existentialist element here—a call to live authentically. "The underlying principle of existential ethics is that one is always morally responsible for who one chooses to be, that is, for the choices of attitude, disposition and character, as well as for one's behavior. One needs to become consciously aware of who one is as a necessary, although not sufficient, step toward reflectively understanding and then deciding whether to change one's life" (May 1991, 243). This is also what Dewey calls the integrated self. This is the self who can discern continuity among all the changes in who one is and act with foresight in the making of the future self.

In general (with these existential and pragmatist exceptions in mind), ethics has focused more on holding others accountable for shortcomings and punishing them. It has focused on responsibility as a subset of accountability and not as a ground for growth. It does not get us beyond a minimum standard of behavior. Hoagland suggests that one reason for this is that we envision responsibility as a one-way process. It does not require me to understand myself or others. She (288) writes, " 'Responsibility', like 'accountability', encourages a one-way process—she's responsible to me; I'm responsible to her. As Maria Lugones notes responsibility encourages us to act to stay in charge. It is one of the ways we manage to keep (some) control over each other. Responsiveness, on the other hand, is two-way and focuses, rather, on the interactive nature of our engagements." To move to responsiveness, to be interactive, requires that we become intelligible to our selves and to others—that we become Dewey's integrated individual.

Marilyn Frye, in her article "A Response to Lesbian Ethics," suggests that in the end Hoagland's "transformation" of ethics should be a call to get beyond ethics altogether. She is right, I think, that inasmuch as ethics is just about telling us how to act, just about what is right and wrong, Hoagland's lesbian ethics does not qualify—nor do existentialist and pragmatist ethics. However, unlike Frye, I think there is value in transforming (replacing) instead of transcending traditional views of ethics.[17] Saying that there is no need for ethics will leave most people clinging to absolutist claims about what is right and wrong.

I would like to see Hoagland's lesbian ethics as still ethics and as an ethics from which we can profit. The ethics of rules and principles has not always been the definitive form for ethics. Richard Taylor in his article "Ancient Wisdom and Modern Folly," argues that notions of right and wrong need not and have not always been a part of ethics. He says (1988, 54),

> The Oxford edition of Aristotle's *Nicomachean Ethics* includes a detailed table of contents wherein every topic touched upon in the work is noted in outline. Nowhere there does one find reference to any distinction between right and wrong, nor to duty or obligation. . . .
>
> The explanation is that the philosophers of antiquity did not think of ethics as having to do with moral right and wrong. It was religion, and the advent of Christianity in particular, which, for better or worse, injected that distinction into philosophical ethics. The moral philosophy of the ancients revolved, instead, around the concepts of virtue, happiness, and justice.

Now, I am not saying that we should return to an Aristotelian virtue ethics, nor even to Alasdair MacIntyre's interpretation of such virtues. What I am suggesting, though, is that there is room for, and perhaps even great need of, an ethics focused not just on right and wrong (accountability and responsibility), but rather on who we are and how we relate to others. Hoagland provides us with a provocative picture of who we might be.

The Pragmatist Feminist Self

Dewey's notion of the integrated self is very helpful for transforming ethics from a focus on rules and principles to a focus on developing a sense of one's self as a dynamic and relating being. However, it has some limitations. For instance, Dewey rarely acknowledges the full strength of entrenched social power present in our habits of race, class, and gender. He

naively, or just hopefully, supposes that habits can be broken by individuals in interaction with their various communities. The attitudes of heteropatriarchy, however, have not yielded to such efforts. Hoagland
recognizes and addresses, in a more realistic way, the pervasive social
norms we face.

She is also more willing to acknowledge separation as a moral choice.
Dewey calls instead for more interaction. In doing this he seems to overlook the real damage that is done to a person in relations of domination
and subordination. Dewey does not seem to realize that one's self can be
lost and that what is taking place is really a one-way monologue. I think
Dewey's integrated individual can be achieved, but not without our more
radically changing our ways of relating.

Why should we try to achieve an integrated self? Where might it take
us? I believe an integrated self is one that can successfully combine the
perspectives of justice and care. While many feminist theorists call for
such a combination (Gilligan, Virginia Held, Joan Tronto), they do not,
I think, realize how much work needs to go into changing our selves if
we hope to change our social situatedness. They seem to ignore that at
least here in the United States we have been brought up with the myth
of the rugged individual and with the social contract/justice perspective
firmly rooted in our sense of our selves, our power, our worth, and our
social institutions. So, if we hope to create a new ethic, a new social
interaction, we must rework the picture of the self that underlies the
ethic.[18]

The selves we have now are gendered and unintegrated selves. The
feminine and masculine voices that Gilligan identifies have caused such
a stir because they do fit the selves many of us now have. To call for the
integration of the masculine and feminine, to get beyond the dualistic
notion of gender, is to create new selves. In order to get beyond the
either/or alternatives of ethics as it has been, and to make real room
for personal agency and social change, we need to begin the process of
reinventing our selves. Dewey and Hoagland give us an interesting place
from which to start.[19]

Notes

1. Examples of the contract/justice model would include Gauthier 1986 and John Rawls 1971.
2. Examples of the organicist/care model would include Bradley 1988 and Noddings 1984.

3. In her book *Pragmatism and Feminism: Reweaving the Social Fabric*, Charlene Haddock Seigfried (1996) points out that pragmatism inherently seeks the perspective of a plurality of voices. There are more than two voices involved in moral discourse, and she argues that we need to acknowledge the mutability and pluralism of both moral discourse and gender. I agree. However, this essay is just a start at breaking down the dichotomy often assumed to exist between justice and care.

4. Both Dewey and Hoagland include a critique of capitalism as an economic system that perpetuates conflict and the relationship of domination/subordination as the norm. To explore this would go beyond the scope of this essay, though I think its relevance is clear.

5. I have been informed that Noddings has a forthcoming book in which a chapter is devoted to an individualized account of the notion of a relational self. This may challenge the reading presented here.

6. It should be noted that the ethic of care represented by Noddings is a feminine ethic of care—it elevates feminine virtues within a patriarchal structure. It may be possible to have a feminist ethic of care, though Hoagland cautions against the belief that using the feminine virtues that were developed under heteropatriarchy will ultimately be liberating. In a recent essay, Carol Gilligan (1995) distinguished between a feminine and a feminist ethic of care:

> Care as a feminine ethic is an ethic of special obligations and interpersonal relationships. Selflessness or self-sacrifice is built into the very definition of care when caring is premised on an opposition between relationships and self-development. A feminine ethic of care is an ethic of the relational world as that world appears within a patriarchal social order: . . .
>
> A feminist ethic of care begins with connection theorized as primary and seen as fundamental in human life. People live in connection with one another; human lives are interwoven in a myriad of subtle and not so subtle ways. A feminist ethic of care reveals the disconnections in a feminine ethic of care as problems of relationship. From this standpoint, the conception of a separate self appears intrinsically problematic, conjuring up the image of rational man, acting out of relationship with the inner and outer world.

Note, however, that even in her description of the feminist ethic of care the individual has little space.

7. On this point, see Williams 1976.

8. Sara Ruddick (1989) makes a similar point in her book *Maternal Thinking: Toward a Politics of Peace*. She says that while much of traditional Western philosophy has sought and worked from a fixed notion of the self, mothering requires the acknowledgment of change. She says that "maternal experience with change and the kind of learning it provokes will help us to understand the changing nature of all peoples and communities. It is not only children who change, grow, and need help in growing. We all might grow—as opposed to simply growing older—if we could learn how" (90).

9. For a rich and interesting account of Dewey's notion of the social self, see chapter 10 of Seigfried's (1996) *Pragmatism and Feminism*.

10. This sounds very much like the spatialist ethics described earlier. However, unlike Hegel and Bradley, Dewey includes a Darwinist perspective. For Dewey, one's particular place is neither static nor fixed, but changing and evolving.

11. Like Dewey, Sara Ruddick (1989) sees the self not as ready-made and fixed, but as emerging and continually working for unification. She says, "As children try on shifting identities, their ability to create a self is inextricably and often painfully mixed with others' ability to recognize the self they are creating. A 'self,' however fixed and personal it may seem, is always in the process of being socially constituted" (92).

12. Ruddick expresses a similar idea in *Maternal Thinking* when she discusses concrete thinking: "Concreteness is opposed to 'abstraction'—a cluster of interrelated dispositions to simplify, general-

ize, and sharply define. To look and then speak concretely is to relish complexity, to tolerate ambiguity, to multiply options rather than accepting the terms of a problem" (1989, 93).

13. In an interesting article, "Fate and Responsibility," Peter French (1992) points out that it is not inconsistent to have a sense of agency about events that are fated to be as they are. He appeals to Frankfurt's critique of the principle of alternate possibilities and to some of the ways people speak about fate and responsibility as not excluding one another.

14. Alain Locke (1989) makes a similar point when discussing the need to focus on Afro-American culture: "[T]here is a necessary internal focusing of culture because true culture must begin with self-culture. Personality, and to a limited extent character also, are integral parts of the equation. In the earlier stages of the development of culture there is pardonable concentration upon self-cultivation. Spiritual capital must be accumulated; indeed, too early spending of the meager resources of culture at an early stage results in that shallow and specious variety which means sham and pretense at the start, bankruptcy and humiliation at the finish" (180).

15. There are obvious connections, which I cannot develop here, to William James's ([1896] 1977) position in "The Will to Believe." James says, "But please observe, now, that when as empiricists we give up the doctrine of objective certitude, we do not thereby give up the quest or hope of truth itself. We still pin our faith on its existence, and still believe that we gain an ever better position towards it by systematically continuing to roll up experiences and think" (726). This process in ongoing and we are forced to think, act, and believe in the face of ambiguity and uncertainty.

16. I do not mean to imply that ethics is not about how we act. However, how we are with one another is as important as what we do. J. L. Austin (1991), in his essay "A Plea for Excuses," makes a similar point when he discusses the "machinery of action." He distinguishes between an executive stage—when we do something—and a stage of appreciation—when we try to understand the situation. He writes: "Many expressions of excuses indicate failure at this particularly tricky stage: even thoughtlessness, inconsiderateness, lack of imagination, are perhaps less matters of failure in intelligence or planning than might be supposed, and more matters of failure to appreciate the situation" (46).

17. I do not mean to dismiss Frye's insight that ethics, at least the ethics that focuses on rules and principles, may be culturally specific and serves mainly to give one a sense of power. This seems quite probable to me.

18. I would like to acknowledge a caution offered by Vincent Colapietro. He notes that this notion of the integrated self may slip into the organicist model and suggests that we need to pay attention to our "fragmentary self with its jagged edges." He points out that not all psychic divisions need to be overcome; the unified self could become a repressive ideal. I take this caution seriously. I also think there are some intriguing possibilities to explore in the "jagged edges" he mentions—in another essay.

19. I would like to thank the National Endowment for the Humanities for support in writing this chapter.

References

Addams, Jane. [1910] 1981. *Twenty Years at Hull-House*. New York: Signet Classic.
Austin, J. L. 1991. "A Plea for Excuses." In *The Spectrum of Responsibility*, edited by Peter A. French, 39–54. St. Martin's Press.
Bradley, F. H. 1988. *Ethical Studies*. Oxford: Oxford University Press.
Card, Claudia. 1991. *Feminist Ethics*. Lawrence: University Press of Kansas.

Dewey, John. [1928] 1984. "Philosophies of Freedom." In *The Later Works*. Vol. 3. Edited by Jo Ann Boydston, 92–114. Carbondale: Southern Illinois University Press.

———. [1929] 1984. *Individualism Old and New*. In *The Later Works*. Vol. 5. Edited by Jo Ann Boydston, 41–143. Carbondale: Southern Illinois University Press.

———. [1935a] 1987. "Future of Liberalism." In *The Later Works*. Vol. 11. Edited by Jo Ann Boydston, 289–95. Carbondale: Southern Illinois University Press.

———. [1935b] 1987. *Liberalism and Social Action*. In *The Later Works*. Vol. 11. Edited by Jo Ann Boydston, 1–65. Carbondale: Southern Illinois University Press.

French, Peter A. 1991. *The Spectrum of Responsibility*. New York: St. Martin's Press.

———. 1992. "Time, Space, and Shame." In *Responsibility Matters*, edited by Peter A. French Lawrence: University Press of Kansas.

Frye, Marilyn. 1991. "A Response to Lesbian Ethics." In *Feminist Ethics*, edited by Claudia Card, 52–59. Lawrence: University Press of Kansas.

Gauthier, David. 1986. *Morals by Agreement*. Oxford: Clarendon Press.

Gilligan, Carol. 1982. *In a Different Voice: Psychological Theory and Women's Development*. Cambridge: Harvard University Press.

Gilman, Charlotte Perkins. 1912. "Our Brains and What Ails Them." *Forerunner* 3 (1–12).

Hoagland, Sarah Lucia. 1988. *Lesbian Ethics: Toward New Value*. Palo Alto, Calif.: Institute of Lesbian Studies.

Jaggar, Alison M. 1991. "Feminist Ethics: Projects, Problems, Prospects." In *Feminist Ethics*, edited by Claudia Card, 78–104. Lawrence: University Press of Kansas.

James, William. [1896] 1977. "The Will to Believe." In *The Writings of William James*. Edited by John J. McDermott, 717–35. Chicago: University of Chicago Press.

Locke, Alain. 1989. "The Ethics of Culture." In *The Philosophy of Alain Locke*. Edited by Leonard Harris. Philadelphia: Temple University Press.

McDermott, John J. 1991. Introduction to *The Later Works*. Vol. 11. Edited by Jo Ann Boydston, xi–xxxii. Carbondale: Southern Illinois University Press.

May, Larry. 1991. "Metaphysical Guilt and Moral Taint." In *Collective Responsibility*, edited by Larry May and Stacey Hoffman, 239–54. Savage, Md.: Rowman and Littlefield.

Mead, George Herbert. 1959. *The Philosophy of the Present*. Edited by Arthur E. Murphy. La Salle, Ill.: Open Court.

Noddings, Nel. 1984. *Caring: A Feminine Approach to Ethics and Moral Education*. Berkeley and Los Angeles: University of California Press.

Rawls, John. 1971. *A Theory of Justice*. Cambridge, Mass.: Belknap Press.

Ruddick, Sara. 1989. *Maternal Thinking: Toward a Politics of Peace*. New York: Ballantine Books.

Seigfried, Charlene Haddock. 1996. *Pragmatism and Feminism: Reweaving the Social Fabric*. Chicago: University of Chicago Press.

Taylor, Richard. 1988. "Ancient Wisdom and Modern Folly." In *Midwest Studies in Philosophy* 13:54–63. Notre Dame: University of Notre Dame Press.

Williams, Bernard. 1976. "Persons, Character, and Morality." In *The Identities of Persons*, edited by Amelie Oksenberg Rorty, 197–216. Berkeley and Los Angeles: University of California Press.

8

Reclaiming the Subject, or A View from Here

Paula Droege

A stark subject/object distinction has often been used by epistemologists to ground perception-based knowledge claims. In this kind of distinction, the subject is isolated from the object of investigation, and so is considered objective and impartial. The subject is also taken to be autonomous, free to seek truth without interference from other things or people. Recently descriptions such as these have come under attack from many and varied fronts. In feminist theory, the notion of an impartial and objective subject has been criticized for claiming an impossible transcendence of worldly ties to body and cultural/political context.[1] In philosophy of mind, many have questioned whether the subject can be taken as the source of any knowledge at all given the influence of social training on perceptual experience.[2] Given these and similar critiques from disciplines as disparate as biology and social/political theory, it is becoming increasingly difficult for the subject, as traditionally described, to find a home in philosophical discourse of any kind.[3] One reason to view this trend as problematic is that a robust (epistemically significant) view of subjects is advantageous to epistemology, especially to feminist epistemology.

My task, therefore, will be to show why the subject—specifically, subjective experience—has been the focus of such criticism and to respond to these objections. First I consider the attraction of an appeal to women's experience as a justification for knowledge claims and a source for critique of traditional epistemologies. Then I juxtapose this view with the postmodernist arguments against any attempt to base knowledge claims on experience. In the second and third sections I will develop Dewey's description of noncognitive and cognitive experience as a feminist pragmatist response to this critique. In the fourth section, then, I consider to what extent the objections have been answered. Since a full defense of the proposed description of experience and its advantages over other experience-based feminist theories cannot be developed here, the goal is not to establish a new epistemology but to argue that experience cannot yet be cast into the heap of failed epistemic devices. In other words, feminist claims for experience need to be reevaluated rather than rejected in order to develop the potential of an experience-based epistemology. My proposal is that if we can define the subject as the locus of experience—which essentially involves organism-environment interaction—then feminist epistemologists can acknowledge social influences while retaining the claim of uniqueness in women's experiences, considered both individually and as a group. What makes this theory 'feminist' is that it shows how the experiences, attitudes, and beliefs of women historically have been omitted in theories of knowledge and explains why this omission is theoretically, as well as ethically and politically, unacceptable.[4] In the same way that women have not been considered political subjects until relatively recently, they have not been valued as epistemic subjects either. Consequently, women's views have been omitted from epistemic theories. Nonetheless, women are epistemic subjects according to the proposed definition of experience, so no theory that leaves out women's experiences is complete.

I. A Critique of Experience

Experience seems an obvious starting point for epistemology, feminist or otherwise, since we broadly attach the label 'experience' to any form of sensory stimulation caused by the world.[5] Epistemologists dispute its significance and interpretation, but 'experience', taken as some sort of sensory relation between a person and the world, consistently figures in epistemic theory. Feminist epistemologists have also utilized notions of experience in arguing that women stand in unique relations to the world by virtue of their social roles. Therefore, women's experiences constitute a potential source for critique of epistemologies based exclusively on man-world relations. Feminist empiricists, for example, have argued that women's experience can provide a challenge to prevailing androcentric norms that distort scientific research, leading to theories based on faulty assumptions and limited data. Alternatively, feminist standpoint theorists have claimed that the experiences of women as victims of oppression provide a privileged perspective from which to critique the dominant ideology.[6]

Not all feminists are convinced of the liberatory potential of an experience-based epistemology, however. Postmodernist feminists in particular have objected to any such attempt to establish a foundation for knowledge. According to this view, the search for firm epistemic ground on which to build a theory of knowledge is at best futile and at worst destructive and debilitating to women. So too, they argue, is the attempt to set up women's experience as a foundation. To the feminist postmodernist, the concept of 'women's experience' is either incoherent or dangerous. If the concept is supposed to include the experiences of women from all classes, races, cultural backgrounds, and so on, then it is incoherent. Given the diversity of interests and activities among these women, there is no sense in which their experiences can be said to form a unitary position from which to critique social or scientific norms. The only way to make an experience-based feminist epistemology work, it seems, is to legislate some feature or description of experience as essential to defining it as 'women's' and use that feature as the block on which to build a feminist epistemology.

Essentialism, however, is dangerous. Historically male-centered theories have often posited such essential female attributes as emotional, body-oriented, and natural, to which are opposed such essential male attributes as rational, mental, and cultural (Ortner 1993, 59–73). The opposition can then be used to justify differential political and social treatment—women are essentially suited to homemaking, essentially unfit for academic work or business, among other things. Essentialism is dangerous because any feature that is picked out as 'essential' can be used to confine women to a social position consonant with that feature.

At first blush, essentialism may seem endemic to feminist theories of experience. In making experience foundational, the only way for feminists to incorporate women into the ground floor of their epistemology as a source of critique is to allocate a special role for women's experience. The definition of some sort of experience as unique to women would seem to require isolating an essential feature of women such that the experience of *this type of person* should be taken as different from the experience of other types of person, namely men. But these experiences could only be different from men's experiences, so the objection goes, if women are in some essential way different from men. To counter this objection, experienced-based theorists have relocated the source of difference in experience between men and women to the social structures within which men and women are positioned rather than in the nature of the sex difference.[7] The place of women outside the androcentric system of norms defines the uniqueness of their experiences. Biological and qualitative features stereotypically used to define the class of women are devices that aid in establishing existing social structures, but the liberatory nature of women's experience is due to the concrete, lived position of women within these structures, not the features used to determine their position. Although experience is foundational for feminist empiricist and standpoint theorists, it need not be static. If we change these structures, we will change the nature of women's experience. Furthermore, experience-based theories need not posit essences in women to distinguish their experience from that of men. The differences are due principally to factors in the society, not essential differences in women. This is not to say that feminist standpoint and empiricist theories never assume essentialist positions, but there is no necessary connection between a feminist theory of experience and essentialism.

Nonetheless, postmodernist worries do not disappear simply by allaying the fear of essentialism. The rejection of experience as a ground of knowledge runs wide and deep. In an extended critique, Joan Scott identifies several points where arguments from experience rest on problematic assumptions, of which three appear central. First, an appeal to experience is taken as evidence for a private domain of subjectivity, immediately accessible through introspection and therefore incorrigible. Second, on the basis of this evidence, an artificial separation between subject/experiencer and historian/observer is established where experience is reality and history is interpretation. Third, both previous claims rely on the unsupported assumption that subjects are coherent, unified entities with an ability to report and evaluate their own experiences. These points will be elaborated in turn.

Scott's first critique, against a private incorrigible domain of evidence, is well taken. Experience has indeed been problematically conceived "as uncontestable evidence and as an originary point of explanation" (Scott 1992, 24). Descartes, the philosopher who got the most theoretical mileage out of this assumption, is regularly accused of leading Western philosophy down a false evidential path.[8] Scott's attack is unique, however, in considering the appeal to subjective experience to be a diversionary tactic. "The evidence of experience becomes evidence for the fact of difference, rather than a way of exploring how difference is established, how it operates, how and in what ways it constitutes subjects who see and act in the world" (Scott 1992, 25).

Experience is used as a political tool to reinforce rather than contest social categories. By focusing on experiences of the members of marginalized groups, such as women or gay men, we must move *within* the categories that have defined them as marginalized. Once we are within these categories, the social structure that generated the categories is rendered invisible and therefore shielded from critique. Furthermore, by developing accounts of experience within existing social/political categories, the bogey of essentialism is reintroduced. Scott notes that "the project of making experience visible precludes analysis of the workings of [the ideological] system and of its historicity; instead it reproduces its terms" (Scott 1992, 25). Experiences are highlighted as those of Woman or Gay Man, effectively lumping together all the experiences belonging to members of the identified group, however diverse they (group members or their experiences) may be. Scott approvingly quotes Denise Riley's comment that the category of 'women's experience' "conflates the attributed, the imposed, and the lived, and then sanctifies the resulting mélange" (quoted in Scott 1992, 31).

Scott's principal concern is the ideological system that produces categories that claim to capture these purportedly essential features. Identification of these features requires some kind of apparatus for distinguishing reality from appearance—the essential features of a group from the features that are merely accidentally common among the members. A second objection Scott raises, then, is that experience assumes the status of the real when it is taken as foundational, creating a dichotomy between experiencer and observer. If the theorist can treat the subject's reports as real, concrete evidence, he can claim for himself the position of neutral observer, removing any need to examine the relevance of his sex, class, race, or sexual orientation to the investigation. "His knowledge, reflecting as it does something apart from him, is legitimated and presented as universal, accessible to all" (Scott 1992, 28).

Scott's final objection gets to the root of her opposition to experience as a foundation of knowledge, and will be the main point I challenge in my attempt to salvage the appeal to experience from these objections. Scott maintains that the secret to avoiding the first two problems, essentialism and transcendental knowledge claims, is to recognize that experience is a social rather than an individual phenomenon. There is no subjective experience because there are no unitary subjects. The mistaken view discussed earlier—that theorists are merely neutral observers—is made plausible by the unquestioned assumption that subjects are isolable from one another by means of their experience. If experience is private, each subject has and reports on her own experience, which no one else shares. In order to assess the epistemic value of experience, therefore, we must first consider the nature of subjects, examining "the complex and changing discursive processes by which identities are ascribed, resisted, or embraced and which processes themselves are unremarked, indeed achieve their effect because they aren't noticed" (Scott 1992, 33). The uncritical assumption of a unitary subject leads naturally to the attribution of experience to individuals. Experience is a psychological operation, so if we are all discrete mental units, then our sets of experiences are discrete units as well. By examining the relation between experience and language, Scott intends to undermine the assumption that subjects or their experiences are in any way discrete. Experiences do not occur in a vacuum, they are situated in and influenced by the particular context of the subject. As an example of the way context figures as an influence on experience, Scott quotes Stuart Hall's description of the way Jamaicans came to speak of themselves as "black." "The fact is 'black' has never been just there . . . [it is] an identity which had to be learned and could only be learned in a certain moment" (quoted in Scott 1992, 33). Language and experience interact. There was no "black" experience waiting for a linguistic label, the experience was shaped by the confluence of historical factors, including changes in language usage. If this description of the effect of context on experience is accurate, then it seems misleading to speak of experience in individualistic terms. Experiences are not isolated, subjective events; they are the result of a dynamic interrelation between subject and context.

In a passage that is illuminating for both its positive and its negative statements, Scott writes: "Subjects are constituted discursively, experience is a linguistic event (it doesn't happen outside established meanings), but neither is it confined to a fixed order of meaning. Since discourse is by definition shared, experience is collective as well as individual" (Scott 1992, 34). On one hand, Scott is reiterating the point already made—language is social, experience is inseparable from language, so experience is social. Yet Scott cannot rest with so bald a position. Immediately following the statement that established meanings are requisite for experience, a qualifying remark allows that meaning need not be fixed. Similarly, Scott classes experience as a form of language, defined as a social medium, but then relents by admitting that experience is individual as well as collective.

While I am in complete agreement with the added subtleties in Scott's description, there seems to be no resource in her position that would justify them. Meanings might be established without being fixed in the sense that words can be used in nonstandard ways to generate new meanings, for example, in conversational implicature and metaphor. Or two groups might establish different meanings for a word, and when the usage conflicts, both meanings are modified, as in the Jamaican usage of *black*. If this form of linguistic conflict is the only tool for meaning change, however, it remains unclear how Scott's discursive analysis would treat the case of a single group reevaluating the meaning of a technical term, such as *subatomic particle*. Such reconsiderations are often sparked by observational data that consistently fail to fit theoretical expectations. But without some sort of appeal to experience outside the realm of established meaning, it is difficult to see how recalcitrant data could manage to pierce the web of theory as Scott has described it. Even if the language of "contested identities" is more appropriate to theoretical analysis than has been previously admitted, it does not follow that the language of experience is thereby rendered incoherent or meaningless.

Furthermore, there seems little reason to attribute experience to the individual at all on Scott's view. Traditionally, experience was taken to serve the function of providing an individual with information about the world so that she could form beliefs and desires appropriate to external conditions. Thus, in the traditional view agency depends on experience for motivating and modifying action.[9] On Scott's account, however, individual subjects are formed as an intersection of social forces within a historical/cultural matrix. While Scott presents her discursive subjects as agents, she consistently uses the passive voice in describing them. They are "subjects whose agency is created through situations and statuses conferred on them."[10] The context in which an individual is situated *confers* agency; salient features of the *context* motivate action rather than an individual's experience.[11]

If, as Scott suggests, agents are more acted upon than acting, there is little for individual experience to do. The society determines what experiences mean, since meanings depend on linguistic practices, and the context motivates individual action. The only sense that remains for experiences to be individual is that one person has them rather than several. If this description is correct, then collective experience must be analyzed as the simultaneous experience by two or more people of tokens of the same linguistic type of experience, the sharing of an experience through its description, or both.[12] Because both forms of experience are essentially social—they depend on linguistic practice for their interpretation—the distinction between individual and collective experience becomes uninteresting, even trivial.

This is Scott's aim. By showing that individual experience depends on the social environment of the subject, Scott intends to defuse attempts to make experience the ground for epistemic justification. This argument and the others in this section have indeed shown that experience cannot be taken as an unmediated access to reality. The simplest forms of categorization require social training, and language is most instructive in this regard.[13] But Scott takes the argument too far when she collapses experience into language. As I will argue in the following section, by distinguishing two forms of experience we can see in what ways (cognitive) experience is shaped through language and in what ways language is in turn shaped by (noncognitive) experience. Once this distinction is clarified, we will then be able to address Scott's objections as well as describe the political advantages of an epistemology grounded in experience over the historicism advocated by Scott and postmodernists.

II. Redefining Experience

To this point I have refrained from defining 'experience', an omission that, as Scott observes, "allows it to function as a universally understood category" (Scott 1992, 32). Since I plan to argue rather than assume that experience serves a useful epistemic function, a definition is in order. My analysis follows John Dewey in distinguishing two levels of experience, noncognitive and cognitive. Noncognitive or primary experience involves the most basic level of sensory interaction between a person and the world. Every creature reacts to features of its environment and in turn the environment responds to this reaction, creating a dialectic of "doings and sufferings" in organism-environment relations (Dewey [1917] 1980, 9). For some creatures, experience consists primarily of this noncognitive type, where the creature functions by adjusting its reactions in response to the environment.

A good example of noncognitive experience in humans is the experience of driving a car. After a few years of practice, the repertoire of necessary skills is firmly in place and requires only periodic adjustment by cognitive processes. Think of highway driving, especially. You pass cars, look at scenery, listen to the radio. Very little of the stimuli experienced can or should be cognitively processed. Few, if any, beliefs are formed during driving (that are about driving, at least). It is this level of experience, I will argue, that can serve a nonessentialist, justificatory function in epistemology.

Cognitive or secondary experience, by contrast, cannot without circularity justify knowledge, because this level serves the function of producing knowledge. At the level of cognitive experience, the creature begins to predict the consequences of its actions in the world, thereby gaining greater control over the environment. Cognitive experience produces beliefs by generalizing over sets of past events in order to assess new situations and solve novel problems. If these cognitive beliefs prove successful, they constitute knowledge. According to Dewey, knowledge is "a matter of the use that is made of experienced natural events [to indicate] what will be experienced under different conditions" ([1917] 1980, 33). The act of knowing allows a person to successfully cope with future situations.[14]

Cognitive experience produces beliefs that are then tested in noncognitive experience. One of Dewey's most significant contributions to epistemology was the realization that the process of knowing forms an arc. Input is processed cognitively and a reaction is generated. The results of that reaction then constitute the next wave of input for analysis (Dewey [1896] 1972, 101f.). By emphasizing the interaction between knowing and doing, Dewey showed how knowledge claims can be justified by their ability to guide action. In other words, the results of cognitive operations count as knowledge if they improve noncognitive functioning. Consider the driving example again. Although few beliefs are formed while one is driving on the highway, several are being tested: beliefs about proper gear-shifting, what the gas gauge means, how to turn the stereo on and off. The beliefs and abilities by which you function in your automotive environment form what Dewey calls the "background" of your experience. Background includes all of the aspects of you and your surroundings that are taken for granted in experience (Dewey [1931] 1985, 11). While driving, you operate on the basis of these beliefs, but they do not need to be reintroduced into cognitive experience. You need not *think* about everything you do, unless something goes wrong. If the gears start making a rumbling noise when you shift to fourth, you will instantly check relevant beliefs to determine which is problematic. Perhaps the belief that fourth is the appropriate gear for a steep hill is faulty. Or there may be no problem with any existing beliefs, but a new belief is required to deal with a new situation. Noncognitive experience tests cognitive beliefs *indirectly*; the environment is the direct test. Noncognitive functioning indicates that the beliefs are true; noncognitive malfunction indicates that the belief system requires revision.[15]

We tend to privilege the cognitive aspect of experience, as it provides us the security of anticipating the consequences of our actions in the environment. But Dewey reminds us that the noncognitive aspect of experience, that which is not known, is just as real as the known. "For in any object of primary experience there are always potentialities which are not explicit; any object that is overt is charged with possible consequences that are hidden; the most overt fact has factors which are not explicit" (Dewey [1925] 1981, 28). We select elements of experience to examine, according to whatever purposes we have at the time. These elements become the objects of cognition and are rightly valued as such, so long as we do not then discard the remainder of experiences as unreal (31).

The remainder of experience, the noncognitive, contains the potentialities and consequences that either reinforce or undermine the results of cognition. Beliefs that fail to achieve the purposes for which they were designed must be reevaluated. When the car gears rumble, a hidden consequence of my faulty (or incomplete) car-driving beliefs is revealed. My noncognitive experience of the car's malfunction signals that my beliefs have failed to accomplish my purpose. In revising my beliefs, I will likely incorporate previously overlooked objects and relations into cognitive experience. But neither I nor anyone could incorporate all aspects of noncognitive experience into a belief system. Noncognitive experience is simply too rich and complex. Although outside cognition, the noncognitive remains a real part of our ongoing interactions with the world and as such constitutes a test of our beliefs in our successfully coping with the world. An important consequence of this bilevel theory is that there are no incorrigible beliefs. Noncognitive experience serves as raw material for the belief-forming mechanisms of cognition, but it is the fallible cognitive processes that store and revise beliefs. There are no noncognitive beliefs, nor could there be. Note that this is a *logical* impossibility. Noncognitive and cognitive experience are defined by their *function*: noncognitive experience involves all nonepistemic elements in organism-environment interaction; epistemic elements are cognitive. Therefore, the same stimulus can figure in either cognitive or noncognitive experience depending on how it is treated. If I simply respond to the pain in my side while driving, the experience remains noncognitive. If I consider the sort of pain it is, say shooting or stinging, cognitive experience is involved.

Be advised, however, that this sort of static description risks misrepresenting the ongoing interaction between noncognitive and cognitive experience. Experience is complex, dynamic and continuous, involving noncognitive and cognitive processes at all times. In the search for understanding, it is appropriate to separate aspects of the knowledge-gathering process according to function and operation, but we should not conclude that intellectual distinctions constitute metaphysically distinct entities.

So the grounding of epistemology I am suggesting is not the same old foundationalist project of sorting indubitable from derived beliefs. No beliefs are indubitable; all are derived from the operations of fallible processes. Rather than positing a set of foundational beliefs, Dewey advocates a belief-forming *process* as the source of justification for our theories. Traditional foundationalist arguments require some absolute epistemic base on which to build knowledge. All beliefs inherit their justification from their relation to this secure base point. Deweyan justification does not fit this model, however. Because the process of belief-formation is the source of justification, no thing (such as sense-data) or belief (such as *cogito*) needs be taken as eternally and absolutely real or true. As should be noted, I have been dealing with simple, empirically oriented beliefs. Accounting for complicated, socially structured beliefs, such as beliefs about equality or social roles, requires an analysis of how the social environment functions in the same sorts of ways as the physical environment. My conviction that this project will prove fruitful rests on a recent spate of arguments showing a continuity between biological and social functioning.[16] Further, there may be different criteria for knowledge claims in different belief contexts, for example, purely formal systems such as logic and mathematics. My aim here is not to show that noncognitive functioning is the only test of beliefs, but that it is a viable test.[17] If I can show that experience can serve as a justification for at least some kinds of belief, then I have shown that the postmodernist move to banish subjective experience from feminist epistemology is premature.

III. Naturalizing Feminism

Now, how can the distinction between noncognitive and cognitive experience prove helpful to feminists? In Section IV, I will detail the specific ways in which this view of experience addresses Scott's objections and suggest a possible grounding of feminist epistemology. In this section I would like to place the proposed theory of experience within the context of contemporary feminist moves toward naturalism. Not all naturalists, or even feminist naturalists, agree on a single definition of naturalism. One unifying thread, however, seems to be a commitment to finding continuity between epistemology and natural science (Maffie 1990). Through this connection with science, naturalism promises a method of justification for belief, making it an a posteriori rather than an a priori process. Feminists have recently turned to naturalism as a middle ground between the impartiality required of empiricism and the relativism inherent in post-modernism. A cousin of pragmatism, naturalist knowledge claims are tested through action, not simply through rational deliberation. Since tests of theory are ongoing, all claims are fallible. Fallibility is useful for feminists in disallowing any claim, androcentric or otherwise, from gaining the status of absolute truth; there is always room for error.

Naturalism takes justification out of the realm of logic and puts it in the fallible physical processes by which we come to know about ourselves and the world.

Nonetheless, some knowledge claims are warranted while others are not, and their warrant comes from their predictive success for the individual.[18] Some might object that only a community can warrant a knowledge claim, given the social nature of knowledge and justification. The communitarian claim is that the standards for determining what counts as successful prediction are set by a given community. It would be misleading, communitarians argue, to pretend that predictive success somehow transcends the particular community in which the test is run. As advocates of naturalism sometimes endorse this view, the point serves as an important distinguishing feature of my proposal. Lynn Hankinson Nelson defends a type of communitarianism in her discussion of Quine's naturalism. Nelson utilizes Quine's analysis of the underdetermination of theory by data to combine feminist claims about the social construction of knowledge with the traditional empiricist insistence on the importance of evidence (Nelson 1993, 174). Because the data available from sensory stimulation is insufficient to specify a single unique theory as the "true theory of nature," other considerations must figure in our endorsement of one account over another. Issues of gender, race, and class are among the often overlooked considerations relevant to our evaluation of scientific theories, as well as social and political theories (Nelson 1993, 178f.). A deep and comprehensive holism in theory building supplements the communitarian argument. Any evidence claim—ranging from claims about subatomic particles to mailboxes—relies on the entire network of shared beliefs and values that determines the standards for what counts as evidence within that community. In the concluding section of the essay, Nelson states the communitarian thesis emphatically: "The primary epistemological agents are groups— . . . the collaborators, the consensus achievers, and, in more general terms, the agents who generate knowledge are communities, not individuals. Individuals do know, of course; but your knowing or mine depends on *our* knowing, for some 'we.' More to the point, you or I *can* only know what *we know* (or could), for some 'we' " (Nelson 1993, 186).

Strong communitarian conclusions such as this are unsettling to people familiar with the way 'we' can be used as a tool of exclusion. 'We' all agree, so *you* must be crazy.[19] Nelson recognizes this problem and uses the term 'we' with qualification (Nelson 1993, 179). Nonetheless, I remain dissatisfied with the claim that communities, not individuals, generate knowledge. Even if very small and diverse groups are taken to count as epistemologically valid communities, no theoretical resources remain for the lone knowledge-seeker in her efforts to critically assess the social system in which she finds herself. She could of course find a group of like-minded individuals. But this move might not be a viable option and does not seem to be the only one available. There ought to be a way that she can evaluate her belief system without necessary recourse to some 'we'. As I will argue, communitarians are correct in pointing out the essential influence of social training in the development of a person's beliefs and values. However, they overstate their case when they claim that a person is not justified in revising those beliefs without social approval.

It may be that individuals rarely engage in social criticism without the support of others. We are, admittedly, social creatures, and our knowledge gathering usually involves negotiations with and encouragement from members of one or another community. If this is all Nelson means in assigning primary status to group activity, then I can agree. But in claiming that individual knowledge *depends* on community knowledge—"I can only know what we know"—Nelson suggests that social sanction is a necessary feature of epistemic warrant. With this stronger claim I definitely disagree; it is possible to determine standards of evaluation in the face of community rejection. Before I defend this objection, however, a few qualifying remarks are in order. First, my claim in the remainder of this section does not deny the necessity of community in the development of language and thought.[20] Although I argue that an individual has the capacity to establish standards on her own, such a capacity assumes a significant amount of social training even to figure out what constitutes a standard. Furthermore, an established symbol system would be required to record the results of inquiry; otherwise it would be impossible to determine whether a standard was applied in the same way on two different occasions. Finally, no standard produced by an individual can be in principle inaccessible to others. That is, I may know what no one else knows, but I cannot know what no one else *could* know. If my fellow researchers fail to accept my results, the reason cannot be the ineffability of the data. They may refuse to accept a premise for theoretical or political reasons; they may be unwilling to learn the conceptual scheme required; or they may find the conclusions too morally reprehensible to even consider the theory. Whatever the reasons that would keep a group from admitting a novel approach, the standards of evaluation and the data they produce must be communicable.[21]

Qualifications aside, the project of reclaiming the subject requires examining the role of social norms and values in shaping experience, while retaining the possibility of individual evaluation and rejection of at least some of these standards. As mentioned earlier, a community provides the conceptual tools that enable us to theorize at all about our experiences, noncognitive as well as cognitive.[22] The context in which we come to learn about the world will set limits on the kinds of projects we find interesting and the problems we choose to solve. We select aspects of experience to investigate and ignore others (Dewey [1925], 31; [1931] 1985, 14). Even so, the interests and experiences of different subjects will lead them to question different elements of commonly held theories. Each of us has, in Dewey's words, "a unique manner of entering into interaction with things" ([1931] 1985, 15). In the course of investigation, one person may find that the results of her research call for radical revision of a deeply entrenched theory. She would generally try to convince those around her to accept her results and will be inclined to reconsider in the face of their rejection. Yet it does not follow that she must reject her own findings if she fails to convince her colleagues or that she would only be justified in accepting the community view. Experimenters following the scientific method construct a path from hypotheses to conclusion. If the conclusion informs the experimenter about connections between experienced things and events, then the method has been useful (Dewey [1925] 1981, 13).

Theories are justified by their predictive value, so a person is warranted in believing an effective theory even in the face of social opposition. Consequently, the power to test theories lies in the hands of any and all subjects of experience, including women. Unlike Cartesian subjects, however, naturalized subjects are not characterized by their impartiality or their separation from the object of investigation. Special interests often spark the inquiry, and those interests will inevitably affect the interaction between subject and object during the course of research. "Harmony with conditions," writes Dewey, "is not a single and monotonous uniformity, but a diversified affair requiring individual attack" ([1930] 1985, 120). In other words, the subject of naturalized epistemology is describing the view from here, the way things are to a person in a place at a time. All knowledge begins in experience as described from one point of view. Dewey considers this subjective aspect of experience to be an inescapable feature of the context of thought, part of the background of experience. "A standpoint which is nowhere in particular and from which things are not seen at a special angle is an absurdity" (Dewey [1931] 1985, 15).

Still, there is a sense in which descriptions from a point of view make a claim to universality. That is, were another person similarly situated, that person would get a similar view. Note that I use the word *similar* rather than *same*. Two people, being distinct, cannot logically occupy the same place at the same time. Furthermore, no two people share the same history: cultural and educational background, formative events and life choices invariably differ. All these factors influence the subject's view and may be relevant to her reports. We determine which factors are relevant and which are not through familiar methods: we compare another person's description of a situation with our own, we consider how the description fits with the rest of what we know about the world, and so on.

If points of disagreement arise, we know something has gone wrong and we must search for the source of the dispute. It may be that the two evaluators are not, as it first appeared, similarly situated in relevant ways. Perhaps some factor involving past experience, such as religious or ethnic history, that seemed irrelevant is in fact important. Or it may be that the original description was faulty, and upon review the subject finds her reports inaccurate.[23] Both of these possibilities affect the claim to universality; they show the claim to be unwarranted. Even so, there are many descriptions that are not in fact disputed, and in these cases the universality claim goes through. It is still a *claim* of universality, for there may remain relevant factors that would limit the claim even though they have not yet surfaced. Nonetheless, in a naturalist theory, the claim to universality has the strength of claims of knowledge, for both types are fallible and may be disproven by future experience. What Nelson and others have effectively shown is that we cannot rule out factors such as gender, race, and class as in principle irrelevant to any given area of investigation. What they have not shown is that a subject cannot in any way evaluate her own experience without the aid of community standards. A subject can evaluate her experience and put forward knowledge claims as candidates for universalization. These claims may prove faulty or fail to generalize beyond her own experience, but they may as well prove themselves by their broad predictive success.

IV. Value of the Subject

In Section II, I set out to redefine experience so as to establish a role for the subject of experience in the justification of her beliefs and values. In the present section, I reconsider Scott's objections to experience as a ground of epistemology in light of the new definition, and I discuss the advantages of an experience-based theory of knowledge.

The first objection—that subjective experience is neither immediately accessible nor incorrigible—can be quickly addressed. Appeals to experience often are taken as incorrigible appeals to a subjective realm, accessible only through introspection. I join Scott in rejecting such a description of experience.[24] In my view, noncognitive experience functions in theory testing rather than in providing a cache of indubitable data. Primary experience is also a source of material for cognition, but in this capacity it serves no justificatory function. The process of theory development forms an arc—input (primary experience) initiates cognitive processes (secondary experience) that lead to actions that either prove the conceptual scheme adequate to the task, or instigate revision procedures. No part of the process depends on incorrigible beliefs, even though some beliefs do prove justified by aiding negotiations with the world.

Scott's second objection, following from the first, is that theories of experience endorse a false dichotomy between the subject of experience and the theorist. One of the negative consequences for historical research that comes from assuming an incorrigible form of experience is the separation of historical subject from historian. The subject's experiences are taken as transcriptions of reality that can be reproduced and analyzed by the researcher. By this move the historian can claim the role of impartial observer; he is simply transcribing public information. Attention is thereby deflected from the gender, race, and class bias that affect the historian's observations and analysis. If, however, we consider experience-based reports as a description of the subject's point of view, not only must we place the subject in a social-historical context, but we must take the context of the researcher into account as well. In evaluating the evidence presented, the historian is also describing a particular point of view, namely, her own view of another person's experiential report.

The historian will no doubt present her view in a way that allows others to find value in her description—she will generalize her results, showing connections between her view and similar research, explaining how her description fits with an accepted theory or points to the inadequacies of a theory. This kind of pull toward objectivity is an important part of theory building, which in turn is an important part of our continuing efforts to understand and cope with the world and one another. Because the experience (cognitive and noncognitive) of each of us is limited, we rely on the methods by which we can share what we have learned from our interactions with the world.[25] Scott worries that the quest for objectivity leads to the call for impartial observers and the consequent concealment of the privilege that accompanies their positions. But objectivity need not involve impartiality.[26]

Louise Antony has argued strongly against the conflation of objectivity and impartiality, a conflation she calls "Dragnet objectivity" (Antony 1993, 206). If objectivity requires an ideal epistemological position—a value-neutral, passive observer who gathers data and mechanically calculates results—then feminists who emphasize the partiality and situatedness of observers must relinquish any claim to objectivity. But, as Antony's queries in the following passage point out, the rejection of both impartiality and objectivity leaves feminists with no grounds on which to critique dominant beliefs and practices. We cannot argue that male bias is problematic in research if we take bias to be inevitable. "Even if it could be established that received epistemic norms originated in the androcentric fantasies of European white males . . . , how is that fact supposed to be elaborated into a *critique* of those norms? All knowledge is partial—let it be so. How then does the particular partiality of received conceptions of objectivity diminish their worth?" (Antony 1993, 210).

Antony concludes that we should reject Dragnet objectivity as false, and instead "begin with whatever it is we think we know, and try to figure out how we came to know it: Study knowledge by studying the knower" (Antony 1993, 210). Once we adopt this approach we will see that no one has in fact ever approximated the ideal of Dragnet objectivity, and that this ideal would not facilitate the production of knowledge. At root, human beings require some conceptual structures with which to organize the incoming sensory flow of information, and concept formation entails sorting out the relevant types of sensory stimulations from the irrelevant ones. So already at the most basic levels of cognition, values and partiality are required to pick "good" information from "bad," as well as to interpret whatever information is selected.

Finally we come to Scott's third and most comprehensive objection—epistemology cannot be grounded in subjective experience because subjectivity is a fiction. Subjects are not individual, autonomous agents with the ability to observe and report on their experiences. Subjects and their experiences are formed by the intersection of cultures, so experience is collective. To take experience as a justification of knowledge, Scott argues, "closes down inquiry into the ways in which female subjectivity is produced, the ways in which agency is made possible, the ways in which race and sexuality intersect with gender, the ways in which politics organize and interpret experience—the ways in which identity is a contested terrain, the site of multiple and conflicting claims" (Scott 1992, 33).

The objection to subjectivity is made on two different grounds. (1) Subjects and subjective experience are constructed by conflicting communities of knowledge. That which is constructed cannot also be the ground of that same construction, so subjective experience cannot ground knowledge. (2) Taking subjective experience as a justification of knowledge leads to the problematic result that political and social influences on experience are obscured. Both of these arguments rely on the assumption that an experience-based epistemology is inconsistent with admitting the social construction of subjective experience. In elaborating a bilevel theory of experience, my aim was to remove this appearance of this inconsistency. Noncognitive functioning is an *indicator* of true theories rather than a *producer* of incorrigible beliefs; noncognitive experience produces no beliefs whatsoever. If beliefs are appropriate to the environment, noncognitive processes will face no problematic situations, and will not activate cognitive belief-revision processes.[27] Consequently, the social influences invoked by Scott apply only to the limits of theory building and do not undermine the justificatory potential of noncognitive functioning.

It is at the level of cognitive experience that social influence enters. Cognitive experience produces beliefs as a response to environmental effects (physical, cultural, historical, and so forth) on noncognitive experience, in other words, problems in noncognitive processing. Even though these beliefs are constructed in part from social forces, society is not the only, nor necessarily the most significant, test of knowledge. Therefore knowledge claims are not limited to the standards of a community; rather they must prove successful in coping with every kind of obstacle presented to noncognitive experience, only one of which is social censure. Still, there remains the possibility that the social and political influences on knowledge production will be overlooked if we admit influences on experience that are not social and political.[28] Dominant groups are likely to adopt the language of experience in justifying their own oppressive belief system. After all, the supposedly "value-neutral" empirical method has been used in scientific theory to "prove" such things as the moral and intellectual inferiority of women and people of color. There is no reason to think that a theory of noncognitive experience will be immune from these kinds of abuses.

While it is a general rule that a tool is only as good as the artisan who wields it, this says nothing against the potential efficacy of the tool. Similarly with the epistemic mechanisms involved in experience— cognitive experience produces beliefs to be checked by noncognitive experience. If factors such as gender or class status systematically shape the beliefs produced by cognitive processes, the result will likely be a theory that maintains rather than critiques oppression. No theory is seamless, however, and oppressed persons are often the ones to identify cracks in an ideology. Therefore, the advantage of an experienced-based epistemology is that the beliefs produced out of the experience of someone with a different gender or class position have warrant to challenge a dominant theory. Members of an oppressed group can critique a theory on the grounds that it fails to aid them in their efforts to cope with their environment, if, for example, they find themselves with more obstacles to overcome in their lives rather than fewer.

This sort of critique is produced when false consciousness is converted into consciousness. Take the tragic case of battered wives. Their beliefs about their situation are in all likelihood shaped by an environment in which men, especially husbands, are granted supreme authority. Often battered women grow up in a household where the mother was battered by the father. Because men occupy positions of power, these women may never have attempted to exercise their own power. One of the reasons that these situations are self-perpetuating is that battered women are often so convinced of their own helplessness that it never even occurs to them to try to get help. Nonetheless, they know that they are having trouble coping with their environment, to say the least. Sadly, battered women are usually convinced by their batterers that the source of the problem is in themselves rather than the abuser. But sometimes—perhaps after a particularly violent attack sparked by a particularly trivial incident—a woman realizes that she is not to blame, that the batterer is at fault. The shock of the inability to function in her environment forces a revision in her belief system, and for some reason—they are the only beliefs left to be challenged, their revision constitutes minimum mutilation to the system, for example—her beliefs about the power and authority of her husband become the object of revision. If she is lucky enough to have some source of independent confirmation of this realization, such as a hotline for battered women, a helpful police officer or a friend, her abilities to critique the beliefs that led to her abuse will be even stronger.[29] Moreover, an experience-based epistemology provides a reason for the dominant group to take this kind of critique seriously. If their theory is inadequate to the experiences of some people (or even one person), it cannot be considered a fully justified theory. This difficulty may instigate a move to classify the offending experiences as invalid— women are irrational, slaves are not persons—but the persistence of contravening evidence eventually precipitates reconsideration of theoretical assumptions. Even batterers are sometimes moved to seek therapy once their spouses have asserted their independence, although the resistance to self-reflection is often unremitting. In science, by contrast, we are witness to the self-corrective capacity of the empirical method. Despite its slow and limited processes, science continually disproves what it had once deemed proven and proves what it had deemed impossible, reinforcing the impression that knowledge gathering is a fallible, but unrelenting, process.

Finally, and perhaps most significantly, an experience-based epistemology admits diversity among women (indeed, among all knowers) while explaining the advantages of affiliation with groups. Each person necessarily is exposed to a unique set of noncognitive experiences, yet common features in the physical and social environments of some people facilitate their communication with one another. Women, therefore, are likely to find other women particularly helpful in developing strategies for negotiating the specific obstacles they mutually face. But this principle cannot be universalized, because other environmental features, such as race or class, may intersect with shared gender-related experiences so that differences overshadow similarities. Nonetheless, the general recommendation for women to seek other women for support and guidance continues to serve as a unifying force for political and social activity.

V. Conclusion

In sum, a bilevel theory of experience incorporates the essential tension between individual and society so as to acknowledge cultural influences while preserving the ability for action and critique by the subject. Social structures such as language, evaluative standards of various kinds, and behavioral norms form a significant part of the environmental forces that shape the beliefs and values resulting from the interaction of noncognitive and cognitive experience. Because this interaction occurs within the individual, though, each person develops a unique point of view out of which her evaluations and accomplishments proceed. Any point of view is inherently limited by the historical and social standpoint in which it is cultivated. Even so, these limitations do not imply that a person is unable to establish standards of evaluation by which to analyze her own experience; they require only that the starting point from which any standards are developed is considered one of the constraints in knowledge gathering.

A naturalized epistemology starts theorizing in the middle of the knowledge-gathering process, assuming that we know things and then figuring out how we might have got this knowledge. Consequently, the context of knowers is immediately relevant to the determination of what can be taken as known and what resources are available for future learning. Given this cyclical description of knowledge gathering, traditional forms of foundationalism can be seen as inappropriate to the project of epistemology. While there are always good reasons to say that some beliefs are more firmly grounded than others, no sense can be made of the theory that some beliefs claim a permanent epistemic status by virtue of their incorrigibility. Because our theorizing begins in the middle of the process, we cannot be certain that any belief will not prove false under future testing. Although we are justified in accepting them, our knowledge claims are fallible.

Where I part company from many other feminists who advocate a naturalized approach to epistemology is in my claim that an individual can be justified in making a knowledge claim, even in the face of community rejection. I take this difference to be an advantage for an experience-based theory over a more Quinean, linguistic-oriented one. By maintaining the possibility of individual knowledge claims, even as we admit contextual influences, we generate a theory that accommodates both individual differences and the forces that bind us together. In this way the power of epistemic warrant can be tapped in various ways, rather than only through community endorsement. A theory of experience that incorporates epistemic flexibility should be appealing to feminists tired of rigid, nomic conceptual systems. Indeed, this theory of experience should be appealing to anyone looking for a description of the way regular people learn about and cope with the world and with one another—and how we can do it better.[30]

Notes

1. See, for example, Scheman 1993, 83–86; Hekman 1987, 65–83; and Scott 1992, 22–40.

2. See Dennett 1991; Kornblith 1988; and Akins 1993.

3. For an argument against individualism in biology and psychology, see Millikan 1993; for a discussion of the mistakes in social and political theory resulting from a sharp subject/object distinction, see Rorty 1991.

4. Linda Alcoff and Elizabeth Potter propose another criterion of adequacy that will also be satisfied: "[A]n epistemology must attend to the complex ways in which social values influence knowledge, including the discernible social and political implications of its own analysis" (1993, 13).

5. Note that I am relying on an intuitive sense of 'experience' for this section to allow for the various ways in which the term has been used to ground feminist epistemology. In Section II, I will define the term as it figures in the view I advocate.

6. Since my aim is primarily to argue against the postmodernist rejection of experience as a possible foundation for knowledge, I will not include an evaluation of my agreements and disagreements with feminist empiricist and standpoint theories. For more discussion of the relation between empiricist and standpoint theories, see Longino 1993 and Harding 1993.

7. This point is made both by Seigfried (1996) in arguing for a feminist pragmatist theory, and by Harding (1993) in her defense of feminist standpoint theory.

8. See, for example, Damasio 1994 and Scheman 1993.

9. An example of the motivating function of experience, in Mentalese: "There's an apple, and I'm hungry. I'd best move my hand to grasp and eat it." An example of the modifying function: "Oops, I missed. I should move my hand farther to the right." Note that the claim is not that experience is the sole source of belief and desire formation, but that it is an important one.

10. Scott 1992, 34; see also 25–26, 28, and 33.

11. It remains a question how the analysis of discursive subject would deal with the mundane examples of agency mentioned in the preceding note. They could be considered stimulus-response reactions rather than cases of genuine agency, but this move leads to a deep mind/body split that is usually objectionable to feminists. More likely, the focus could be on the contextual factors that create beliefs and desires and the opportunities that allow their satisfaction. Still, this analysis needs some explanation of how environmental cues manage to translate into individual action.

12. Scott does not define these terms herself; these conjectures are based on her general analysis of experience.

13. Wittgenstein's (1958) private-language argument and its attendant literature ably defends this point, albeit to extreme in points.

14. Epistemologists may object that knowledge claims must be more than successful, they must be true. Dewey would agree with this, but would analyze 'true' as 'warranted assertability', in other words, the belief is justified by its success and its fit with other beliefs. See Section III for a discussion of justification as it figures in the proposed theory of experience.

15. What form the revision will take depends on the belief system and the problem at hand. The holism involved in a naturalized epistemology will be further discussed in Section III.

16. See Millikan 1993; Dennett 1991; Dretske 1995; and Neisser 1993.

17. I believe that arguments can, and eventually will, be made to show that other criteria for knowledge rest more or less directly on noncognitive functioning. These arguments will not be developed here, however, as my attempt is only to show the justificatory potential of experience for feminist epistemology.

18. Other factors may be important to determining warrant. Richmond Campbell (1994) adds observation independence and explanatory power in his defense of scientific methods. For the purposes of illustration, I will only discuss predictive success.

19. The problem of defining sanity and insanity within feminist theory is an interesting question and deserves more careful analysis than can be provided here. For an examination of this problem in the context of ethics, see Morgan 1987.

20. As is shown by, for example, Dewey's emphasis on the role of historical and social context in shaping thought, Wittgenstein's private-language argument, and reams of feminist sociological, psychological, and philosophical literature on the connections between mothering and cognitive development.

21. This rule applies to the data of subjective experience as well. I may not be able to have the experience of being a bat (or another person), but I can talk about what that experience must be like given what I know about bat (human) abilities and psychological processes. See Akins 1993.

22. We cannot theorize about noncognitive experiences while we are having them; that makes them cognitive. But we can theorize about them in the same way we can theorize about another person's subjective experience—we can talk about them even though we are not having them. Witness the description of a noncognitive driving experience.

23. While the pragmatist does not require a theory to be true beyond its warranted assertability, she does distinguish between what appears warranted and what is. The appearance/reality distinction does not disappear, but it moves to the level of evidence. Nothing beyond available evidence is required for a knowledge claim to be warranted, but all available evidence must be included. In other words, there is such a thing as a mistaken knowledge claim.

24. While this issue is easily settled between Scott and myself, I realize that many feminist empiricists and standpoint theorists would object to the move to desanctify experience. An objection on this point, however, leaves open the full arsenal of postmodern critique, against which I see few lines of defense.

25. See also Dewey: "Everything discovered belongs to the community of workers" ([1930] 1985, 115).

26. Again, see Dewey [1916] 1980, 152–55.

27. There may be other reasons that cognitive processes are activated, however. One of the by-products of being reflective creatures is that we do not always wait for a problem before reevaluating our beliefs. Curiosity is as much a motivator of cognition as is problem solving.

28. One might argue that every influence is social and political because every perception is shaped by norms and values. But this is to confuse the source with the result. The source or cause of some aspect of experience may be entirely nonsocial, for example, a physical thing such as a tree. The result or consequence of a person's interaction with the tree will combine her various past and present experiences, including their social dimension.

29. For a feminist pragmatist description of spousal abuse that emphasizes the important role of community in supporting such belief revision, see Seigfried 1996, 163f.

30. Earlier drafts of this essay have benefited from the comments of Lynn Hankinson Nelson, Jane Duran, Elise Springer, Keya Maitra, Sarah Willie, Gloria Chun, and especially Diana T. Meyers, whose encouragement gave me the fortitude to carry the analysis through to its final stage. Charlene Haddock Seigfried provided invaluable comments and citations to help me mine the riches of Dewey's work. A brief version of this essay was presented at the "enGendering Rationalities" conference and the Central Division meeting of the American Philosophical Association, both in April 1997.

References

Akins, Kathleen A. 1993. "A Bat Without Qualities?" In *Consciousness*, edited by Martin Davies and Glyn W. Humphreys, 258–73. Oxford: Basil Blackwell.

Alcoff, Linda, and Elizabeth Potter. 1993. *Feminist Epistemologies*. New York: Routledge.

Antony, Louise M. 1993. "Quine as Feminist: The Radical Import of Naturalized Epistemology." In *A Mind of One's Own*, edited by Louise M. Antony and Charlotte Witt, 185–225. Boulder, Colo.: Westview Press.

Campbell, Richmond. 1994. "The Virtues of Feminist Empiricism." *Hypatia* 9 (1): 90–115.

Damasio, Antonio R. 1994. *Descartes' Error: Emotion, Reason, and the Human Brain*. Kirkwood, N.Y.: G. P. Putnam.

Dennett, Daniel C. 1991. *Consciousness Explained*. Boston: Little, Brown.

Dewey, John. [1896] 1972. "The Reflex Arc Concept in Psychology." In *The Early Works*. Vol. 5. Edited by Jo Ann Boydston, 96–109. Carbondale: Southern Illinois University Press.

———. [1916] 1980. *Democracy and Education*. Vol. 9 of *The Middle Works*. Edited by Jo Ann Boydston. Carbondale: Southern Illinois University Press.

———. [1917] 1980. "The Need for a Recovery of Philosophy." In *The Middle Works*. Vol. 10. Edited by Jo Ann Boydston, 3–48. Carbondale: Southern Illinois University Press.

———. [1925] 1981. *Experience and Nature*. Vol. 1 of *The Later Works*. Edited by Jo Ann Boydston. Carbondale: Southern Illinois University Press.

———. [1930] 1985. "Individuality in Our Day." In *The Later Works*. Vol. 5. Edited by Jo Ann Boydston, 111–23. Carbondale: Southern Illinois University Press.

———. [1931] 1985. "Context and Thought." In *The Later Works*. Vol. 6. Edited by Jo Ann Boydston, 3–21. Carbondale: Southern Illinois University Press.

Dretske, Fred. 1995. *Naturalizing the Mind*. Cambridge: MIT Press.

Harding, Sandra. 1993. "Rethinking Standpoint Epistemology: What Is 'Strong Objectivity'?" In *Feminist Epistemologies*, edited by Linda Alcoff and Elizabeth Potter, 49–82. New York: Routledge.

Hekman, Susan. 1987. "The Feminization of Epistemology: Gender and the Social Sciences." *Women and Politics* 7 (3): 65–83.

Kornblith, Hilary. 1988. "How Internal Can You Get?" *Synthese* 74:313–27.

Longino, Helen. 1993. "Subjects, Power, and Knowledge: Description and Prescription in Feminist Philosophies of Science." In *Feminist Epistemologies*, edited by Linda Alcoff and Elizabeth Potter, 101–20. New York: Routledge.

Maffie, James. 1990. "Recent Work on Naturalized Epistemology." *American Philosophical Quarterly* 27 (4): 281–93.

Millikan, Ruth. 1993. *White Queen Psychology and Other Essays for Alice*. Cambridge: MIT Press.

Morgan, Kathryn. 1987. "Women and Moral Madness." In *Science, Morality, and Feminist Theory*, edited by Marsha Hanen and Kai Nielsen. Calgary: University of Calgary Press.

Neisser, Ulric. 1993. *The Perceived Self: Ecological and Interpersonal Sources of Self-Knowledge*. Cambridge: Cambridge University Press.

Nelson, Lynn Hankinson. 1993. "A Question of Evidence." *Hypatia* 8 (2) :172–89.

Ortner, Sherry B. 1993. Is Female to Male as Nature Is to Culture? In *Women and Values*. 2d ed., edited by Marilyn Pearsall, 59–72. Belmont, Calif.: Wadsworth.

Rorty, Richard. 1982. *Consequences of Pragmatism*. Minneapolis: University of Minnesota Press.

———. 1991. *Objectivity, Relativism, and Truth*. Cambridge: Cambridge University Press.

Scheman, Naomi. 1993. *Engenderings*. New York: Routledge.

Scott, Joan W. 1992. "Experience." In *Feminists Theorize the Political*, edited by Judith Butler and Joan W. Scott, 22–40. New York: Routledge.

Seigfried, Charlene Haddock. 1996. *Pragmatism and Feminism*. Chicago: University of Chicago Press.

Wittgenstein, Ludwig. 1958. *Philosophical Investigations*. 3d ed. Translated by G. E. M. Anscombe. New York: Macmillan.

Part Four

Objectivity and Truth

9

The Pragmatic Ecology of the Object

John Dewey and Donna Haraway on Objectivity

Eugenie Gatens-Robinson

Introduction

To the nonscientist, the objects of modern science may seem to be exotic fictions: quarks, gluons, transfer RNA, neurotransmitters, retroviruses, black holes, and white dwarfs. How is one to integrate these things with ordinary items of lived experience, such as sunsets, sick children, periods of deep sadness, and the passage of time? Philosophers of science in the twentieth century have tried to explicate a theory of objectivity that can support taking scientific entities as the legitimate progeny of valid empirical inquiry and as the ultimate explanations of our everyday experiences. The struggle over the ontological status of such objects is ongoing and has generated a bevy of realist and antirealist positions from Bas van Fraassen's "constructive empiricism" (1980) to Hilary Putnam's "internal realism" (1987) to Paul Churchland's "eliminative materialism" ([1979] 1986).

The questions concerning the reality of the objects that function in our theories has led to questions about the objects of everyday experience. These everyday things are just as contaminated with our "folk" theoretical expectations as are the more exotic denizens of the microscopic and subatomic world. Recently, in a conversation with a moderately well known philosopher of science, I found myself called upon to defend my apparently naive belief in the existence of sycamore trees. Their homey presence beyond the window before which we talked did not seem to undermine his charge that I was in the grip of naïve realism concerning natural kinds and species. I did not fare well in this discussion, since I found myself wanting to have it both ways. First, the world really does break down into sycamores and nonsycamores. Second, this way of looking at the world, the sycamore-identifying way, is mediated by an interested human perspective, situated in a specific historical, cultural world, and is as fine grained as it needs to be for the purposes at hand. Is our way of classifying plants objective? Is that classification socially constructed? I want my answers to these two questions to be yes and yes, respectively.

The problem of giving an account of objectivity that goes beyond the failed project of sense certainty is one that John Dewey and Donna Haraway share. It is a problematic that Dewey carried through the first half of the twentieth century and that Haraway carries into the next century. Both want to understand how we can learn things about the natural world, actually come to know its objects, while affirming the creative, mediating capacities of an active inquiring intelligence, an intelligence that "needs" to know. In this essay, I will make use of this shared problem in order to connect Dewey's and Haraway's understandings of objectivity and the object of knowledge in ways that may be mutually enriching for both pragmatic and feminist thought. Haraway's "situated" view of knowledge can draw skeins of Deweyan pragmatic naturalism into "postmodern" conversations in ways that may make them more accessible and hopeful. A careful reading of Dewey's view of the scientific object can also enliven and enlighten feminist discussions of objectivity, taking them in positive directions unavailable within the context of the current debates that seem to force a choice between a social constructivist relativism or a neorealist determinism.

Donna Haraway is pragmatic in her view of objective inquiry. She says that we need a world that is knowable, transformable, and real. "For political people, social constructionism cannot be allowed to decay into the radiant emanations of cynicism. . . . We would like to think our appeals to real worlds are more than a desperate lurch away from cynicism and an act of faith like any other cult's, no matter how much space we generously give to all the rich and always historically specific mediations through which we and everybody else must know the world" (Haraway 1991, 184–85).

In juxtaposing Haraway's "situated" account of objectivity with Dewey's view of the object of knowledge, I hope that it is possible to draw on the strengths of both and give some direction to this search for a way a knowing that is liberating rather than alienating. Dewey's pragmatic optimism, uncontaminated with information-age cynicism, and Haraway's postmodernist edginess, informed by an expert facility in the discourses of the information age and the biological sciences, are strange partners. But this may be just the kind of partnership needed at this particular juncture in our search for a way of knowing that allows for a shared, pluralistic and democratically open, form of scientific inquiry.

What Is the Problem for Objectivity?

Within the modern scientific view, objectivity has been taken as the capacity of the passive mirrorlike mind to take in, know, or reflect a set of mind-independent and prestructured "objects" out there in nature. It is important for the objectivist that the activities of the human mind have as little as possible to do with "forming" the objects of knowledge. The object must not be a projection of the inquirer's expectations or needs. To the end of objective observations, the biases, prejudices, expectations, and needs of the human knower or the needs of the extrascientific community in which he or she exists are to be eliminated or filtered out by the right sort of methodology or the proper disciplines of education. The gaze of the scientist must be a view from approximately no-where.

This characterization of "objectivity" has fallen under modern and postmodern attacks that point out that all observation is theory laden and thus never innocent. There is no neutral level of observation upon which the objectivity of theory can be grounded. On Paul Churchland's ([1979] 1986) view, observation is theory laden all the way through. There is no privileged level of observational practices that allow for a clear test of theory against pure unmediated data. The distinction be-tween direct observation and theory, upon which accounts of objectivity have traditionally relied, is impossible to make. Since there is no theo-retically unbiased level of perceptual knowledge, there simply is no ob-jectivity of the sort we have thought we needed. Churchland opts not to give up the project, but to embrace a view he calls "eliminative material-ism." The preferable course is to laden our observations with the best theories available right from the start and eliminate the old common-sense theories. For Churchland these "best" theories are the successful theories of the physical sciences. Churchland claims that what science must do is to provide us with a superior and perhaps profoundly different conception of the world, even at the perceptual level ([1979] 1986, 2). We would no longer see the sky redden at sunset, but would see "wave-length distribution of incoming solar radiation shift towards the longer wavelengths" (29). We ought to abandon our folk perceptions as infor-mation that is poor and inefficient. He claims that our sensations simply teem with objective intentionalities that we fail to "exploit" unless we reformulate common sense to embody our best modern physical theory. Our commonsense categories are not to be reduced to or augmented by these theoretical modes of perception. They are to be replaced by them. Our old modes of seeing are objectively information poor and in that sense objectively faulty if not straightforwardly false. A "science without experience" seems to be the endgame of the objectivist project. "Sensa-tions are just causal middle-men in the process of perception, and one kind will serve as well as another so long as it enjoys the right causal connections. (So far then, in principle they might even be dispensed with, so far as the business of learning and theorizing about the world is concerned. As long as there remain systematic causal connections be-tween kinds of states of affairs and kinds of singular judgements, the evaluation of theories continue to take place . . .)" (Churchland [1979] 1986, 15).

In order to have maximum objective contact with the world, the mediation of human sense experience under this model must be rendered merely as means. The human perceiver becomes a cluster of "interpretation functions" for taking in objective information about the physical world in order to exploit it efficiently.

I have sketched Churchland's position briefly as a radical example among others of where traditional objectivism seems to lead. Churchland is not alone in this sort of rendering of objectivity and the objects of inquiry. One need only look at the later Popper's (1972) evolutionary epistemology, which gives us an "epistemology without a knowing subject," all in the name of objectivity. As Hilary Putnam claims, "The strength of the 'Objectivist' tradition is so strong that some philosophers will abandon the deepest intuitions we have about ourselves-in-the-world, rather than ask (as Husserl and Wittgenstein did) whether the whole picture is not a mistake" (Putnam 1987, 15). What is immensely troubling about this picture is that the connection of "pure objective information" to what it means for lived human experience is left unmade. We are at a loss about what to do or not do with all this information. Build a bomb? Clone a genius? DNA-test a rapist? Use prenatal testing to identify the sex of the fetus? Patent a genome? It is with this problem in mind that I turn to John Dewey and Donna Haraway for a different picture of the character of scientific objectivity.

Haraway warns,

> The degree to which the principle of domination is deeply embedded in our natural sciences, especially in those disciplines that seek to explain social groups and behavior, must not be underestimated. . . . Nor must we lightly accept the damaging distinction between pure and applied science, between use and abuse of science, and between nature and culture. All are versions of the philosophy of science that exploits the rupture between subject and object to justify the double ideology of firm scientific objectivity and mere personal subjectivity. (1991, 8)

In a similar vein, Dewey says that "theories which have set science on an altar in a temple remote from the arts of life . . . are part of the technique of retaining a secluded monopoly of belief and intellectual authority." He warns that until they are properly integrated into education, morality, and industry they have little to do with life but to serve as

" the heavy hand of the law upon spontaneity" and to invoke "necessity and mechanism to witness against generous and free aspiration" (Dewey [1925] 1988, 310).

The view of the objective mind and its "object" as somehow passive leads many feminists to shy away from doctrines of scientific objectivity. The "objective" object of this sort "refreshes the power of the knower, but any status as agent in the production of that knowledge is denied the object. It—the world—must be objectified as a thing, not as agent" (Haraway 1991, 199). Haraway points out, "Accounts of such objects can seem to be either appropriations of a fixed and determined world reduced to resource for the instrumentalist projects of destructive Western societies, or they can be seen as masks for interests, usually dominating interests" (Haraway, 1991, 197).

It is the experience of many women and other subjugated people that the pure "objects" of scientific knowledge are just the ones that have functioned as means of surveillance and domination in their own lives. Further, it is because they are this particular kind of object, the silent objects of scientific scrutiny, that there is little recourse against them. They are what constitute the truth within the dominant form of discourse. For example, the technology of genetic engineering, with its objects of genome and enzyme, attempts to give us a fixed definition of organic normality and disease, even within an increasingly abnormal genetic and social environment, which the practice itself helps to constitute via its powerful technology.

In speaking of her study of primatology, Haraway says, "[T]heories are accounts of and for specific kinds of lives" (1989, 8). Feminist philosopher of science Evelyn Fox Keller claims that "somewhere in the project of genetics there is already contained not only the possibility, but the expectation, of eugenics, just as the anticipation of explosive power is somewhere contained in the project of nuclear physics" (Keller 1992, 77). It is important, in fact vital, for us to understand how some of the stories told by science about the world could be "true" stories, and empowering stories as well, and how they might enhance the meaning of other equally true stories and serve as vehicles for emancipatory change.

In the two sections that follow, I will examine first Dewey's and then Haraway's views of objectivity and the "objects" of scientific inquiry in order to begin to understand how they might help construct a pragmatic ecology of the object.

Dewey's Object: The End of Inquiry

In rejecting the dualisms of object and subject, mind and world, Dewey struggled to express himself through a language in which those distinctions are built in. For his pragmatic objectivity, the knower is in the world; knowing is a natural process. His or her knowledge of the world arises in active involvement with the environment. Knowing is always an interaction, a doing. It is not a mere state, or to use Dewey's words, "a kodak fixation" (Dewey [1908] 1977, 129). His metaphors of knowing are richly organic. "Knowledge, like the growth of a plant and the movement of the earth, is a mode of interaction; but it is a mode which renders other modes luminous, important, valuable, capable of direction, causes being translated into means and effects into consequences" (Dewey [1925] 1988, 435). Thus knowledge is not achieved by withdrawing from the world, but by participating in it. In explicating Dewey's view, Raymond Boisvert claims, "Humans (not mere knowers) are participants in the general scheme of things. They are not subjects contemplating objects from a posture of detachment. Practice thus becomes the most accurate expression of the relationship of humans to their enveloping world" (Boisvert 1989, 180–81).

For Dewey, the scientific object is the end of an inquiry, which is both its aim and its completion. It is an achievement of meaning. For him, meaning is what the mind, the word, and the world have in common. He says, "The name object will be reserved for subject-matter so far as it has been produced and ordered and in settled form by means of inquiry; proleptically, objects are the objective of inquiry" (Dewey [1938] 1986, 122). An object of knowledge is not some thing encountered in its immediacy. In fact, such an encountered thing is "had," not known. It is enjoyed or suffered and may constitute the beginning of inquiry. A known object, in contrast, is a work. The known object is an answer to an interrogation of the environment. It is the result of a history of interaction between the inquirer and the world that began from within the context of a problematic situation, a situation in which meanings are initially unstable. In fact, it is this instability that calls for thought. Any trivial thing may "swell and swell, if it bothers us. . . . The immediately precarious, the point of greatest immediate need, defines the apex of consciousness" (Dewey [1925] 1988, 236). Thus an object of knowledge for Dewey is thoroughly historical and dynamic. It arises and is constituted by a temporal interaction between the community of inquiry and the subject matter. Dewey tells us that an object "is a set of qualities treated as potentialities for specified existential consequences. . . . A piece of iron is now a sign of many things of which it was not once a sign. . . . The greater the number of interactions, of operations, and of consequences, the more complex is the constitution of a given substantial object" (Dewey [1938] 1986, 132). Thus each object has (is) a history of interaction. It is this history of interaction that constitutes its substantial existence and simultaneously our knowledge of it. For Dewey, an object is always contextual. "An object or event is always a special part, phase or aspect, of an environing experienced world—a situation. The singular object stands out conspicuously because of its especially focal and crucial position at a given time in determination of some problem of use or enjoyment that the total complex environment presents. There is always a field in which observation of this or that object or event occurs" (Dewey [1938] 1986, 72–73).

Dewey has refused the demand for a distinction between the real qualities of things, their primary qualities, and those that are mere projections, secondary qualities. He says, "If we recognize that all qualities directly had in conscious experience apart from use made of them, testify to nature's characterization by immediacy and finality, there is ground for unsophisticated recognition of use and enjoyment of things as natural, as belonging to the things as well as to us. Things are beautiful and ugly, lovely and hateful, dull and illuminating, attractive and repulsive. Stir and thrill in us is as much theirs as are length and breath and thickness" (Dewey [1925] 1988, 91).

He distinguishes the existents immediately suffered or had in experience from the scientific object. The latter he tells us is an instrument, a tool. Scientific objects such as the quark or the gene are nature in its instrumental character, "the bald and dry" objects of mathematico-mechanical systems. Like refined ore, they are purified and rarified to those characteristics that allow us to make stable connections with other things (Dewey [1925] 1988, 109). On first reading, this characterization of the scientific object might give us pause. Is Dewey positing the object of science as a stable reality behind the natural appearance of things? He explicitly denies this. The objects of science are not metaphysical rivals to ordinary experience. The final objects of experience for Dewey are the ends or fulfillments of natural histories. The scientific object is a tool or a means to just those fulfillments. It is "an order of relationship which serves as a tool to effect immediate having and being" (Dewey [1925] 1988, 110). "To link the things which are immediately and apparitionally had with one another by means of what is not immediately apparent and thus to create new historic successions with new initiations and new endings depends in turn upon the system of mathematical-mechanical systems which form the proper objects of science as such" (Dewey [1925] 1988, 112).

The objects of physics function to weave together otherwise discon-nected beginnings and endings into a consecutive history. He claims that to treat the object of physics as a complete and self-sufficient object is to burden ourselves with an unnecessary and insoluble problem. This gives us a new way of thinking about the bald and dry objects of scientific thought. They are ways of getting a handle on things. It is through them that we gain the ability to "take hold of things right end up" (Dewey [1908] 1977, 130). They are refined instruments for the exploration of meaning. In the end they lead us to the ultimate human good, shared experience. In his emphasis on the centrality of shared experience, Dewey makes the connection between the knowledge that arises in in-quiry and the shared life of a community, a pluralistic community of multiple voices where nonetheless experience is shareable.

For the nonpragmatic objectivist, the worry is that Dewey courts and succumbs to idealism in his characterization of the scientific object. If the objects of science are "mere" tools to human ends, are they then totally mind-dependent creations? I agree with Boisvert that this is to misread Dewey and to miss the power of his interpretation. Boisvert says that for Dewey, "[t]here is no object out there waiting for a subject in here to contemplate its inner being. There are, rather, participants involved in varied kinds of interactions, with their surroundings" (Boisvert 1989, 182).

A mind, for Dewey, is not something separate from the world that must come into conformity to it in the process of objective inquiry. It is only when consciousness is taken as something separated from nature that knowing is a mystery. " When consciousness is connected with na-ture, the mystery becomes a luminous revelation of the operative inter-penetration in nature of the efficient and the fulfilling" (Dewey [1925] 1988, 265). It is not that the inquiring mind and nature never corre-spond. Rather, that is exactly what they do in a more literal sense. Fur-thermore, the response that takes us "off the track . . . is, existentially speaking, perfectly real, [but] is not *good* reality" (Dewey [1908] 1977, 136). We are looking for certain kinds of objects, for the real objects we can get somewhere with. They must be objects we can trust. These are what Dewey calls "sincere things." This is the "good reality" we are after in experience. It should not surprise us that Dewey's objects have a moral dimension, since they are interactions, changes. They are features of interactions of a certain sort. That knowledge makes a difference in reality does not deny its objectivity. "[C]hange in environment made by knowing is not a total or miraculous change. Transformation, readjustment, reconstruction, all imply prior existences: existences which have characters and behaviors of their own which must be accepted, consulted, humored, manipulated or made light of, in all kinds of differing ways in the different contexts of different problems" (Dewey [1908] 1977, 141).

The challenge to a pragmatic objectivity is to make clear that scientific objects are not "fictions" or "instrumental" in a positivistic sense, mere means for prediction and control. For example, the "gene" is certainly something real. It has been a successful mode of participation in the world for almost a hundred years. But the gene as an object of knowledge is dynamic and historical. What it means within experience and how it has funded experience has evolved. It is a way of taking up certain aspects of the human environment that have a history and a beginning. It is not just about natural history. It is itself a natural history interwoven with others. It is one of what Dewey calls "nature's affairs." The gene as a weaving of consciousness and nature is a way of trying to bring consciousness home. As such, it can also go astray. Knowledge signifies events "so discriminately penetrated by thought that mind is literally at home in them" (Dewey [1925] 1988, 128).

For Dewey, seeing an object, like the gene, as some fixed entity whose real structure is first discovered and then applied to human needs is courting disaster. It seems that Dewey's understanding of the scientific object is organic in a literal sense. It is a means, but a means as an organ is a means. It is a way of taking up the problematic objects of ordinary experience and rendering them usable in the achievement of ends to which they are organically connected. The separation of means (the instrumental) from ends (the final) is constitutive of the problem of experience itself for Dewey. This is so because where instrument and end are not part of a continuous process, the problem that initiated inquiry is not solved. Bare physical and brute relationships have not been brought into connections with meaning that are characteristic of the possibilities of nature. The natural end of the objective process is that "we [come to] live on the human plane, responding to things in their meaning." This means that we do not merely suffer experience; rather, experience is "charged with meaning" in which we understand things in terms of their histories and futures. Thus, the end of scientific inquiry for Dewey, that for which it is the organ, is to make of this world a home for consciousness (Dewey [1925] 1988, 128). As Thomas Alexander points out, to miss what Dewey means by use and the instrumental is to miss the point of his whole philosophy (Alexander 1987, 199). Use in his pragmatism is not mere instrumentality, but the use of appropriate tools for meeting the most characteristic human need, the expansion of meaning. Yet the feeling that has become most pervasive, as science becomes more and more powerful in its capacity to affect and control the natural world via atomic physics and molecular biology, is not one of the growth of meaning and connection, but of alienation and fear.

Although Dewey's admiration for science is obvious, his worries about its practice come from the possibility of the separation of the potent scientific object from its end for experience. Science is the difficult work we must do to make experience genuinely meaningful. If science is practiced in such a manner that the scientific object is not an organ to that end then science can become purely and simply a mode of domination for a consciousness that is less and less at home in this world. Genuine science is the intelligent use of the stable in things in the service of the enjoyment of the contingent and the precarious.

Dewey's object can be seen to have three historical stages, stages that are never merely sequential, but constantly interwoven and recurrent. The first is the natural entity as it is had in primary experience. This is the experience that is like that of the young child, the pure having of qualitative experience. "Existences are not given to experience. Their giveness is experience" (Dewey [1938] 1986, 509). Such experience is not cognitive. It becomes so only through the work of scientific inquiry. The scientific object is a refinement of the initial situated interaction, refined in order to take advantage of the stable within it. In doing this we must leave its qualitative immediacy, give up having it for the moment, in the interest of making it a means of connecting it with other things. Boisvert contrasts the Aristotelian view that the highest form of knowledge is theoretical and lies in contemplation and Dewey's view with its emphasis on knowledge that is a kind of making, a techne (Boisvert 1988, 102–3). This making is instrumental to a further end. The end of this

project is to have events filled with meaning. This last stage of the objective process Dewey, claims is, art. Science is for the service of art. In the
end, the scientific object is an object that can speak with its own voice.
It is an aesthetic object. It is the ultimate means of shared experience
and thus it is a home for consciousness. Dewey claims, "Thought, intelligence, science is the intentional direction of natural events to meanings
capable of immediate possession and enjoyment: this direction—which
is operative art—is itself a natural event in which nature otherwise partial
and incomplete comes fully to itself; so that objects of conscious experience when reflectively chosen, form the 'end' of nature" (Dewey [1925]
1988, 269).

The aesthetic object for Dewey is not a cognitive object in the sense
that the refined scientific object is. Nevertheless, it is not devoid of
knowledge. It is the experience that intelligent consciousness makes possible wherein "the contingent and ongoing no longer work at cross purposes with the formal and the recurrent but commingle in harmony"
(Dewey [1925] 1988, 269).

Donna Haraway's Object: The Coding Trickster

A central part of the feminist epistemological project has been to articulate just the kind of nondualistic, nonabsolutist view of natural objectivity that I have explicated earlier. As I mentioned at the outset, feminist
thought has a deep suspicion of the "object" of nonpragmatic objectivism. Feminism has a long-standing suspicion of nature as it has been
thematized by science as a mode of determination and suppression in
relationship to female experience and powers. The world given to women
and Third World peoples through scientific discourse is often an alien
world that, for them, does not constitute an organ of shared experience.
While welcoming the debunking of objectivism by the social constructiv-
ists and postmodernists, feminist positions have tended to "let science
be science," and remained cynical about natural knowledge except as
technology. Donna Haraway is clear that this is not a safe option. She
claims that feminists have "allowed our distance from science and technology to lead us to misunderstand the status and function of natural
knowledge. We have accepted at face value the traditional liberal ideology of social scientists in the twentieth century that maintains a deep

and necessary split between nature and culture," and in doing that we have allowed that "natural knowledge is reincorporated covertly into techniques of social control instead of being transformed into sciences of liberation" (Haraway, 1991, 8).

It is clear to Haraway that our need for a new object for scientific objectivity is a practical and urgent need. She says that we need a science that is not built on the object/subject split that has functioned in legitimating domination. It is interesting to note that Haraway begins her book on reinventing nature with the statement that " 'nature' and 'experience' [are] two of the most potent and ambiguous words in English" (Haraway 1991, 1). On this she and Dewey are obviously of one mind.

For Haraway as for Dewey, science is inherently about meanings. For both, objectivity is situated knowing that is of necessity perspectival. This stands the traditional view of objectivity on its head. To be objective, for Haraway, is to "be somewhere in particular." Thus it involves "mobile positioning" and "passionate detachment." To be objective is to be locatable and thus responsible for how one comes to see. Objectivity cannot be the dream of the transcendent intellect, a view from nowhere. Such a neutral perspective would constitute no view at all. Haraway points out that the "active" vision of modern scientific optical instrumentation, the visualizing of the world exemplified in the electron microscope or the camera in the rocket, are always partial ways of organizing the world. "These technologies are ways of life, social orders, practices of visualizations" (Haraway 1991, 194). She points out that the vital questions, How to see? Where to see from? What to see for? Whom to see with? are suppressed by the view that the object of scientific knowledge is what it is independently of how we come to see it and to what purpose. For Haraway, the object is always historical. She says that objectivity cannot be about fixed vision simply because "what is to count as an object is precisely what world history turns out to be about" (Haraway 1991, 195).

Haraway fills out this idea of historicity in her exploration of the object of the biological sciences as it changes form from the pre–World War II "organism-to-be-managed" to the post–World War II, postcommunication revolution that views nature as "cybernetic system." On this latter view, "Nature is structured as a series of interlocking cybernetic systems, which are theorized as communications problems." With the advent of sociobiology, molecular genetics, with its metaphors derived from information theory, became the central level of meaning of objectivity in biology. The organism is taken as an expression of the encoded messages in the gene. The population or society becomes, for Richard Dawkins (1982) or E. O. Wilson (1975), replicatory strategies for reproducing, a mechanism for investment to maximize genetic profit in the next generation. These objects of the life sciences allow biology to become an engineering science, "a science that studies system design, with an eye to human-mediated improvement of potentially outmoded natural control systems" (Haraway 1991, 65). Control systems to what end? Since nature and human scientific activity still stand separately in this objective structure, to an engineering strategy there are no moral limits. As Haraway sees it, this objective strategy constitutes "a capitalist and patriarchal analysis of nature which requires domination, but in a very innovative form" (1991, 67). Haraway claims that we have the science we have made historically. Thus it is possible to choose different modes of interactions with the world, which would constitute a different form of knowledge. In fact, Haraway claims that we have a responsibility to do just that. She says that "natural history—and its offspring, the biological sciences—has been a discipline based on scarcity. Nature, including human nature, has been theorized and constructed on the basis of scarcity and competition." She goes on to say, " I do not know what life science would be like if the historical structure of our lives minimized domination. . . . basic knowledge would reflect and reproduce the new world, just as it has participated in maintaining the old" (Haraway 1991, 68). Perhaps, to use Dewey's language, the objects we are engaging are not ones we can trust.

Her insight is a genuinely pragmatic one. Our knowledge of the world is what it is within the context of certain forms of human relationships. It is always a situated knowledge. Communities of inquiry give rise to forms of knowledge that are reflective of the forms of life within them. Sociobiology is a reflection of a capitalistic and patriarchal form of life funded by scarcity. If the forms of life are hierarchical and competitive, the objects that are their "objective" will be mirrors of that social life and function to reproduce it. It is the denial of that connection between the subjective and social existences of the inquirer and the existence of the objects within experience that Haraway claims forms "the anti-liberation core of knowledge and practice in our sciences" (Haraway 1991, 8).

Thus, ways of seeing objects are ways of being in the world, ways of life. As with Dewey, we must find a defense against the charge that Haraway's objects are not real natural objects because they are the "result" of a rather complicated interaction with the world rather than a simple mirroring of it as it is in itself. Like Dewey's objects, they have a moral and political dimension. For Haraway the world that is encountered in the process of inquiry is not only always embedded in the context of a situation, but it is also an active entity within that situation. Rather than being the passive object open to the innocent exploitative gaze of the objective mind, the world is responsive to various forms of address. The world can be induced to speak. Haraway uses an image of nature as witty agent, as the coyote or trickster of the native American Southwest. This image she suggests can show us how we might give up the idea of control as the goal and validation of objectivity and seek a form of fidelity, "knowing all the while we will be hoodwinked." Scientific objects are not merely ideological constructs. They are, says Haraway, "material-semiotic generative nodes" (1991, 208). In a recent book with an E-mail address for a title she claims, "Objects like the fetus, chip/computer, gene, race, ecosystem, brain, database, and bomb are stem cells of the technoscientific body. Each of these curious objects is a recent construct or material-semiotic 'object of knowledge,' forged by heterogeneous practices in the furnace of technoscience. To be a construct does not mean to be unreal. . . . Out of each of these nodes or stem cells, sticky threads lead to every nook and cranny of the world" (Haraway 1997, 129).

So for her as for Dewey, an object of scientific knowledge is dynamic, historical. It is a tool for generating new meaningful connections between things. Haraway says that "bodies, minds and tools" have a lot in common. Scientific objectivity is not about distanced stances for making discoveries about preexisting objects. But this does not mean that the gene or the virus is some "ghostly fantasy." They are rather more or less effective ways in which we have learned to correspond with a real world that is a "coding trickster" (Haraway 1991, 209). Haraway and Dewey invite elements both of humor and enjoyment into the notion of objectivity.

Both Dewey's object and Haraway's witty agent revise the old object of objective thought in a way that enlivens it. I would like to connect this last image of nature as "witty agent" with Dewey's view of the object in a way that will be useful in approaching an ecology of the object in the last section of this essay. As for Haraway, the object for Dewey has an "animate" characteristic. Nature and our experience of it are dramatic. Our knowledge is something that happens in the world. It is an important way in which the world changes. Meanings are not something in peoples' heads. But peoples' "heads" are, nonetheless, in the world. Meanings are modes of natural interaction for Dewey. He says that they are primarily properties of behaviors and secondarily of objects (Dewey [1925] 1988,

141). Meanings thus arise within the world and are not imposed on it. Just as does Haraway, Dewey claims that the meaning of a word is a sign of something in common between persons and an object. It signifies a community of partaking ([1925] 1988, 145). This animistic talk, Dewey explains, does not refer to some mental properties existing independently in natural objects (any more than our consciousness is something existing independently in us). Rather, such aspects of things arise because of certain kinds of interaction with them. In labeling them, giving them names, we call forth an answer from them. Knowing an object is a way of giving that thing a voice. Such objects are "more lifelike, than were antecedent states of natural existence" (Dewey [1925] 1988, 286). He says of using language to discriminate the traits of things: "This "objectification" is not a miraculous ejection from the organism or soul into external things, or an illusory attribution of psychical entities to physical things. The qualities never were 'in' the organism; they always were qualities of interactions in which both extra-organic thing and organism partake" (Dewey [1925] 1988, 198).

V. The Ecology of the Object

Dewey's ontology is modeled on post-Darwinian biology (Boisvert 1989, 183). Haraway's ontology takes seriously the information-theory biology of the late twentieth century. Both have what can be called an ecological view of the object of the natural sciences. If one takes seriously the liberating refusal of the subject-object split and refuses as well the dangerous dichotomy, dangerous from both Dewey's and Haraway's perspectives, between the pure and applied sciences, then knowing and experience can be seen as happenings within nature. Haraway would no doubt want us to deconstruct/reconstruct the category of nature, to make meanings that are more effective for our lives. This seems a necessary project, but one that need not take Haraway's postmodern condition as a given. Dewey points out that all the epistemological quandaries generated from within traditional philosophy might be sidestepped if one paid serious note to the fact that consciousness arises in this world, not in general. We are not, he says, like "little gods" outside of "nature." And thus it seems obvious that mind is attuned to its environment in such a manner that knowing is one of its fundamental activities. "The world is the subject-matter for mind because mind has developed in that world" (Dewey [1925] 1988, 221). He tells us that we are "about something, and it is well to know what we are about" ([1925] 1988, 29). What seems implausible is that the mind and subjective experience should have come into existence in a world with which it had nothing in common. Dewey says, "When intellectual experience and its material are taken to be primary, the cord that binds experience and nature is cut. That the physiological organism with its structures, whether in man or in the lower animals, is concerned with making adaptations and uses of material in the interest of maintenance of the life-process, cannot be denied" (Dewey [1925] 1988, 29).

Dewey never meant to "naturalize" epistemology in the reductive manner of many contemporary evolutionary epistemologists (Hull 1989; Campbell 1974). These philosophers are still trying to salvage the old empiricism by defining knowledge as a natural product of a deterministic sort. For Dewey, scientific understanding allows for something new, something more than the mere undergoing of experience of some animals. It is a way of taking experience in hand to the end of enriching it. Instead of the merely having of objects in experience, scientific inquiry allows for the connections that might make those havings intelligent and not merely enjoyed or suffered. It would allow us to enter consciously into their histories. Thus scientific objects are ecological objects in a literal sense. They are objects by which we attempt to render the world a home, *oikos*, for consciousness, by the way of understanding. In being historically wrought modes of interaction, they may serve better or worse in that function.

Haraway says that what we need is "an account of radical historical contingency for all knowledge claims and knowing subjects, a critical practice for recognizing our own 'semiotic technologies' for making meanings, *and* a no-nonsense commitment to faithful accounts of a 'real' world, one that can be partially shared and friendly to earth-wide projects of finite freedom, adequate material abundance, modest meaning in suffering, and limited happiness" (Haraway 1991, 187).

It is tempting to analogize the forms of understanding embodied in the scientific entities, described by Dewey and Haraway, to environmental niches. Haraway prefers the metaphors of cybernetics and embryology: cyborgs and stem cells. I wonder if a switch in the form of the narrative to that of ecology might take us on a different tack, one closer to home and more democratically accessible. If we follow biologist R. C. Lewontin (1982) in his view of the organism-environment relationship the analogy may be genuinely helpful. He claims that traditional Darwinian thought has taken the environment as a prestructured given to which organisms must adapt, just as post-Cartesian thought has taken material reality to be a fixed mind-independent realm. Thus environments begin as something preexisting and alien to the organism to which they must adapt. In fact, Lewontin tells us, one can never describe an environment without reference to an organism, nor can one give a coherent description of an organism totally out of the environmental context within which it has evolved. Organisms are not forms that are passively fashioned by the environment. The relationship between organism and environment is dialectical. The environment becomes an environment for an organism partly because of the changes in that environment resulting from the organism's presence. The stream becomes a fishing pond through the activity of the beaver. The forked tree branch becomes a support for a nest, the field of grasses a source of building supplies. These are all real possibilities that take on environmental meanings only in the presence of organisms of certain kinds. And equally, the organism becomes this organism partly because of the changes brought on by its interactions with a particular environment. The moth grows darker in color after a few generations of living in an industrial, smoggy environment. The chimpanzee gets smart and learns to use a stick as a tool in the presence of termite feasts unreachable with fingers. The organism and the environment mutually intend one another, in the sense of giving each other meaning. What is a hoof or hand but a living response to an environment of a certain sort? There is nothing mysterious in this, but perhaps something wonderful. They are just instances of what Dewey calls nature's affairs. Everything that happens is an interaction, and there is never a "passive" side to a genuine interaction. Both sides must be changed.

Yet humans, who are in some ways the most environment affecting of all organisms, struggle not to see their own intellectual work as part of the environment that they have participated in making and that in turn makes them. In our accepting Dewey's and Haraway's view of the scientific object, it becomes very important to understand more clearly how scientific objects are really natural objects. We have the science we make, and that making occurs within nature. The theoretical connections of scientific practices weave us into the world in a particular way. Taking the gene as the primary object of scientific connection for understanding fetal development and organic disease and for defining human individuality leads us to have certain kinds of lives. It leads to certain kinds of changes in what is. Haraway points out that the present project to map the human genome is part of our attempt to make a meaningful object of the organic individual. "An act of canonization to make the theorists of the humanities pause, the standard reference work called the human genome would be the means through which human diversity and its pathologies could be tamed in the exhaustive code kept by the national and international genetic bureau of standards. . . . Access to this standard of 'man' will be a matter of international financial, patent, and similar struggles" (Haraway 1991, 215).

Haraway helps us see that other types of lives are possible if connections undisclosed or even forbidden within our current "objectivity" were engaged. For her, scientific objects are material-semiotic generative nodes. "Their boundaries materialize in social interaction; 'objects' like bodies do not pre-exist as such. Scientific objectivity (the siting/sighting of objects) is not about dis-engaged discovery, but about mutual and usually unequal structuring, about taking risks" (Haraway 1991, 208).

The kind of risks Haraway wants us to take are disconcerting to say the least, but they might be ones Dewey would find just the kind we need to get on with what we are about. She suggests that we let go of the boundary, not only between nature and culture, but also between human and machine. She suggests that the high-tech culture has challenged dualisms in a new way. "It is not clear who makes and who is made in the relation between humans and machine" (Haraway 1991, 177). She wants to take the technological "in" and recognize that it is already us. She wants us to get friendly with our tools. We are already, she claims, cyborgs, hybrids, chimeras, in both an organic and an inorganic sense. She asks us to give up dreams of organic holism supported by genetic identity and immune system defense mechanisms against non-self and to fray the boundaries in all directions. And we might ask whether this fraying must not be done with thoughtful caution. There are reasons to maintain a pragmatic ecologist's eye on the scene.

We must engage in a form of knowing or a network of knowledges that allows for translation among very different kinds of communities, and not just human communities and not only within the self-consciously postmodern mind. "We need the power of modern critical theories of how meanings and bodies get made, not to deny meanings and bodies but in order to live in meanings and bodies that have a chance for a future" (Haraway 1991, 187). And finally, as Dewey tells us, we must minister to "the unfinished processes of existence so that frail goods shall be substantiated, secure goods be extended, and the precarious promises of good that haunt experienced things be liberally fulfilled" (Dewey [1925] 1988, 68). If we are going to fray, we also had better learn how to weave. There is a world outside my window in which sycamore trees promise fragrance, the peppery aroma of their species. It is a good that is woven securely into my experience, my interactions in the world. It is a secure good that might be enriched and deepened by an understanding of the tree's peculiar chemistry, not as neutral information, but as further and potent connections within experience.

References

Alexander, Thomas M. 1987. *John Dewey's Theory of Art, Experience, and Nature: The Horizons of Feeling.* Albany: State University of New York Press.

Boisvert, Raymond. 1988. *Dewey's Metaphysics.* New York: Fordham University Press.

———. 1989. "Rorty, Dewey, and Post-modern Metaphysics," *Southern Journal of Philosophy* 27:173–93.

Campbell, Donald. 1974. "Evolutionary Epistemology." In *The Philosophy of Karl Popper,* edited by Paul Schilpp. La Salle, Ill.: Open Court.

Churchland, Paul. M. [1979] 1986. *Scientific Realism and the Plasticity of Mind.* Cambridge: Cambridge University Press.

Dawkins, Richard. 1982. *The Extended Phenotype: The Gene as the Unit of Selection.* Oxford: Oxford University Press.

Dewey, John. [1908] 1977. "Does Reality Possess Practical Character?" In *The Middle Works.* Vol. 4. Edited by Jo Ann Boydston. Carbondale: Southern Illinois University Press, 125–42.

———. [1925] 1988. *Experience and Nature.* Vol. 1 of *The Later Works.* Edited by Jo Ann Boydston. Carbondale: Southern Illinois University Press.

———. [1938] 1986. *Logic: The Theory of Inquiry.* Vol. 12 of *The Later Works.* Edited by Jo Ann Boydston. Carbondale: Southern Illinois University Press.

Haraway, Donna. 1989. *Primate Visions: Gender, Race, and Nature in the World of Modern Science.* New York: Routledge Press.

———. 1991. *Simian, Cyborgs, and Women: The Reinvention of Nature.* New York: Routledge.

———. 1997. *ModestWitness@SecondMillennium.FemaleMan©MeetsOncoMouse™.* New York: Routledge.

Hull, David. 1989. *Science as Process.* Chicago: University of Chicago Press.

Keller, Evelyn Fox. 1992. *Secrets of Life, Secrets of Death: Essays on Language, Gender, and Science.* New York: Routledge Press.

Lewontin Richard. 1982. "Organism and Environment." In *Learning, Development, and Culture,* edited by H. C. Plotkin. New York: John Wiley and Sons.

Popper, Karl. 1972. *Objective Knowledge: An Evolutionary Approach.* Oxford: Clarendon Press.

Putnam, Hilary. 1987. *The Many Faces of Realism.* La Salle, Ill.: Open Court.

van Fraassen, Bas. 1980. *The Scientific Image.* Oxford: Clarendon.

Wilson, E. O. 1975. *Sociobiology: The New Synthesis.* Cambridge: Harvard University Press.

10

The Need for Truth

Toward a Pragmatist-Feminist Standpoint Theory

Shannon Sullivan

Because of the located, perspectival corporeality of all human knowers, the objectivist claim that objectivity is attained when humans know the world as impartial, neutral observers is extremely problematic. In the wake of deconstructions of objectivism, however, many have worried that the only remaining epistemological position is judgmental relativism.

This essay is a modified version of chapter 6 of my *Living Across and Through Skins: Transactional Bodies, Pragmatism, and Feminism* (Bloomington: Indiana University Press, 2001). My thanks go to Phillip McReynolds, Del McWhorter, Charlene Haddock Seigfried, and Dee Mortensen for their suggestions on earlier drafts of the essay and chapter.

Given the importance of both the recognition of human situatedness and the need for epistemological standards, it is crucial that deconstruction of traditional notions is followed by reconstruction of a new ideal of objectivity. If feminists and pragmatists deconstruct objectivity without providing a subsequent reconstruction of standards of judgment, we risk reinforcing the conclusion that no alternative to objectivism exists but relativism. If we avoid a discussion of how we might make distinctions between various perspectives, we offer no resources for undermining the false dilemma between the two epistemological positions. In that way, we leave the dilemma, and thus our choices in the face of it, intact. Admittedly, moving "beyond objectivism and relativism"[1] may seem to imply a paradox, since it requires us to acknowledge the importance of objectivity at the same time that we benefit from objectivism's deconstruction. But we need not accept the false dilemma of objectivism and relativism. To move beyond objectivism and relativism, feminists and pragmatists must construct a notion of objectivity that is based upon the many perspectives that constitute human beings as located and embodied knowers.

Sandra Harding's development of feminist standpoint theory offers one of the most significant attempts to reconstruct objectivity in philosophy today. In what follows, I briefly explain Harding's position, concentrating on the three definitions of "strong objectivity" that can be found in her work and the problematic metaphysics of the third and main definition of strong objectivity as "less partial and distorted." While Harding's development of feminist standpoint theory takes pains to distance itself from foundational claims found in earlier versions, her account implicitly relies upon some of those same claims to justify the epistemological privilege given to women's lives. In the second half of this essay, I use Dewey's pragmatism in an attempt to improve the situatedness of feminist standpoint theory and its account of objectivity, sketching the development of a pragmatist-feminist standpoint theory that holds greater promise for leading beyond objectivism and relativism.

Feminist Standpoint Theory

Harding's account of feminist standpoint theory claims that knowledge can be conceived as objective without assuming a disinterested, impersonal "God's eye" point of view only if philosophical, scientific, and other kinds of research start from the perspective of women's lives. Unlike men, whose view of the social relations of our patriarchal society is distorted by their position as "master," women have a privileged perspective on reality because they are marginalized. Their marginalization means that they have less interest in ignoring or remaining oblivious to a society's gender inequalities and thus that their perspective can provide the starting point for accounts of knowledge that are undistorted by gender loyalties (Harding 1986, 191).

Harding (1991, 276) makes a distinction between a standpoint, in which experience is socially mediated through politics and critical inquiry, and a mere perspective, which is provided by unmediated experience. Women's experiences and stories are valuable for what they reveal about a patriarchal social order, but like all human beings, women are shaped by patriarchy and thus can espouse sexist views. For that reason, Harding does not use the mere stories and experiences that constitute women's perspectives to ground her position. The critical standpoint developed out of them anchors it instead. As a critical standpoint, feminist standpoint theory includes standards for judgment and discrimination, which a mere injunction to listen to women does not (Harding 1989, 279; 1991, 286–87; 1993, 54).

Central to Harding's feminist standpoint theory is her concept of strong objectivity. Harding (1993, 150–51) chooses this term to distinguish her conception from traditional notions of objectivity, which, she claims, by drawing from a masculine perspective only are not objective enough. The contrast Harding between her position and objectivism's narrowness of perspective implies that her notion of objectivity is defined as a type of pluralism: a broadening of perspectives so that those other than white, heterosexual, middle-class males are included in the starting point for scientific and other research. Harding herself often suggests that such a pluralism of perspectives is what she means by strong objectivity:

> The goal of maximizing the objectivity of research should require overcoming *excessive* reliance on distinctively masculine lives and making use *also* of women's lives as origins for scientific problematics, sources of scientific evidence, and checks against the validity of knowledge claims. (Harding 1991, 122–23, emphasis added)

> Listening carefully to different voices and attending thoughtfully to others' values and interests can enlarge our vision and begin to correct for inevitable enthnocentrisms [sic]. (152)

For men, the view from women's lives can illuminate their own lives by creating a broader context and contrasting perspective from which to examine critically the institutions and practices within which occur their own beliefs and behaviors, social relations and institutions. (286)

"Pluralist" objectivity, as I will call it, increases objectivity by maximizing the number of different perspectives allowed to contribute to knowledge claims. Its pluralism is what makes Harding's formulation of objectivity stronger than that of objectivism.

Distinct from but related to pluralist objectivity is the second sense of objectivity implied by Harding: objectivity as "background-revealing." According to Harding (1991, 149, 151), to operate under the directive of strong objectivity means also to critically examine one's own position from the viewpoint of another. Becoming objective requires the ability to see the background beliefs that inform one's position, beliefs that are usually so familiar to and thus hidden from oneself that it takes another to help one identify them. Harding's account of strong objectivity recognizes that people—and men, in particular—are not self-transparent and thus they need the perspectives of others to root out the biases that exist in their worldviews. Harding's position thus "starts thought in the perspective from the life of the Other, allowing the Other to gaze back 'shamelessly' at the self who had reserved for himself the right to gaze 'anonymously' at whomever he chooses" (150). In that way, feminist standpoint theory "makes strange what had appeared familiar" (150), that is, makes the very familiarity of a man's perspective seem strange to him.

Background-revealing objectivity is similar to pluralist objectivity in that both require multiple perspectives to maximize objectivity. As developed by Harding, however, background-revealing objectivity goes further than pluralist objectivity in specifying which background assumptions need examination and thus which perspectives are to be listened to so that objectivity is increased. Or, rather, to the extent that pluralism may suggest a judgmental or epistemological relativism in which all perspectives are equally valid, Harding distances herself from pluralism with her definition of objectivity as background-revealing. According to Harding (1991, 152), while "listening carefully to different voices can enlarge our vision," we must take note that "the dominant values, interests, and voices are not among these 'different' ones." The "Other" is not just anyone who occupies a different perspective from one's own. It is the person in a position marginalized by society. Because Western culture is patriarchal, it is the hidden beliefs of patriarchy that have been exempt from critical examination and are in need of exposure. Furthermore, since we have all, Western men and women alike, been shaped by the dominant masculine perspective in Western culture, for each of us, women included, the perspective of the "Other" is the perspective from women's lives. For these reasons, women and men both need to listen to and start from the particular perspective of women.[2]

In addition to revealing hidden background beliefs, starting from the particular perspective of women maximizes objectivity in another distinct, but related, way. Harding implies a third definition of strong objectivity, in which the perspective of marginalized women produces less partial and distorted knowledge than does the view from a dominant, masculine perspective. The definition of objectivity as "less partial and distorted" is distinct from pluralist objectivity because "distorted" is *not* meant by Harding as a synonym of "partial." It is not the case that the masculine perspective is distorted *because* it is partial, as pluralist objectivity could claim. Rather, *apart from* or *in addition to* its partiality, it is also distorted. As Harding (1991, 273) states, "[T]he unselfconscious [masculine] perspective claiming universality is in fact not only partial but also distorting in ways that go beyond it partiality." According to Harding (xi), knowledge generated by starting from women's lives is less partial and distorted than the dominant perspective because research based on women's lives provides "less false" claims to knowledge than does research based on that of men.

This last claim distinguishes Harding's less and partial and distorted objectivity from not only pluralist, but also background-revealing, objectivity. Less partial and distorted objectivity does not merely claim that the perspective from women's lives allows one to highlight background assumptions in one's culture's belief system. It also claims that this perspective provides truer accounts of our world than does the dominant perspective. This does not mean that the perspective from women's lives is completely impartial or undistorted. On Harding's account, all perspectives are partial and distorted by relations of domination. Thus for Harding (1991, 59), there is no Archimedian point of absolute infallibility from which to begin one's account of the world. But Harding (187) argues that just because there is no one true account of the world, one is not then forced to give up attempts to distinguish between more and less false accounts of the world. According to Harding (1987, 83), one can still judge some accounts to be less false than others even though no account is absolutely true.

Harding's argument about "less false" claims is a result of her efforts to combine the postmodern claim that there is no one true story about the world with the feminist need to distinguish between better and worse, sexist and nonsexist accounts of the world. Harding's (1991, 106n) self-described "semi-rapprochement between standpoint and postmodernist tendencies" is motivated by postmodern criticisms of earlier versions of feminist standpoint theory made by those such as Jane Flax and Donna Haraway. Flax (1990, 56) charges feminist standpoint theory with assuming the existence of "a reality that is out there waiting for our representation" and that "the oppressed have a privileged (and not just different) relation and ability to comprehend" it. Likewise, Haraway criticizes feminist standpoint theory for relying upon the dual notion of a reality capable of accurate reflection and a feminist standpoint that is pure and innocent enough to produce such reflection (McCaughey 1993, 77). And indeed, early versions of feminist standpoint theory, such as that of Nancy Hartsock, made these very assumptions, if not explicit claims, when arguing that a metaphysical hierarchy of activity explains women's privileged location. Adopting Marx's distinctions between dual levels of reality, Hartsock (1983, 288) claims that "reality itself consists of 'sensuous human activity, practice.'" Unlike men's work, the work of women is immersed in concrete, sensuous, material processes, and so knowledge developed from women's activity is more closely linked to reality and thus is able "to go beneath the surface of appearances to reveal the real but concealed social relations" (304). Because of the emphasis it gives to the particular material activity of maternity, Hartsock's account suggests that men could never inhabit an epistemologically privileged perspective as well as women, if they could inhabit it at all, because they could never be as fully embedded in material activity as women.

By rejecting the claim that "our 'best' representations of the world are transparent to the world—that is, are true," Harding (1991, 185) attempts to distance herself from notions of truth as faithful mirroring of the world. Harding asserts that her position does not need to maintain that claims made from women's perspectives are true, that is, transparently represent the world independently of human beings. All her position needs, she claims, is a criterion of less falsity in which all claims are admittedly distorted and thus not true representations of the world, but in which some claims can be shown to represent the world in a less false manner. Along these lines, Harding (1992, 586, 587) thus rhetorically asks, "But once the idea of absolute falsity also [in addition to absolute truth] becomes indefensible, what could be the use of the concept of truth? The notion [of truth] is inextricably linked to objectivism and its absolutist standards. . . . Who needs truth in science? Only those who are still wedded to the neutrality ideal."

Harding's move from a criterion of absolute truth to one of less falsity does not, however, distance her from foundational notions of truth as faithful mirroring, as she had hoped. Just as the question "What makes something true?" needs explanation, so does the question "What makes something less false than another thing?" The shift from absolute truth or falsity to degrees of truth or falsity does not eliminate Harding's dependence upon and need for an account of what truth is.[3] Because Harding does not explicitly develop a notion of truth as something other than mirroring reality, she implicitly relies upon the very same notion to justify why women's perspectives are less false than those of men. Her claim that some perspectives, such as those of women, do so better than others, such as those of men, and thus are less false is able to function only by means of the standard of transparency supplied by an account of truth as faithful mirroring. Since for Harding, *distorted* is not a mere synonym for *partial*, describing claims as more or less distorted implies that her position judges various perspectives on their greater or lesser ability to clearly present the world. Harding's claim that no perspective can represent the world completely and accurately does not diminish the fact that the standard by which greater and lesser degrees of representation are measured remains that of truth as mirroring reality.

Continued reliance in Harding's work upon a foundational ideal of truth as mirroring is evident in much of the language she uses to describe the advantages of feminist standpoint theory, as well. Sounding much like Hartsock, Harding (1991, 126, 127) claims that research starting from women's lives will provide us with "clearer and more nearly complete visions of social reality" and that feminist struggles can allow us to "begin to see beneath the appearances created by an unjust social order to the reality of how this social order is in fact constructed and maintained." The problematic distinction between dual levels of reality and the troubling dependence upon a material hierarchy that functioned in early versions of feminist standpoint theory continues to operate in Harding's mature development of her position. Rather than disrupt the dichotomy between absolute truth and falsity, Harding's appeal to a criterion of "less false" merely locates her claims between them (Hekman 1997a, 354).

The problem with Harding's continued reliance upon hierarchies of truth and falsity is not only its dependence upon foundational metaphysics and epistemology, per se. More important, such reliance merely reverses the traditional, unjustified metaphysical privileging of a male perspective over a female one. As Daniel Conway (1993, 121; 1997, 9) has suggested, such a reversal risks being "an inverted, matriarchal version of patriarchal objectivity" that merely replaces the patriarchal "god-trick" with a "goddess-trick" of Harding's own design. Without an alternate account of what truth is, appeal to women's perspectives as "less false" is just as arbitrary and problematic as is a sexist culture's assumption that a masculine perspective should be privileged over a feminine one. Even when made with the good intention of pointing out what reality is really like for women, such appeals do not eliminate the oppressive effects of the claim to have a truer view of reality than another (Seigfried 1996, 152). Harding resists providing an alternative account of truth because she erroneously assumes that truth can only mean what traditional philosophy has said it does. But truth is not necessarily tied to objectivism and absolutism, and thus it is not the case that only those who are wed to the neutrality ideal need truth. Feminist standpoint theory needs an alternative account of truth precisely so that it can divorce itself from the neutrality ideal and the type of epistemic justification that it allegedly provides.

My suggestion that Harding's work needs an alternative account of truth does not misconstrue the aims and purposes of feminist standpoint theory as epistemological, as opposed to the political. Harding has expressed this concern when summing up the aims of her standpoint theory in response to her readers. Replying to criticisms of her reliance upon a concept of "true reality," Harding (1997, 382) has insisted that feminist standpoint theory concerns "relations of power and knowledge" and thus is distorted when it is characterized as a project "of figuring out how to justify the truth of feminist claims to more accurate accounts of reality." Precisely because politics and epistemology are inseparable but not identical, however, feminist standpoint theory must not flinch from the fact that it is and should be in the business of providing epistemic justification. This does not mean that epistemic justification must be conceived traditionally. It can be conceived in a variety of different ways, and how feminists should conceive it is precisely what is at issue here. Epistemic justification is crucial to Harding's position because only with it can feminist standpoint theory avoid merely "preaching to the choir" and inadvertently supporting the relativism it wants to avoid.[4] Without epistemic justification, Harding's account has no response to the nonpersuaded who might ask, "Why start with women's lives if I have sexist rather than feminist sympathies?" And without a response, Harding cannot avoid playing into a judgmental relativism that claims, "You have your political commitments and thus your starting point for research, I have mine, and there is no basis on which you can claim yours is better than mine."

Harding (1991, 218–48) seems to recognize this problem and the corresponding need for epistemic justification in her discussion of conflicting First and Third World perspectives on the role and effects of modern science and technology. As she claims in that context, "Given the different frameworks of the two stories" about Western science, "defenders of each [story] can claim that the other is partial and distorted" (239). But while Harding acknowledges that "what is needed [are] . . . standards competent to distinguish between" the stories, she is only able to respond to that need with the admission that "at present, it is difficult to locate such standards" (239). The inability to provide such standards is an effect of Harding's continued reliance upon foundational notions of truth. This inability severely jeopardizes, if not completely undermines, feminist standpoint theory, including its attempt to provide an account of knowledge that is both objective and situated in women's lives. Feminist standpoint theory must pay further attention to the epistemic justification for starting with women's lives it offers through its criterion of the "less false." Only by explicitly providing an account of truth that is not based on mirroring reality can it provide justification for its starting point of women's lives that does not implicitly appeal to representational accounts of reality. Precisely so that feminist standpoint theory can avoid being a project of justification by means of appeal to a true reality, it must focus on the issue of truth.

Pragmatic Truth

The nonfoundational standards for justification and the alternative account of truth needed by feminist standpoint theory can be found in the pragmatism of John Dewey. My choice of Dewey as a partner for feminist epistemology may seem ironic, since Dewey argues that philosophy is not primarily a way of gaining knowledge but a way to make life more rich and meaningful. Because Dewey's pragmatism puts epistemology and its standards to work in the service of life, however, it can provide feminist standpoint theory with nonfoundational justification for its emphasis upon women's lives.

Much of philosophy, including much that claims to eschew epistemology,[5] continues to operate with a definition of truth as perfectly mirroring a reality divorced from human experience. This concept of truth admittedly often seems satisfactory, if only because it is so deeply ingrained in philosophical explanations. The problem with a definition of truth as that which corresponds to reality, however, is that it fails to acknowledge that in human experience truth claims are not used merely to describe states of affairs, nor are they useful for mere description of existing facts. Knowledge and truth have the purpose of putting existing facts and events to use in the transformation of the world. In contrast to much of traditional philosophy, Dewey's pragmatism recognizes the connection of knowledge to life and thus puts truth to work in service of human existence by defining it as that which produces "the richest and fullest experience possible" (Dewey [1925] 1988, 308). In this way, Dewey radically transforms traditional philosophy's ideas of knowledge and truth.

According to Dewey ([1925] 1988, 307), philosophy's "proper task" is that "of liberating and clarifying meanings" in human life. This view of philosophy leads Dewey ([1908] 1977, 138n) to redefine many traditional philosophical concepts so that they are saved from "that species of intellectual lock-jaw called [traditional] epistemology." Knowledge continues to play an important role in Dewey's philosophy, but its role is that of a means for reorganizing experience, not that of cataloguing data or constructing systems of abstract knowledge. For Dewey, knowing is not something human beings do merely for its own sake, but rather for the sake of securing the changes that they wish to effect in the world. Knowledge is the result not of perfect mirroring, but of a method of experimental inquiry in which people investigate the problems with which they are confronted in order to develop possible solutions to them that are then tested in experience to see if the desired results occur (Dewey [1910b] 1985, 236–41). By defining knowledge in this way, Dewey's pragmatism transforms knowing from being a passive recording of the features of the world to being a way that people guide their participation in the world.

Like knowledge, the concept of truth needs reconceptualization so that it is seen as a judgment of the success of attempts to reorganize experience. Dewey ([1911] 1985, 67) argues that "truth, in the final analysis, is the statement of things 'as they are,' not as they are in the inane and desolate void of isolation from human concern, but as they are in a shared and progressive experience." A judgment or belief is true not if it matches the state of affairs it attempts to report, but rather if, when acted on, it produces the transformation of experience that was desired by those engaged in that experience. In that way, truth refers to the future career of a judgment and, in particular, the ability of that judgment to effect an improved transaction between living beings and their environments. Truth must pass the test of experience. Claims to truth are not to be considered true until "tested in the satisfaction of the most intimate and comprehensive of human needs" (66). When considering the truth of a claim, one is not asking whether it mirrors reality, but instead whether it satisfies desires and needs. While the specifics of what those needs are will and should vary based on the particular situation in question, the fundamental value guiding the ends-in-view in the situation is that of satisfaction. Only those ends that have passed the test of the satisfaction of needs and desires of those in question are ones that count as true. (Precisely whose needs and desires are in question is an issue to which I shall return later.) While Dewey's philosophy is instrumental in that it focuses on the means by which one might achieve one's desired ends, it is not viciously instrumental, because it includes a critique of ends as well—not just any end is satisfactory, on Dewey's account.

In addition to serving as the broad end that shapes the specific ends to be attained in specific problematic situations, satisfaction in experience also plays an important role in the initial identification of a situation as problematic. Lack of satisfaction indicates why a situation is troubling and thus in need of inquiry so that it might be transformed. Admittedly, the specifics of why a situation is unsatisfactory will vary depending on the particular situation, but the lack of satisfaction, broadly speaking, is what spurs one to experimentally inquire into a situation in the first place. By relating the need for knowledge to the concept of satisfaction, Dewey's philosophy thus connects epistemology to the problems experienced in everyday life, explaining how felt difficulties in life, and not the problems of academic epistemology, are to generate the problems of knowledge into which one inquires.

Given the importance of satisfaction to Dewey's account of truth, it is crucial to recognize that when Dewey speaks of "satisfaction," he does so in a rich sense of flourishing that is not reducible to a utilitarian definition of happiness as the maximization of pleasure. Happiness or satisfaction in a quasi-utilitarian or crudely instrumental sense is inadequate, since, in Dewey's ([1922] 1988, 202) words, "to 'make others happy' except through liberating their power and engaging them in activities that enlarge the meaning of life is to harm them." The quality of human experience is composed not merely of its agreeableness, but more important of its promotion of continuing growth and further expansion of experience, which often involves unpleasantness and pain (Dewey [1938] 1991, 13, 19). Something becomes true when it encourages flourishing, which is to say that it becomes true when it promotes the liberation of powers, the enlargement of life's meaning, and the growth of experience through enriched transactions with the world.

A word or two about the concept of experience as used by Dewey is also in order. The term does not refer merely to human experience, since the test of experience that truth must pass involves more than just human life. Or, rather, because of Dewey's concept of the self as transactional, human experience always already involves more than human beings considered as isolated from their environments and the other living organisms that populate them. Truth can be achieved only through transaction with one's environments, since there is no self apart from the world in which it exists. As Dewey ([1925] 1988, 324) claims, "If man is within nature, not a little god outside . . . , interaction is the one inescapable trait of every human concern." Human beings are not set apart from an independent reality as detached spectators, but are always already participants in a world that is in part shaped by them. The transactional relationship between humans and their various environments means that Dewey's definition of truth as transactional flourishing necessarily includes the flourishing of those other than humans, for example, animals, plants, soil, and other components of the nonhuman environment.[6] All human activity, as well as any satisfaction found in it, is a matter of mutual transformation of the self and its world, human and nonhuman alike.

At the same time that Dewey includes the nonhuman, however, he often makes statements of the sort that claims to truth should not be considered true until "tested in the satisfaction of the most intimate and comprehensive of human needs" (Dewey [1911] 1985, 66; see also [1925] 1988, 331). In that his claim is that truth is a matter of satisfaction in the here and now of this world, rather than the otherworldly, his point is well taken. In his attempts to steer his readers away from an objectivist notion of truth, however, Dewey risks overemphasizing human organisms at the expense of nonhuman ones. While Dewey's emphasis on human needs should be heard in the context in which it was intended, it remains too strong. This is especially true in his ([1926] 1988) writings on animal experimentation. Pragmatist feminism requires more explicit inclusion of the needs of nonhuman needs and interests than Dewey tends to provide.

In addition, when what are at issue are human needs in particular, pragmatist feminism requires more explicit focus on the question of who counts as human than Dewey tends to offer. Women of all races, men of color, lesbians and gay men, and people with physical and mental disabilities are just some of the human beings who historically have been and currently often are discounted as not being fully human. The reconceptualization of truth as transactional flourishing not only must include the ideal of maximum inclusion of various human and nonhuman organisms' needs, interests, and desires. It also must include a historical awareness of who is likely to be left out of the attempt to produce richer experiences. In addition, it must include a contemporary awareness of who actually is being left out in the particular situation in question. Awareness of exclusion should be funded with historically based, general guidelines that help one identify likely habits of exclusion and oppression. At the same time, it should gear those guidelines to specific situations, since patterns of inclusion and exclusion can be particular to and thus vary in specific situations. Of course, such guidelines cannot ensure that habits of exclusion and oppression will be identified and corrected for in all situations, since no ironclad guarantees are possible in a world populated by fallible, embodied knowers. The point here is not to engage in the quest for certainty, but to attempt to expand awareness of past patterns of exclusion to improve the chances of increased inclusion in the present and future.

The co-constitution and co-transformation of humans and their environments means that Dewey's account of truth is not a correspondence theory. On the occasions he uses the word *correspondence* in connection with his account, Dewey does so not in the sense of mirroring reality, as the correspondence theory of truth does. Rather, he uses the word "in the sense in which two friends correspond, that is, interact as checks, as stimuli, as mutual aids and mutual correctors" (Dewey [1911] 1985, 45). Truth occurs when humans and their environments respond to and transact with one another in such a way that flourishing is achieved for both humans and their environments. As Dewey ([1910a] 1985, 10) claims, "What the pragmatist does [with her account of truth] is to insist that the human factor must work itself out in *cooperation* with the environmental factor, and that their coadaptation *is* both 'correspondence' and 'satisfaction.' " Pragmatism thus does not agree with traditional philosophy that truth is a matter of humans' "fitting" their beliefs to the world. Truth is not a matter of matching internal representations to external reality; rather it is a mutual negotiation and transformation of a relationship between humans and their environments that promotes the thriving of both.[7]

An important implication of the transactional nature of both the self and truth is that Dewey's account of pragmatic truth does not deny a "reality" that at times objects to human purposes or requires people to modify their beliefs and plans. By tying truth to human interests, needs, satisfactions, and purposes, Dewey has not turned truth into a hollow standard in which "anything goes" because everything is "merely subjective." Such concerns reflect the operation of a dichotomy of objective and subjective that the pragmatist rejects with her account of transaction: "Once [we] recognize the human factor [in truth] . . . , pragmatism is at hand to insist that the believer must accept the full consequences of his beliefs, and that his beliefs must be tried out, through acting upon them, to discover what is their meaning or consequence. Till so tested, [the pragmatist] insists that beliefs, no matter how noble and seemingly edifying, are dogmas, not truths" (Dewey [1910a] 1985, 10–11, emphasis in original).

Because they are intimately connected to human need and human transaction with an ever changing world, truths are neither timeless nor unchanging. They are historically and temporally situated, capable of revision based on the changing needs of the particular human and nonhuman beings in question. In addition, the fact that situations change means that our truths are not just capable of, but often in need of, transformation. Pragmatism not only supports the idea of change in truth; it also morally obliges people to reexamine and update their truths if they no longer serve the interests for which they were designed. This obligation does not mean that pragmatism endorses a Cartesian razing of all established beliefs. As pragmatists have long argued, it is not possible for us to reject all our currently accepted truths at once (Seigfried 1992, 153). Doubt is not universal. It is specific to particular problematic situations. The need to critically examine and revise various truths arises from them, producing context-dependent inquiry that transforms accepted truth piece by piece, situation by situation.

Just as truths are not timeless or unchanging, neither are the selves whose interests, desires, and needs truth involves. In the attempt to transform a problematic situation, one transforms not just the situation, but the selves formed through transaction in it as well. Desires and interests are constitutive of the self in that when one attempts to change a situation so as to provide greater satisfaction, one not only changes the situation but also changes oneself through its transformation. Dewey ([1932] 1989, 296) puts the relationship of self and desire well when he says that "[a] self changes its structure and its value according to the kind of object which it desires and seeks; according, that is, to the different kinds of objects in which active interest is taken." As a result, to pursue a particular desire through the transformation of experience is to pursue a particular self. The self is always in the process of remaking itself, and in doing so, it becomes what it desires (Garrison 1997). Both the self and its desires and interests change as a result of inquiry, which means that the truths one pursues, that is, the satisfaction of desires and enriching of experiences that one attempts to achieve, must continually change as well.

The appeal of Dewey's pragmatic notion of truth is that it allows for distinctions between better and worse claims without appeal to a foundationalist notion of truth as faithful mirroring. As Charlene Haddock Seigfried (1992, 144) has claimed, pragmatism's originality may be said to consist precisely in its ability to "demonstrat[e] that true appearances can be distinguished from false ones without one's ever appealing to a reality hidden beneath appearances." With Dewey's pragmatism, claims can be judged to be true or false based on the degree to which they promote flourishing in and through transactions with the world, not on the degree of their transparency to reality. Dewey replaces traditional Western philosophy's appeal to mirroring with a method of experimental inquiry. That method allows one to arrive at historical, socially situated, fallible, *and* warranted truths that have been tested in experience for their ability to promote flourishing. In this way, pragmatic truth leads beyond objectivism and relativism. One can reject the false dilemma of having either absolute truth or a complete inability to make epistemological judgments, as well as the false dilemma of our having either the rigor of "objective," impersonal standards or the "anything goes" of mere "subjective," biased pseudostandards. Dewey's method of experimental inquiry and emphasis on transactional flourishing provide standards for objectivity that are situated in human existence and not located in an extrahistorical or presocial realm.

Toward a Pragmatist-Feminist Standpoint Theory

Complementing feminist standpoint theory with Dewey's pragmatism creates what I will call a pragmatist-feminist standpoint theory. Such a theory helps feminists move away from questions about which standpoint describes reality in less distorting ways, to questions about which standpoints can help promote flourishing transactions. The shift away from foundational justifications for beginning with women's rather than men's lives does not sacrifice the ability to make judgments about better and worse starting points. A pragmatist-feminist standpoint theory allows one to make those judgments on contextual instead of absolute grounds. This shift is important because it allows standpoint theory to avoid merely endorsing the reverse side of the same sexist coin that claimed privilege for a masculine perspective.

The move away from foundational metaphysics is also important because it allows standpoint theory to better focus on the otherwise hidden question, Who is the "we" deciding upon "our" goals and, more to the point, what if "we" do not agree? Harding's account of feminist standpoint theory can provide an answer as long as the question is understood to be one of conflict between homogenous feminine and masculine perspectives. Harding apparently resolves oppositions between conflicting standpoints and their goals by assigning metaphysical priority to women's description of reality, and thus also to the goals generated from it. Aside from the problematic implications of priority, Harding's position becomes even more difficult once she no longer essentializes women (or men) and instead acknowledges the complexity of all subject positions. Once multiple marginalized standpoints and thus multiple liberatory projects are involved, it is not clear how feminist standpoint theory can handle conflicting claims of liberatory epistemologies. As critics of Harding (McCaughey 1993, 78; Pinnick 1994, 656) have pointed out, her position never resolves the problem of conflict and has no answer to this question other than the thin suggestion that one welcome this tension as a source of creativity.

Dewey's pragmatism is better equipped to handle such tension and to use it as a source of creativity. There is no need to appeal to true(r) descriptions of reality to resolve opposition between conflicting claims. Indeed, such an appeal tends to shut people with perceived "less true" perspectives out of the conversations and communities needed to resolve conflict. Instead of declaring at the outset that some people have "less false" perspectives, all parties in a problematic situation should have a voice in the project of creating perhaps as yet unforeseen solutions that accommodate the needs and encourage the flourishing of all the parties involved. Dewey's answer to the question of who gets to resolve conflicting claims about what counts as flourishing, as well as conflicting answers to the question, Flourishing for whom? is, in a significant sense, "everyone." Those in both the so-called center and margins need to be involved in the process of resolving opposition. This process must take into account the needs of all "locations," not just the needs of the marginalized groups at the expense of the dominating one(s) or vice versa.[8]

This is not to claim that including all relevant parties, or even determining who the various parties in an issue are will be an easy or, ultimately, successful project. Nor is it to claim that all parties have the same sort of access to or power within the rhetorical and physical spaces that delimit whose voices are heard (Code 1995). But is to claim that radical inclusion should be the ideal toward which feminists, pragmatists, and others work, even if they fall short of it. Indeed, it should be a working ideal even if one necessarily falls short of it due to the exclusions that seem inevitable in the process of securing space for greater inclusion (Butler 1993, 193). I have in mind here the example of the seeming necessity to exclude members of violent white supremacist groups from public space for the purpose of broadening it to include black, Latino, and Native persons and other people of color. Like all cultural spaces, spaces of radical democratic inclusion are constituted by vectors of power and thus paradoxically might require exclusion as a condition for the possibility of their existence. Yet the possibility of the practical necessity of such types of exclusion does not invalidate the ideal of always seeking to be as inclusive in one's dealing as possible. Nor does it warrant an a priori declaration that exclusion of those who themselves exclude is necessary. In some problematic situations, this may be so, but in others not. Each particular situation must be examined for what it requires to maximize inclusion.

The possibility and power of radical inclusion is well illustrated by

Daryl Davis (1998), a black man who has spent years seeking to understand and combat racism by pursuing conversations with, attending ral-
lies and marches of, and even developing friendships with members of
the Ku Klux Klan. Many people in general, and probably most black
people in particular, see the Klan as a group that must be excluded from
the polis to secure the inclusion of black people. Rather than dismiss,
avoid, or attempt to silence Klan members, however, Davis listened to
their views on the world even though they often angered him. He did
not attack or badger them with his own, different views, but instead
ventured his opinions only after a level of trust and common ground
between the Klan members and himself had been established. The result
of Davis's transactions with the Klan was not just an improved understanding of the Klan's racism. Nor was it merely the unexpected discovery
of some similar beliefs and commitments between Klan members and
himself, or the development of friendships, one of which resulted in
Davis' becoming the godfather of the daughter of the Imperial Wizard of
the Ku Klux Klan. It also was a change in opinion about black people on
the part of some Klan members, occasionally accompanied by their quit-
ting the Klan altogether.

This transformation occurred because even though he vehemently dis-
agreed with them, Davis was willing to treat Klan members as people who
are potentially worthy of respect, honesty, and fair treatment. He included those who seemed most deserving of exclusion and his gesture of
goodwill transformed the lives of some members of the Klan. Of course,
Davis's example does not mean that the ideal of radical inclusion can be
put into practice in every situation. Davis did not get along with every
Klan member he met, and his book is not intended as a how-to manual
for fighting racism. What Davis's life demonstrates is the importance of
the ideal of radical inclusion as a guide for practice. It also shows how
inclusion can sometimes be extended in beneficial ways beyond that
which currently seems conceivable or possible. The ideal of inclusion
needs to be one in which as many people as possible struggle over what
counts as a satisfactory resolution of a problematic situation, such as that
of racial conflict, even if the ideal cannot always be put into practice.

The reason that everyone must be involved in such struggles, both
ideally and as far as can be accomplished practically, is that the self is
not atomistic. Because the self is transactional, everyone's capacity to
flourish affects and is affected by every other one in the society. To adopt
an agricultural metaphor, since the "soil" that each of us "grows" in is

shared by others in the society, the more everyone in the society thrives, the more any individual self is able to thrive. To neglect the needs of any group is to deprive all groups of a crucial condition for the possibility of their flourishing.[9]

To emphasize here the needs of the dominating group(s) is not to claim that because resolution of conflicting perspectives must include perspectives from men's lives as well as those of women, such resolution must include sexist as well as nonsexist components. Conceiving of the dialogue between perspectives in this way is to base one's conception on an atomistic notion of the perspectives involved. The transactional nature of the self means that the meanings of claims put forward, as well as the solutions that may be generated from them are not the private property of their originators, but are jointly constructed with others.[10] It thus entails what Lorraine Code (1995, 55) has called a "resourceful" skepticism, which is not a denial of all claims but a wariness of hasty conclusions and a readiness to reconsider one's own proposals. With Dewey's pragmatism, dialogue with another becomes a process of mutual transformation effected by experimental inquiry and in which claims are offered as hypotheses that are open to modification by the other.

A further implication of the transactional nature of the self is not only that everyone *should* be, but also that everyone *is* involved to some degree in the mutual process of creating solutions, even if that involvement takes the form of ignoring or refusing to listen to another. The needs of both dominating and dominated are at issue and part of any solution any time there is conflict. Recognizing this fact shifts the focus of one's epistemological projects in a positive way. The question is never one of whether everyone is to be involved or not, but whether everyone will be involved in ways that either promote or limit their flourishing. That is, the choice is not whether to include certain people and their perspectives, but whether to include them by conceiving of their various needs in a static, isolated way that demands rejecting one person's needs for that of another, or by means of a creative solution that incorporates all needs through their mutual transformation.

On a pragmatist-feminist account, such mutual transformation is welcome, rather than troublesome, because no party is self-transparent and thus all parties need one another to help them see themselves. The insistence upon mutual transformation suggests that a pragmatist-feminist standpoint theory differs from Harding's position by emphasizing more strongly the self-opacity of all people. Harding's account of feminist standpoint theory rightfully stresses the lack of self-transparency on the part of the dominating, in her claim that marginalized perspectives are needed to uncover hidden assumptions that the dominating cannot see. But Harding implies that self-opacity is relatively one-sided, that it is much more characteristic of the dominant than the marginalized perspective. In its claim that the projects developed from women's lives are less partial and distorted, Harding's standpoint theory implies that someone speaking from a feminist standpoint has relatively little need for the help of others in seeing the hidden assumptions and background beliefs of her own position. While it does not promise absolute infallibility, feminist standpoint theory claims to provide the most certain foundation available and thus discourages context-sensitive questions about the benefits of beginning with women's lives. A pragmatist-feminist standpoint theory, in contrast, holds open the possibility that all perspectives and standpoints may be in need of transformation through dialogue with another. Operating with a thoroughgoing fallibilism, a pragmatist-feminist standpoint theory assumes that no perspective or standpoint is self-transparent. Even someone speaking from a feminist standpoint—as well as a pragmatist-feminist standpoint—may have problematic, hidden assumptions that she cannot see on her own and thus needs others to help her uncover.

Because pragmatism's appeal to experience does not treat experience as a transparent, self-evident ground for epistemological claims, a pragmatist-feminist standpoint that draws on Dewey's epistemology does not treat the category of experience foundationally.[11] Dewey's rejection of the privatization of experience means that no one person can claim absolute authority for her experience and the perspective generated from it. This does not mean that a woman's perspective is necessarily false. It instead means that, like men's perspectives, women's perspectives are finite and capable of revision based on reflective interpretations of it, provided by women and men alike (Seigfried 1996, 153). One can and should affirm the distinctiveness of women's perspectives from those of men at the same time that one acknowledges the need for the transaction of many different perspectives to counter the limitation of each of them (213).

Another reason that pragmatism's treatment of experience is not foundational is that the process of experimental inquiry transforms the initial experience that presented itself as problematic. The experience with which we begin our inquiry is not the same one with which inquiry concludes. The experience that is modified by inquiry and action, not the initial experience itself, serves as a testing ground for the truthfulness of attempted changes to a problematic experience. Pragmatists do not treat experience as a static, infallible foundation on which to base knowledge. By distinguishing between the experiences that initiate inquiry and the transformed experiences that are the result of it, a person can both acknowledge the reality and importance of her experiences and critique her initial understandings and conceptions of them (Seigfried 1996, 154). In this way, pragmatism recognizes and validates our experiences without relativizing or uncritically accepting them. On this approach, women's experiences do not have to be used as a starting point only. Their experiences as transformed by inquiry also can be used as a testing point for the value of the changes made to a situation.

To this point, I have emphasized the needed transformations of feminist standpoint theory that Dewey can help effect, but feminism has important contributions to make to pragmatism as well. While everyone may need to be involved in creating solutions to conflict through mutual transformation, Harding suggests that such creativity is more likely to come from a marginalized than from a dominant point of view, since the former offers a fresh perspective. If one is genuinely concerned about the flourishing of all, one should tend to start one's projects from the view of women's, rather than men's, lives. Feminist standpoint theory provides a compelling further reason to do so: Western culture has a long history of dominant perspectives' silencing marginal perspectives by attempting to speak for them or claiming to know what is best for them. To help increase the likelihood not only that they are allowed to speak but that they are heard, marginalized rather than dominant perspectives should tend to be the first place to which a pragmatist-feminist standpoint theory turns and on which it focuses in its search for solutions to problematic situations.

By including the words *tend to* in a pragmatist-feminist injunction to start from women's lives, this injunction, like all pragmatist-feminist injunctions, is a working hypothesis, a general guideline with which to direct inquiry. It is not an inviolable rule or directive that can never admit of exception. Its appropriateness will vary in different situations. The fruitfulness of working with this guideline will be tested and retested in every experience and situation to which it is applied, and it is always open to modification based on future experience. The past flourishing produced by use of this guideline has established its truth, but that truth is historical, contextual, and flexible and may change if experience shows the need for its revision. In this way, a pragmatist-feminist standpoint theory urges philosophers and others to begin from women's lives, because doing so currently is the best working hypothesis for producing the flourishing of all. But it also cautions them not to treat that hypothesis as an unquestionable rule. They—we—should remain open to the changes in and improvements of the injunction to start with women's lives that future experience may suggest.

Conclusion

Implicit in the preceding sketch of a pragmatist-feminist standpoint theory is the suggestion that we tease out the pragmatist elements of Harding's position.[12] While Harding's account of feminist standpoint theory, and its third definition of objectivity as less partial and distorted in particular, suffers from dependence upon a problematic definition of truth as mirroring reality, other sides of her position complement pragmatist-feminist standpoint theory. Harding's notion of objectivity as pluralistic is a valuable resource. Although Harding attempts to distance herself from pluralism, worried that it necessarily entails judgmental relativism, the broadening of perspectives is an important goal recognized by both Harding and pragmatist feminism. And since Dewey's pluralism does not entail a lack of criteria with which to make distinctions between better and worse reconfigurations of our sexist culture, pluralism is a key component in a reconstructed notion of objectivity.

Additional pragmatist strains in Harding's work make her position even more amenable to pragmatism. While the tone of her work often suggests that the injunction to start from the lives of the oppressed need not be questioned by feminists, Harding (1991, 142, 144) says at one point that one needs "to determine which social situations tend to generate the most objective knowledge claims" and that "some [social values and interests] have systematically generated less partial and distorted beliefs than others." When she does so, she indicates that her injunction is a flexible guideline that is to be relied upon not because of an unquestionable faith in it, but because of the fruitful results of doing so to this point. In addition, Harding's description of the type of claims provided by science, and by extension feminist standpoint theory, agrees with Dewey's account of truth as flexible, nondogmatic, and ever changing. When Harding (1997, 387) claims that "scientific claims are supposed to be held not as true but, only provisionally, as 'least false' until counter-evidence or a new conceptual framework no longer provides them with the status of 'less false' than those against which they have been tested," she describes science in a way that complements Dewey's notion of truth as hypothetical. Because she continues to operate with a notion of truth as mirroring reality, Harding (387) insists that "science never gets us truth," but with Dewey's (re)definition of truth one might say that her description of science demonstrates precisely how truth is always a matter of working hypotheses.

Intersecting Harding's feminist standpoint theory with Dewey's pragmatism helps feminists better achieve Harding's goal of reconstructing objectivity. A pragmatist-feminist standpoint theory will not, however, provide easy answers to questions about how to deal with the complex problems that erupt in a post-Enlightenment world. Broadening the number of viewpoints that are to be included in the processes of negotiating human flourishing makes these processes more complicated than does Harding's feminist standpoint theory. But the ability to make theories messy is an asset, not a liability, of Dewey's pragmatism. Tempting though they may be, overly tidy answers usually only gloss over the difficulties that must be dealt with if any meaningful improvements to lived experience are to be made. By enabling feminist standpoint theory to shift away from a criterion of distortion to a criterion of transactional flourishing, Dewey's pragmatism eliminates the comfortable security that a claim to a clearer vision of reality offers. Rather than provide such comfort, it demands the hard work of negotiating a satisfactory solution to social, political, and other problems, including even those who are in part responsible for those very problems.

Notes

1. I take this phrase from Bernstein (1983), who gives an excellent account of the false dilemma in question but stops short of the work of constructing this "beyond" itself.

2. This allows Harding to deflect Donna Haraway's criticism of her version of feminist standpoint theory that it assumes the oppressed are somehow "innocent," that is, untouched by the oppressive society they live in (McCaughey 1993, 77). A more serious problem arises as a result, however, as Susan Hekman notes: if the perspective of the oppressed is admittedly distorted by oppression, then it can no better provide a valid starting point for epistemology than can that of the oppressor (McCaughey 1993, 77). This problem is related to the foundational ideal of truth that

continues to function in Harding's position, an issue that will be discussed in more detail in the following section.

3. Thus Tannoch-Bland (1997, 171n) misses the central thrust of Conway's (1993) criticism of Harding in her response to him. While Tannoch-Bland is correct that Harding claims that the oppressed can help us gain not a completely pure, but a purer picture of the world, Conway remains right that this claim still operates with a notion of pure truth as its standard for objectivity.

4. McCaughey (1993, 77–78) also notes that without something other than political grounds for privileging women's claims, feminist standpoint theory collapses into relativism. If Conway (1993, 116, 122) is right that Donna Haraway offers only political grounds for the support of her postmodern feminist epistemology, then Haraway's project is likewise in danger of such collapse. Contra Conway (1993, 114, 122), feminist epistemology should not base itself solely on a political agenda in which politics is separated from epistemology. It needs epistemic justification, albeit not in the sense of "old-style" epistemological legitimacy, the search for which would forever defer feminism's political goals, as Conway (1993, 123) rightly argues.

5. Neopragmatist Richard Rorty must be included in this category. While Rorty (1979) rightfully criticizes the conception of truth as mirroring reality, his response to traditional epistemology is to reject it and substitute for it "conversations" that have no epistemological basis or function. In his very rejection of epistemology, however, Rorty implicitly validates and thus helps sustain a definition of truth as mirroring nature by offering no alternative to it. This is a crucial problem in Rorty's version of pragmatism, which explains my preference for that of Dewey.

6. For some of the implications of pragmatism for environmental philosophy, see Light and Katz 1996.

7. I thus disagree with Tannoch-Bland (1997, 167) when she claims that those redefining objectivity "can still retain a notion of correspondence, or fit with the world." At a minimum, such a redefinition must be accompanied by an account of correspondence alternative to what the tradition has provided. Otherwise, those who are attempting to redefine objectivity leave the "old" definition of correspondence in place and, in doing so, undermine their attempts to transform objectivity by suggesting a return to a definition of truth as mirroring reality.

8. Conway (1993, 117) suggests that Donna Haraway's postmodern feminist epistemology agrees that the standpoint of the oppressor must be included in refashioned notions of objectivity.

9. See Sullivan 1997a for a more detailed explanation of the reasons for Dewey's democratic commitments.

10. I have elsewhere described this process in more detail as one of "hypothetical construction" (Sullivan 1997b and 2001).

11. See Grant 1987 for an overview and critique of the foundational treatment of experience in some feminist philosophy.

12. And those of other standpoint theorists, such as Evelyn Fox Keller, as well. Keller suggests a move toward pragmatism when she explicitly rejects a "copy" theory of truth for the position that "some representations are clearly better (more effective) than others" because of "the practices they facilitate" (Soble, 1994, 522–23). Because she gives only political and not also epistemic reasons for preferring some practices to others, however, she is open to criticism that her criterion of "better" begs the question (523). A pragmatic notion of truth would allow Keller to effectively support her criterion of "better" against those such as Soble, and, just as important, do so without slipping back, as Keller occasionally does, into claims that science includes "maximally reliable (even if not [completely] faithful) representation[s] of nature" (525).

References

Bernstein, Richard J. 1983. *Beyond Objectivism and Relativism: Science, Hermeneutics, and Praxis*. Philadelphia: University of Pennsylvania Press.

Butler, Judith. 1993. *Bodies That Matter: On the Discursive Limits of "Sex."* New York: Routledge.

Code, Lorraine. 1995. *Rhetorical Spaces: Essays on Gendered Locations.* New York: Routledge.

Conway, Daniel W. 1993. *"Das Weib an Sich:* The Slave Revolt in Epistemology." In *Nietzsche, Feminism, and Political Theory,* edited by Paul Patton, 110–29. New York: Routledge.

———. 1997. *"Circulus Vitiosus Deus?* The Dialectical Logic of Feminist Standpoint Theory." *Journal of Social Philosophy* 28 (1): 62–76.

Davis, Daryl. 1998. *Klan-Destine Relationships: A Black Man's Odyssey in the Ku Klux Klan.* Far Hills, N.J.: New Horizon Press.

Dewey, John. [1908] 1977. "Does Reality Possess Practical Character?" In *The Early Works.* Vol. 4. Edited by Jo Ann Boydston, 125–42. Carbondale: Southern Illinois University Press.

———. [1910a] 1985. "A Short Catechism Concerning Truth." In *The Middle Works.* Vol. 6. Edited by Jo Ann Boydston, 3–11. Carbondale: Southern Illinois University Press.

———. [1910b] 1985. *How We Think.* In *The Middle Works.* Vol. 6. Edited by Jo Ann Boydston, 177–356. Carbondale: Southern Illinois University Press.

———. [1911] 1985. "The Problem of Truth." In *The Middle Works.* Vol. 6. Edited by Jo Ann Boydston, 12–68. Carbondale: Southern Illinois University Press.

———. [1922] 1988. *Human Nature and Conduct.* Vol. 14 of *The Middle Works.* Edited by Jo Ann Boydston. Carbondale: Southern Illinois University Press.

———. [1925] 1988. *Experience and Nature.* Vol. 1 of *The Later Works.* Edited by Jo Ann Boydston. Carbondale: Southern Illinois University Press.

———. [1926] 1988. "The Ethics of Animal Experimentation." In *The Later Works.* Vol. 2. Edited by Jo Ann Boydston, 98–103. Carbondale: Southern Illinois University Press.

———. [1932] 1989. *Ethics.* Vol. 7 of *The Later Works.* Edited by Jo Ann Boydston. Carbondale: Southern Illinois University Press.

———. [1934] 1989. *Art as Experience.* Vol. 10 of *The Later Works.* Edited by Jo Ann Boydston. Carbondale: Southern Illinois University Press.

———. [1938] 1991. *Experience and Education.* In *The Later Works.* Vol. 13. Edited by Jo Ann Boydston, 1–62. Carbondale: Southern Illinois University Press.

Flax, Jane. 1990. "Postmodernism and Gender Relations in Feminist Theory." In *Feminism/Postmodernism,* edited by Linda J. Nicholson, 39–62. New York: Routledge.

Garrison, Jim. 1997. *Dewey and Eros: Wisdom and Desire in the Art of Teaching.* New York: Teachers College Press.

Grant, Judith. 1987. "I Feel Therefore I Am: A Critique of Female Experience as the Basis for a Feminist Epistemology." *Women and Politics* 7 (3): 99–114.

Haraway, Donna. 1988. "Situated Knowledges: The Science Question in Feminism and the Privilege of Partial Perspective." *Feminist Studies* 14 (3): 575–99.

Harding, Sandra. 1986. *The Science Question in Feminism.* Ithaca: Cornell University Press.

———. 1989. "How the Women's Movement Benefits Science: Two Views." *Women Studies International Forum* 12 (3): 271–83.

———. 1991. *Whose Science? Whose Knowledge? Thinking from Women's Lives.* Ithaca: Cornell University Press.

———. 1992. "After the Neutrality Ideal: Science, Politics, and 'Strong Objectivity.' " *Social Research* 59 (3): 567–87.

———. 1993. "Rethinking Standpoint Epistemology: 'What Is Strong Objectivity?' " In *Feminist Epistemologies*, edited by Linda Alcoff and Elizabeth Potter, 49–82. New York: Routledge.

———. 1997. "Comment on Hekman's 'Truth and Method: Feminist Standpoint Theory Revisited': Whose Standpoint Needs the Regimes of Truth and Reality?" *Signs: Journal of Women in Culture and Society* 22 (2): 382–91.

Hartsock, Nancy C. M. 1983. "The Feminist Standpoint: Developing the Ground for a Specifically Feminist Historical Materialism." In *Discovering Reality*, edited by Sandra Harding and Merrill B. Hintikka, 283–310. Boston: D. Reidel.

Hekman, Susan. 1997a. "Reply to Hartsock, Collins, Harding, and Smith." *Signs: Journal of Women in Culture and Society* 22 (2): 399–402.

———. 1997b. "Truth and Method: Feminist Standpoint Theory Revisited." *Signs: Journal of Women in Culture and Society* 22 (2): 341–65.

Light, Andrew, and Eric Katz. 1996. *Environmental Pragmatism*. New York: Routledge.

McCaughey, Martha. 1993. "Redirecting Feminist Critiques of Science." *Hypatia* 8 (4): 72–84.

Pinnick, Cassandra L. 1994. "Feminist Epistemology: Implications for Philosophy of Science." *Philosophy of Science* 61:646–57.

Rorty, Richard. 1979. *Philosophy and the Mirror of Nature*. Princeton: Princeton University Press.

Seigfried, Charlene Haddock. 1992. "Like Bridges Without Piers: Beyond the Foundationalist Metaphor." In *Antifoundationalism Old and New*, edited by Tom Rockmore and Beth J. Singer, 143–64. Philadelphia: Temple University Press.

———. 1996. *Pragmatism and Feminism: Reweaving the Social Fabric*. Chicago: University of Chicago Press.

Soble, Alan. 1994. "Gender, Objectivity, and Realism." *Monist* 77 (4): 509–30.

Sullivan, Shannon. 1997a. "Democracy and the Individual: To What Extent Is Dewey's Reconstruction Nietzsche's Self-Overcoming?" *Philosophy Today* 40 (2): 296–308.

———. 1997b. "Domination and Dialogue in Merleau-Ponty's *Phenomenology of Perception*." *Hypatia* 12 (1): 1–19.

———. 2001. *Living Across and Through Skins: Transactional Bodies, Pragmatism, and Feminism*. Bloomington: Indiana University Press.

Tannoch-Bland, Jennifer. 1997. "From Aperspectival Objectivity to Strong Objectivity: The Quest for Moral Objectivity." *Hypatia* 12 (1): 155–78.

Part Five

Social and Political Philosophy

11

How Practical Is John Dewey?

Lisa Heldke

The philosophy which interests me most results from observations anyone can make
every hour of [one's] daily life, and not on those technicalities which can only be
considered by specialists furnished with technical devices. Certain judgments are forced
on [a person] by the situation in which [one] finds [oneself]. The present tendency is to
feel that philosophy should be based on scientific observations.
. . . Shall philosophy start with the common materials near at hand or with the more
abstract intellectual results of thinking? I think that philosophy should start with
common experiences.

> —John Dewey, "A Resume of Four Lectures on Common Sense, Science, and
> Philosophy"

I

Reading this passage, a feminist philosopher just discovering Dewey feels
her heart leap in her chest. "At last," she thinks, as she reads Dewey's

Enormous thanks go to Scott Pratt, who gave me transformatively helpful comments on an earlier
version of this essay. Thanks also to the members of the Feminism and Pragmatism reading group,
which existed for a brief, shining moment in the summer of 1996 at the University of Oregon; to
Felicia Kruse, who commented on an earlier version of it; and to Peg O'Connor, who made comments on the most recent version.

valorization of "common experiences" and "daily life observations," "at last a male figure from the history of Western philosophy who might take 'women's work' seriously. At last a traditional philosopher who might just understand that the daily, routine work women historically have done to maintain human lives from day to day is worthy of philosophical attention—indeed, might be the work from which philosophy ought to originate!"

And to a considerable extent, this feminist philosopher's optimism is well founded. John Dewey stands as an exemplar of the view that philosophy ought to place "common experience," "common materials," and daily activity at its center. He regularly exhorts us to make our theorizing return to the practical problems that launch it.[1] Dewey is seriously committed to reconnecting the practice of philosophy to ordinary concerns—the emotional, intellectual, and practical affairs of daily life. Furthermore, his examples regularly mention activities such as farming, carpentry, and even dishwashing.[2] Thus, while Dewey never gives a precise definition of what he means to include in the realm of "common experience," the feminist philosopher is certainly not leaping to unreasonable conclusions to think that it includes women's work in the home.

Dewey's philosophical project impels a radical rethinking of the way that philosophical attention has been distributed among human endeavors—a distribution that, since Plato, has tended to privilege "head work" to the exclusion of "hand work," theory making to the exclusion of practice. He presents his readers with motive, means, and opportunity to bring the practical and the everyday into the scope of philosophy—to make philosophy genuinely address the "common materials" of everyday life.

However, Dewey did not fully avail himself of the opportunity. As our feminist philosopher reads longer and deeper in Dewey, she becomes struck by the fact that, despite his willingness to use examples drawn from women's—and laboring men's—work, he doesn't seem to *do* all that much with those examples. Dewey's framework argues for making daily life—its subject matters and methods—central to the doing of philosophy. Arguably, it is women in their homes (and in other people's homes) whose lives are most taken up by just this sort of dailiness. Nevertheless, Dewey's philosophical writings tend to leave that daily life on the periphery, the source of useful examples and inspirations, but only examples—not defining, constitutive elements of his theory of inquiry.[3]

That role he reserves for the scientific method—the experimental method. Admittedly, Dewey defines the experimental method very broadly, so that to say that it figures as his chief model of inquiry is not to say that he believes that only the physical sciences can overcome the separation between knowing and doing that has plagued intellectual life since the Greeks. But I would suggest that even his expansive definition of the experimental method could benefit from the incorporation and challenge of other kinds of methods and practices of inquiry, methods drawn from everyday activities such as growing and cooking food. Such methods *may* be reducible to the experimental method—but they may not be best or only understood thus.[4]

Charlene Haddock Seigfried, writing on the relations between pragmatism and feminism, helps illustrate the "something more" I am seeking in Dewey's treatment of everyday activities. She (1966, 146) cites Dewey's clear and powerful assessment of the dualistic thinking of philosophy, which places theory above practice, minds above bodies and constancy above change. She (149) notes, however, that "although Dewey recognized and criticized the dominating dualisms . . . he did not recognize that the hierarchy of the public realms . . . also rested on a gender hierarchy. His language reveals a male bias even as he exposes a bias of classical philosophy when he contrasts the philosophical valorizing of the ideal over 'the world in which men act and live.' " "For all his sensitivity to different angles of vision," Seigfried (169) writes, "Dewey does not finally recognize how much his philosophic perspective derives its strength from the fact that it is a view from a privileged center"—from a privileged male standpoint. This perspective, I suggest, is at least partially responsible for the fact that he took note of women's daily-life activities on the periphery, but did not bring them into the center of philosophic discourse.

Lorraine Code makes a similar point in "Feminists and Pragmatists: A Radical Future?" Code (1998, 23) asks "what feminist epistemologists could gain from making common cause with pragmatists"—particularly with Dewey. In answering this question, she observes that the "legacy" of Dewey's theory of experience is mixed. While Dewey and other pragmatists challenge the separation of facts from values, and theories from practices, they largely fail "to contest the public man/private woman dichotomy that still infects the societies in which pragmatists and feminists devise and enact their theories of knowledge"—a dichotomy, I suggest, that circumscribes the ways in which Dewey can make good on his promise to ground philosophy in common experiences (Code 1998, 25). And while Code (25) agrees that it is inappropriate to call Dewey to task for "failing to think in a conceptual frame that is not of . . . his time," nevertheless "the time-boundedness of a social emancipatory project that overlooks the possibility of emancipating itself from these assumptions also has to be addressed, particularly when its articulator is on record for his openness to innovation [and] experimentalist thinking."

Dewey's philosophy promises to be useful to feminist philosophers interested in thinking about "women's work," manual labor, and other activities traditionally ignored or scorned by philosophers because of their connections with bodies, with temporality, and with practicality. His philosophy suggests that we may be able to understand such work not only as providing relevant illustrations of inquiry (for example), but as the starting point, the source, for models and methods of inquiry. That he does not fully live up to this promise is a fact that does not warrant approbation—but does merit attention.

This essay represents my attempt to press Dewey to be more Deweyan, to challenge him to expand the framework he uses to conceptualize methods of inquiry. In part II, I expand my claim that Dewey's own description of his philosophical project makes it reasonable for us to expect him to make common experiences and practical activities central strands of his theory of inquiry. I note here his valorization of practice and the practical, and also his expansive definition of the experimental method. I also discuss the significant fact that practical activities occupy pride of place in Dewey's educational philosophies, as enterprises aimed at children's intellectual development. Children learn about inquiry by cooking, sewing, working with wood, and so on. But as they mature into adult inquirers, they leave these activities behind, and replace them with (it seems) more "mature" forms of inquiry—science, for example. Why does Dewey sideline these practical activities when he turns to discuss "grownup philosophy?" This question leads me to part III.

In part III, I ask how we might understand Dewey's sidelining of women's work. I suggest that gender as well as class bias, in "benign" forms, are significantly responsible for Dewey's failure to expand the circle of philosophically relevant activities in serious ways. I also suggest that Dewey seems to regard women's work as something that can provide useful insight into inquiry for children, and for cultures early on—but that such work seems to be supplanted by other, theoretically richer, forms of inquiry. As I've already noted, the kinds of practices in which I'm interested are those often labeled women's work—and also slaves', servants', or laborers' work. Such work is the work of "keeping body and soul together," of providing for one's own and others' most basic needs by growing food, cooking, providing nurturance, and so on. Dewey uses various terms to refer to these and other activities; among them are "common sense," "common experience," "practice" and "the practical."⁵ In asking why he leaves the activity of daily life on the periphery, I'm asking why Dewey leaves the sphere of philosophically relevant material organized in a way that systematically marginalizes activities done by people who are themselves marginalized in this culture—particularly women, and also men who are manual workers. I'm also asking why he continues to give fairly limited importance to practices vital to the very being of human being—that are life sustaining in both literal and symbolic senses. Why does Dewey think cooking and woodworking are activities worth investigating when the subject is the education of children, but are only useful as the sources of examples—not sources of methods of intellectual engagement with the world—when we turn to the adult activity of philosophy?

I understand my project in this essay to be in the spirit of John Dewey; I mean to challenge and expand his view in just the ways that he calls for philosophy to do, to be self-critical and reconstructive. It is reasonable to expect a sustained exploration of everyday practical activity from Dewey; such treatment would bring the practical into the scope of philosophy. But while Dewey has not fully undertaken such explorations, he has devised a position that allows us to do so.

II

In this section, I first look at two aspects of Dewey's discussion of experience—namely, his treatment of practice and his understanding of the experimental method—to show why and how his philosophy of experience makes practical activities centrally important, at least in principle. I then look briefly at his philosophy of education and the work of the Dewey School, in which these activities are given pride of place in the curriculum as ways in which children can do inquiry—can engage in intelligent interactions with their environments. The aim of part II is not to construct a watertight argument showing Dewey to be inconsistent or negligent for his treatment of practical, everyday activities. However, it is meant to show why centering such activities would be a natural— and indeed a highly useful—move for him to make, given his philosophical commitments. And it is intended to leave the reader with the sense that, on Dewey's own terms, an explanation for his lack of detailed attention to practical activity *is* in order.[6]

One important element of Dewey's investigation of experience is his analysis of the nature of practice and the practical. Dewey exposes the wrongheadedness of philosophy's traditional neglect of practical activity, its "depreciation of action, of doing and making" ([1929] 1980, 4). Central to Dewey's analysis is his critique of the hierarchical dichotomy of theory and practice. Questions about why theorizing has been separated from practice, and what the consequences of that separation have been, are a recurrent theme in *The Quest for Certainty*, among other works. Throughout this work, Dewey explores the consequences for philosophy of this separation, and of the accompanying elevation of theorizing above practice. He argues for reconciling the separation, and points to experimental science as the endeavor in which the theoretical and practical— knowing and doing—have been most fully integrated.

Dewey also points out that the denigration of practical activity did not originate with philosophy; rather, philosophy provided justification for an attitude already in place.[7] Philosophy has posited that "practical action, as distinct from self-revolving rational self-activity [theorizing], belongs in the realm of generation and decay, a realm inferior in value as in Being" ([1929] 1980, 29). Humans wanted and continue to want perfect certainty. But such certainty is unattainable in one's dealings with practical matters, so philosophy has deemed these matters inferior. This "quest for certainty," ancient though it is, continues to compel us today, motivating the philosophical neglect and denigration of practical activity.

For Dewey, in contrast, theorizing and practice may most usefully be regarded as two forms of practice; in fact, given the way he formulates their relations, it might be appropriate to rename theorizing "thinking about practice," or even "thoughtful practice."[8] Dewey's reconceptualization of the relation between theory and practice brings him to praise science, an activity that has traditionally occupied a position of importance in philosophy. Dewey's praise of science differs, however, in that he focuses not purely on its nature as a theoretical activity, but on the ways in which theory and practice intertwine in it. It is, he suggests, the activity that has most "completely surrendered the separation between knowing and doing" ([1929] 1980, 78–79). For Dewey, the experimental method, as it has been realized in the sciences, stands as a model for how other activities, from ethical decision making to teaching children, can be made more intelligent.

Dewey's definition of the experimental method is expansive enough to encompass all manner of practical activity; we start with the stuff of the ordinary world, and act upon that stuff in a way that allows us to determine how to control the changes it undergoes. Similarly, he (1938b, 104–5) defines inquiry as "the controlled or directed transformation of an indeterminate situation into one that is so determinate in its constituent distinctions and relations as to convert the elements of the original situation into a unified whole."[9]

Other theorists have noted the flexibility and inclusiveness of Dewey's conception of the experimental method. As Robert Westbrook (1991, 141) says, for Dewey, "scientific thinking . . . was but a refinement of the ordinary procedures for fixing belief." And, as John Herman Randall (1991, 82) points out, "Dewey's experimentalism is not primarily based on the method of the laboratory. It is at once the experimentalism of practical common sense, and the coming to self-awareness of the best and most critical techniques and concepts of the social sciences." William Gavin (1980, 22) notes in this regard that "Dewey advocates that the form of [the experimental method], as opposed to any specific content, serve as a model." According to Gavin, characteristics of such a method include its future-orientedness, its interpenetrating use of thought and action, its communal nature, and its capacity for self-correction. Dewey argues for the superiority of an *approach*—not for the superiority of the subject matter of experimental science. Any human enterprise could be treated experimentally in this general sense.[10]

To Dewey, writing early in the twentieth century, it is clear that science is the form of inquiry most successful at developing and implementing the experimental method. But its claim to this achievement is neither exclusive nor guaranteed; this is also clear to him. Its privileged status stems from the fact that scientists are the most successful users of the experimental method—not from anything inherent to the subject matter of the sciences. (However, *something* separates the sciences from commonsense practical activity. Dewey [(1949) 1988, 343] suggests that "commonsense knowing is enmeshed in the individual situation. Scientific knowing liberates itself from the individual situation and its pressing practicality. This liberation does not destroy the practical possibilities of scientific knowing; it is the very source of its practical power.")

It is science to which the experimental method in some sense "belongs"—science, an activity already highly regarded by philosophy as a theory-making enterprise. In making the experimental method the prime example of an activity that undermines the knowing/doing split, does Dewey actually do as much as he could to argue for the importance of practice? While his reconceptualization of science prompts Dewey to *reshape* the way it is categorized by philosophy, it does not impel him to attend to other activities that have been regarded as merely practical and have for that reason remained outside the purview of philosophy. Ought he not also discuss the ways in which foodmaking, farming, child care (and other activities normally regarded *only* as untheoretical practices) could *or do* employ the experimental method? Or how they employ a method that is not experimental, but that offers us insight into how to surrender the separation of knowing and doing?

Dewey's reconception of theory and practice as "kinds of practice" invites us to attend to a whole host of human activities that have long been neglected by philosophy. In undermining the distinction between theory and practice, Dewey gives us reason to overlook the philosophical justifications frequently given for ignoring "practical" activities such as foodmaking and child rearing, and to examine these activities to see what insights they can give us about the methods of inquiry, of thoughtful practice, intelligent activity. What might such examinations unearth? In this essay, I gesture toward an answer to that question; obviously a genuine answer requires a fully fleshed-out discussion of several such activities.[11]

Practical, daily activities—such as caring for a toddler or shopping for and cooking dinner—can give us methodological suggestions for undercutting the dichotomies that have plagued much of Western philosophy. Seigfried (1996, 146) identifies four dichotomies: "(1) the depreciation of doing and making and the overevaluation of pure thinking and reflection, (2) the contempt for bodies and matter and praise of spirit and immateriality, (3) the sharp division between practice and theory, and (4) the inferiority of changing things and events and the superiority of a fixed reality." Daily activities show us how to undercut these dichotomies differently from science at least in part because they are presumed to be on the "other side" of the dichotomies in the first place.

In the case of the first and third dichotomies, science is presumed to be theoretical, and (for at least some sciences) primarily a reflective enterprise, so Dewey must show how it is also practical, by focusing on its experimental nature. Cooking dinner, by contrast, is presumed to be utterly practical, so undercutting the dichotomy requires us to show how it is also theoretical—to show that the practice of foodmaking is indeed a thoughtful practice. Examining cooking gives us an understanding of how theorizing informs practice in an activity that may appear to be simply "rote"—how a bread maker reflects on the dough in order to determine when to add more flour to it. With respect to the second and fourth dichotomies, while it would be ridiculous to suggest that sciences are not concerned with bodies and matter, or that they do not address change over time, it is true that the bodies in which they are interested are "theoretical bodies," and the changes they are interested in are presumed to have stable, measurable, predictable rates. Cooking dinner, however, situates us in a bodily realm in which bodies are anything but generalizable over time (or space): the size of family members' appetites yesterday is no reliable indicator of today's; the bread that rises in two hours in July will take considerably longer in January; and while this tomato is dead-ripe, the one right next to it on the vine has begun to rot.

Explorations of daily activity can also suggest ways to challenge what Dewey calls the "intellectualist fallacy," which separates the world of doing and living (under which category fall the moral, religious, emotional, and aesthetic aspects of life), from the world of knowing. Cooking dinner for one's family is an arena in which the aesthetic and the moral, of necessity, intertwine with knowing. Preparing a meal that looks delicious to everyone, from the picky four-year-old to the eat-anything teenager, balancing one's budgetary constraints with one's desire to avoid factory-farmed meat and vegetables sprayed by insecticide and picked by workers who don't earn minimum wage—the cook must somehow address all these concerns each time she enters the kitchen to make the evening meal.

In one arena, Dewey recognizes the instructive potential of daily activities, namely his philosophy of education, in which he employs cooking and carpentry to introduce children to inquiry. His philosophy of education treats ordinary practices with considerable seriousness. His use of household activities in the education of children assigns those activities an integral role in that education—not "just" as "vocational training," but as tools for intellectual development, for teaching inquiry, as well.

Robert Westbrook (1991, 101) describes Dewey's pedagogy as calling for teachers to reinsert the subject matter of the curriculum into the ordinary experience from which it has been extracted. The task of teachers is to create a situation "in which the present activities of the child would be confronted with problematic situations in which the knowledge and skills of science, history, and art would be required to resolve these difficulties"—that is, to introduce formal inquiry by way of practical problems.

On the Deweyan model, this pedagogical challenge was to be met in the schools in part through the introduction of so-called manual activities. Cooking, sewing, carpentry, and gardening were among the occupations engaged in by children at the "Dewey School"—the Laboratory School at the University of Chicago, directed by Dewey. Dewey describes the function of these manual activities in the curriculum: "[T]he child comes to school to *do;* to cook, to sew, to work with wood and tools in simple constructive acts; *within* and about these acts cluster the studies—writing, reading, arithmetic, etc."[12] Doing and thinking come together for the child in the classroom through the vehicles of familiar, everyday activities.

In saying they come together, I mean to emphasize the fact that for Dewey, the role of manual activities is not (simply) to increase students' dexterity, to entertain them, or to provide them with a marketable skill. Rather, in the Deweyan classroom, such enterprises as gardening, cooking, weaving, and carpentry are the theoretical-and-practical activities through which students' intellectual skills are developed even as their hands develop facility.[13] Furthermore, returning to the matter of the integration of formal knowledge and practical problems, "[t]here is nothing in the elementary study of botany which cannot be introduced in a vital way in connection with caring for the growth of seeds. Instead of the subject matter belonging to a peculiar study called botany, it will then belong to life" ([1916] 1980, 208). Practical activities here function as the loci in which daily life and abstract knowledge come into focus.

When actually carried out in the classroom, such philosophical convictions about the nature of education have a genuinely transformative result—a concrete result manifesting the transformation of the theory/practice dichotomy that Dewey seeks in his writings on experience and inquiry. For example, Susan Laird (1988, 120) notes that at the Laboratory School,

> [s]tudents . . . first experienced science laboratories as classes in cooking: all children learned to experiment as they took part in preparing a weekly luncheon for themselves and guests. . . . Furthermore, the curriculum treated such domestic pursuits—especially cooking and textile arts—along with heavier industrial activities not as mere vocational skills, but actually as highly valued forms of culture, setting them always in the context of historical studies.

The respect for practical activity that Dewey expresses abstractly in his writings on inquiry is clearly and specifically manifested in the organization and work of the school;[14] cooking and sewing are recognized as activities that employ the experimental method, and also as activities that hold an esteemed place in culture, thus warranting serious academic attention. Indeed, Dewey ([1916] 1980, 209–10) suggests that they are the best vehicles with which to introduce children to social life and to the experimental method.

Laird emphasizes that the Laboratory School was fully coeducational; boys and girls learned cooking and carpentry alongside each other, and no activities were restricted to one sex. But it was also coeducational—and cut across class lines as well—on a deeper level, because of its very inclusion of manual activity in the "academic" classroom. "Whereas Plumfield [the school in Louisa May Alcott's *Little Men*] segregated its academic work (in Professor Bhaer's schoolroom) from Jo's playful domestic sphere (everywhere else) . . . the Laboratory School's curriculum actually treated the home as a central concept around which all its play and learning activities were organized, even those in science and history" (1988, 120). The point is not just that little boys got to sew and little girls got to build clubhouses; it is not even that little professors' kids got to sew and build clubhouses. By placing the home at the center of education, the Laboratory School undercut a more deeply ingrained sexism and class bias in education, namely, the schema that places the practical, manual work of women and laborers firmly outside the purview of "intellectual activity" (men's work). Dewey drags the kitchen into the middle of the school, and circles the classrooms around it.[15]

This method of organizing learning stands as a concrete alternative to the hierarchy that places abstract thinking above manual trades. Practical activities are best suited to introducing students to more abstracted disciplines, for it is from these activities that the disciplines emerge *and to which they return*. In Dewey's writing on education, and in the school he oversaw, the practical activities of everyday life are full facets of the *intellectual* development of students. Why do these activities move to the periphery when Dewey writes about grown-ups' work as inquirers?

III

No doubt there is a multitude of reasons why Dewey's discussion of inquiry tends to sideline, rather than foreground, the methods and practices of homemaking and other work traditionally assigned to women and laboring men. Here, I will concern myself only with one reason: Dewey's benign, but nonetheless troublesome sexism and class bias. It is more than coincidental that Dewey's philosophical commitments point so clearly to the importance of women's work as a source of models of methods, of practices of inquiry—but that his own discussions of such work tend to place it on the fringes, or in the elementary school classroom.

Dewey was not at all insensitive to the existence of sexism, racism, and class bias as structures of social life. He was involved in social movements such as the settlement house movement and was active in the founding of the NAACP. He wrote articles, and made comments in other writings, which might be described as feminist and at the very least are supportive of women.[16] Nor was he unaware of the ways in which structures of oppression have shaped the way philosophy has been done; recall his claim, in The Quest for Certainty, that Greek philosophy reified an existing social distinction between theory and practice, a distinction that denigrated slaves and serfs because of the work they did, and that recognized as full human beings only those who did theory (Dewey [1929] 1980, 4–5).

Nonetheless, it cannot be denied that to a considerable extent, Dewey's philosophy accepts prevailing sexist, class-biased assumptions about which human activities are to be accorded philosophical value. He does not succeed in showing how child rearing, foodmaking and carpentry might be accorded similar value by philosophers. Although he gives us different reasons for ascribing value to the experimental sciences than do the modern philosophers he criticizes, the fact remains that he continues to focus the majority of his attention on those activities. He does not make significant efforts to show how philosophers might find similar value in the practices of child rearing, foodmaking, or carpentry.

Dewey's philosophy of education makes similar assumptions—a fact that is surprising, considering the amount of attention he gives practical activity in some of his writings about education, and in the emphasis on such activity in the curriculum of the Laboratory School. Westbrook (1991, 111) points out that "Dewey was interested in the educative potential of 'women's work' for both boys and girls, yet he never challenged the notion that homemaking was women's special sphere." Thus, while little boys at the Dewey School might be photographed baking cookies, Dewey would argue in print that coeducation was helpful to women in providing training for their "distinctive career" as household managers.[17] And, as Laird (1988, 115) points out, while the Laboratory School "was radically and consciously *coeducational*, indeed far more dramatically so than almost any school practices today," nevertheless "Dewey does not once mention this unusual experiment in coeducation in his *Ladies' Home Journal* article ['Is Coeducation Injurious to Girls?']." At best—in the curriculum of the Dewey School—Dewey's thoughts regarding "women's work" and its role in education are undeveloped—supportive of the dismantling of hierarchies between men's work and women's work, between manual and intellectual work, but unreflective about the significance of that support. At worst—the *Ladies' Home Journal* article, for example—Dewey "implicitly supports the female subordination sold in the many domestic-product advertisements" found in that magazine.

What is the significance of Dewey's sometimes uncritical acceptance of the sexual division of labor, when considered alongside the coeducational experiment of the Laboratory School? Laird (1988, 119) puts it in the form of a question: "What is the sense of cultivating egalitarianism and mutuality among children while maintaining male privilege among adults [through the advocacy of 'domestic roles' for women]"? I would add, What is the sense of cultivating a respect for the intellectual worth of practical, "women's work" in children's education, while leaving little room for such work in his theory of ("grownup") inquiry?[18]

Suggesting that Dewey accepted certain sexist and class-biased philosophical assumptions in formulating his theories of both inquiry and education leads me to consider one other reason for his selective neglect of practical activities. Dewey's writings about inquiry and about education can tend to leave one with the feeling that practical activity is something that is "outgrown"—by an individual (as they leave elementary school), or by a culture (as it develops science).

Recall that, for Dewey, artisans were the first experimental knowers. It is the work of practical craftworkers, he argues, that leads to the development of the modern experimental method, with its emphasis on doing. According to Dewey, experimental science has its roots not in the science of the ancients—a science that contemplated fixed and unchanging reality—but rather in their crafts, which aimed at manipulating and controlling a changing material world.[19] This is the aim of contemporary science as well—to *make* sure. Science has brought refinement, systematization, and method to the artisans' making. But as science has refined and reformed the work of the craftworkers, it has also surpassed that work, making its study irrelevant to the modern-day epistemologist. Examining the historical roots of contemporary experimental science in the work of the ancient cook or carpenter is useful; examining the methods and practices of the contemporary cook or carpenter is no longer particularly useful or important. The value of these enterprises has already been realized and absorbed by experimental science; it is to this field that our theorizing about inquiry must now turn its attention. Contemporary practical activities can no longer provide insight into the nature of knowing, or into the dismantling of the theory/practice dichotomy.[20] While the Greeks should have paid more theoretical attention to their practical activities, it seems it is not necessary for contemporary philosophers to do so.

It would appear that, for Dewey, some version of Haeckel's law[21] holds true; inquirers, as they mature, go through developmental stages that parallel the stages through which societies have moved. Like societies, philosophers (at least if they are men) eventually outgrow practical activities and must seek their insights into the nature of inquiry elsewhere. Children begin learning science through cooking, but as they get older, such practical activities are dropped from their curriculum, replaced by more "theoretical" activities. Homemaking is "baby science," useful for introducing children to scientific reasoning, but dispensable once they are able to tackle the "real stuff."

In advancing this attitude toward practical, domestic activities, whether in the classroom or in the history of epistemology, Dewey sometimes seems to suggest that these activities are useful *only* insofar as they are protosciences, employing crude approximations of the scientific method. Beyond this, they have no particular worth as methods of in-quiry—and their educational worth is vocational, limited to women who work in the home. That practical activities might provide insights other than, or as supplements to, the insights of experimental science, is a possibility he does not fully or seriously consider. (Thus, for example, in *Democracy and Education* [(1929) 1980, 284], he explains that such activities as agriculture and household occupations are "instinct with applied science," but that "many of those who now engage in them are not aware of the intellectual content upon which their personal actions depend.")

IV

Dewey's attempt to make philosophy "start with the common materials near at hand" does not dig deeply enough to root out the sexism and class bias inherent in philosophy's devaluing of daily life activities, and in its neglect of the people who engage in them. But his work does provide a useful framework from which to undercut sexism and class bias, by developing tools for undertaking a philosophical reconsideration and revaluation of practical activities. (To get a sense of what this might mean, imagine ignoring the values presently attached to human activities by philosophy, and instead attending to them using Dewey's conception of inquiry, with its particular understandings of the relation between theory and practice and of the nature of the experimental method. If one could actually undertake such an exercise, it is clear that the map of philosophically relevant human activity would look considerably different from the way it now does. Where would gardening line up, in relation to, say, particle physics? Child care and developmental biology?)

In the spirit of Dewey, I suggest that feminist philosophers interested in expanding the received conception of inquiry—a conception that, at present, tends to rest heavily on the model of physical science, and physics in particular—can profit from reflecting on the tasks and occupations that have constituted the fabric of daily life for many women (and men) throughout history. What value—intellectual value, but always (as Dewey would argue) also ethical, social and aesthetic value—can we draw from them? Far from being narrow, restricted, and provincial, the concerns that emerge when one reflects upon the daily tasks of making dinner, weeding the garden, or shopping for groceries are in fact of broad, deep significance for human lives. Such activities can be the sources of considerable insight into the way that intelligent action in the world (inquiry) integrates practical, intellectual, ethical, and aesthetic concerns.

Examples of this kind of undertaking already exist from Dewey's own time. Seigfried (1966, 194–201) discusses some of the women, feminist and nonfeminist, who influenced and were influenced by Dewey and who took up and used his pragmatist understanding of the experimental method in their own daily work. She points to the work of the Dewey School, as chronicled in Katherine Camp Mayhew and Anna Camp Edwards's book, *The Dewey School*, as one example. Mayhew and Edwards detail the ways in which all members of the school worked to make its program deliberately and self-consciously experimental in Dewey's sense—a sense that in fact evolved for him as a consequence of this pedagogical experiment.

Seigfried also identifies Jane Addams's Hull House as an example of a feminist use and expansion of Dewey's notion of experimentalism. Writing about the settlement house in *Twenty Years at Hull House*, Addams describes the ways in which the pragmatist feminists working there "came to respect, seek, and use as their touchstone the hard-won knowledge of the immigrant poor among whom they worked and the actual effects on them of their experimental efforts" (Seigfried 1996, 199). For Addams, "the experimental method was literally one of learning from mistakes," but it was "not just a piecemeal trial-and-error affair. It was the expression of a pragmatist feminist interpretive framework . . . summed up in a phrase frequently used by both women and men pragmatists: 'sympathetic understanding' " (200).

What about contemporary examples of this pragmatist feminist project to expand the meaning of inquiry by reflecting in and on women's work? One arena (Heldke 1988 and 1992) I have explored is cooking, particularly recipe creation and exchange; how can these activities illuminate, expand, and challenge a "science-centric" conception of inquiry? I would suggest that cooking (in part because it has been ignored by philosophers) provides a fresh way to challenge certain apparently insoluble problems that plague a conception of inquiry that has borrowed heavily from the physical sciences. For example: everyday cooking challenges the theory/practice dichotomy—it surrenders the separation of knowing and doing in ways that science cannot (even if it could in the past). Cooking affords us an example of inquiry that is deeply emotional and erotic, and that is also deeply and necessarily bodily. Cooking draws our attention to consequences—the meal on the table, the satisfaction and health of the diner. The mindful cook recognizes that her activity is always an ethical/ social political one, that puts her in connection with persons all over the globe, and also animals and the earth itself. Is cooking somehow uniquely situated to illuminate these aspects of inquiry? No, probably not. Nevertheless the striking ways in which it does so suggest to me that if we are serious about realizing the promise of Dewey's reconception of inquiry, we will give cooking, farming, and other such activities our serious attention.

In "Common Sense and Science," Dewey (1948, 207) suggests that one of the most important philosophical problems he sees "concerns the possibility of giving directions to this return-wave [of science, its methods and conclusions, into daily life] so as to minimize evil consequences and to intensify and extend good consequences." He (1948, 208) goes on to say, "[I]t is hard to see what concern [philosophy] can take for its distinctive care and occupation save that of an attempt to meet the need just indicated." Thus, he concludes, "perhaps the simplest way of getting rid of the dualisms in which philosophy has been bogged down is to recur to the concerns, cares, affairs, etc. of common sense." I would agree with his recommendation, and would further assert that a feminist philosophy directed at the exploration of the everyday activities of women's work is one highly appropriate way in which to carry it out.

Notes

1. See, for example, Dewey 1938a; [1920] 1948; 1958.

2. This is particularly true of the later works. See, for example, Dewey 1938b.

3. Charlene Haddock Seigfried disagrees. She argues that the everyday examples Dewey uses throughout *How We Think* function as the theme of the book, not merely as illustrations of it. I shall interweave her critique of my view throughout the notes of this essay.

4. James Campbell (1995) quotes Dewey as saying that the society he inhabited had developed a method " 'of cooperative and experimental science which expresses the method of intelligence' (LW, 11:58). It is important to recognize from the beginning that for him the notion of a method is better understood as a *mentality* for approaching and dealing with problems than a *protocol* for setting out in advance our responses to possible conditions" (18). Again, I will grant the expansiveness of the terms *scientific* and *method*. Nevertheless, I want to suggest that it is unproductive—un-Deweyan!—to give the scientific method such an exclusive position of privilege. I believe that to do so runs the risk of overlooking or rejecting the unique contributions of methods of intelligent practice that do not look at all like the scientific method, or of contorting all such methods in order to show that they are in fact instances of the scientific method.

5. While these terms are not synonymous, they do share common threads. I've quoted his use of

the term *common experience* above. Dewey has this to say about common sense: "We may summarize the matters which fall within the common-sense frame of reference as those of the uses and enjoyments common to mankind, or to a given community" (1948, 200). Water, considered as it is used to wash things, float boats, nourish crops, and so on is a commonsense concern. Verbs that denote activities involving a "union of self-and-thing"—"occupy," "engage," "busy," "concern"—are those with which common sense is concerned. His use of the terms *practice* and *practical* will be discussed in some detail during the course of the paper.

6. An anonymous reviewer of an earlier draft of this essay suggests that it rests on "a misunderstanding"; according to this reviewer, "Dewey's point . . . was always that insofar as our activities require reflection, it should take the form of experimental intelligence." For this individual, "it was enough for him to point out (as he did repeatedly) that all successfully executed crafts implicitly embody experimentalism, and he in fact provides many examples." But this precisely misses my point. I am suggesting that to restrict the development of experience and inquiry to the experimental method, *no matter how expansively we define the latter*, is to restrict it unduly, to fail to recognize that other activities (including practical activities) come with their own methods—methods that may not be usefully understood by translating them into the language of experimentalism.

7. See, for example, Dewey [1929] 1980, 4–5.

8. See Dewey 1958, 314–15, for his description of the relation between theory and practice.

9. Bertrand Russell points to the inclusiveness of Dewey's definition of experimental inquiry as evidence of its weakness: "I cannot but think that this definition does not adequately express Dr. Dewey's meaning, since it would apply, for instance, to the operations of a drill sergeant in transforming a collection of raw recruits into a regiment, or of a bricklayer transforming a heap of bricks into a house, and yet it would be impossible to say that the drill sergeant is 'inquiring' into the recruits, or the bricklayer into the bricks" (1930, 143).

10. Dewey recommends, for example, that the use of the experimental method be extended to moral thinking. See, for example, chapter 7 of *Reconstruction in Philosophy*. Furthermore, his description of the historical emergence of inquiry and knowing explicitly addresses the role played in that emergence by practical activity. Westbrook (1991, 333) points out that, for Dewey, "Artisans were the world's first knowers. The sciences, in turn, were children of the useful arts." Science emerged from craftwork, and it has grown into a set of disciplines that in turn bear an intimate relation to the technologies they support. (See 1957, 41; [1925] 1958, 128; [1916] 1980, 324–25.)

11. Elsewhere, I begin to undertake this project, by thinking about foodmaking activities. See "Recipes for Theory Making," and "Foodmaking as a Thoughtful Practice," for examinations of foodmaking that are informed by Dewey.

12. Quoted in Westbrook 1991, 102. My emphasis on "within."

13. See Dewey [1916] 1980, 208–9.

14. Laird also points out that the organization and workings of the school were very much the collective effort of all the teachers who taught there—most of whom were women. Thus, much of the development of Dewey's ideas about the role of practical activity in education cannot be credited to Dewey—or at least not to him alone—but must be credited to the women who took his ideas and made them operational. For a detailed account of the Laboratory School, see Mayhew and Edwards 1936.

15. See, for example, Dewey [1916] 1980, chapter 20.

16. For a summary of these writings, see Westbrook 1991, 167. For a summary of analyses of Dewey's feminism, see Laird 1988, 111–12. For a detailed exploration of Dewey's feminism, see Seigfried 1996 and Chapter 3 in the present volume.

17. See Westbrook, 1991, 111, and Laird 1988. Westbrook also notes, however, that Dewey does not see women as *locked* into a role as domestic managers; women who choose other occupations are not deviants and should be accorded full rights in their chosen careers (167).

18. Seigfried disagrees with this analysis of Dewey's understanding and use of women's practical

activities. She writes: "Dewey is perhaps unique in the annals of professional philosophy for incorporating the insights he gained from working with women and children into every aspect of his philosophy. . . . [T]hey provide the warp and woof of his philosophical perspective. He is explicit that his theory of education is a theory for life and not something for children that should be left behind" (personal correspondence). Seigfried has tracked down many of the specific and profound ways that Dewey was influenced by the women philosophers and activists around him. Nevertheless, I maintain that the ways in which Dewey incorporates those influences tend to erase, or at the very least to minimize, the degree to which they emerge from and return to the experiences of women. Furthermore, the women with whom Dewey worked were far from "ordinary" women engaged in everyday women's work; on the contrary, they were exceptional, sometimes extraordinary, women, whose work lives were quite different from the lives of full-time homemakers, for example. And so, I suggest, the fact that they bore a powerful impact on Dewey still leaves him at one remove from that daily activity.

But my argument presupposes that it would have been appropriate for Dewey to discuss women's work more directly—that it would have been useful and worthwhile for him to explore and examine activities in which he did not himself participate. But, as Seigfried points out, many of the feminists who surrounded Dewey would have felt very differently about the matter; they would have supported the "cultural feminist belief that women should be the ones liberating women. As long as men supported their efforts and acknowledged their right to be full intellectual partners, that was more than enough" (Seigfried, personal correspondence). Dewey's role, for these feminists, was not to analyze women's work in his own theories of inquiry, but to be supportive of women's efforts to explore their own work—aided, perhaps, by his theories, just as he was aided by theirs.

19. "It is pertinent to note that in the history of the race the sciences grew gradually out from useful social occupations" (Dewey [1916] 1980, 208).

20. Further down in the passage quoted above, Dewey [1916] 1980, 209) says as much: "Mathematics is now a highly abstract science; geometry, however, means literally earth-measuring. The practical use of number in counting to keep track of things and in measuring is even more important to-day than in the times when it was invented for these purposes. Such considerations . . . are not arguments for a recapitulation of the history of the race or for dwelling long in the early rule-of-thumb stage."

21. Haeckel's law holds that ontogyny recapitulates phylogyny; that is, that the development of individual organisms recapitulates the evolution of its species. Thanks to Felicia Kruse for pointing out this connection.

References

Addams, Jane. 1910. *Twenty Years at Hull House*. New York: Macmillan.
Aptheker, Bettina. 1989. *Tapestries of Life: Women's Work, Women's Consciousness, and the Meaning of Daily Experience*. Amherst: University of Massachusetts Press.
Campbell, James. 1995. *Understanding John Dewey*. Chicago: Open Court.
Code, Lorraine. 1998. "Feminists and Pragmatists: A Radical Future?" *Radical Philosophy* 87:22–30.
DeVault, Marjorie. 1991. *Feeding the Family: The Social Organization of Caring as Gendered Work*. Chicago: University of Chicago Press.
Dewey, John. 1910. "The Influence of Darwin on Philosophy." In *The Influence of Darwin on Philosophy and Other Essays in Contemporary Thought*. New York: Henry Holt.
———. 1911. "Is Coeducation Injurious to Girls?" *Ladies' Home Journal* 28:22ff.

———. 1916. "An Added Note as to the 'Practical.' " In *Essays in Experimental Logic*. Chicago: University of Chicago Press.

———. [1916] 1980. *Democracy and Education*. Vol. 9 of *The Middle Works*. Edited by Jo Ann Boydston. Carbondale: Southern Illinois University Press.

———. [1920] 1948. *Reconstruction in Philosophy*. Boston: Beacon.

———. [1925] 1958. *Experience and Nature*. New York: Dover.

———. [1929] 1980. *The Quest for Certainty: A Study of the Relation of Knowledge and Action*. New York: G. P. Putnam's Sons.

———. 1932. "A Resume of Four Lectures on Common Sense, Science, and Philosophy." *Bulletin of the Wagner Free Institute of Science of Philadelphia* 7:12–16.

———. 1934. *Art as Experience*. New York: Perigee.

———. 1938a. *Experience and Education*. New York: Collier.

———. 1938b. *Logic: The Theory of Inquiry*. New York: Holt, Rinehart and Winston.

———. 1948. "Common Sense and Science: Their Respective Frames of Reference." *Journal of Philosophy* 45 (8): 197–208.

———. [1949] 1988. "Appendix 1: The Unfinished Introduction to Experience and Nature." In *The Later Works*. Vol. 1 (*1925*). Edited by Jo Ann Boydston. Carbondale: Southern Illinois University Press.

Gavin, William. 1980. The Importance of Context: Reflections on Kuhn, Marx, and Dewey. *Studies in Soviet Thought* 21:15–30.

Hartsock, Nancy. 1983. "The Feminist Standpoint: Developing the Ground for a Specifically Feminist Historical Materialism." In *Discovering Reality: Feminist Perspectives on Epistemology, Metaphysics, Methodology, and Philosophy of Science*, edited by Sandra Harding and Merrill B. Hintikka. Boston: D. Reidel.

Heldke, Lisa. 1988. "Recipes for Theory Making." *Hypatia* 3 (2): 15–30.

———. 1992. "Foodmaking as a Thoughtful Practice." In *Cooking, Eating, Thinking: Transformative Philosophies of Food*, edited by Deane Curtin and Lisa Heldke Bloomington: Indiana University Press.

———. 1994. "Interaction in a World of Chance: John Dewey's Theory of Inquiry." In *Modern Engenderings: Critical Feminist Essays in the History of Western Philosophy*, edited by Bat-Ami Bar On. Albany: State University of New York Press.

Laird, Susan. 1988. "Women and Gender in John Dewey's Philosophy of Education." *Educational Theory* 38 (1): 111–29.

Mayhew, Katherine Camp, and Anna Camp Edwards. 1936. *The Dewey School*. New York: D. Appleton-Century.

Randall, John Hermann. 1939. "Dewey's Interpretation of the History of Philosophy." In *The Philosophy of John Dewey*, edited by Paul Arthur Schilpp. The Library of Living Philosophers, vol. 1. Evanston: Northwestern University Press.

Ruddick, Sara. 1980. "Maternal Thinking." *Feminist Studies* 6:342–67.

Russell, Bertrand. 1939. "Dewey's New *Logic*." In *The Philosophy of John Dewey*, edited by Paul Arthur Schilpp. The Library of Living Philosophers, vol. 1. Evanston: Northwestern University Press.

Seigfried, Charlene Haddock. 1996. *Pragmatism and Feminism: Reweaving the Social Fabric*. Chicago: University of Chicago Press.

Sherman, Ann L. 1984. "Genderism and the Reconstitution of Philosophy of Education." *Educational Theory* 34 (4): 321–25.

Smith, Dorothy. 1979. "A Sociology for Women." *The Prism of Sex: Essays in the Sociology of Knowledge*, edited by Julia Sherman and Evelyn Torton Beck. Madison: University of Wisconsin Press.

————. 1987. *The Everyday World as Problematic: A Feminist Sociology*. Boston: Northeastern University Press.

Westbrook, Robert. 1991. *John Dewey and American Democracy*. Ithaca: Cornell University Press.

12

Deepening Democratic Transformation

Deweyan Individuation and Pragmatist Feminism

Judith M. Green

When women who are not mere students of other persons' philosophy set out to write it, we cannot conceive that it will be the same in viewpoint or tenor as that composed from the standpoint of the different masculine experience of things.

—John Dewey, "Philosophy and Democracy"

Upon the whole, economics has been treated as on a lower level than either morals or politics. Yet the life which men, women and children actually lead, the opportunities open to them, the values they are capable of enjoying, their education, their share in all the things of art and science, are mainly determined by economic conditions. Hence we can hardly expect a moral system which ignores economic conditions to be other than remote and empty. Industrial life is correspondingly brutalized by failure to equate it as the means by which social and cultural values are realized. That the economic life, thus exiled from the pale of higher values, takes revenge by declaring that it is the only social reality, and by means of the doctrine of materialistic determination of institutions and conduct in all fields, denies to deliberate morals and politics any share of causal regulation, is not surprising.

—John Dewey, The Quest for Certainty

Our increasingly globalized social world at the beginning of the twenty-first century is in the midst of a breathtakingly rapid process of "democratization" that should be both celebrated and regarded with grave concern by those who understand democracy as John Dewey understood it, including feminists who recognize the significance for our mutual flourishing of insights and values that arise within women's experience and who support women's opportunities for full development of diverse potentials. We should celebrate democratization insofar as this concept refers to popular movements in differing places, such as South Africa, Central Europe, and the member nations of the former Soviet Union, that have over-thrown oppressive regimes that maintained control through violence, apartheid, censorship, cronyism, and promotion of social distrust. How-ever, many leaders of newly posttotalitarian societies have equated de-mocratization with rapid transition to a capitalist economy and liberal political institutions on the assumption that the political economies of wealthy, powerful, and relatively stable Western nations offer defining, final models of democracy in its fully actualized form. This misguided equation should be cause for grave concern because antidemocratic po-tentials within both the developed political economies it treats as models and the posttotalitarian developments it has been guiding make transi-tion to a deeper kind of democracy more difficult. For example, most of the emerging, expert-guided institutional models of posttotalitarian "democratization" in Central European nations are market structured and minimally participatory in character, achieving very little change in long-established social practices and attitudes while opening up these nations to Western investment, rapidly privatizing and downsizing for-merly state-owned industries, and cutting large holes in the social safety net. Aggregate measures of social welfare show that these changes have led to significant increases in gross domestic product (GDP), yet "minor-ity" problems are emerging everywhere, originally enthusiastic electoral participation already has dropped to the low levels that have become increasingly common in the West, and many families and whole regions face poverty.[1]

Meanwhile, effective commitment to girls' education and women's lit-eracy is declining worldwide. A recent UNICEF study, "The State of the World's Children 1999," reports that nearly one-sixth of humanity still cannot read or write, and predicts that illiteracy rates will steadily in-crease, because only one child in four attends school in the poorest na-tions, and more than half of those denied education are girls. It has been clear for some time that women's education levels are directly linked to poverty, overpopulation, environmental degradation, and various adverse health indicators, including infant mortality. As women's education lev-els rise, these critical problems decrease. According to the UNICEF re-port, "a 10-percentage-point increase in girls' primary enrollment can be expected to decrease infant mortality by 4.1 deaths per 1,000, and a simi-lar rise in girls' secondary enrollment by another 5.6 deaths per 1,000. . . . This would mean concretely, in Pakistan for example, that an extra year of schooling for 1,000 girls would ultimately prevent roughly 60 infant deaths." Levels of illiteracy are highest in countries that also have a high rate of population growth, but fertility drops sharply as women's education rises. In Brazil, for example, "illiterate women have an average of 6.5 children," whereas "mothers with secondary-school education have an average of 2.5 children."[2]

Women's widespread economic marginalization, as expressed by disproportionately high rates of unemployment (as high as 90 percent in industrial areas of the posttotalitarian Ukraine) as well as by women's underemployment and by continuing social barriers to women's career choice and leadership in decision making in both "experienced" and "developing" democracies, reflects the untransformed power of patriarchal cultures.[3] Such cultures restrict the emergence and effective employment of women's talents, aspirations, and social contributions to a subset of those of which women are capable, often at great cost to their families as well as their individual welfare. Violence against women is shockingly common worldwide in the forms of domestic abuse, clitoridectomy and genital mutilation, "honor" killings, and rape as a weapon of war, yet currently dominant institutional models of democratization are silent about these traditional practices.[4] Moreover, both "experienced" and "developing" democracies ignore or radically underfund research and public interventions concerning other important threats to the health of women and their families: prenatal care, familial exposure to AIDS, "women's cancers," and social constructions of women's beauty that lead to anorexia and bulimia, as well as dangers created by inadequate nutrition, sanitation, housing, and air and water quality.

John Dewey's conception of democracy offers a way of framing, analyzing, and transforming these and other millennial problems of democratization that is more inclusive of women's voices, values, and experience-based visions for a preferable future than is the expert-guided institutional model of capitalist liberal democracy. For Dewey, democracy is an ideal quality of community life that reflects open-minded, diversity-inclusive, and actively participatory attitudes, beliefs, social habits, and characteristic decision processes. This "deeper" democracy serves as basis, guide, and goal for ongoing evolutionary development of democratic institutions (Green 1999a). Democracy so understood has never been fully actualized, though it has been partially achieved at certain times and places, giving rise to certain institutional forms that have the potential to promote its fuller realization. The right of all citizens to vote is one of these, as are public education, free exchange of information through the press, and trust-based citizen deliberation within the social transactions of daily life. Still to be achieved is full sharing of diverse values and responsibilities within all of the institutions of adult life, including families, churches, workplaces, and community planning processes.

As Dewey's activist philosophical legacy suggests to pragmatist feminists of our own era, women can and must play a key role in deeply democratic changes in character, culture, and institutional structures of social cooperation in ways that direct global change processes toward a more desirable future. Dewey's deeper model of democracy offers diverse feminists a common ground and guide for collaborative transformative action to relieve the suffering and promote the flourishing of women, their loved ones, and their valued communities worldwide. At the same time, transformations of values and institutional visions that have emerged within many women's daily experience, as well as within feminists' cross-difference collaborative efforts to transform community life, offer necessary insights for reconstructing Dewey's pragmatist philosophical practices and hypothetical generalizations about democracy in order to make them helpful guides to locally differing yet globally interlinked democratization processes in the years ahead.

Dewey's Deep Conception of Democracy

Dewey's insightful conception of democracy differs from presently dominant economistic institutional models in a key way. Dewey focuses on participatory and educative requirements for continuing processes of personal growth and individuation, as well as for ongoing social and institutional transformations that make possible a more desirable quality of each member's individual experience within a shared social life that is mutually beneficial and mutually valued. In contrast, economistic liberal and libertarian models of democracy simply aim to coordinate the unexamined preferences of differing, separate, fundamentally unchanging individuals in ways that avoid violent conflict while maximizing aggregate holdings of primary social goods, especially income and wealth.[5] According to economistic theorists of institutional democracy, individuals in their actual differences serve as the final measure and goal of the coordinating institutions of social life. There is and could be no shared public value in terms of which various actual individuals' values could be assessed, they claim, other than freedom from interference with and by other individuals in one's pursuit of whatever conception of the good one finds motivating. Thus, they take actual preferences, talents, and distributions of means as unanalyzable givens. They assess institutions as "democratically effective" insofar as these protect individuals' freedom from others' interference while enhancing individuals' opportunities to rationally optimize their welfare (however they conceive the good) without worsening others' welfare.

According to this economistic conception of democracy, capitalist markets that are structured and protected by liberal legal and political institutions are paradigmatically democratic institutions because they coordinate individual choices into more desirable outcomes than individuals could otherwise achieve while minimizing sociopolitical interference with individual freedom of choice. Thus, democratization processes so conceived guide changes in law and public policy through the goal of increasing the mediating role of markets in allowing individuals' preferences, talents, and assets to determine the production and distribution of primary social goods, as well as the practical relationships of daily social life. Markets are so important within this model of democratization both because of their putative effectiveness in advancing aggregate welfare, as represented by the income and wealth that allows individuals to pursue their various conceptions of the good, and because, in comparison with still-fresh memories of state censorship and centralized planning, markets minimize political interference with individuals' pursuit of whatever "good" motivates them.[6] This model treats the universal human right of citizens to vote as important because it protects individual freedom and promotes the general welfare so understood. Similarly, it treats universal education as important because it prepares all citizens to compete in the marketplace, as well as to protect their own and others' freedom through their use of the franchise. Finally, it treats a stable, fair, and impersonal framework of laws that protects private property and establishes "transparent" ground rules for financial institutions and productive enterprises as important because such a legal framework allows markets to operate efficiently while allowing individuals to act freely and knowledgeably as investors, labor contractors, and consumers.

Dewey's deeper conception of democracy agrees with this economistic institutional conception in affirming that societies that can rightly be called democratic structure their institutions so as to actually benefit all of their citizens within the changing conditions of global life, treating them as equals and educating them to recognize their mutual stake in assuring orderly social change. "A society which makes provision for participation in its good of all its members on equal terms and which secures flexible readjustment of its institutions through interaction of the different forms of associated life is *in so far democratic*. Such a society must have a type of education which gives individuals a personal interest in social relationships and control, and the habits of mind which secure social changes without introducing disorder" (Dewey [1916] 1980, 105, emphasis mine). However, Dewey suggests that the background rationale for democratic institutions and change processes within the economistic institutional model is fundamentally flawed by the acontextual, static conception of the goals and potentialities of individuals that it shares with its eighteenth-century theoretical antecedents.

Instead of being equal, autonomous centers and choosers of value from their moments of birth or their attainment of social adulthood, Dewey argues, fully formed individuals are the goal and the continuing outcome of *a process of ongoing growth* that allows them interactively to develop and to deploy many of their diverse potentials within a democratic social context that supports or at least allows such a multifaceted actualization to occur—unlike the social contexts in which most people have lived historically and most people, including most women, still live. "The ground of democratic ideas and practices is faith in the *potentialities of individuals*, faith in the capacity for positive developments *if proper conditions are provided*. The weakness of the philosophy originally advanced to justify the democratic movement was that it took individuality to be something given ready-made; that is, in abstraction from time, instead of as *a power to develop*" (Dewey [1940] 1988, 113, emphases mine). Many eighteenth-century democratic theorists, like their contemporary liberal and libertarian inheritors, emphasized noninterference with individuals understood as self-contained centers of personal goals as well as context-independent, birth-originating specific talents. In contrast, Dewey argues that effective democratic societies must create the kinds of real conditions that will allow diverse, interlinked desirable potentialities of each of their members to emerge and to develop within institution-structured, cooperative processes of guiding their shared course within ongoing change processes toward future outcomes that are both individually and mutually desirable.

Creating more ideally democratic conditions in real historical contexts requires what we now call democratization in both experienced and developing democracies, within which Dewey would emphasize eliminating arbitrary past barriers to individuals' development of their potentials and constructing positive opportunities for their emergence and active deployment.

> Democracy signifies, on one side, that every individual is to share in the duties and rights belonging to control of social affairs, and on the other side, that social arrangements are to eliminate those external arrangements of status, birth, wealth, sex, etc. which restrict the opportunity of each individual for full development of himself [or herself]. On the individual side, it takes as the criterion of social organization and of law and government release of the potentialities of individuals. On the social side, it demands cooperation in place of coercion, voluntary sharing in a process of mutual give and take, instead of authority imposed from above. (Dewey [1932] 1985, 348–49)

Both the infinite worth of diverse, fully formed individuals and the precariousness of the processes and conditions through which they can develop and flourish make our experienced democracies relatively desirable and historically progressive. However, their actual imperfections as conditions for democratic individuation and for cooperative social transformation show that democracy is still an ideal goal guiding transformative struggle, rather than an accurate description of any actual society or set of existing institutions of political economy.

Nonetheless, its ideal character does not make Dewey's conception of democracy utopian, in the sense of being an unrealistic or even antirealistic guide to social and individual transformation. Rather, Dewey's focus on the transformation-guiding implications of the democratic ideal realistically thematizes our shared human need to develop certain diverse potentialities that each of us finds to some extent already immanent and motivating within us. It also expresses a widely shared, experience-based awareness that some patterns of social relations, even in experienced democracies, tend to be more favorable to development of the complex and valuable potentialities of some individuals than of others: "As an ideal, it expresses the need for progress beyond anything yet attained; for nowhere in the world are there institutions which in fact operate equally to secure the full development of each individual, and assure to all individuals a share in both the values they contribute and those they receive"

(Dewey [1932] 1985, 349). Thus, the democratic ideal serves both *a critical role* in clarifying just what is wrong when some of a society's members are prohibited by arbitrary social structures and processes from actualizing their most valued and valuable potentials, and *a reconstructive role* in guiding the reshaping of existing social institutions and processes.

Perhaps the greatest practical difference that Dewey's deeper conception of democratization makes, as compared to the advice that has so often been derived from economistic institutional conceptions, concerns the importance for individual development as well as outcome effectiveness of active citizen participation in shaping new institutions and processes.

> The best guarantee of collective efficiency and power is liberation and use of the diversity of individual capacities in initiative, planning, foresight, vigor and endurance. . . . This fact fixes the significance of democracy. . . . It is but a name for the fact that *human nature is developed only when its elements take part in directing things which are common*, things for the sake of which men and women form groups—families, industrial companies, governments, churches, scientific associations and so on. (Dewey [1920] 1982, 199–200, emphasis mine)

Dewey makes a two-part claim here for his deeper, more actively participatory conception of democracy: that it is necessary to the development of the diverse valuable potentialities of individual persons, and that such an approach is "the best guarantee of collective efficiency and power." It is best because it brings about the well-coordinated inclusion of highly developed, diverse personalities who contribute dispersed insights, disparate skills, differently located yet cooperative criticisms, and alternative imaginative syntheses, as well as loyal commitment and hard work to assure the ongoing success of collaborative processes. This suggests that our central concern in promoting the general welfare must be the development of human persons within valued cooperative institutions, which requires the reliable availability of means to support their individual and mutual growth and flourishing. Aggregate growth in GDP is inadequate as an indicator of improvement in human welfare apart from these democratically inclusive, distributive, and developmental dimensions.

In fact, the shift of attention in the now-dominant economistic institutional model—from human development and effective cooperation to

growth in GDP and increase in profits as indicators of efficacy in achieving the purpose of democracy—seemed to Dewey both to *cause* and to
hide the catastrophic impacts of actual capitalist liberal political economies in the lives of real human individuals. Capitalistic economies allow
a few to pursue selfish, shallow goals at the cost of most people's opportunities to develop, to enjoy, and to contribute many of their unique and
desirable potentials (Dewey [1930] 1984). The manufactured appearance
of necessity, even desirability, of the increasingly dominant institutions
of liberal capitalist political economy and of extreme, market-intensified
actual differences in socioeconomic power make it very difficult for many
people to believe that a more desirable institutional model that would
facilitate fuller development of diverse human potentialities is practically
possible. Many doubt the potential efficacy of ordinary citizens to cooperatively transform existing and increasingly world-dominant liberal capitalistic institutions, given existing power disparities and institutional
biases as well as inequalities both in developed understandings of how
political economies work and in skills in making them do what the less
powerful regard as desirable (Dewey [1929] 1984, 65).

However, if most of the members of these experienced democracies
feel excluded from developing the capacities that would allow them to
believe that they can and do actively participate in guiding their societies
in ways that work to their individual and mutual benefit, this fact is
nothing less than *a systematic failure relative to the criterion of democracy*
that is alleged to guide these societies' institutional structures and processes.

> Government, business, art, religion, all social institutions have a
> meaning, a purpose. That purpose is to set free *and to develop* the
> capacities of human individuals without respect to race, sex, class,
> or economic status. And this is all one with saying that the test
> of their value is the extent to which they educate every individual
> into the full stature of his [or her] possibility. Democracy has
> many meanings, but if it has a moral meaning, it is found in re-
> solving that the supreme test of all political institutions and in-
> dustrial arrangements shall be the contribution they make to *the
> all-around growth of every member of society.* (Dewey [1920] 1982,
> 186, emphases mine)

Widespread failure of democratic faith in people's practical capacities for
self-governance suggests that expert-guided transformation to increase

the role of markets and to diminish the planning role of government is not the true meaning of democratization, and may even create new obstacles to democracy. Instead, democratization processes in both experienced and developing democracies must be guided by the goal of evoking and inclusively educating the diverse human potentials that members of a society will need to employ if they are to achieve and to believe in self-governance within and through all of the various social institutions that shape adult life.

Why Deeper Democratization Needs Women, and Women Need Deep Democracy

Women of diverse and sometimes antagonistic backgrounds must become key players in such deeper democratization processes, for their own sake as well as to optimize the collective efficiency and power of their larger communities. In his prophetic suggestion of the future contributions women would someday make to philosophy as well as to the deeper democratization that he believed would bring truly modern societies into existence for the first time, Dewey focused on the first of these considerations. Dewey suggests that women's diverse experiences and viewpoints will contribute differing, much-needed values and insights that will benefit whole societies through their participation in the wider "public" sphere from which many societies' traditional gender systems have excluded them in earlier historical eras. This great social good can only be achieved, however, if women undertake (and are supported or at least tolerated in undertaking) the kinds of active participatory roles within all of the institutions of adult life that will allow them to develop many of the diverse and desirable potentialities that have usually remained latent, perhaps unknown to many women themselves.

If, as Dewey ([1916] 1980, 82) argues, human potentialities are actualized primarily through the rub of social interaction, rather than from an independent, internal imperative, the importance of this lifelong educative dimension of women's participatory experience cannot be overstated. Women need to actively participate in economic, political, social, cultural, athletic, agricultural, and artistic pursuits, activities, and interactions with others in order to actualize particular valuable, complex potentialities that will not arise out of them in any other way. There is no way to determine in advance of such active participation whether and to what extent a particular woman or women in general may be capable of developing such potentials—no test, no questionnaire, no social scientific or biogenetic study. To become fully aware, energized, active, creative, and effective in particular valuable dimensions of their actuality, women need to engage in the kind of educative growth that is brought forth by the stimulation, role modeling, and interactive engagement of their own imaginative desire to improve something, to transform something, or to make something new within valued transformative activity with others (Dewey [1940] 1988, 110–11).

As women develop their valued, context-relevant, participatory capacities over time, they become increasingly capable of effectively playing increasingly responsible, trust-grounded leadership roles and of contributing on-point creative insights for the guidance of a collaborative process. Such guiding insights concern long-term goals as well as new strategies, methods, and means for actualizing desirable social relations, for stabilizing needed resources, and for further educating new and continuing members of the group. Of course, women are not blank slates when they first enter a new participatory context. They already have values, experiences, and previously developed skills, as well as beliefs, doubts, fears, hopes, memories, and habits. Some of these "contents on arrival" may be the kinds of valuable insights and desirable ways of being that Dewey and other feminists have prophesied women as a group would bring to the various "public" spheres of cooperative social activity as they increasingly became full participating members. These include relational skills, caring, concern for the vulnerable, intergenerational vision, and experience-grounded appreciation of the importance of basic bodily and psychological needs. Some women's other contents on arrival may be less desirable: lack of confidence in their own voices and visions, lack of skill in thinking impersonally and analytically, lack of knowledge of the history and current operative processes of these public spheres, and specific wounds from past processes of exclusion and diminishment on grounds of race, ethnicity, religion, nation, and class as well as gender that may have left a well of pent-up anger or its twin, depression.

Thus, women's specifically "womanly" contents on arrival in new collaborative transformative contexts are and can be expected to be a mixed bag. Women who are new to collaborative public projects may combine fuller development of certain valuable human potentialities than is typical of men (because of the gender roles to which they were assigned, restricted, or validated in their particular cultures) with lesser development of others. Newcomers may also experience and express mixed feelings about themselves and about participating in unaccustomed activities, including fear of the new and of the previously wounding, inexperienced hopes for less or for more than is possible, only partially awakened awareness of their own complex potentialities, and still-unfocused aspirations to develop these in order to contribute in ways of which they have not yet specifically dreamed. What is typical of womanly contents on arrival as participants in collaborative public efforts to transform various dimensions of differing societies changed greatly over the course of the twentieth century and will continue to change. So will the contents of those intersecting dimensions of individual women's overlapping differences related to race, culture, class, caste, sexual orientation, and other aspects of our embodiment amid the commonalities that interactively create overlapping patterns of family resemblances we evoke when we use the experience-based and experience-regulative collective concept of "women."[7]

However, there is no reason to assume that all these changes must or will be desirable, or that progress is inevitable in the absence of women's active and effective efforts to make them so. Many global currents give reason for anxiety about the future at the beginning of a new millennium. Not least among these is the threat to women's literacy, which has profoundly adverse implications, especially in traditional societies in which women play the primary role in raising children and are limited in their access to diverse opportunities to participate in the public sphere. The reversal of gains in women's literacy worldwide threatens not only the future development of women themselves, but also of their families, classes, castes, cultures, and nations. Literacy opens up infinitely more relational connections and prepares women for further relational participatory development through the stimulus to their desire for growth as well as the through access to the specific contents of others' diverse experiences that they can make their own through the mediation of books, newspapers, and the Internet. Literacy is the first step into a broader world of direct, cross-difference interactions that can actualize valuable individual potentialities that would otherwise remain vague and latent.

Unless these potentialities are actualized, women will live their lives as different individuals from those they might have become, and the different future that might have come to pass as a result of the more deeply democratic transformative role they might have played will be replaced by a different, less desirable social actuality. "While progress is not inevitable, it is up to men [and women] as individuals to bring it about. Change is going to occur anyway, and the problem is the control of change in a given' direction. The direction, the quality of change, is a matter of individuality" (Dewey [1940] 1988, 113). This is the vulnerability of the democracy project Dewey acknowledged when he recognized that it depends on contingent individual development. "Individuality conceived as a temporal development involves uncertainty, indeterminacy, or contingency. Individuality is the source of whatever is unpredictable in the world" (111). Thus, the democratic global future in which diverse women participate as equals in shaping the values, the goals, and the outcomes of cooperative social institutions and processes can only come into being if women in this less-than-democratic world act for their own transformation. This will require transgressing countervening traditions to enter into new public contexts of cooperative cross-difference efforts to guide the inevitable change process in desirable directions— contexts that will, in turn, provide the stimulus, the interactive partners, the experience-based information, and the time process they need to become effective and powerful enough in their diverse individual actualizations to introduce something new into their families, races, classes, castes, cultures, and nations that can change the current direction of history.

Contrary to the frequently raised objection that women's present inequalities and historically generated, still-living racial, cultural, class, caste, and national antagonisms constitute practical and moral obstacles to women's cross-difference collaborative participation in social transformation, such collaborations are both a possible and a morally necessary step toward transforming these inequalities and antagonisms. Those who teach a purely oppositional history and politics of difference tell a false story that is also disempowering. The true story of democratic struggle we must reclaim also includes Cornel West's litany of boundary transgressors who offer a symbol of the kind of cross-difference collaboration toward which we must strive.

> Yet I hear a cloud of witnesses from afar—Sojourner Truth, Wendell Phillips, Emma Goldman, A. Philip Randolph, Ella Baker, Myles Horton, Fannie Lou Hamer, Michael Harrington, Abraham Joshua Heschel, Tom Hayden, Harvey Milk, Robert Moses, Barbara Ehrenreich, Martin Luther King, Jr., and many anonymous

others who championed the struggle for freedom and justice in a prophetic framework of moral reasoning. They understood that the pitfalls of racial reasoning are too costly in mind, body, and soul—especially for a downtrodden and despised people like black Americans. The best of our leadership recognized this valuable truth—and more must do so in the future if America is to survive with any moral sense. (West 1994, 48–49)

In their life witnesses of educative growth toward individuation and efficacy, and of cross-difference partnerships that led both to successes and to failures, these boundary transgressors offer us the beginnings of an empirical basis for a general model of transformative collaboration and community building amid social formations of inequality and adversarial relations. Their stories of struggle include high costs of pain, because these boundary transgressors embodied their real conditions of limit and contradiction within them and not just between them. Nonetheless, their accounts suggest that such great prices in pain have been and can again be transformed and made meaningful by convergent cross-difference needs, interests, and hopes, by hard work carried out, by risks undertaken, and by many small achievements won.

Likewise, Jane Addams, the other women of Hull House, and the new American immigrants they worked with in Chicago a century ago offer us hopeful models of deep, mutual individual transformations within cross-difference collaboration that are crucial to cooperative efficacy.[8] Their experience shows that *mutual individual changes* make it possible for cross-difference collaborators, who began with class-based, culture-based, and gender-based misconceptions about one another and about their own needs and potential, to continue to work together on levels of progressively deeper, experience-based trust. In turn, this earned trust is the key to the mutual commitment to one another and to the ongoing collaborative project that creates both the time process and the opportunities for stimulating and coordinating the development and active employment of their individual potentialities for particular skills, effective vision, and committed hard work that Dewey argued offers "the best guarantee of collective efficiency and power." As Charlene Haddock Seigfried has effectively documented, Dewey developed many of his insights about the practical meaning and means of deeper democratization within his theoretical and practical collaboration with Jane Addams.[9] He may have had Hull House in mind when he stressed the importance of the individual-transforming opening up of others' differing experiences as sources of expanded awareness, reorientation, and stimulation to actualize still-latent potentialities that occurs within active participation in collaborative activities whose important purpose engages one's imagination and desire of grow in understanding and skills.

> Active connections with others are such an intimate and vital part of our own concerns that it is impossible to draw sharp lines, such as would enable us to say, "Here my experience ends; there yours begins." In so far as we are partners in common undertakings, the things which others communicate to us as the consequences of their particular share in the enterprise blend at once into the experience resulting from our own special doings. The ear is as much an organ of experience as the eye or hand; the eye is available for reading reports of what happens beyond its horizon. Things remote in space and time affect the issue of our actions quite as much as things which we can smell and handle. They really concern us, and consequently, any account of them which assists us in dealing with things at hand falls within personal experience. (Dewey [1916] 1980, 194)

Through the windows of one another's differing experience that we transformatively encounter in written and visual forms, but even more powerfully through interactive, multifaceted living testimony, women who have been both benefited and harmed by interactive systems of inequality can learn from one another's intergenerational stories. They can revise and extend their own stories in light of them, can discover what they deeply desire and are able to gain only by working together, and can begin to actualize their potentialities for trust-based cross-difference collaboration. As Jane Addams reminds us, unless women become sufficiently trustworthy as individuals to others who are rightly suspicious of some of the inequality-transmitting group-related contexts of our formation such as race, class, caste, culture, and nation, the kind of deep and lasting mutual commitment of collaborative effort that will allow them to actualize complementary potentialities will not occur. The preferable future that might have come from it will not be realized. Thus, selective, warranted, mutual trust must be the first goal and achievement of potentially effective cross-difference collaborations among those who realize how much is at stake for individual women, their beloved others, and our shared global future. We must realize that such a deeper, individual-developing, cross-difference collaboration-building, group-transforming, and eventually institution-reconstructing democracy is the path of progress out of the terrible dangers of our present time and toward a preferable future. Without such deeper transformations in women's understandings, characters, and practical skills, as well as the transformations in the present formations of race, class, caste, culture, and nation in which women must participate, current change processes will continue to diminish the practical liberty and opportunities for development of most human beings, but especially the world's poor, including disproportionate numbers of women and children, and with them, our global ecosystem.

Women can and must play a key role in fostering deeper democratization in characters, cultures, and institutional structures of social cooperation in ways that direct global change processes toward a more desirable future. We will make mistakes—we will hurt one another and be deeply hurt on future occasions as we have in the past, and we will do our best together and still be wrong sometimes. Nonetheless, we will grow wiser and do better than if we refused to take the risks of working together and opening ourselves to one another's influence; and the values at stake are so great that we must continue to pick ourselves up, learn from both aspects of our experience, and revise our efforts accordingly. We must work together to sustain our individual self-esteem and our critically loyal pride in the group traditions that made our present achievements and our new efforts possible. At the same time, we must recognize the need to learn from one another, to grow, and to set the future courses of our diverse traditions in compatible, sometimes convergent, always diversity-celebrating directions that reflect the fruitfulness of our experiences of individual growth through cooperative, cross-difference processes of democratic transformation.

Notes

1. Most Western philosophers, economists, and democratic theorists have paid too little attention to these developments, though the mainstream Western press has reported them; see, for example, Edmund L. Andrews, "Poland Opens Door to West, and Chills Blow Both Ways," *New York Times*, June 21, 1999, A1. For retrospective and prospective economic, political, cultural, educational, and philosophical analyses of these developments by participants in an international conference in Krakow, Poland, sponsored by the Jagiellonian University and the Friedrich Neumann

Foundation, see Miklaszewska 1999 and Green 1999b. See also Singer and Koczanowicz, forthcoming.

2. See Crossett 1998. In Afghanistan, an effective effort to end girls' education and women's employment outside the home on the basis of the revolutionary Taliban faction's conception of Islamic law has already worsened this situation while at the same time offering a frightening model path to an even less democratic future with terrible implications for women, the environment, and international peace.

3. Concerning causes and implications of the 1999 unemployment rate of 90 percent among women in industrial areas of posttotalitarian Ukraine, see Ukrainian feminist theorist Kutova (1999).

4. At the 1999 Eastern Division meetings of the American Philosophical Association, Uma Narayan argued that it is possible to practice "female circumcision" in minimal ways and in sterile conditions that would make it no more objectionable than common practices of male circumcision that are virtually uncriticized in the West. Narayan's analogy misfires, because current widespread practices of clitoridectomy and other forms of female genital mutilation, often in unsanitary conditions, are closer in one important respect to male castration than to male circumcision—they bar the girls who are subjected to them from ever experiencing sexual pleasure due to genital stimulation. However, I agree with Narayan's general view that women's universal rights have a culturally contextual dimension that must be taken into account in international debates, including her argument that Third World women must be respected in their direction of location-specific efforts to transform their own cultures in ways and at a pace that will make them more responsive to women's needs and potentials; see, for example, Narayan 1997.

5. By "economistic liberal and libertarian theorists of institutional democracy," I have in mind a large group of thinkers in economics, politics, and philosophy who have interactively shaped currently dominant views about democratization, who disagree among themselves about various details, but who hold converging views that treat democracy largely in terms of institutional forms and principles and that treat individuals as fundamentally separate and finished in their development when they reach social adulthood. These thinkers include, among others, Friedrich Hayek, Milton Friedman, Margaret Thatcher, Ronald Reagan, John Rawls, and Jeffrey Sachs, whose *Poland's Jump to the Market Economy* (1993) expresses many of these thinkers' shared assumptions and convergent methods in a brief and highly influential form that reflects his own role in the early 1990s as an expert economic adviser about democratization processes in central and eastern Europe. For historically contextualized criticisms of the dominant view as it has been applied in Poland, see Slay 1994. For technical criticisms of many of Sachs's assumptions and recommendations by an equally respected mainstream economist who until recently served as chief economist for the World Bank, see Stiglitz 1994.

6. See, for example, Sachs 1993; Johnson and Loveman 1995; and Winiecki 1997.

7. The ontological and linguistic perspective from which I argue that we should understand the concept of "women" is both descriptive and regulative, involving overlapping patterns of commonalities amid various differences, rather than a shared essence or set of universal necessary and sufficient characteristics, and draws on Ludwig Wittgenstein's (1958) analysis of games.

8. See Jane Addams's discussion of "Charitable Effort" in *Democracy and Social Ethics* (1902). See also her *Twenty Years at Hull House* (1910).

9. See Seigfried's (1996) insightful discussion of Addams's methods, her contributions to the development of classical American pragmatism, and the resources she offers for contemporary pragmatist feminism.

References

Addams, Jane. 1902. *Democracy and Social Ethics*. New York: Macmillan.
———. 1910. *Twenty Years at Hull House*. New York: Macmillan.

Crossett, Barbara. 1998. "UNICEF Study Predicts 16% World Illiteracy Rate Will Increase," *New York Times*, December 9, 1998, A11.

Dewey, John. [1916] 1980. *Democracy and Education*. Vol. 9 of *The Middle Works*. Edited by Jo Ann Boydston. Carbondale: Southern Illinois University Press.

———. [1919] 1982. "Philosophy and Democracy." In *The Middle Works*. Vol. 11. Edited by Jo Ann Boydston, 41–53. Carbondale: Southern Illinois University Press.

———. [1920] 1982. *Reconstruction in Philosophy*. In *The Middle Works*. Vol. 12. Edited by Jo Ann Boydston, 77–201. Carbondale: Southern Illinois University Press.

———. [1929] 1984. *The Quest for Certainty*. Vol. 4 of *The Later Works*. Edited by Jo Ann Boydston. Carbondale: Southern Illinois University Press.

———. [1930] 1984. "What I Believe." In *The Later Works*. Vol. 5. Edited by Jo Ann Boydston, 267–78. Carbondale: Southern Illinois University Press.

———. [1932] 1985. *Ethics*. Rev. ed. With James H. Tufts. Vol. 7 of *The Later Works*. Edited by Jo Ann Boydston. Carbondale: Southern Illinois University Press.

———. [1940] 1988. "Time and Individuality." In *The Later Works*. Vol. 14. Edited by Jo Ann Boydston, 98–114. Carbondale: Southern Illinois University Press.

Green, Judith M. 1999a. *Deep Democracy: Community, Diversity, and Transformation*. Lanham, Md.: Rowman and Littlefield.

———. 1999b. "Deepening Democracy in Central Europe: A Radical Pragmatist Perspective from the American Experience." In *Democracy in Central Europe, 1989–1999: Comparative and Historical Perspectives*, edited by Justyna Miklaszewska, 101–30. Krakow: Meritum.

———. 2001. "Guiding Post-totalitarian Economic Democratization Through Deweyan Radical Pragmatism." In *Democracy and the Post-totalitarian Experience*, edited by Beth J. Singer and Leszek Koczanowicz. Amsterdam: Central-European Value Studies, Editions Rodopi.

Johnson, Simon, and Gary Loveman. 1995. *Starting Over in Eastern Europe: Entrepreneurship and Economic Renewal*. Cambridge: Harvard Business School Press.

Kutova. Natalia. 1999. "Gender Equality in Ukrainian Democratic Discourse." In *Democracy in Central Europe, 1989–1999: Comparative and Historical Perspectives*, edited by Justyna Miklaszewska, 343–52. Krakow: Meritum.

Miklaszewska, Justyna. 1999. "Public Choice Theory and Politico-economic reforms in Poland." In *Democracy in Central Europe, 1989–1999: Comparative and Historical Perspectives*, edited by Justyna Miklaszewska, 87–99. Krakow: Meritum.

Narayan, Uma. 1997. *Dislocating Cultures: Identities, Traditions, and Third World Feminism*. New York: Routledge.

Sachs, Jeffrey. 1993. *Poland's Jump to the Market Economy*. Cambridge: MIT Press.

Seigfried, Charlene Haddock. 1996. *Pragmatism and Feminism: Reweaving the Social Fabric*. Chicago: University of Chicago Press.

Singer, Beth J., and Leszek Koczanowicz, ed. *Democracy and the Post-totalitarian Experience*. Amsterdam: Central-European Value Studies, Editions Rodopi, 2001.

Slay, Ben. 1994. *The Polish Economy: Crisis, Reform, and Transformation*. Princeton: Princeton University Press.

Stiglitz, Joseph E. 1994. *Whither Socialism?* Cambridge: MIT Press.

West, Cornel. 1994. *Race Matters*. New York: Vintage Books.

Winiecki, Jan, ed. 1997. *Institutional Barriers to Poland's Economic Development: The Incomplete Transition*. New York: Routledge.

Wittgenstein, Ludwig. 1958. *Philosophical Investigations*. 3d ed. Translated and edited by G. E. M. Anscombe. London: Basil Blackwell and Mott.

13

Jane Addams's Critique of Capitalism as Patriarchal

Marilyn Fischer

In the 1970s, socialist feminists, by synthesizing elements of Marx's critique of capitalism with radical feminism's insights into patriarchy's pervasiveness, argued that capitalism is patriarchal. Jane Addams, feminist and pragmatist of the Progressive Era, also analyzed industrial capitalism as patriarchal. In this essay I will point out affinities and distinctions in the two analyses.

But why an article on capitalism as patriarchal in a book about Dewey? In *Pragmatism and Feminism*, Charlene Haddock Seigfried (1996, 10) points out many respects in which pragmatist and feminist perspectives

are closely aligned. She decries the paucity of feminist literature on pragmatism and brings to our attention many women from the late nineteenth and early twentieth century who worked within the pragmatist
tradition. Seigfried (1993, 5) writes, "Although Addams's philosophy is
virtually neglected in classical pragmatist writings, there is more evidence
for her contributions to pragmatism than for any other woman I have
discovered so far."

This essay is a response to Seigfried's invitation to explore historical
writings of women within the pragmatist tradition. In the first part, I
show how Dewey's and Addams's shared appreciation of evolutionary perspectives, concrete experience, context, and sympathetic understanding
led them to similar conceptions of social democracy and similar critiques
of industrial capitalism. In Part II, I explain how Addams's critique of
industrial capitalism goes beyond Dewey's in explicitly linking capitalism
with philanthropy as then practiced, and criticizing both as patriarchal.
In Part III, I compare Addams's account to that of socialist feminists, and
show that while there are clear differences in their accounts, there are
also many affinities.[1]

I. Commonalities in Dewey and Addams

Addams and Dewey had a long and close association. Alice Hamilton
([1945] 1985, 65), a longtime resident of Hull House, speaks of Dewey as
one of Addams's "closest friends and counselors." In her writings, Addams mentions Dewey frequently, with both appreciation and humor.
Acknowledging Dewey's tenure as a Hull House trustee, Addams (Lasch
1966, 177) notes, "Unlike many trustees, he actually worked on the job."
Dewey used Addams's book *Democracy and Social Ethics* as a text in his
teaching and cites Addams and the work of Hull House as contributing
significantly to his conceptions of democracy and education (Seigfried
1996, 74). Without a detailed history of their collaboration, it is impossible to say how and from whom these ideas originated. No doubt they
emerged in true pragmatist fashion from the remarkable mix of activity
and reflection that Addams and Dewey shared with the residents of Hull
House and colleagues from the University of Chicago.

Both Addams and Dewey write from an evolutionary perspective.
Working within the tradition of Auguste Comte's evolutionary ethics,

Addams describes in some detail stages she calls individual ethics, and social ethics or social democracy (Fischer 1995). This evolutionary perspective gives Addams a pattern for ethical analysis. As social organization changes, so ethical codes and values should adapt accordingly. Values of a previous stage should not be discarded, but adjusted and supplemented to meet the challenges of newly evolving circumstances. Addams often analyzes ethically troubling situations, not in terms of right and wrong or good and evil, but in terms of maladjustment, where values and codes of earlier times have not been readjusted with changing social conditions and newly emerging values.

For Dewey, Darwinian evolutionary theory shifted philosophical thinking profoundly. For two thousand years, knowledge, goodness, beauty, and truth had been understood in terms of transcendence, perfection, and static permanence (Dewey [1910] 1977, 3). Post-Darwin, Dewey claims, knowledge and truth should be sought in patterns of change and growth. Philosophical inquiry should focus on specific organisms in constant interaction with concrete and complex environments, constantly doing and undergoing, initiating and responding (Dewey [1917] 1980, 26). Since "every occurrence is a concurrence," the context of change is crucial. Here, context includes the spatial and temporal environment within which the organism functions, as well as culture, traditions of interpretation, and values. The philosopher's stance cannot be that of an external, objective observer. Dewey calls this "view from nowhere" an absurdity. Rather, the philosopher should adopt an artist's perspective, shaping ideas and theories with care, concern, and affection (Dewey [1931] 1985, 9–15).

With this orientation, philosophy, like science, should be experimental. In ethics, moral principles are not eternal verities, but hypotheses to be tested, adapted, readjusted, and verified by experience (Dewey [1922] 1988, 164–65). Deliberation is a form of experimentation, which takes place in the imagination (132). Rather than simply providing commentary on other philosophical theories, philosophy should address perplexing issues of its own time.

Like Dewey, Addams begins with the premise that moral perception and knowledge must be based on concrete, lived experience. She acted on this premise in founding Hull House, a settlement house in Chicago located in an immigrant neighborhood of Russians, Polish people, Germans, Greeks, Italians, and others. In her article "A Function of the Social Settlements" Addams is explicit that Hull House was founded as a pragmatist test: to verify that the truth of an idea lies in its application. Those founding a settlement are motivated by "a desire to use synthetically and directly whatever knowledge they, as a group, may possess, to test its validity and to discover the conditions under which this knowledge may be employed" (Addams [1899] 1994, 77; see Seigfried 1996, 196–201). Addams and the residents of Hull House were careful not to be identified with any religious and political doctrine. They feared such identification might cloud their perceptions in reading experience and hinder their ability to respond with flexibility (Addams et al. [1893] 1970, 22–23).

Both Dewey and Addams conceptualize people as inherently social beings, organically interconnected. In *Democracy and Education* Dewey ([1916] 1980, 129) writes, "What one is as a person is what one is as associated with others, in a free give and take of intercourse." Intelligence itself is inherently and contextually social (see Seigfried 1996, 95–101). Addams shares this perspective, and adds to it a belief in "universal brotherhood." She was deeply influenced by Tolstoy's conception of early Christianity, interpreted simply as love for all humankind, without dogma or theology. Addams (Addams et al. [1893] 1970, 19–20) believes that "love is the creative force of the universe, the principle which binds men together and by their interdependence on each other makes them human." Here Addams ([1902] 1964, 63) blends a pragmatist commitment to action as the test of knowledge with Tolstoy's belief that faith must be enacted. Solidarity among all humankind is undergirded by compassion for the vulnerable, extending to worthy and unworthy alike.

Thus, both Addams and Dewey write of entering imaginatively and sympathetically into the perspective of others. Addams is careful to pair sympathetic understanding with carefully acquired facts. She and her colleagues were emphatic that a first step to addressing social concerns was to gather accurate information and statistical data. Addams (1906, 160, 10) gives detailed accounts of how the charitable impulse uninformed by knowledge can be cruel and disastrous; without concrete knowledge, she claims, sheer sentiment is blind. Yet without sympathy, one cannot gain access into how others perceive and experience a situation; that is, one cannot know about the event or context. Sympathy is itself an entrance requirement for understanding. Sympathetic knowledge, Addams (1912b, 11) writes, "is the only way of approach to any human problem."

Dewey's and Addams's conceptions of democracy are strikingly similar. For both, democracy is far more than a way of governing; it is a way of associated living. Dewey ([1916] 1980, 88–93) would assess a democracy by asking how freely and fully the people associate, and how many and varied are the interests they share.

Addams would ask the same questions. For Addams, social democracy is the ethics suitable to an urban, industrial society. Addams viewed her own society as one in which traditional kinship-village patterns had been replaced by complex, reciprocal, industrial interdependencies. For Addams, social democracy is a mode of association, concomitant with this complex interdependency. However, this interdependency is far more than economic. Repeatedly, Addams (1906, 64ff.) points out what her immigrant neighbors can teach more-assimilated Americans; how their customs, art, and conceptions of justice and sociability can enrich understanding and social life immeasurably.

Democratic values of equality and freedom are best understood in terms of growth and reciprocity. In contrast to social contract theorists who view persons as bundles of rights and duties, Addams (1906, 38) sees the person dynamically, as ever growing and evolving. Each person is a source of social power, "a creative agent and a possible generator of fine enthusiasm," with something of unique value to contribute (Addams [1902] 1964, 179).

Addams ([1910] 1990, 258) and Dewey (Gouinlock 1994, 190–92, 208, 223) both assess democracy, not in terms of political or legal rights, but by whether all members of a community have the opportunity to develop their capacities, to share in the community's economic wealth and cultural inheritance, and to contribute to the community's enrichment. Thus, for both Addams and Dewey, social democracy should pervade all aspects of life: in industry, community, and family, as well as in government. Hull House provided the experimental testing grounds. Addams (Addams et al. [1893] 1970, 10) writes, "The social and educational activities of a Settlement are but differing manifestations of the attempt to socialize democracy, as is the existence of the settlement itself."

But in late nineteenth- and early twentieth-century Chicago, social democracy did not pervade industrial life. Addams's knowledge of industrial capitalism grew from her experience with its effects on her immigrant neighbors, many of whom worked fourteen hours a day in Chicago factories and sweatshops. She recounts these experiences in poignant detail. Little girls refused candy at a Hull House Christmas party, because they "worked in a candy factory and could not bear the sight of it" (Addams [1910] 1990, 117). Scarlet fever broke out in rural areas from coats sewn in infected city sweatshops; children were injured and killed for lack of inexpensive factory safety equipment (117). Factory workers were "heavy and almost dehumanized by monotonous toil," their days "filled with monotonous and deadening drudgery" (Addams 1964, 207, 189–90). Modern industry, Addams ([1910] 1990, 219) writes, is "needlessly ruthless and brutal to her own children."

Both Addams ([1902] 1964, 206–7) and Dewey ([1934] 1987, 345ff.) write about how workers need an artist's perception; they need to have a sense of industry as a whole and to know and appreciate what they contribute to that whole. Many of the immigrants' children in Addams's neighborhood worked in textile factories; many of the parents had been weavers and spinners in Europe, yet neither saw continuity between their endeavors. Addams called this chasm "unnecessarily cruel and impassable," and sought some way of bridging the distance between Americanized children and immigrant parents, while showing to both the continuity of their labor. Addams recounts how she first discussed her ideas with Dewey and then started a labor museum that gave a living history of textile production from the immigrants' traditions. The museum served both of Addams's purposes. Workers could see historic continuity from spinning wheels and hand looms to industrial textile production, and the immigrants' children found new pride in their parents' craft (Addams [1910] 1990, 139–41).

Seeing one's role in the whole of production is but a part of transforming industry into social democracy. Dewey and Addams were also concerned by workers' lack of control over the machines they tended. Dewey writes of how workers do not contribute to deciding what the machines are to be used for; they do not understand how the machines work, hence they have no care and concern for the purposes to be achieved. Labor becomes a burden rather than active fulfillment (Dewey [1922] 1988, 100, 86–87). Addams ([1909] 1972, 128) adds that machines should function as tools, controlled by the workers' creative intelligence, rather than the workers being controlled by the machines.

Addams and Dewey are troubled by the class-based division of labor in industrial capitalism. Dewey ([1916] 1980, 346) states explicitly that class divisions between those who labor with their muscles and those who freed from such labor are the source of classic philosophical dualisms: rational-empirical, universal-particular, intellect-emotions, and so on. Addams ([1902] 1964, 195) provides a historical perspective: "Apparently we have not yet recovered manual labor from the deep distrust which centuries of slavery and the feudal system have cast upon it." Addams (1906, 116) adds race and ethnicity to her class-based analysis, noting how modern industry exhibits contempt for the worker, not unlike contempt for the slave, and much of the physical and psychological burden falls on the immigrants.

II. Addams's Critique of Capitalism as Patriarchal

We have seen how many similarities there are in Dewey's and Addams's critiques of industrial capitalism. But Addams goes beyond Dewey in explicitly linking capitalism with philanthropy as then practiced, and in using the patriarchal family as a model for arguing against both. For Addams, the salient traits of the patriarchal family are hierarchical authority, where the subordinate is expected to respond with gratitude, and social responsibility limited by the boundaries of the family.

Experiences with her own family and with her immigrant neighbors gave Addams rich materials to draw upon in understanding the patriarchal character of families. In "Filial Relations" Addams ([1902] 1964, chapter 3) describes the tensions between parents and their adult daughters in families of some social standing. These parents expect their sons to enlarge their fields of interest and endeavor beyond the family, but when their daughters respond to the ethical claims of the larger world, the family accuses them of being selfish. "It is always difficult for the family to regard the daughter otherwise than as a family possession," Addams (82) notes. The family here is patriarchal in that the parents feel they have the authority to restrict their daughters' activities to the family realm, and they do not feel their daughters' responsibilities should extend beyond the family to larger social needs.

In "Household Adjustment" Addams ([1902] 1964, chapter 4) gives a lengthy analysis of domestic service, focusing primarily on young, unmarried women as isolated, live-in servants to a household. Addams's analysis of the patriarchal family is appropriate here, even though the "mistress" and "the servant," as they were then called, are unrelated biologically and are both women.

Many dimensions of this relationship are undemocratic; Addams points them out in considerable detail. The mistress functions patriarchally in that she is in a position of relatively unbounded authority over the servant and there is not even the pretense of contractual limits to what she may ask the servant to do. Excessive demands in terms of hours and tasks may be imposed at whim. The servant is expected to be grateful for any consideration or affection. Also, from the mistress's point of view, the servant's obligations are defined and limited by the mistress's dedication to her own family. The servant's obligations beyond those limits, to her own aged parents or even for her own independent social life, for example, are of little account. Addams ([1902] 1964, 124) notes the irony in how the mistress's demands come from her "zeal to preserve her own family life intact," without noticing that she is denying the same to the servant.

This patriarchal pattern of authority and responsibility belongs to the stage in evolutionary ethics that Addams calls "individual ethics." Addams did not conceptualize the individual in terms of natural or contractual rights and duties, as did Locke, nor in terms of individual autonomy, as did Kant. Instead, "the individual" is a social unit that functions like a patriarchal family, regardless of the sex or blood relationship of the members of the unit.

In the examples given here, the parents' and the mistresses' moral codes are within this stage of individual ethics. The adult daughters and the servants, with their broader perspective of social ethics or social democracy, do not reject their obligations to family and employer, but wish to redefine those obligations democratically. Addams writes that these two moral stances are "maladjusted." The answer is not to discard either, but to adjust both claims, so that "neither shall lose and both be ennobled" (Addams [1902] 1964, 75).

While Addams does not name Andrew Carnegie, his highly influential essay, "The Gospel of Wealth," published in 1889, provides a context for her critique of industrial capitalism and philanthropy as patriarchal. Carnegie's thesis was that the wealthy should not squander their wealth on personal indulgence; instead, they should use it for public betterment. He gives a clear utilitarian argument for capitalism, and adds that it ensures the survival of the fittest. Like Adam Smith ([1776] 1993, 10, 177), Carnegie ([1889] 1992, 130) claims that the poor under capitalism are far better off than they otherwise would be, even though the increasing inequality between rich and poor leads to class friction.

Carnegie advocates philanthropy as a way of extending opportunities to the "deserving poor." He is clear that decisions about how to use their wealth belong to wealthy persons themselves, given their superior wisdom and judgment. By contributing to projects such as universities, public libraries, hospitals, museums, concert and lecture halls, public parks, and so on, the wealthy provide "ladders on which the aspiring can climb" (Carnegie [1889] 1992, 140). This path would reconcile the rich and the poor, enabling them to live in social harmony (Carnegie [1889] 1992, 136). For Carnegie, then, the path to social betterment is capitalism plus philanthropy, working together.[2]

It is a patriarchal family in literature that provides Addams with a model for how capitalism is patriarchal, and explains why Carnegie's solution of capitalism plus philanthropy will not lead to social betterment and harmony. In A Modern Lear, Addams draws a parallel between King Lear's troubled relation with his daughter, Cordelia, and George Pullman's troubles with his striking workers. Of this work Dewey (Lasch 1965, 176) wrote, "It is one of the greatest things I ever read both as to its form and its ethical philosophy." Although written in 1894, the work was not published until 1912, because it was so controversial. George Pullman, manufacturer of railroad cars, had built a model town for his employees, with decent houses, beautiful parks, and other amenities. Thus he functioned both as capitalist employer and as philanthropist toward his employees. In the summer of 1894 the Pullman workers, who were not allowed to unionize, went on strike over a reduction in wages. The American Railway Union, under the leadership of Eugene Debs, called a nationwide sympathy strike. Addams ([1910] 1990, 126), as a representative of Chicago's Citizens' Arbitration Committee, served in arbitration efforts.

As is typical of Addams's writings, she took a concrete case that she knew intimately and used it to make a larger, theoretical point. King Lear, as owner of the kingdom, had the authority to dispose of his riches as he saw fit. He was indulgent, ready to bestow his wealth lavishly upon his daughters. Pullman was indulgent toward the workers, far beyond expectations of the time. Both had dictatorial relations in regard to their subordinates; both expected gratitude and deference in return. Both assigned their beneficence in terms of their own independent assessment of their subordinates' needs and deserts, without involving them in the decision process or viewing the situation from the perspective of the subordinates' moral sensitivities (Addams 1912a).

Cordelia and Pullman's workers were responding to a wider arena of moral concern. Addams describes Cordelia's refusal to declare her devotion in the way Lear expected as "the awkward attempt of an untrained soul to be honest, to be scrupulous in the expressions of its feelings." Rather than responding solely as a dutiful daughter, she answered Lear as "a citizen of the world," with moral obligations beyond that of mere gratitude to her father. Likewise, Pullman's workers were joining in the worldwide movement toward social justice for the working class, desiring international solidarity. Their work-related moral obligations were not limited by the boundaries their employer imposed; with other workers they "had learned to say in many languages that 'the injury of one is the concern of all'" (1912a, 134, 135). Addams (132) notes, "Historically considered, the relation of Lear to his children was archaic and barbaric, holding in it merely the beginnings of a family life, since developed. We may in later years learn to look back upon the industrial relationships in which we are now placed as quite as incomprehensible and selfish, quite as barbaric and undeveloped, as was the family relationship between Lear and his daughters."

Thus, Addams shows how the pattern of authority and responsibility characteristic of the patriarchal family is also descriptive of late nineteenth-century philanthropy and industrial capitalism. From their perspective of individual ethics, philanthropists such as Carnegie and Pullman feel entitled to select recipients of their largesse and to determine what their needs are. Recipients are considered blameworthy if they do not respond with gratitude. Similarly, private-property ownership gives capitalists hierarchical authority to manage employees' activities as they see fit and to retain profits. It also limits their scope of responsibility, assuming that they have no obligation for the well-being of the community or workers outside the factory walls. But in fact, industrial production is inherently and complexly social, characterized by interdependence and reciprocity of effort and contribution by all. The form of the factory is social, the ends anachronistically individual (Addams [1902] 1964, 139). Addams (2–3) writes, "To attain individual morality in an age demanding social morality, to pride one's self on the results of personal effort when the time demands social adjustment, is utterly to fail to apprehend the situation."

Like the rest of society, the workplace should be characterized by social democracy. At that time, government regulation of industry was virtually nonexistent, and with other Hull House residents Addams worked tirelessly for legislation regarding hours, wages, sanitary conditions, and restrictions on child labor. But that was just the beginning of her concern.

She compares the emancipation of workers with the emancipation of slaves and advocates that together, employees and employers should labor cooperatively. In production, all parties should be motivated by affection and social justice. Like Dewey (Morris and Shapiro 1993, 170), Addams envisions labor as a medium for understanding, self-expression, and self-development. The goal, Addams (1912a, 136) writes, is "the complete participation of the working classes in the spiritual, intellectual and material inheritance of the human race."

Seigfried (1996, 150) suggests that the pragmatist approach becomes more pragmatist when women's experiences are included. Although their analyses of industrial capitalism are similar in many respects, Addams's knowledge of women's experiences in families of many configurations strengthens her critique. Dewey, in contrast to many canonical philosophers, also uses the family as a model and source of insight. Dewey (Morris and Shapiro 1993, 64) speaks of the family as an ethical community, in which individuality is not lost, but in which there is "unity of interest and purpose," and he then proposes that industry should function analogously. Now for Dewey to use the family as a model for industry is itself remarkable, but the model is limited by his idealized conception of the family (see Seigfried 1996, 95–104). By contrast, many of Addams's experiences were with troubled families, with drunken husbands, neglectful fathers, troubled and troublesome children, and women who naively and cheerfully put up with domestic abuse. Because of her concrete experience with many families and her awareness of women's varied experiences within families, Addams has a clearer, more nuanced perspective for understanding and evaluating industrial capitalism.

III. Addams and Socialist Feminism

In the 1970s, socialist feminists developed sophisticated critiques of capitalism as patriarchal by synthesizing, in varying ways and degrees, a Marxist critique of capitalism with a radical feminist critique of patriarchy. Socialist feminist thinking continues to be refined and revitalized by work on intersections of gender, race, class, and sexuality.[3] Since Addams was writing in an earlier time and out of a different theoretical orientation, her critique of capitalism as patriarchal of course differs from more recent socialist feminist critiques. I will indicate some of these differences and also note points of affinity between Addams's and socialist feminists' critiques of capitalism as patriarchal.

Historically, socialist feminism developed out of Marxism. The social-ist movement was vibrantly alive in Chicago's immigrant communities in the last decade of the nineteenth century. Addams studied socialism intensely and worked closely with many socialists on union issues and social reform measures. Florence Kelley, who lived at Hull House for seven years and, according to her son, regarded Addams as her "dearest and most intimate friend," was a committed socialist (Linn 1938, 138). Kelley corresponded with Engels and had translated his "Conditions of the Working Class in England" before coming to Hull House (Addams [1910] 1990, 116). Addams credits Kelley with directing Hull House's focus toward research and social reform (Seigfried 1996, 78).[4]

Addams was not a socialist, although people often associated her and Hull House with radical movements. In fact, chapters 9 and 10 of *Twenty Years at Hull House* can be read as Addams's pragmatist reply to socialism. She ([1910] 1990, 110) deeply appreciated the socialists' dedication to relieving poverty and to promoting solidarity among the working poor through union activity. Addams also found great value in the endless theoretical discussions on socialism held at Hull House. These discus-sions aroused the community's conscience and helped settlement workers "learn the difference between mere social unrest and spiritual impulse" (116).

Addams uses her concrete experience in the Hull House neighborhood to test socialist theories. Working in the midst of great poverty and social chaos, she reminisces, "I also longed for the comfort of a definite social creed." But parallels between then current theoretical discussions on so-cialism and her childhood ruminations about the doctrine of foreordina-tion troubled her. Neither doctrine placed at its center "the essential provisionality of everything" that day-to-day experience reveals (116).

Addams lived through many strikes, negotiated many of them, and gave solace to the broken bodies and spirits left in their aftermath. In *A Modern Lear*, although Addams's sympathies are clearly with the workers, she chides them. Just as Cordelia needed to go back to her father, "so the emancipation of working people will have to be inclusive of the employer from the first or it will encounter many failures, cruelties and reaction" (Addams 1912a, 137).

Knowing how variable people are, and how intertwined cooperative efforts must be, Addams (1906, 86) gently rebukes the socialists, saying,

"Their orators are busily engaged in establishing two substitutes for human nature which they call 'proletarian' and 'capitalist.' They ignore the fact that varying, imperfect human nature is incalculable, and that . . . in time 'the proletarian' and 'the capitalist' will become the impedimenta which it will be necessary to clear away in order to make room for the mass of living and breathing citizens with whom self-government must eventually deal."[5] Addams advocates social change through "associated effort," rather than class struggle, with cooperative, full participation of all those affected. Progress will be slower, but deeper, as the process creates sympathetic understanding among all those involved (1912a, 137).

Addams's critiques of both capitalism and socialism exhibit her pragmatist methodology. As a pragmatist she focuses on how industrial capitalism actually functions, rather than on its theoretical lineage. While she criticizes political liberalism as an inadequate theory, she does not argue against capitalism for being based on that inadequate theory. She examines the meaning and impact of industrial capitalism on concrete lives and finds its patriarchal character by analogy with the concrete experience of living in patriarchal families. The limitations of socialism that concern her are the ones revealed likewise through pragmatist examination of socialism as lived and tested by concrete experience and sympathetic understanding. For Addams ([1902] 1964, 273), "action is indeed the sole medium of expression for ethics." Addams would be encouraged by moves in contemporary feminism away from totalizing theory toward more localized, nuanced analyses in terms of race, class, ethnicity, and historical and geographical location. She would approve the emphasis on context, but would be concerned if the results were to entrench differences more deeply.

However, in many respects Addams's work anticipates contemporary socialist feminist perspectives. Addams did not intend her reform measures as mere tinkering with the political-economic system already in place. Her conception of social democracy shares more affinity with the socialist vision than with that of classical liberalism. While not a socialist, Addams also was not a classical political liberal, and she criticizes liberalism for many of the same reasons that socialists do. Addams (1906, 31–33) criticizes the social contract tradition vigorously, centering her pragmatist critique on its lack of sympathetic understanding and its vast distance from concrete experience. Experience reveals, for example, how political liberalism has failed immigrants by defining democracy in terms of political rights and the franchise. Addams (1906, 42–43) reveals her pragmatism, her clarity, and her scorn in writing: "As children who are allowed to amuse themselves with poker chips pay no attention to the real game which their elders play with the genuine cards in their hands, so we shut our eyes to the exploitation and industrial debasement of the immigrant, and say, with placid contentment, that he has been given the rights of an American citizen, and that, therefore, all our obligations have been fulfilled."[6] Addams's conception of humans as inherently social, as changing historically, and as having creative potential to develop through association all resonate with a socialist feminist approach.

Jaggar (1983, 132) points out, "The one solid basis of agreement among socialist feminists is that to overcome women's alienation, the sexual division of labor must be eliminated in every area of life." Addams's writings and political activity are not this sweeping. She never discusses the politics of reproduction and does not suggest that men share child-care responsibilities equally with women; Addams (1912b, 115) at one point refers to child rearing as women's "supreme social function." However, Addams knew of and sought to change many dimensions of the sexual division of labor, both in the home and in the workplace.

Addams does not make the liberal distinction between private and public spheres, but like socialist feminists, sees continuity and interpenetration between family and community. Because the Hull House neighborhood was not only multiethnic, but also "multihistorical" in the sense that for many of her neighbors, centuries-old, historical traditions were vital ways of life, Addams watched the lines and tasks of public and private waver, overlap, and become redrawn. Like socialist feminists, Addams views the family as an historically evolving institution, and notes how women's responsibilities have changed accordingly.

Addams's analysis of the stages of individual ethics and social ethics needing adjustment can be applied here. Before industrialization, women defined their responsibilities in terms of the family, in the stage of individual ethics. Since the home was a center of economic activity, women's work included textile production, agriculture, and often administrative responsibilities directing the work of many others (Addams [1902] 1964, 104–5). But through industrialization those tasks have been socialized by their being moved into the factory and placed under industrial and municipal control. As a result, women lost administrative and productive control over the processes necessary for caring for their own families. The old line between family and society is maladjusted to current industrial conditions. It was painfully evident to Addams that a Victorian mother, tending only to her separate sphere, could not possibly succeed in the Hull House neighborhood. Addams ([1910] 1990, 172) tells of a neighbor, single-mindedly devoted to keeping her own home clean, who could not stop typhoid from claiming her daughter. A city, Addams writes, is in many respects "enlarged housekeeping." Clean milk, untainted meat, and adequate garbage collection are both civic matters and intimate family concerns. Women cannot care adequately for their families unless they are also involved in civic affairs (Addams 1906, chapter 7).

Hull House tried many experiments, seeking to help families adjust to industrial conditions. One of its first undertakings was a day nursery; young and old alike were welcome while their family members worked in factories (Addams [1910] 1990, 100). Hull House also experimented with a community kitchen. Knowing that women in the sewing trades did not have time to prepare nutritious meals, the residents gathered data and methods on large-scale food preparation and sold nutritious stews and soups to factories and households. The results of this experiment were mixed. Addams summarized many neighbors' attitudes in her account of how one woman rejected the community-kitchen products, the woman explaining that she preferred to eat "what she'd ruther." A coffeehouse, which gave neighbors an alternative to the saloon for social gatherings, was more successful. Addams comments on how this experiment reinforced the need for sympathetic understanding. Hull House residents should be responsive to the neighbors' own assessment of their needs, rather than deciding what is good for them (Addams [1910] 1990, 78–79).

Guiding Addams in these and other experiments was her understanding of the family, not as a private haven, but as intertwined with the community. "The sacredness and beauty of family life do not consist in the processes of the separate preparation of food, but in sharing the corporate life of the community, and in making the family the unit of that life" (Addams [1902] 1964, 110). This understanding was no doubt developed and reinforced by life in Hull House, itself offering a kind of family. There were male as well as female residents at Hull House, but it was clearly a female-led and -dominated space. Addams ([1910] 1990, 89–90; 255–58; see also Seigfried 1996, 73–79) drew great strength, intellectual stimulation, and activist collegiality from living there.

Addams also worked to ameliorate the impact of the sexual division of labor in industry. Many of her female neighbors worked in sex-segregated sweatshops and factories. Addams and her colleagues helped to organize many women's unions and a workingwomen's living cooperative. Hull House residents and neighbors worked tirelessly for legal regulation of factory safety and sanitary conditions and for child-labor restrictions (Addams [1910] 1990, chapter 10).

Because Addams was both activist and theorist, and wrote as both simultaneously, it is difficult to ascertain just how deeply she understood the sexual division of labor in the family and in industry. Many of her female neighbors finished their twelve-to-fourteen-hour factory shift, only to begin their heavy domestic responsibilities. Addams advocated protective labor legislation for women, which would have restricted women to a forty-eight-hour work week and prohibited them from working at night. Was she more concerned that the workplace not incapacitate women from meeting gender-assigned obligations to the family than with achieving male and female equality before the law? In contrast to much of the rhetoric supporting protective legislation at the time, Addams ([1910] 1990, 103) writes that women do not need protection because of physical inferiority. But she ached for her neighbor who late every night scrubbed office floors, the pail water mixed with flowing milk because she could not nurse her infant. We have since seen how such legislation worked against women's interests. But at the time, wage equality with men was not a politically viable option, and many thought that protective legislation for women would be a wedge opening the way to improving men's working conditions as well (Kessler-Harris, 1982, chapter 7). Often, Addams had "the sickening sense of compromise," which activists must experience if they are to work *with* the people, rather than seeking to impose their vision of the good society. What mattered most to Addams were the needs of overworked, impoverished women who needed relief right then and who could not wait until gender roles within family, workplace, and law were reconfigured equitably.[7]

Addams's critique of capitalism as patriarchal is a study that richly demonstrates the mutually supportive resources of pragmatism and feminism. By centering her analysis on women's experiences, Addams was able to refine and enrich Dewey's critique of industrial capitalism. Also, Addams's linking of capitalism and philanthropy is particularly useful today as the political debate regarding the poor (and most often, poor women) is so often cast in terms of government welfare programs versus the efforts of nonprofit voluntary associations. Both alternatives embody the same structure as the patriarchal family; both suffer the same fundamental flaws. Finally, comparison with the socialist feminist critique of capitalism illustrates how many affinities Addams's pragmatist approach has with more contemporary scholarship.

Notes

1. Throughout *Pragmatism and Feminism* (1996) Seigfried points out many affinities between pragmatist and feminist perspectives. See especially chapters 7 and 9.

2. Alice Hamilton ([1943] 1985, 6–7), who investigated industrial poisons, comments in her autobiography, "I used to despair of relief for the overworked, underpaid immigrant laborers. . . . It was they who did the heavy, hot, dirty, and dangerous work of the country. In return for it they met little but contempt from more fortunate Americans. . . . The Carnegie Company's principle of a high tariff to shut out cheap foreign-made goods, and a wide-open door to let in cheap foreign labor, resulted in the building up of great fortunes; but measured in terms of human welfare it was cruel and ruthless."

3. See Eisenstein 1979 and Jaggar 1983, chapter 6; also Tong's (1989) overview of socialist feminism. Hennessy and Ingraham 1997 gives selections from the 1970s into the 1990s.

4. See Sklar 1995, chapters 8–12, for a history of Kelley's years at Hull House.

5. Addams's arguments against socialism here parallel her arguments for pacifism; regardless of the justice of the cause, the actual struggle between opposing sides causes great misery and further entrenches hatred and divisions (see Fischer 2000).

6. Chapter 2 of *Democracy and Social Ethics* (Addams [1902] 1964) can be read as a critique of the social contract tradition, which Addams calls "eighteenth century philosophy."

7. Theorist-activists are well acquainted with this dilemma, which Addams faced daily. In discussing whether we should work to reform society or to transform it, Jaggar (1994, 25–26) writes, "Feminists should embrace both horns of this dilemma. . . . Feminists should continue to struggle for women to receive a fair share of the pie, carcinogenic though it ultimately may be," and at the same time seek more thoroughgoing social transformation.

See Seigfried's (1996, 262–68) discussion of how feminists, in setting their research and activism agendas, should not let the aesthetics of theoretical purity overshadow the needs of the most vulnerable.

References

Addams, Jane. [1899] 1994. "A Function of the Social Settlement." In *Jane Addams on Education*. Edited by Ellen C. Lagemann, 74–97. New Brunswick, N.J.: Transaction.

———. [1902] 1964. *Democracy and Social Ethics*. Reprint, with an introduction by Anne Firor Scott, Cambridge: Harvard University Press.

———. 1906. *Newer Ideals of Peace*. New York: Macmillan.

———. [1909] 1972. *The Spirit of Youth and the City Streets*. Reprint, Urbana: University of Illinois Press.

————. [1910] 1990. *Twenty Years At Hull House*. Reprint, Urbana: University of Illinois Press.

————. 1912a. A Modern Lear. *Survey* 29:131–37.

————. 1912b. *A New Conscience and an Ancient Evil*. New York: Macmillan.

Addams, Jane, et al. [1893] 1970. *Philanthropy and Social Progress*. Reprint, Montclair, N.J.: Patterson Smith.

Carnegie, Andrew. [1889] 1992. "The Gospel of Wealth." In *The Andrew Carnegie Reader*. Edited by Joseph F. Wall, 130–54. Pittsburgh: University of Pittsburgh Press.

Dewey, John. [1910] 1977. "The Influence of Darwinism on Philosophy." In *The Middle Works*. Vol. 4. Edited by Jo Ann Boydston, 3–14. Carbondale: Southern Illinois University Press.

————. [1916] 1980. *Democracy and Education*. Vol. 9 of *The Middle Works*. Edited by Jo Ann Boydston. Carbondale: Southern Illinois University Press.

————. [1917] 1980. "The Need for a Recovery of Philosophy." In *The Middle Works*. Vol. 10. Edited by Jo Ann Boydston, 3–48. Carbondale: Southern Illinois University Press.

————. [1922] 1988. *Human Nature and Conduct*. In *The Middle Works*. Vol. 14. Edited by Jo Ann Boydston. Carbondale: Southern Illinois University Press.

————. [1931] 1985. "Context and Thought." In *The Later Works*. Vol. 6. Edited by Jo Ann Boydston, 3–21. Carbondale: Southern Illinois University Press.

————. [1934] 1987. *Art as Experience*. Vol. 10 of *The Later Works*. Edited by Jo Ann Boydston. Carbondale: Southern Illinois University Press.

Eisenstein, Zillah. 1979. "Developing a Theory of Capitalist Patriarchy and Socialist Feminism." In *Capitalist Patriarchy and the Case for Socialist Feminism*, edited by Zillah R. Eisenstein, 5–40. New York: Monthly Review Press.

Fischer, Marilyn. 1995. "Philanthropy and Injustice in Mill and Addams." *Nonprofit and Voluntary Sector Quarterly* 24:281–92.

————. 2000. "Jane Addams's Pragmatist Pacifism." In *Peacemaking: Lessons from the Past, Visions for the Future*, edited by J. Presler and S. Scholz, 207–17. Amsterdam: Rodopi Press.

Gouinlock, James, ed. 1994. *The Moral Writings of John Dewey*. New York: Prometheus Books.

Hamilton, Alice. [1943] 1985. *Exploring the Dangerous Trades*. Reprint, Boston: Northeastern University Press.

Hennessy, Rosemary, and Chrys Ingraham, eds. 1997. *Materialist Feminism: A Reader in Class, Difference, and Women's Lives*. New York: Routledge.

Jaggar, Alison. 1983. *Feminist Politics and Human Nature*. Totowa, N.J.: Roman and Allanheld.

————. 1994. "Sexual Difference and Sexual Equality." In *Living with Contradictions: Controversies in Feminist Social Ethics*, edited by Alison Jaggar, 18–28. Boulder, Colo.: Westview Press.

Kessler-Harris, Alice. 1983. *Out to Work: A History of Wage-Earning Women in the United States*. New York: Oxford University Press.

Lasch, Christopher, ed. 1965. *The Social Thought of Jane Addams*. New York: Bobbs-Merrill.

Linn, James. 1938. *Jane Addams: A Biography*. New York: D. Appleton-Century.

Morris, Debra, and Ian Shapiro, eds. 1993. *John Dewey: The Political Writings*. Indianapolis: Hackett.

Seigfried, Charlene Haddock. 1993. "Shared Communities of Interest: Feminism and Pragmatism." *Hypatia* 8(2): 1–14.

——. 1996. *Pragmatism and Feminism*. Chicago: University of Chicago Press.

Sklar, Kathryn Kish. 1995. *Florence Kelley and the Nation's Work*. New Haven: Yale University Press.

Smith, Adam. [1776] 1993. *The Wealth of Nations*. Edited by Laurence Dickey. Indianapolis: Hackett.

Tong, Rosemary. 1989. *Feminist Thought: A Comprehensive Introduction*. Boulder, Colo.: Westview Press.

Select Bibliography

Addams, Jane. *Democracy and Social Ethics*. 1902. With an introduction by A. F. Scott. Cambridge: Harvard University Press, 1964. Reprint, with an introduction by Charlene Haddock Seigfried, Champaign: University of Illinois Press, 2001.
———. "A Function of the Social Settlement." 1899. In *Jane Addams on Education*. Edited by Ellen C. Lagemann, 74–97. New Brunswick, N.J.: Transaction Publishers, 1994.
———. *The Long Road of Women's Memory*. New York: Macmillan, 1916. Reprint, with an introduction by Charlene Haddock Seigfried, Champaign: University of Illinois Press, 2001.
———. *A New Conscience and an Ancient Evil*. New York: Macmillan, 1912.
———. *Newer Ideals of Peace*. New York: Macmillan, 1906.
———. *The Spirit of Youth and the City Streets*. 1909. Reprint, Urbana: University of Illinois Press, 1972.
———. *Twenty Years at Hull-House*. 1910. New York: Signet Classic, 1981.
———, et al. *Philanthropy and Social Progress*. 1893. Reprint, Montclair, N.J.: Patterson Smith, 1970.
Alcoff, Linda, and Elizabeth Potter. *Feminist Epistemologies*. New York: Routledge, 1993.
Alexander, Thomas M. *John Dewey's Theory of Art, Experience, and Nature: The Horizons of Feeling*. Albany: State University of New York Press, 1987.
Antler, Joyce. *Lucy Sprague Mitchell*. New Haven: Yale University Press, 1987.
Antony, Louise M. "Quine as Feminist: The Radical Import of Naturalized Epistemology." In *A Mind of One's Own*, edited by Louise M. Antony and Charlotte Witt, 185–225. Boulder, Colo.: Westview Press, 1993.
Aptheker, Bettina. *Tapestries of Life: Women's Work, Women's Consciousness, and the Meaning of Daily Experience*. Amherst: University of Massachusetts Press, 1989.
Bernstein, Richard J. *Beyond Objectivism and Relativism: Science, Hermeneutics, and Praxis*. Philadelphia: University of Pennsylvania Press, 1983.
Boisvert, Raymond. *Dewey's Metaphysics*. New York: Fordham University Press, 1988.
———. "Rorty, Dewey, and Post-modern Metaphysics." *Southern Journal of Philosophy* 27 (1989): 173–93.
Butler, Judith. *Bodies That Matter: On the Discursive Limits of Sex*. New York: Routledge, 1983.
———, and Joan W. Scott, eds. *Feminists Theorize the Political*. New York: Routledge, 1992.

Campbell, Donald. "Evolutionary Epistemology." In *The Philosophy of Karl Popper*, edited by Paul Schilpp. La Salle, Ill.: Open Court, 1974.

Campbell, James. *Understanding John Dewey*. Chicago: Open Court, 1995.

Campbell, Richmond. "The Virtues of Feminist Empiricism." *Hypatia* 9, no. 1 (1994): 90–115.

Card, Claudia. *Feminist Ethics*. Lawrence: University Press of Kansas, 1991.

Chen, Constance M. *"The Sex Side of Life"*: *Mary Ware Dennett's Pioneering Battle for Birth Control and Sex Education*. New York: New Press, 1996.

Code, Lorraine. "Feminists and Pragmatists: A Radical Future?" *Radical Philosophy* 87 (1998): 22–30.

———. *Rhetorical Spaces: Essays on Gendered Locations*. New York: Routledge, 1995.

———. *What Can She Know? Feminist Theory and the Construction of Knowledge*. Ithaca: Cornell University Press, 1991.

Cooper, Anna Julia. *A Voice from the South*. 1892. New York: Oxford University Press, 1988.

Cornell, Drucilla. "Toward a Modern/Postmodern Reconstruction of Ethics." *University of Pennsylvania Law Review* 133 (1985): 291–380.

Damasio, Antonio R. *Descartes' Error: Emotion, Reason, and the Human Brain*. Kirkwood, N.Y.: G. P. Putnam, 1994.

Dewey, Jane M. "Biography of John Dewey." In *The Philosophy of John Dewey*, edited by Paul Arthur Schilpp. Evanston: Northwestern University Press, 1939. Reprint, Chicago: Open Court, 1990.

Dewey, John. "Address to the National Association for the Advancement of Colored People." In *The Later Works*. Vol. 6, *1931–32*. Edited by Jo Ann Boydston, 224–30. Carbondale: Southern Illinois University Press, 1985.

———. *Art as Experience*. Vol. 10 (*1934*) of *The Later Works*. Edited by Jo Ann Boydston. Carbondale: Southern Illinois University Press, 1987.

———. "The Basic Values and Loyalties of Democracy." In *The Later Works*. Vol. 14, *1939–1941*. Edited by Jo Ann Boydston, 275–77. Carbondale: Southern Illinois University Press, 1988.

———. "Context and Thought." In *The Later Works*. Vol. 6, *1931–1932*. Edited by Jo Ann Boydston, 3–21. Carbondale: Southern Illinois University Press, 1985.

———. " 'Contrary to Human Nature.' " In *The Later Works*. Vol. 14, *1939–1941*. Edited by Jo Ann Boydston, 258–61. Carbondale: Southern Illinois University Press, 1988.

———. "Creative Democracy: The Task Before Us." In *The Later Works*. Vol. 14, *1939–1941*. Edited by Jo Ann Boydston, 224–30. Carbondale: Southern Illinois University Press, 1988.

———. *Democracy and Education*. Vol. 9 (*1916*) of *The Middle Works*. Edited by Jo Ann Boydston. Carbondale: Southern Illinois University Press, 1980.

———. "Does Reality Possess Practical Character?" In *The Middle Works*. Vol. 4, *1907–1909*. Edited by Jo Ann Boydston, 125–42. Carbondale: Southern Illinois University Press, 1977.

———. *Ethics*. Vol. 5 (*1908*) of *The Middle Works*. Edited by Jo Ann Boydston. Carbondale: Southern Illinois University Press, 1978.

———. *Ethics*. Vol. 7 (*1932*) of *The Later Works*. Edited by Jo Ann Boydston. Carbondale: Southern Illinois University Press, 1985.

———. "The Ethics of Animal Experimentation." In *The Later Works*. Vol. 2, *1925–*

1927. Edited by Jo Ann Boydston, 98–103. Carbondale: Southern Illinois University Press, 1984.

————. *Experience and Nature*. Vol. 1 (*1925*) of *The Later Works*. Edited by Jo Ann Boydston. Carbondale: Southern Illinois University Press, 1981.

————. "Future of Liberalism." In *The Later Works*. Vol. 11, *1935–1937*. Edited by Jo Ann Boydston, 289–95. Carbondale: Southern Illinois University Press, 1987.

————. *How We Think*. In *The Middle Works*. Vol. 6, *1910–1911*. Edited by Jo Ann Boydston, 177–356. Carbondale: Southern Illinois University Press, 1978.

————. *Human Nature and Conduct*. Vol. 14 (*1922*) of *The Middle Works*. Edited by Jo Ann Boydston. Carbondale: Southern Illinois University Press. 1983.

————. "In Defense of Mary Ware Dennett's *The Sex Side of Life*." In *The Later Works*. Vol. 17. Edited by Jo Ann Boydston, 127 and 560n. Carbondale: Southern Illinois University Press, 1990.

————. *Individualism Old and New*. In *The Later Works*. Vol. 5, *1929–1930*. Edited by Jo Ann Boydston, 41–143. Carbondale: Southern Illinois University Press, 1984.

————. "The Influence of Darwinism on Philosophy." In *The Middle Works*. Vol. 4, *1907–1909*. Edited by Jo Ann Boydston, 3–14. Carbondale: Southern Illinois University Press, 1977.

————. "Intelligence and Morals." In *The Middle Works*. Vol. 4, *1907–1909*. Edited by Jo Ann Boydston, 31–49. Carbondale: Southern Illinois University Press, 1977.

————. *John Dewey: The Political Writings*. Edited by Debra Morris and Ian Shapiro. Indianapolis: Hackett, 1993.

————. *Liberalism and Social Action*. In *The Later Works*. Vol. 11, *1935–37*. Edited by Jo Ann Boydston, 1–65. Carbondale: Southern Illinois University Press, 1987.

————. *Logic: The Theory of Inquiry*. Vol. 12 (*1938*) of *The Later Works*. Edited by Jo Ann Boydston. Carbondale: Southern Illinois University Press, 1986.

————. "The Need for a Recovery of Philosophy." In *The Middle Works*. Vol. 10, *1916–1917*. Edited by Jo Ann Boydston, 3–48. Carbondale: Southern Illinois University Press, 1980.

————. "Philosophies of Freedom." In *The Later Works*. Vol. 3, *1927–1928*. Edited by Jo Ann Boydston, 92–114. Carbondale: Southern Illinois University Press, 1984.

————. "Philosophy and Democracy." In *The Middle Works*. Vol. 11, *1918–1919*. Edited by Jo Ann Boydston, 41–53. Carbondale: Southern Illinois University Press, 1982.

————. *The Quest for Certainty*. Vol. 4 (*1929*) of *The Later Works*. Edited by Jo Ann Boydston. Carbondale: Southern Illinois University Press, 1984.

————. "The Reflex Arc Concept in Psychology." In *The Early Works*. Vol. 5, *1895–1898*. Edited by Jo Ann Boydston, 96–109. Carbondale: Southern Illinois University Press, 1972.

————. "The Senate Birth Control Bill." In *The Later Works*. Vol. 6, *1931–32*. Edited by Jo Ann Boydston, 388–89. Carbondale: Southern Illinois University Press, 1985.

————. "A Symposium on Woman's Suffrage [Statement]." In *The Middle Works*. Vol. 6, *1910–1911*. Edited by Jo Ann Boydston, 153–54. Carbondale: Southern Illinois University Press, 1978.

————. "War's Social Results." In *The Later Works*. Vol. 17, *1885–1953*. Edited by Jo Ann Boydston, 21–25. Carbondale: Southern Illinois University Press, 1990.

————. "What I Believe." In *The Later Works*. Vol. 5, *1929–30*. Edited by Jo Ann Boydston, 267–78. Carbondale: Southern Illinois University Press, 1984.

Du Bois, W. E. B. *The Autobiography of W. E. B. Du Bois*. New York: International, 1980.
———. *Darkwater: Voices from Within the Veil*. With an introduction by Herbert Aptheker. Millwood, N.Y.: Kraus-Thomson, 1975.
———. *Dusk of Dawn: An Essay Toward an Autobiography of a Race Concept*. New York: Harcourt, Brace, 1940.
Eldridge, Michael. *Transforming Experience: John Dewey's Cultural Instrumentalism*. Nashville: Vanderbilt University Press, 1998.
Fischer, Marilyn. "Jane Addams's Pragmatist Pacifism." In *Peacemaking: Lessons from the Past, Visions for the Future*, edited by J. Presler and S. Scholz. Amsterdam: Rodopi Press, 2000.
———. "Philanthropy and Injustice in Mill and Addams." *Nonprofit and Voluntary Sector Quarterly* 24 (1995): 281–92.
———. *On Addams*. Belmont, Calif.: Wadsworth, 2001.
Flax, Jane. "Postmodernism and Gender Relations in Feminist Theory." In *Feminism/Postmodernism*, edited by Linda J. Nicholson, 39–62. New York: Routledge, 1990.
Flexner, Eleanor. *Century of Struggle*. Cambridge: Harvard University Press, 1975.
Follett, Mary Parker. *Creative Experience*. New York: Longmans, Green, 1930.
———. *The New State*. New York: Longmans, Green, 1926.
Freire, Paolo. *The Pedagogy of the Oppressed*. New York: Continuum, 1970.
French, Peter A. *The Spectrum of Responsibility*. New York: St. Martin's Press, 1991.
———. "Time, Space, and Shame." In *Responsibility Matters*, edited by Peter A. French. Lawrence: University Press of Kansas, 1992.
Frye, Marilyn. "A Response to Lesbian Ethics." In *Feminist Ethics*, edited by Claudia Card, 52–59. Lawrence: University Press of Kansas, 1991.
Garrison, Jim. *Dewey and Eros: Wisdom and Desire in the Art of Teaching*. New York: Teachers College Press, 1997.
Gauthier, David. *Morals by Agreement*. Oxford: Clarendon Press, 1986.
Gavin, William. "The Importance of Context: Reflections on Kuhn, Marx, and Dewey." *Studies in Soviet Thought* 21 (1980): 15–30.
Gilligan, Carol. *In A Different Voice: Psychological Theory and Women's Development*. Cambridge: Harvard University Press, 1982.
Gouinlock, James, ed. *The Moral Writings of John Dewey*. New York: Prometheus Books, 1994.
Grant, Judith. "I Feel Therefore I Am: A Critique of Female Experience as the Basis for a Feminist Epistemology." *Women and Politics* 7, no. 3 (1987): 99–114.
Green, Judith M. *Deep Democracy: Community, Diversity, and Transformation*. Lanham, Md.: Rowman and Littlefield, 1999a.
———. "Deepening Democracy in Central Europe: A Radical Pragmatist Perspective from the American Experience." In *Democracy in Central Europe, 1989–1999: Comparative and Historical Perspectives*, edited by Justyna Miklaszewska, 101–30. Krakow: Meritum, 1999b.
———. "Guiding Post-totalitarian Economic Democratization Through Deweyan Radical Pragmatism." In *Democracy and the Post-totalitarian Experience*, edited by Beth J. Singer and Leszek Koczanowicz. Amsterdam: Central-European Value Studies, Editions Rodope, forthcoming.
Greene, Maxine. Diversity and Inclusion: Toward a Curriculum for Human Beings. *Teachers College Record* 2 (1995): 211–21.

Hamilton, Alice. *Exploring the Dangerous Trades*. 1943. Reprint, Boston: Northeastern University Press, 1985.

Haraway, Donna. *ModestWitness@SecondMillennium.FemaleMan©MeetsOncoMouse™*. New York: Routledge, 1997.

———. *Primate Visions: Gender, Race, and Nature in the World of Modern Science*. New York: Routledge Press, 1989.

———. *Simians, Cyborgs, and Women: The Reinvention of Nature*. New York: Routledge, 1991.

———. "Situated Knowledges: The Science Question in Feminism and the Privilege of Partial Perspective." *Feminist Studies* 14, no. 3 (1988): 575–99.

Harding, Sandra. 1992. "After the Neutrality Ideal: Science, Politics, and 'Strong Objectivity.' " *Social Research* 59, no. 3 (1992): 567–87.

———. "Comment on Hekman's 'Truth and Method: Feminist Standpoint Theory Revisited': Whose Standpoint Needs the Regimes of Truth and Reality?" *Signs* 22, no. 2 (1997): 382–91.

———. "How the Women's Movement Benefits Science: Two Views." *Women Studies International Forum* 12, no. 3 (1989): 271–83.

———. "Rethinking Standpoint Epistemology: 'What Is Strong Objectivity?' " In *Feminist Epistemologies*, edited by Linda Alcoff and Elizabeth Potter, 49–82. New York: Routledge, 1993.

———. *The Science Question in Feminism*. Ithaca: Cornell University Press, 1986.

———. *Whose Science? Whose Knowledge? Thinking from Women's Lives*. Ithaca: Cornell University Press, 1991.

Hartsock, Nancy C. M. "The Feminist Standpoint: Developing the Ground for a Specifically Feminist Historical Materialism." In *Discovering Reality*, edited by Sandra Harding and Merrill B. Hintikka, 283–310. Boston: D. Reidel, 1983.

Hekman, Susan. "The Feminization of Epistemology: Gender and the Social Sciences." *Women and Politics* 7, no. 3 (1997): 65–83.

———. "Reply to Hartsock, Collins, Harding, and Smith." *Signs* 22, no. 2 (1997): 399–402.

———. "Truth and Method: Feminist Standpoint Theory Revisited." *Signs* 22, no. 2 (1997): 341–65.

Heldke, Lisa. "Foodmaking as a Thoughtful Practice." In *Cooking, Eating, Thinking: Transformative Philosophies of Food*, edited by Deane Curtin and Lisa Heldke. Bloomington: Indiana University Press, 1992.

———. "Interaction in a World of Chance: John Dewey's Theory of Inquiry." In *Modern Engenderings: Critical Feminist Essays in the History of Western Philosophy*, edited by Bat-Ami Bar On. Albany: State University of New York Press, 1994.

———. Recipes for Theory Making. *Hypatia* 3, no. 2 (1988): 15–30.

Hoagland, Sarah Lucia. *Lesbian Ethics: Toward New Value*. Palo Alto, Calif.: Institute of Lesbian Studies, 1988.

Hull, David. *Science as Process*. Chicago: University of Chicago Press, 1989.

Jaggar, Alison. "Feminist Ethics: Projects, Problems, Prospects." In *Feminist Ethics*, edited by Claudia Card, 78–104. Lawrence: University Press of Kansas, 1991.

———. *Feminist Politics and Human Nature*. Totowa, N.J.: Roman and Allanheld, 1983.

———. "Sexual Difference and Sexual Equality." In *Living with Contradictions: Controversies in Feminist Social Ethics*, edited by Alison Jaggar, 18–28. Boulder, Colo.: Westview Press, 1994.

————, and Susan R. Bordo, ed. *Gender/Body/Knowledge: Feminist Reconstructions of Being and Knowing.* New Brunswick: Rutgers University Press, 1989.

Keller, Evelyn Fox. *Secrets of Life, Secrets of Death: Essays on Language, Gender, and Science.* New York: Routledge Press, 1992.

Kellogg, Paul. "Twice Twenty Years at Hull-House." In *Eighty Years at Hull-House,* edited by Allen F. Davis and Mary Lynn McCree. Chicago: Quadrangle Books, 1969.

Kessler-Harris, Alice. *Out to Work: A History of Wage-Earning Women in the United States.* New York: Oxford University Press, 1983.

Kloppenberg, James T. "Pragmatism: An Old Name for Some New Ways of Thinking?" *Journal of American History* 83, no. 1 (1996): 100–138.

Lasch, Christopher, ed. *The Social Thought of Jane Addams.* New York: Bobbs-Merrill, 1966.

Lewontin Richard. "Organism and Environment." In *Learning, Development, and Culture,* edited by H. C. Plotkin. New York: John Wiley and Sons, 1982.

Light, Andrew, and Eric Katz. *Environmental Pragmatism.* New York: Routledge, 1996.

Linn, James. *Jane Addams: A Biography.* New York: D. Appleton-Century, 1938.

Locke, Alain. "The Ethics of Culture." In *The Philosophy of Alain Locke.* Edited by Leonard Harris. Philadelphia: Temple University Press, 1989.

Longino, Helen. "Subjects, Power, and Knowledge: Description and Prescription in Feminist Philosophies of Science." In *Feminist Epistemologies,* edited by Linda Alcoff and Elizabeth Potter, 101–20. New York: Routledge, 1993.

Lugones, María. "Purity, Impurity, and Separation." *Signs* 19 (Winter 1994): 458–79.

May, Larry. "Metaphysical Guilt and Moral Taint." In *Collective Responsibility,* edited by Larry May and Stacey Hoffman, 239–54. Savage, Md.: Rowman and Littlefield, 1991.

Mayhew, Katherine Camp, and Anna Camp Edwards. *The Dewey School: The Laboratory School of the University of Chicago, 1896–1903.* New York: D. Appleton-Century, 1936.

McCaughey, Martha. "Redirecting Feminist Critiques of Science." *Hypatia* 8, no. 4 (1993): 72–84.

Mead, George Herbert. *The Philosophy of the Present.* Edited by Arthur E. Murphy. La Salle, Ill.: Open Court, 1959.

Millikan, Ruth. *White Queen Psychology and Other Essays for Alice.* Cambridge: MIT Press, 1993.

Minnich, Elizabeth. "Liberal Learning and the Arts of Connection for the New Academy." Washington, D.C.: Association of American Colleges and Universities, 1995.

Mitchell, Lucy Sprague. *Two Lives.* New York: Simon and Schuster, 1953.

Morgan, Kathryn. "Women and Moral Madness." In *Science, Morality, and Feminist Theory,* edited by Marsha Hanen and Kai Nielsen. Calgary: University of Calgary Press, 1987.

Narayan, Uma. *Dislocating Cultures: Identities, Traditions, and Third-World Feminism.* New York: Routledge, 1997.

Neisser, Ulric. *The Perceived Self: Ecological and Interpersonal Sources of Self-Knowledge.* Cambridge: Cambridge University Press, 1993.

Nelson, Lynn Hankinson. "A Question of Evidence." *Hypatia* 8, no. 2 (1993): 172–89.

Noddings, Nel. *Caring: A Feminine Approach to Ethics and Moral Education.* Berkeley and Los Angeles: University of California Press, 1984.

Ortner, Sherry B. "Is Female to Male as Nature Is to Culture?" In *Women and Values*. 2d ed., edited by Marilyn Pearsall, 59–72. Belmont, Calif.: Wadsworth, 1993.

Pinnick, Cassandra L. "Feminist Epistemology: Implications for Philosophy of Science." *Philosophy of Science* 61 (1994): 646–57.

Popper, Karl. *Objective Knowledge: An Evolutionary Approach*. Oxford: Clarendon Press, 1972.

Pratt, Scott. *Native Pragmatism*. Indianapolis: Indiana University Press, 2001.

Putnam, Hilary. *The Many Faces of Realism*. La Salle, Ill.: Open Court, 1987.

Rooney, Phyllis. "Gendered Reason: Sex Metaphor and Conceptions of Reason." *Hypatia* 6, no. 2 (1991): 97–98.

Rorty, Richard. *Consequences of Pragmatism*. Minneapolis: University of Minnesota Press, 1982.

———. *Objectivity, Relativism, and Truth*. Cambridge: Cambridge University Press, 1991.

———. *Philosophy and the Mirror of Nature*. Princeton: Princeton University Press, 1979.

Ruddick, Sara. "Maternal Thinking." *Feminist Studies* 6 (1980): 342–67.

———. *Maternal Thinking: Toward a Politics of Peace*. New York: Ballantine Books, 1989.

Scheman, Naomi. *Engenderings*. New York: Routledge, 1993.

Scott, Joan W. "Experience." In *Feminists Theorize the Political*, edited by Judith Butler and Joan W. Scott, 22–40. New York: Routledge, 1992.

Seigfried, Charlene Haddock. "Advancing American Philosophy," *Transactions of the Charles S. Peirce Society* 34 (Fall 1998): 807–39.

———. "Beyond Epistemology: From A Pragmatist Feminist Experiential Standpoint." In *Engendering Rationalities*, edited by Nancy Tuana and Sandi Morgen, 99–121. Albany: State University of New York Press, 2001.

———. "The Dilemma of Democracy: Diversity of Interests and Common Experiences." In *Renascent Pragmatism: Studies in Law and Social Science*, edited by Alfonso Morales. Brookfield, Vt.: Ashgate, 2002.

———. "Feminist Ethics and the Sociality of Dewey's Moral Theory." *Transactions of the Charles S. Peirce Society* 36 (Fall 2000): 529–34.

———. "Like Bridges Without Piers: Beyond the Foundationalist Metaphor." In *Antifoundationalism Old and New*, edited by Tom Rockmore and Beth J. Singer, 143–64. Philadelphia: Temple University Press, 1992.

———. "Perspectives on Pragmatism: A Reply to Lorraine Code." *Radical Philosophy* 92 (November/December 1998): 25–27.

———. *Pragmatism and Feminism: Reweaving the Social Fabric*. Chicago: University of Chicago Press, 1996.

———. "Socializing Democracy: Jane Addams and John Dewey." *Philosophy of the Social Sciences* 29 (June 1999): 207–30.

———, and Hans Seigfried. "Individual Feeling and Universal Validity." In *Rhetoric, Pragmatism, Sophistry*, edited by Steven Mailloux, 139–54. Cambridge: Cambridge University Press, 1995.

Sklar, Kathryn Kish. *Florence Kelley and the Nation's Work*. New Haven: Yale University Press, 1995.

———. "Hull House *Maps and Papers*: Social Science as Women's Work in the 1890s." In *Gender and American Social Science: The Formative Years*, edited by Helene Silverberg. Princeton: Princeton University Press, 1998.

Smith, Dorothy. *The Everyday World as Problematic: A Feminist Sociology*. Boston: Northeastern University Press, 1987.

———. "A Sociology for Women." In *The Prism of Sex: Essays in the Sociology of Knowledge*, edited by Julia Sherman and Evelyn Torton Beck. Madison: University of Wisconsin Press, 1979.

Sullivan, Shannon. "Democracy and the Individual: To What Extent Is Dewey's Reconstruction Nietzsche's Self-Overcoming?" *Philosophy Today* 40, no. 2 (1997): 296–308.

———. "Domination and Dialogue in Merleau-Ponty's *Phenomenology of Perception*." *Hypatia* 12, no. 1 (1997): 1–19.

———. *Living Across and Through Skins: Transactional Bodies, Pragmatism, and Feminism*. Bloomington: Indiana University Press, 2001.

Taft, Jessie. *The Woman Movement from the Point of View of Social Consciousness*. Menasha, Wis.: Collegiate Press, George Banta, 1915.

Tannoch-Bland, Jennifer. "From Aperspectival Objectivity to Strong Objectivity: The Quest for Moral Objectivity." *Hypatia* 12, no. 1 (1997): 155–78.

Tong, Rosemary. *Feminist Thought: A Comprehensive Introduction*. Boulder, Colo.: Westview Press, 1989.

West, Cornell. *The American Evasion of Philosophy: A Genealogy of Pragmatism*. Madison: University of Wisconsin Press, 1989.

———. *Race Matters*. New York: Vintage Books, 1994.

Westbrook, Robert B. *John Dewey and American Democracy*. Ithaca: Cornell University Press, 1991.

Wilson, E. O. *Sociobiology: The New Synthesis*. Cambridge: Harvard University Press, 1975.

Woodson, G. Carter. *The Mis-education of the Negro*. 1933. Washington, D.C.: Associated Publishers, 1990.

Contributors

ANA M. MARTÍNEZ ALEMÁN is an assistant professor of education at Boston College. Her research activities focus on the impact of gender, race, and ethnicity on college teaching and learning. She is currently at work on an examination of the ideal of community in higher education and the challenge of multiculturalism.

PAULA DROEGE is a visiting assistant professor in the Philosophy Program at Bard College. In addition to her work in feminist epistemology, she is currently completing a manuscript in philosophy of mind, entitled *Caging the Beast: A Theory of Sensory Consciousness*.

MARILYN FISCHER is an associate professor of philosophy at the University of Dayton. She has published several articles on Jane Addams and draws on Addams's and Dewey's philosophy in developing an ethical decision-making model for fund-raisers in her book, *Ethical Decision Making in Fund Raising* (John Wiley).

EUGENIE GATENS-ROBINSON began her academic life in biology, doing research in cell biology and finishing a masters in zoology at the University of Wyoming. She completed her Ph.D. in philosophy at Southern Illinois University at Carbondale, where she is now a faculty member. Genie researches, teaches, and publishes in the areas of feminism, pragmatism, and philosophy of science. She, her husband, and daughter live and garden at the edge of the Shawnee Forest.

JUDITH M. GREEN is associate professor of philosophy at Fordham University in New York City and a principal of GreenWoods Associates, a consulting firm specializing in community building. She received her Ph.D. from the University of Minnesota and has published essays on pragmatism, democratic theory, feminism, African American philosophy, environmental ethics, and Native American philosophy. She is the author of *Deep Democracy: Community, Diversity, and Transformation*.

LISA HELDKE writes and teaches pragmatist feminist philosophy at Gustavus Adolphus College. She is the co-editor of *Cooking, Eating, Thinking: Transformative Philosophies of*

Food, and the author of Let's Eat Chinese: Theorizing Cultural Food Colonialism, a work in progress. She also co-edits the quarterly 'zine Philosophers on Holiday.

ELLEN CONDLIFFE LAGEMANN is president of the Spencer Foundation in Chicago and professor of history and education at New York University. She currently also serves as president of the National Academy of Education. Her latest book, An Elusive Science: The Troubling History of Education, was published by the University of Chicago Press in 2000.

ERIN McKENNA is associate professor and chair of the philosophy department at Pacific Lutheran University. Her work, while always in the pragmatist and feminist vein, ranges over a wide array of topics: social contract theory, pedagogy, housework, vegetarianism, biomedical research on great apes. She shares her life with two dogs and two horses.

MARJORIE C. MILLER is professor of philosophy and women's studies and coordinator of the Philosophy Board of Study at Purchase College, State University of New York. She co-edited Contributions and Controversy in Feminist Philosophy (Metaphilosophy, 1996). Several of her recent articles on both feminism and pragmatism have been translated into Chinese and published in China.

ELIZABETH KAMARCK MINNICH is professor of philosophy and women's studies, the Graduate School for Interdisciplinary Arts and Sciences, at the Union Institute. She writes, speaks, and consults about the implications of contemporary scholarship for more inclusive curricula and the arts of democratic civic life. Her book, Transforming Knowledge, was awarded the Frederic Ness Prize for best book on liberal education.

CHARLENE HADDOCK SEIGFRIED is professor of philosophy and American studies and a member of the Women's Studies Committee at Purdue University. Her recent work includes Pragmatism and Feminism and introductions to Jane Addams's Democracy and Social Ethics and The Long Road of Woman's Memory (Illinois University Press, 2002). She is a past president of the Society for the Advancement of American Philosophy and was the 1998 Lecturer of the John Dewey Society.

SHANNON SULLIVAN is assistant professor of philosophy and women's studies at Penn State University. She teaches and writes on feminist theory, pragmatism, Continental philosophy, and critical race theory. She recently published Living Across and Through Skins: Transactional Bodies, Pragmatism, and Feminism (Indiana University Press, 2001) and is currently working on a manuscript tentatively Race, Space, and Place: Pragmatist-Feminist Reflections on Racial Experience.

Index